Day by Day
in the Psalms

EDITED BY

Arthur T. Shearman
John Heading

PRECIOUS SEED PUBLICATIONS

First printed 1986
Reprinted 1991, 2000

©Copyright Precious Seed Publications

ISBN 1 871642 03 5

The illustrations on the
cover are by courtesy of
Creative Publishing, Bath, UK

Printed by Redwood Books Ltd, Trowbridge

Preface

THE GENEROUS RECEPTION given by many believers to our two books *Day by Day through the Old and New Testaments* has encouraged us to produce another: *Day by Day in the Psalms*. In this book it is hoped that readers will capture some of the beauties contained in the Psalter. This is not a straight-through, systematic reading of the Psalms, but an unfolding of some of the major themes contained therein. Its aim therefore is not so much exegetical or expositional, although both of these aspects are not lacking. But the main intent of the publication is practical and devotional, designed to touch the heart with some of the spiritual treasures enshrined in these "songs from experience".

It will be noticed that many Psalms are used several times. We make no apology for this repetition. We are sure that it will be appreciated that Psalms looked at from different angles, and handled by different authors, will prove to bring out features that reveal the abundant values of truth taught in these Old Testament portions. Our desire is that, in the reading and study of the Psalms, some of the many contemporary needs of the people of God may be daily met, and that faith, hope and love may be stimulated and deepened.

Our deep gratitude is due to those who have given freely of their time to write the daily studies. We are privileged to have the ministry of godly teachers, busy men who share willingly with others the fruits of their study. Some have written for our previous works; others are new to *Precious Seed Publications*. We give our sincere thanks to all. We are also greatly indebted to Michael Jones of Cardiff who, together with the two editors, carefully read and corrected the galley proofs.

As an aid to the profitable use of the book, a comprehensive list of all Psalms dealt with is provided at the beginning; every Psalm has been touched on at least once. The index will help in following out truths contained in the daily readings.

We commend this publication to the Lord Himself who, walking with two disconsolate and downcast disciples one day long ago, so unfolded such scriptures to them, that burdened spirits were exchanged for burning hearts, and the truths in the Psalms "concerning himself" were illuminated. May the glory and the praise be His! (A.T.S.; J.H.)

List of Contents

List of Psalms 5

The Psalmist's God
by A. E. Phillips (West Moors) . . . 9

What is Man?
by A. T. Shearman (Worcester) . . 41

Prayer, Trust, Confidence in God
by D. Lawrence (Ammanford) . . 71

Righteousness, Justice, Judgment
by B. Osborne (Dinas Powis) . . . 103

The Blessings of Mercy, Lovingkindness and Compassion
by T. Renshaw (Manchester) . . . 134

Glory
by H. Barnes (Bromborough) . . . 166

The House of the Lord and Worship
by J. Heading (Aberystwyth) . . . 197

Hallelujah, Praise and Thanksgiving
by D. Newell (Glasgow) 229

The Word of God
by R. V. Court (Isle of Wight) . . . 261

Christ in the Psalms
by D. Clapham (Birmingham)
M. Horlock (Cardiff)
J. Mitchell (Cardiff)
D. Roberts (Cardiff) . . . 292

Experiences of the Covenant People
by K. T. C. Morris (Southampton) . . 324

Prospects, Hopes and Aspirations
by S. Emery (Workington) . . . 355

Index 387

List of Psalms

	Page
1 Chron. 29	217
Psalm 1	70, 262
Psalm 2	70, 304, 311
Psalm 3	206
Psalm 4	94, 124, 207, 356
Psalm 5	95, 211
Psalm 6	49
Psalm 7	108, 130
Psalm 8	42, 167, 320
Psalm 9	125
Psalm 10	322
Psalm 11	23, 108, 109, 110
Psalm 12	264
Psalm 13	72
Psalm 14	44
Psalm 15	45, 128, 203
Psalm 16	308, 309
Psalm 17	99, 133, 135, 274
Psalm 18	35, 69, 109, 132, 325
Psalm 19	37, 39, 168, 263
Psalm 20	326
Psalm 21	327
Psalm 22	43, 230, 305
Psalm 23	209, 316, 357
Psalm 24	46, 169, 320, 358
Psalm 25	58, 73, 136, 137, 359
Psalm 26	129, 131, 170, 205
Psalm 27	25, 74, 212, 360
Psalm 28	361
Psalm 29	25, 171, 199
Psalm 30	231
Psalm 31	64, 75, 138, 307
Psalm 32	62, 139, 140
Psalm 33	38, 115, 232, 233, 275
Psalm 34	56, 141, 142
Psalm 35	76, 122, 301
Psalm 36	143

	Page
Psalm 37	63, 66, 123, 279
Psalm 38	50
Psalm 39	362
Psalm 40	56, 77, 204, 273, 291, 295
Psalm 41	303
Psalm 42	12, 35, 208, 363
Psalm 43	12
Psalm 44	328
Psalm 45	118, 172, 300, 314
Psalm 46	98, 221
Psalm 47	20, 26, 32
Psalm 48	222, 234
Psalm 49	55, 364
Psalm 50	111, 173, 269, 329
Psalm 51	78, 126, 144, 145
Psalm 52	200
Psalm 53	44
Psalm 54	79
Psalm 55	54, 80, 210
Psalm 56	100
Psalm 57	146, 147, 174, 235
Psalm 58	112
Psalm 59	64, 81
Psalm 60	330
Psalm 61	82
Psalm 62	35, 83, 365
Psalm 63	148, 366
Psalm 64	53
Psalm 65	28, 216
Psalm 66	236
Psalm 67	40, 237
Psalm 68	22, 201, 310, 312
Psalm 69	226, 297, 302, 306
Psalm 70	84
Psalm 71	85, 116
Psalm 72	121, 175, 331
Psalm 73	176, 332, 367
Psalm 74	223, 333
Psalm 75	120, 238

	Page
Psalm 76	177, 334
Psalm 77	29, 65, 149, 368
Psalm 78	11, 178, 198, 270, 280, 299, 335, 336
Psalm 79	150, 179
Psalm 80	24, 214, 317, 337, 369
Psalm 81	239, 338, 339
Psalm 82	113, 114
Psalm 83	52, 340
Psalm 84	68, 180, 220, 370
Psalm 85	151, 152, 181, 268
Psalm 86	13, 153, 182
Psalm 87	60
Psalm 88	49, 86, 371
Psalm 89	14, 15, 17, 183, 240, 241, 318, 321, 341
Psalm 90	47, 184, 293
Psalm 91	16, 101, 225, 298, 319
Psalm 92	104
Psalm 93	293, 342, 372
Psalm 94	33, 87, 282, 373
Psalm 95	242, 374
Psalm 96	185, 202, 243, 244, 375
Psalm 97	119, 186, 343
Psalm 98	245
Psalm 99	228
Psalm 100	246
Psalm 101	61
Psalm 102	187, 285, 294, 376
Psalm 103	27, 154, 247, 248, 320
Psalm 104	188, 294
Psalm 105	22, 344, 345, 377
Psalm 106	105, 189, 346, 347
Psalm 107	31, 88, 249, 250, 276
Psalm 108	155, 190
Psalm 109	89
Psalm 110	313, 315
Psalm 111	18, 19, 281
Psalm 112	58
Psalm 113	14, 156, 191, 251
Psalm 114	57, 348

	Page
Psalm 115	90, 192, 349, 378
Psalm 116	67, 157
Psalm 117	252
Psalm 118	127, 227
Psalm 119	117, 265, 266, 267, 271, 272, 278, 283, 284, 287, 288, 289, 290, 291, 296
Psalm 120	91
Psalm 121	30, 92, 379
Psalm 122	215, 350
Psalm 123	93
Psalm 124	97
Psalm 125	96
Psalm 126	158, 351
Psalm 127	218
Psalm 128	59
Psalm 129	51
Psalm 130	159, 380
Psalm 131	381
Psalm 132	219, 323, 352, 382
Psalm 133	383
Psalm 134	213
Psalm 135	10, 353
Psalm 136	34, 160
Psalm 137	224, 354
Psalm 138	161, 193, 286
Psalm 139	21, 43, 384
Psalm 140	53
Psalm 141	102, 106
Psalm 142	107
Psalm 143	162
Psalm 144	48
Psalm 145	36, 163, 164, 165, 194, 253, 385
Psalm 146	254
Psalm 147	255, 256, 277
Psalm 148	195, 257, 258
Psalm 149	196, 259
Psalm 150	260, 386

The Psalmist's God

THE NAMES and titles of God express His Person and character, for they tell out His nature. They carry their own sweet messages to every enquiring heart, bringing strength to the weak, succour to the bereft, companionship to the lonely, and encouragement to the downcast. To be meditating thereon will be inditing a good matter.

All the Old Testament names of God are for us. They have not been eclipsed by the supreme revelation of God as Father by our Lord. ("I have made known unto them thy name", John 17. 26 R.V.) Paul preserved the name "the Lord Almighty" of the Old Testament even when speaking of the Father, 2 Cor. 6. 18, for though we know "one God, the Father", 1 Cor. 8. 6, yet His names are eternal. For example, "Jehovah-Jireh" ("the Lord will provide") is to be read, as it were, between the lines of Romans 8. 32, which echoes Genesis 22. 14 where that compound name is found.

We should notice that these revelations of God by His names are always appropriate to the actual circumstances of the writers of the psalms. They are not abstract ideas or theological niceties. Often they are expressed poetically, but they are not speculative flights of fancy, but they are for us right now and just where we are.

As we read our English Book of Psalms, we could note, for example, that "Lord" means Sovereign-Lord and Owner. But "LORD" speaks of Jehovah who Is, the I AM, the covenant-keeping and unchanging One.

As in other Old Testament Scriptures, the psalms indicate that God was to be revealed in the Messiah. In Psalm 2, He is the eternal Son—"my Son". In Psalm 89. 27, He is "my firstborn". Psalm 110 shows Christ sharing the solitary throne of Deity consequent on His triumph. No angel could share that throne, Heb. 1. 13. It is His by right of eternal equality, and by His triumphant redemptive work of the cross.

Through the inspired psalmists, the Spirit calls him "God" in the full meaning of that word, Psa. 45. 6; Heb. 1. 8-10. In Psalm 68. 18, God's ascent is the Son's ascent, as Ephesians 4. 8-11 clearly asserts. Yet we also see His coming in true Manhood, Psa. 8. 4; Heb. 2.6; this led to the cross and His perfect sacrifice, Psa. 40. 6-8; Heb. 10. 5-9.

9

January 1st

READING: **Psalm 135**

GOD ABOVE ALL GODS (PART 1)

GOD MADE man in His own image. Eventually man was making gods after his own likeness, thereby expressing his debased thoughts in images cast from the moulds of his passions and darkness. The inspiring spirit behind these varied products was the evil one himself. They were "abominations", "lies" and "vanities". They that made them were like unto them. So were they that trusted them, for they became "vanities" in life, lived a "lie", and worshipped they knew not what, Psa. 135. 18; Isa. 40. 20; John 4. 22.

But "our God is above all gods", Psa. 135. 5. Whatsoever He does is of His own pleasure and purpose, v. 6. The idol was nailed down, being limited to their petty thoughts, Isa. 46. 7; it had been a burden to its makers and to those who carried it. In contrast, the Lord is the One who bares and carries even to old age, vv. 1-4. In due time, Messiah would have "borne our sins, and carried our sorrows", 53. 4.

God's Name (His character, nature and renown) had been revealed, and it was His memorial throughout all generations, Psa. 135. 13; Exod. 3. 15. He is the Self-revealing and Self-sustaining God, who in the fulness of the times was fully revealed in His beloved Son, John 1. 18.

Of His own purpose, God has chosen Israel, making them His peculiar treasure and giving them an inheritance, Psa. 135. 4, 12. So our psalmist calls repeatedly for praise and blessing from the congregation, and the priests and Levites, vv. 1, 19, for such was pleasant, v. 3.

We have the more reasons so to do, being priests unto God, showing forth the praises of Him who predestinated us after the counsel of His own will, to the praise of the glory of His grace, 1 Pet. 2. 9; Eph. 1. 11; Heb. 13. 15.

> Rise our hearts, and bless the Father,
> Ceaseless song e'en here begun,
> Endless praise and adoration
> To the Father and the Son.
> (Centra Thompson)

10

READING: **Psalms 78. 34-40, 54-58**

GOD ABOVE ALL GODS (PART 2)

ABRAM, THE PROGENITOR of Israel, was called from the idolatry of Ur, and Israel became God's witness against polytheism, Isa. 43. 10. Alas, in this they utterly failed, and suffered the captivity. Worse still, they could attempt to link God's Name to a golden calf, to the brazen serpent, and to other idolatries. In all this, they "turned back, and dealt unfaithfully like their fathers: they were turned aside like a deceitful bow", Psa. 78. 57-58.

In great mercy God brought back a repenting remnant from the captivity. They were cured of outward idolatry.

But their renewed orthodoxy generated a Pharisaical spirit; they prominently wore broad phylacteries wherein the major text was "The Lord our God is one", but they were blind leaders of the blind. Their legalistic pedantry was their substitute for true worship.

Did a Pharisee ever imagine that greed for riches was an abomination, that is, idolatrous?, Luke 16. 14-15; cf.Matt. 24. 15. Did the exemplary young ruler realize that he loved something beyond the Lord his God, Luke 18. 22. The Lord is a jealous God; He is to be loved beyond the nearest, Matt. 10. 37.

Besides these, there were "idols" made by errorists such as "another Jesus", "another spirit", associated with "another gospel", 2 Cor. 11. 4; Gal. 1. 6-7. In such a context, the last surviving apostle pertinently and affectionately exhorts, "keep yourselves from idols", 1 John 5. 21.

Jacob's pilgrimage began when he realized God's presence, and himself as the object of heaven's attention. He called the place Bethel. After years of spiritual decline, the call came to get back to that significant place. This he did, but only after the idols were buried under a tree. At Bethel, he found the *God* of Bethel, Gen. 28; 35. 1-7.

When God is as the dew in freshness to the soul, we ask, "What have I to do any more with idols?", Hos. 14. 5-8.

"We are in him that is true, even in his Son Jesus Christ. This is the true God, and eternal life", 1 John 5. 20.

11

January 3rd

READING: **Psalms 42 & 43**

THE LIVING GOD

WHEN THE gospel came in power and much assurance to the pagan Thessalonians, it caused them to turn to the living God from dead idols. The order is significant. "The expulsive power of a new affection" turned them around to love Him, to labour for Him and to long for His return, 1 Thess. 1. 9-10. They ate of the living bread, drank of the living waters, heard the living oracles, became children of the living God and living stones in God's house, and received a living hope. Henceforth lifeless religious formality and carnal excitement would never satisfy. Their springs were in Him, Psa. 87. 7.

Our psalmist recalls the sweet fellowship of past days when he went with fellow-worshippers to God's appointed gathering centre. Yea, he led them there with joy and praise, 42. 4 R.V. The living God was in the midst, and rejoiced to listen and record their spiritual conversation, Mal. 3. 16.

But now the psalmist is afflicted and away in the northern parts of the land. "Where is thy God?", the enemies taunt. Ten times he asks, "Why?".

His naked faith now has nothing outward to sustain it. Hitherto had he been carried along by the enthusiasm of others? No, for as the hart pants after the waterbrooks, so his soul pants after the living God whom he had known before. Why be cast down and disquieted? Is He not the living One of present circumstances? He is the health of your present countenance. You shall yet praise Him, 42. 11. His light and truth shall yet lead you back to your former fellowship, 43. 3. With exceeding joy you shall have the soul refreshing of erstwhile altar-experiences, 43. 4; Heb. 13. 10.

The hand of faith stretches out to grasp the harp of God to tune it to praise, whilst anticipating the time when, gathered around the throne, he and all the redeemed will sing of the worthiness of the Lamb, Rev. 5. 8-10.

"We also joy in God through our Lord Jesus Christ, by whom we have now received the reconciliation", Rom. 5. 11 *lit.*

12

READING: **Psalm 86**

THOU ART GOD ALONE

DEDUCTIONS evidencing the uniqueness of God can be made from the uniformity of the universe, which shows the work of the one all-wise Creator, and from the intuitive demands of conscience in a common humanity. There is also the one culminating revelation of God in the Person of His Son. All these have their value as evidence.

But our psalmist bases his conviction of God's uniqueness on the fact that He *alone* can meet his soul's need. He is poor (without any merit) and needy, yet is holy because set apart to God by grace. Moreover, he is trustingly serving his Lord and Owner, daily seeking mercy so that his joy may alone be in the Lord, vv.1-5.

Come what may, he is convinced that God is good and plenteous in mercy, vv. 5-7. Even whilst still in adversity, v. 17, he determines to offer praise with all his heart, v. 12. This is most fitting, and is the fruit of active faith.

With God alone before him, he rightly desires a heart that is united in reverence to God's Name, for he knew how conflicting loyalties would pull in differing directions, v. 11. Elsewhere he can affirm that his heart is fixed, Psa. 108. 1, and again, "my heart is fixed, O God, my heart is fixed", 57. 7. His eye is single; his whole self is full of light.

On this he soliloquized, "I have said unto the Lord, Thou art my Lord: I have no good beyond thee", Psa. 16. 2 R.V. "Whom have I in heaven but thee? and there is none upon earth that I desire beside thee ... God is the strength of my heart, and my portion for ever", Psa. 73. 25-26.

All his springs, both in motive and action, were in God, Psa. 87. 7. So one thing only did he desire of the Lord, namely, to dwell in the Lord's house for ever, and to behold the beauty of the Lord, Psa. 27. 4. His whole heart was directed to the supreme Object, 119. 2, 10, 58.

How diverse are the multiple cravings of the world system! But it is passing away, with the sum total of it having no eternal value. But he who pursues the single, integrated will of God abides for ever, *"all that is in the world ... is not of the Father. And the world passes away ... but he that doeth the will of God abideth for ever"*, 1 John 2. 16-17.

READING: **Psalms 89. 1-6; 113. 1-9**

THE INCOMPARABLE GOD

(1) "Who in the heaven can be compared unto the Lord?". Consider the glories of His heavenly temple, the myriads of holy angels who excel in strength and who do His commandments, hearkening unto the voice of His word, that do His pleasure, Psa. 103. 20-21. He "maketh his angels spirits; his ministers a flaming fire", 104. 4.

The cherubim of His righteous demands, and the seraphim ("burning ones") of His holiness antiphonally crying, "Holy, holy, holy"; all speak of His power and glory. But He alone is God, "thou art God, even thou alone", Isa. 37. 16; 44. 6. He is incomparable in the heaven, so that He humbles Himself to behold the things in heaven, Psa. 113. 6(a).

Moreover, He graciously humbles Himself to behold the things in the earth, Psa. 113. 6(b). He heard the cry wrung from the oppressed in Egypt, and came down to deliver His people, Exod. 3. 7-8. In due time, His co-equal Son made Himself of no reputation, taking upon Him the form of a servant, becoming obedient unto death, and *that* the death of the cross, Phil. 2. 7-8. All this was in order to raise up the poor, to seat them with princes of His believing people, Psa. 113. 7; Eph. 2. 6. Even now they reign in life through Him who came to give His life a ransom for many, Rom. 5. 17.

(2) Who is like Him who delivers the poor believing ones from him that is too strong for them?, Psa. 35. 10. These are they who tremble at God's Word, and make no claim to any merit. They know that the strong evil one can only be met by the stronger One who is able to save to the uttermost, and to keep from falling, for "greater is he that is in you, than he that is in the world", 1 John 4. 4; "when a stronger than he shall come upon him, and overcome him, he taketh from him all his armour wherein he trusted", Luke 11. 22; Heb. 2. 14-15; 7. 25. This is our incomparable Saviour.

Well may we join in the first song in Scripture, when the redeemed were asking, *"Who is like unto thee, O Lord ... who is like thee, glorious in holiness, fearful in praises, doing wonders?"*, Exod. 15. 11.

January 6th

READING: **Psalm 89. 1-17**

GOD IS GREATLY TO BE FEARED

THE PSALMISTS had a deep sense of the reverence due to so great a God, v. 7. Long before their time, the patriarchs had known God as "the Fear", Gen. 31. 53 R.V.

The tabernacle, and later the temple, inculcated this solemn truth by the meticulous ritual of approach, in the demands of holiness, as well as by the holy judgments exacted, Lev. 10. 1-3. "I will be sanctified in them that come nigh me" and "ye shall be holy; for I am holy" were the demands of unutterable holiness, Lev. 11. 44.

The Lord most high is terrible (awesome) in His sanctuary, for "holiness becometh thine house, O Lord, for ever", Psa. 93. 5. Hence, "Serve the Lord with fear", Psa. 2. 11, and "be ye clean that bear the vessels of the Lord", Isa. 52. 11.

In such collective worship, the psalmist would be a companion of all that fear the Lord, Psa. 119. 63. They would often speak together in reverence as they thought on His Name, Mal. 3. 16. In this exercise they would discover the truth that "the secret of the Lord is with them that fear him", and what a rich heritage there is for those that fear the Lord's Name, Psa. 25. 14; 61. 5. Moreover, their posture would indicate their spiritual state, and their careful use of the Name would show how holy and how greatly to be revered it is, 95. 6; 111. 9.

In N.T. times, there is no diminishing of the demands of the same fear of the Lord. The Father has been revealed, the Spirit of sonship has been given, and the believer encouraged to draw near with boldness into the holiest, even to the mercy seat, Heb. 10. 19; 4. 16. The new covenant has brought in full blessings, but an essential of that covenant is the fear of God in hearts, Jer. 32. 40.

Thus as pilgrims we are to pass the time of our sojourning in fear, even as we call on the *Father*, 1 Pet. 1. 17. Praying that His Name be hallowed, we are to perfect holiness in the same fear, and to work out our salvation in fear and trembling, 2 Cor. 7. 1; Phil. 2. 12.

"Wherefore we receiving a kingdom which cannot be moved, let us have grace, whereby we may serve God acceptably with reverence and godly fear: for our God is a consuming fire", Heb. 12. 28-29.

15

January 7th

READING: **Psalm 91**

GOD ALL SUFFICIENT

THE PSALMIST first states his own experience, vv. 1-2. Then he addresses himself in testimony to individual listeners, vv. 3-13. Finally, God confirms the truths affirmed, vv. 14-16.

The writer had experimentally known God by entering into the message of the Name, v. 14. The "most High" is the One above all the conflicts without, v. 1. This reduces the enemies to their real size! The "Almighty" (Shaddai) is the all-sufficient One, v. 1. "The Lord" is the unchanging One, Mal. 3. 6.

For the writer, this was not just knowing God in a general way, but learning all this in the secret place which is known only to faith, v. 1. It is the place of warming love, which softly cherishes away from the harshness of the rough world, v. 4; Deut. 32. 11; Matt. 23. 37, and becomes his own refuge and fortress in which he determines to trust, v. 2. By making it his habitual resort, it becomes his habitation, v. 9.

The terrors without are real and active both by night and day, vv. 5-6. But no evil shall attain its object, v. 10. Not a hair of the head shall perish or be singed by the fire, even if slain for the Lord's sake, Luke 21. 16-18; Dan. 3. 27. God's promise is explicit, "I will be with thee ... I will deliver him", Psa. 91. 15.

The lion of open opposition goes about seeking whom he can devour; the subtle adder silently strikes. But faith sees the victory in Him who has overcome them, and who asserts that "the God of peace shall bruise Satan under your feet shortly", Psa. 91. 13; Rom. 16. 20; Eph. 1. 22. To this end, He shall give His angels command to be ministering spirits to these heirs of salvation, Heb. 1. 14; Psa. 91. 11-16.

But the cunning serpent, whilst avoiding the verses of our Psalm which indicate his coming doom, can misuse and misquote the Scripture, as at the temptation of our Lord, Matt. 4. 5-7; Psa. 91. 11-12. "Do something to attract attention to yourself! Put God to the test in your own demonstrative way" were the implied meanings of his subtle suggestions! Forsake the secret place of simple faith and obedience? Never! Our Lord's one thrust with the sword of the Spirit was simple and effective. *"It is written ... "*, Matt. 4. 4, 7, 10.

READING: **Psalm 89. 1-10**

THE FAITHFUL GOD

In O.T. times, believers instinctively knew that God could not be inconsistent with His holy nature. What He promised in His love and mercy must be fulfilled. No word from Him can fruitless fall. So they gloried in His steadfastness, and in His unchanging covenant and oath thereon. He was the faithful God that kept covenant, Deut. 7. 9; Psa. 111. 5.

They desired to show forth His lovingkindness in the morning, and His faithfulness every night, 92. 2. God's testimonies concerning His purposes for them were very faithful, 119. 138. His commandments are faithful, for with the command the enabling obedience is given, for He works in them both to will and to do of His good pleasure, 119. 138; Phil. 2. 13.

"Thy faithfulness reacheth unto the clouds" —to the very throne of God, Psa. 36. 5. God was His own witness of His integrity. Now we know of One who was made like unto His brethren that He might be a merciful and faithful High Priest upon the throne. He is the "yea" and "amen" to all the promises of God which are *by us* to the glory of God, 2 Cor. 1. 20; Rev. 3. 14.

Is there suffering for Christ's sake? Commit the keeping of your souls to Him in well-doing as unto a faithful Creator, 1 Pet. 4. 19, assuredly knowing that no testing overtakes you but such as man can bear: but God is faithful who will make a way of escape, 1 Cor. 10. 13. If necessary, be faithful unto death so that a crown of life shall be yours, Rev. 2. 10. (Do we pray for suffering believers?)

The psalmist accepted his suffering from the hand of God, "thou in faithfulness hast afflicted me", Psa. 119. 75. "If we confess our sins, he is faithful and just to forgive us our sins, and to cleanse us from all unrighteousness", 1 John 1. 9. We must know the truth of this so as to be useful to Him.

"God is faithful, by whom ye were called into the fellowship of his Son", 1 Cor. 1. 9. In response, it is required that we are found faithful in the absence of our Lord, so that He will gladly show His approval in that day: "Well done, thou good and faithful servant", 1 Cor. 4. 2; Matt. 25. 21.

"Confide in Jehovah ... feed on faithfulness", Psa. 37. 3
J.N.D.

January 9th

READING: **Psalm 111**

THE ONLY WISE GOD

"HIS UNDERSTANDING is infinite", Psa. 147. 5, is a truth that every believer gladly confesses. By wisdom He made the heavens, 136. 5, and by the wisdom of grace He is making a people prepared for that heaven.

These are "children of wisdom", Matt. 11. 19. Their wisdom began with the fear of the Lord, Psa. 111. 10. They rejected the wisdom that is from below, James 3. 15; 1 Cor. 1. 20, and as babes accepted God's revelation of the Person of His Son, Matt. 11. 25-27.

The world by its philosophic wisdom knew not God, but it pleased God by the (seeming) foolish message of the cross to deliver them that believe. Thus Christ became their wisdom, 1 Cor. 1. 24. Even after sin had held sway, in repentance one could affirm "in the hidden part thou shalt make me to know wisdom", Psa. 51. 6. They are renewed in knowledge after the image of Him who recreated them, Col. 3. 10, and exclaim "to him that is of power to stablish you ... to God only wise, be glory through Jesus Christ for ever", Rom. 16. 25-27.

Having found the Lord as our Wisdom, we are to walk in wisdom. For this God "gives counsel", Psa. 16. 7, by His testimonies, 119. 24, as we let the Word of God dwell in us in all wisdom, Col. 3. 16. But a teachable spirit is necessary, for it is the meek that He teaches His way, Psa. 25. 9. The meekness of wisdom, James 3. 13, will be in the spirit of the Lord who was meek and lowly in heart, and whose yoke is accepted, Matt. 11. 29. So "a good understanding have all they that do his commandments", Psa. 111. 10.

Whilst so walking wisely, we should be assured that the all-wise One is guiding by His counsel, and afterwards will receive us to glory, Psa. 73. 24. *He* knows the way we take, Job 23. 10. He knows our frame, Psa. 103. 14. He guides by the skilfulness of His hands, and according to the integrity of His *heart*, 78. 72. He cannot fail: being omnipotent, all things are possible with Him; being all-wise, He plans and works for our highest good. Our wisdom is willingly to accept this; then as children of wisdom, we shall vindicate God, Matt. 11. 19.

"O the depth of the riches both of the wisdom and knowledge of God", Rom. 11. 33.

18

January 10th

READING: **Psalm 111**

THE WORKS OF THE LORD

GOD HAS shown His works in His wonderful universe. He rested on the seventh day, for all was "good" and "very good". But the sabbath was broken by man's sin. Henceforth God would be working for man's recovery. Daily He rose early and all day long stretched forth His hands imploring men to return, for they made Him serve with their sins and wearied Him, Jer. 7. 13; Isa. 43. 24; Rom. 10. 21. This ceaseless activity through His prophets was continued by the Lord Jesus, as He stated, "My Father worketh hitherto, and I work", John 5. 17.

These spiritual works of the Lord are great, and are sought out of all them that have pleasure therein, Psa. 111. 2. As we so do, we exclaim, "Oh that men would praise the Lord for his goodness, and for his wonderful works to the children of men!", Psa. 107. 21-22. Sacrifices of thanksgiving will follow, and the declaring of His works in testimony. Especially in the remembrance feast will His works be recalled, Psa. 111. 4.

As believers, we gladly own that "it is he that hath made us, and not we ourselves", Psa. 100. 3, for we are "his workmanship, created in Christ Jesus", Eph. 2. 10. Thus "if any man be in Christ there is a new creation", 2 Cor. 5. 17 R.V. marg, in which "all things are of God", v. 18; Eph. 4. 24.

Such a perfect work of God in re-creation moves the heart to pray, "strengthen, O God, that which thou hast wrought for us", Psa. 68. 28, and "let thy work appear" in our lives, Psa. 90. 16, so that Christ may be formed in us, Gal. 4. 19.

To this end God is working in us that which is wellpleasing in His sight, Phil. 2. 13; Heb. 13. 21. He who saved us apart from our works, calls us unto good works, Eph. 2. 10, concerning which we are to be zealous, Titus 2. 14, diligently maintaining them, 3. 8. So we shall justify the faith that alone justified us, James 2. 17, for faith works by love, Gal. 5. 6. Whilst so working, our prayer will be, "establish thou the work of our hands", Psa. 90. 17.

We shall also lift up our eyes on the harvest fields, praying the Lord to thrust forth labourers into the harvest, knowing that a man who sleeps in harvest is one that causes shame, Prov. 10. 5.

"Work: for I am with you, saith the Lord", Hag. 2. 4.

19

READING: **Psalm 47**

THE MOST HIGH GOD

THIS TITLE of God, v. 2, asserts His transcendence, being above all, and beyond all. "When the wicked spring as the grass, and when all the workers of iniquity do flourish ... thou, Lord, art most high for evermore", Psa. 92. 7-8. He is the high and lofty One that inhabits eternity, Isa. 57. 15.

His sovereign purposes are evidenced in this title: "When the most High divided to the nations their inheritance, when he separated the sons of Adam, he set the bounds of the people according to the number of the children of Israel", Deut. 32. 8. He is the Governor of history, for "the most High ruleth in the kingdom of men", Dan. 4. 17, 25, 32; 5. 21.

When Isaiah saw Judah's throne empty, he "saw *also* the Lord sitting upon a throne, high and lifted up", Isa. 6. 1. And Ezekiel's vision was of a chariot-throne, awesomely high, and undeviatingly making its straight course, Ezek. 1. 9, 19-21. Yet upon that throne was the likeness of a Man, v. 26. We see Jesus who ascended on high, Psa. 68. 18. The eternal years of the right hand of the most High are his who was cut off in the midst of His years, 77. 10; 102. 24; Heb. 1. 10-12.

But though He is high, He has respect unto the lowly, Psa. 138. 6; Isa. 57. 15. The lowly amongst men know that man was made to look up beyond self to the most High. In saving them, God has broken their yoke of bondage and made them go upright, Lev. 26. 13. The woman, who was "bowed together, and could in no wise lift up herself" for eighteen long years, at the Lord's touch, was made straight, Luke 13. 11-13. She looked up to her Deliverer's face. "I will cry unto God most high", says the psalmist, Psa. 57. 2. Even the Lord, in dependent Manhood (yet knowing that He had come from God), "lifted up his eyes to heaven", John 17. 1.

This gives a new dimension to the soul, for it now dwells in the secret place of the most High, Psa. 91. 1. Hence "I will set him on high", says the most High, v. 14, "because he hath set his love upon me ... because he hath known my name". He is "the rock that is higher than I", Psa. 61. 2.

Instead of the believer cleaving to the dust, Psa. 119. 25, his feet will be like hind's feet; "*he will make me to walk upon mine high places*", Hab. 3. 19.

January 12th

READING: **Psalm 139**

GOD'S THOUGHTS

The All-knowing God, vv. 1-6.

David loved the fellowship of God's worshipping people. But he did not neglect to sit alone before the Lord, 2 Sam. 7. 18, as can be seen in the personal "I" and "me" throughout this psalm. Meditation is searching and enriching, for it does not represent a vacuum, but is the consideration of God's thoughts from His Word.

The daily activities (downsitting and uprising), thoughts before they have been formulated, the paths proposed, the words before they are articulated: God knew them altogether! Such knowledge is too high for us, and very searching, but to those who live in its light, "the living one who seeth me" becomes a well of refreshing, Gen. 16. 14 R.V. marg.

The Ever-present God, vv. 7-12.

God's omnipresence is a further arresting thought. Neither height nor depth, neither east nor west, can become a hiding place from Him. From the time of man's attempted hiding from God in Eden, guilty men (both wise and foolish) have attempted to do so, Jonah 1. 3; Rev. 6. 16. But our psalmist finds that the truth of God's prevailing presence brings great comfort to him. Conscience would put the Lord at a distance ("Depart from me"), but mercy would drive us to Him ("fell down at Jesus' knees"), Luke 5. 8.

The Ever-planning God, vv. 13-18

David is convinced that the God who knew him and fashioned him in his prenatal state, has also recorded all His purposeful thoughts towards him. "How precious also are thy thoughts unto me, O God! how great is the sum of them!", he exclaims.

His life was planned by an overruling Providence (see Jer. 1. 5; Gal. 1. 15). Whom God foreknew, He also foreordained to be conformed to the image of His Son. In view of this, "all things work together for good", Rom. 8. 28-29. Such counsels of the Lord stand for ever, for they are the thoughts of His *heart* to all generations, Psa. 33. 11, and they are to us-ward who believe, Psa. 40. 5; Eph. 2. 7.

"*We have the mind of Christ*", 1 Cor. 2. 16;

"*Set your mind on the things that are above*", Col. 3. 2 R.V.

21

January 13th

READING: **Psalms 68. 28-35; 105. 1-5**

GOD MY STRENGTH

THIS TITLE is found in Psalm 18. 2. Believers always remember that the Lord saved them when they were without strength. Their rescue, with all that was involved in it, was of God by His power, Rom. 5. 6.

The working of God in the resurrection of His Son was the working of His mighty power. Nothing less than *that* is the measure of His power to us-ward who believe. This is true both in our initial salvation, and in His continuous keeping, until by the power whereby He is able to subdue all things He will conform us to the image of His Son, changing our body of humiliation so that it may be fashioned like unto His glorious body, Eph. 1. 19-20; Phil. 3. 21.

We can now read the inspired psalmist's statements with the added dimension of the completed Scriptures, as scribes instructed therein and finding treasures new and old, Matt. 13. 52.

The Lord is the One who "giveth strength and power unto his people", Psa. 68. 35, so we can assert, "thou art the God of my strength", 43. 2. "The Lord hath *commanded* thy strength", 68. 28. We are the strong ones with whom our Lord shares the spoils of His death and victory, Isa. 53. 12.

This is blessedly true, but it must be realized daily in some measure. To this end, "Seek the Lord, and his strength: seek his face", 105. 4, and pray, "strengthen, O Lord, that which thou *hast* wrought for us", 68. 28, for our cry is, "My flesh and my heart faileth: but God is the strength of my heart", 73. 26. If physical weakness is felt, be assured that the Lord will strengthen such upon the bed of weakness, 41. 3.

In service for God, however small it may seem, His empowering is indispensable. "I will go in the strength of the Lord God", says the psalmist, 71. 16. "Go in this thy might", said God to a trembling Gideon, Jud. 6. 13-14. God's strength is made perfect in weakness, for man's felt weakness can be the vehicle of His strength. But self-sufficiency can be His rival, 2 Cor. 12. 9; 4. 7. Remember that the primary object of being strengthened is that Christ may dwell in the heart through faith, Eph. 3. 16-17.

"I will love thee, O Lord, my strength", Psa. 18. 1.

January 14th

READING: **Psalm 11**

THE GOD WHO TESTS

A SERIOUS crisis had developed for the psalmist. The wicked were targetting their assult upon him, and *that* in the night season. The foundations of his faith were in danger. What can he do?

Well-intentioned friends (or foes) suggest his fleeing to the mountains. But he had already committed both himself and the danger to the Lord, v. 1. His priorities were right, for faith asserts itself before the keenness of the trial is felt: otherwise, it could be overwhelming. He had set the Lord always before him, so he would not be moved, Psa. 16. 8. Flight can put him in the firing line of those arrows of unbelief. He must take the shield of faith, having kept it oiled for such an eventuality, 2 Sam. 1. 21 R.V.; Eph. 6. 16. For this warfare, his hand had been taught by his Lord, Psa. 144. 1. (Contrast the low state of the people when no shield was available, for Deborah sang, "was there a shield or spear seen among forty thousand in Israel?, Jud. 5. 8.)

But the trial was real. Although it was of the enemy, yet it was to be used by the Lord, and must be accepted as such, Psa. 11. 5. Faith, being more precious than gold, when passing through the refining fire can be unto praise, honour and glory, 1 Pet. 1. 7. Therefore, "count it all joy when ye fall into divers temptations", because the trying of faith works endurance, James 1. 2-3.

"The Lord's throne is in heaven", Psa. 11. 4, and Jesus the Author and Finisher of faith is there! Thus, looking off from self, and steadfastly to Him who endured to the end, we see the outcome of our faith, Heb. 12. 2-3; 1 Pet. 1. 9.

For those exercised by the trial, the discipline of the trial is evidence of sonship, and is for profit, so that there will be a partaking of God's holiness, Heb. 12. 7-11. Although God shows hard things to His people, yet at the same time He gives them a banner to be displayed because of the truth of all God's ways, Psa. 60. 3-4.

The ultimate issue is to "behold his face", Psa. 11. 7 R.V., and to be able to bless the hand that guided and the heart that planned. Look for the token of good in the trial, for the Lord is good, Psa. 86. 5, 17.

READING: **Psalm 80**

GOD DWELLING BETWEEN THE CHERUBIM

THE ARK in the tabernacle and temple of old was the symbolic throne of God. At either end of the mercy seat was a golden cherub, looking downwards towards the seat. Our psalmist speaks of God as seated between these cherubim, Psa. 80. 1; see Hebrews 9. 4-5. God is seated upon "the throne of his holiness", 47. 8. Justice and judgment are the foundation of that throne, 89. 14 R.V.; 97. 2.

On the yearly Day of Atonement, the blood of propitiation was sprinkled upon the seat, Lev. 16. By this it became the "mercy seat", for mercy and truth met together, righteousness and peace kissed each other, Psa. 85. 10. It was God who provided the sacrifice, Lev. 17. 11.

To us it is written: "Herein is love, not that we loved God, but that he loved us, and sent his Son to be the propitiation for our sins", 1 John 4. 10, and "God has set forth Christ Jesus a mercy seat through faith in his blood, for the showing forth of his righteousness", Rom. 3. 25 J.N.D. Thus the God who dwells between the cherubim can be just and the justifier of him that believes, Rom. 3. 26. We rightly joy in God through the Lord Jesus Christ through whom we received the reconciliation, 5. 11 R.V.

The ark also spoke of God's presence with His pilgrim people, leading them and seeking a place of rest for them, Num. 10. 33; Josh. 3. 14. "I am a stranger", said the psalmist, but more, "a stranger with thee", Psa. 39. 12.

In Psalm 80, the writer speaks of the oppression of the enemy. Prayer seems unavailing; "How long?", is the cry, v. 4. He recalls that there was to be a vine for God's delight and testimony, v. 8. His prayer is for restoration to fruitfulness and to be able to sense afresh the glory and presence of God who dwelt between the cherubim, so that God's face may shine upon him, vv. 1, 3, 7, 19.

By the Spirit of prophecy, the writer is directed to the Man of God's right hand who was upheld in His faithful service, v. 17; Isa. 42. 1. Recourse to Him can quicken him (and us) so that he would never go back from God, Psa. 80. 18.

"I chose you ... that ye should go and bear fruit, and that your fruit should abide", John 15. 16 R.V.

24

READING: **Psalm 27. 1-4; 29. 1-11**

THE BEAUTY OF THE LORD

IN THE Scriptures, glimpses of the eternal throne are given with a sense of the inadequacy of human language to express its beauty. The sapphire-like throne was seen on a sapphire-like pavement, Exod. 24. 10; Ezek. 1. 26.

In this world's creation, God has made everything beautiful in its time, Eccl. 3. 11, as all will confess.

The tabernacle and temple were structures where "strength and beauty" were evident, Psa. 96. 6. They were beautiful in symmetry and in colour. The temple site was beautiful for situation, the joy of the whole earth, 48. 2. In fact, it was the perfection of beauty, 50. 2.

The high priest's garments were for glory and beauty, Exod. 28. 2, 40. The tabernacle's inner covering, the veils with their intricate weaving, the buds and flowers of the lampstand, all had beautiful meanings to anointed eyes. "In his temple every thing saith, Glory", Psa. 29. 9.

In the salvation of the believing one, the Lord has done everything well (i.e., beautifully), for "he will beautify the meek with salvation", Psa. 149. 4; Mark 7. 37. Such an one is perfect in Him, because of the comeliness that He has put upon him, Ezek. 16. 14. The Lord is taking unlovely sinners, making them members of His church which will yet be seen as a radiant church, without stain, wrinkle or any blemish, Eph. 5. 27.

The heart's response should be *praise*, for this is comely, Psa. 33. 1, and *"worship* in the beauty of holiness", 29. 2. "One thing have I desired of the Lord ... to behold the beauty of the Lord, and to enquire in his temple", says the psalmist, 27. 4.

In the world, the believer's life is to be consistent with the profession that he has made, so that it adorns (shows the beauty of) the teaching of grace, Titus 2. 10. "Let the beauty of the Lord our God be upon us", Psa. 90. 17. To this the reply of the Word is, "put on thy beautiful garments", Isa. 52. 1, "so shall the king greatly desire thy beauty", Psa. 45. 11.

From the womb of the day of the new birth, believers should be free-will offerings in the beauties of holiness, 110. 3 R.V. marg. Holiness is spiritual wholeness.

"The dayspring from on high hath visited us", Luke 1. 78.

25

January 17th

READING: **Psalm 47**

GOD THE SOURCE AND OBJECT OF LOVE

THE PEOPLE of God are described in many ways, but supremely they are "beloved of God", as was "Jacob whom he loved", v. 4; Rom. 1. 7. Solomon ("peace") was given an even better name, Jedidiah ("beloved of the Lord"), 2 Sam. 12. 25; Neh. 13. 26.

God set His love upon Israel, Deut. 7. 8, not only because of their pitiable state in Egypt, but because of His own purpose and grace long before. The reason could only be found in God's own heart. They were not more numerous or more cultured than others.

God had wooed them by putting His love in them, Hos. 2. 19; He had drawn them with cords of love, and He remembered their espousals, Jer. 2. 2. With what grief of heart then did He hear their steely question when they proved unfaithful: "Wherein hast thou loved us?", Mal. 1. 2. Their sin was not only against His law, but against His heart, Hos. 11. 8.

The truly pious ones well knew that the proper response was to love the Lord their God with all the heart. "My *heart* followeth hard after thee", Psa. 63. 8, and "Whom have I in heaven but thee? and there is none upon earth that I desire beside thee", 73. 25, were suitable spiritual responses.

The whole heart would express its love, 119. 2, 10, 58. Thus "my heart is fixed", 57. 7; 108. 1; 112. 7.This was not by outward legal obedience, but by God's cords of love, Jer. 31. 3. Those so drawn deeply desired others to love Him, "O love the Lord, all ye his saints" were the words of their urging, Psa. 31. 23.

God's perfect love is perfected (it had found its object) when we love one another, 1 John 4. 12. When doing so, we love the habitation of God's house, the place where His honour dwells, Psa. 26. 8. This love for fellow-believers is a proof of having passed from death unto life, 1 John 3. 14, and is the answer to the love that sent the beloved Son for our sins, vv. 10, 11. Further, it is proof of our love to God who is invisible. (A psalmist, perhaps, would have appended a "Selah" at such a statement—"stop and think".)

"As the Father hath loved me, so have I loved you: continue in ye in my love", John 15. 9.

READING: **Psalm 103**

GOD OUR FATHER

THE PSALMIST makes a very meaningful and tender statement: "Like as a father pitieth his children, so the Lord pitieth them that fear him", v. 13. Again, concerning the orphan, the psalmist speaks of God as a father of the fatherless, thus showing His tender care, 68. 5.

Yet not even David the psalmist could address God as "Father". These touching analogies were anticipating the time when the sublime truth of the Father would be revealed by *the* Son. "I have manifested thy name unto the men which thou gavest me out of the world", He said to the Father, John 17. 6.

"Show us the Father, and it sufficeth us", said Philip, John 14. 8. Such a revelation is supremely satisfying. *That* is the believer's portion now, for "now are we children of God", 1 John 3. 2 R.V. The Spirit of sonship in our hearts witnesses to this, leading us to cry, "Abba, Father", the very address that our Lord used in Gethsemane, Mark 14. 36; Gal. 4. 6.

"Wherefore thou art no more a servant, but a son", Gal. 4. 7; the prodigal would have been content to be a servant, but the Father's heart would be content with nothing less than a son in the family and near His heart. The son would serve, but in a true spirit of sonship.

How delighted our Father is in hearing us address Him thus in all meaningful sincerity! When we are delivered from the sophistries of the world's thoughts about God, it is as babes that we receive the Father's revelation, Luke 10. 21.

In time of need, "your Father knoweth what things ye have need of, before ye ask him", Matt. 6. 8, yet "Give us this day our daily bread" is the prayer of a dependence which is truly felt. Our Father who feeds the sparrows and clothes the flowers will much more attend to our needs. To doubt His heart is to be as pagans, and earns His rebuke, "ye of little faith", v. 30.

In time of severe trial, "Abba, Father, all things are possible unto thee" acknowledges His illimitable power; "nevertheless not what I will, but what thou wilt" owns His perfect wisdom, Mark 14. 36. How good to see these expressed in perfect harmony in the life of the Son.

In fellowship with other members of the same family of believers, *"let brotherly love continue"*, Heb. 13. 1; Eph. 3. 15.

January 19th

READING: **Psalm 65**

THOU THAT HEAREST PRAYER

THE LATTER part of this psalm depicts God mercifully meeting the great need in time of drought. In Israel's case, this occurred through departure from God, Deut. 28. 24.

The awe-inspiring renewal of nature came about upon confession of the cause of the drought—the transgression which had prevailed against them, v. 3. God is the One who hears such prayer, and restores, so that the soul, like the land, can be fruitful again.

The Book of Psalms breathes an atmosphere of prayer. Prayer is a looking up beyond self to a higher sphere, 5. 3; a lifting up the eyes in desire for spiritual vision, 123. 1; a lifting up of the very soul unto the Lord, 25. 1.

It is waiting only on God, 62. 2, even when the eyes fail while so doing, 69. 3, assured that none that wait shall be put to shame, 25. 3, but shall be enriched, 37. 9. Therefore, "Wait on the Lord: be of good courage, and he shall strengthen thine heart: wait, I say, on the Lord", 27. 14.

Importunity in prayer is inculcated by our Lord, whose busy life was also a life of prayer, Luke 11. 1-13. In the agony of the garden, He repeated prayer, for this did not constitute "vain repetitions", Matt. 6. 7.

Prayer is a drawing near to God, and as such is productive and good, Psa. 73. 28; 65. 4. But it is to be with the whole heart, 119. 58, and it must not be out of feigned lips, 17. 1. Therefore confession will be made, for "If I regard iniquity in my heart, the Lord will not hear me", 66. 18. In this spirit, prayer is definitely not double-minded, James 1. 6-8.

Prayer pleads the promises and faithfulness of the Lord, "in thy faithfulness answer me", 143. 1. "Remember the word unto thy servant, upon which thou hast caused me to hope".

Present prayer finds encouragement from past answers, "I love the Lord, because he hath heard my voice ... therefore will I call upon him as long as I live", 116. 1, 2. Faith is to be active, for God is the confidence of the ends of the earth, 65. 5. Humility is not absent, "thou hast heard the desire of the humble", 10. 17. Moreover, set times for prayer show an ordered life, "Evening, and morning, and at noon, will I pray", 55. 17.

"Let your requests be made known unto God", Phil. 4. 6.

January 20th

READING: **Psalm 77**

THE GOD THAT DOETH WONDERS

THE PSALMIST commences by acknowledging that the Lord had answered his prolonged prayers, v. 1. He then recounts those trying times. This is the proper order in all testimony.

His hand had been outstretched in prayer in the night, and did not slacken in sustained importunity, v. 2 R.V. He recalled God's way in sacred history, and in the songs of joy that he himself had experienced in past seasons of darkness. But God seemed so inactive right now, so the remembrance of His past doings made the present more inexplicable. The psalmist refused to be comforted!

But he bestirs himself to challenge his latent unbelief: *can* God cast off for ever? Is His unfailing love totally finished? Has He expunged me from His memory? Can His plighted word fail? Has He closed the affection of His heart?

"No!" is the only answer to these rhetorical questions. God cannot fail or be inconsistent with Himself. The infirmity is that of the speaker; the breakdown is his alone, v. 10.

Having so confronted himself, he will remember the right hand of the most High, and the wonders of old, together with His doings *now*. As the psalmist does so, the "I", so prominent hitherto, gives place to "thou". God comes into focus, and problems are reduced to their real relative size.

He can now exclaim, "who is so great a God ... that doest wonders", the wonder of making a great obstacle (the Red Sea) to become a way of deliverance, vv. 16, 19, the wonders of His leading, providing and keeping in the desert ahead. Surely all things work together for good.

For the psalmist in his present experience, the greatest wonder from the God that does wonders is that "so great a God" patiently bore with him, and was turning his melancholy into quiet assurance, v. 13. Yea, "many, O Lord my God, are thy wonderful works which thou hast done, and thy thoughts which are to us-ward", 40. 5.

What further persuasion can we, who live this side of the Lord's cross and entrance into glory, bring to bear upon life's perplexities? *"That thy name is near thy wondrous works declare"*, Psa. 75. 1.

January 21st

READING: **Psalm 121**

GOD THE KEEPER

WE ALL realize the need of being kept safe in an evil and cruel world, and the more so as we know the latent, perfidiousness of our own hearts. Our Lord knew our need in such a scene as he prayed, "these are in the world ... Holy Father, keep through thine own name those whom thou hast given me", John 17. 11.

In this psalm, the writer no less than six times uses the word "keep" (R.V.). From wherever the help comes, it comes from the Lord whose omnipotence and omniscience have servants ready to do His bidding, vv. 1-2. His unwearied love and continual set purpose assure unbroken preservation of God's own, v. 4.

The Lord (Jehovah, the unchanging One) is the shade from the simmering heat. Such ministry is at the right hand in strong support. Satan had been at the right hand to accuse (the usual position for the counsel for the prosecution in a court). But the Judge Himself is now the Upholder of the justified one, Zech. 3. 1; Rev. 12. 10; Rom. 8. 33.

The supporting right hand reminds us that we are kept by the power of God unto salvation, 1 Pet. 1. 5, for "I ... will hold thine hand, and will keep thee", says the Lord, Isa. 42. 6. Moreover, the complete company of the kept-ones is preserved as one inviolable entity, to be admired in that day, John 17. 11; 2 Thess. 1. 10.

The Lord's keeping is not only in His power, but also in exquisite tenderness, "Keep me as the apple of the eye", Psa. 17. 8. The Lord had promised this very thing, Deut. 32. 10, (*lit.* "the little man in the eye"—the reflection. The same idiom exists in the Chinese language).

The good of all this should be enjoyed daily in the believer's life. Those whose minds are stayed on the Lord in faith, He will keep in perfect peace, Isa. 26. 3.

So *"In nothing be anxious; but in everything by prayer and supplication with thanksgiving let your requests be made known unto God. And the peace of God, which passeth all understanding, shall guard your hearts and your thoughts in Christ Jesus"*, Phil. 4. 6-7 R.V.

January 22nd

READING: **Psalm 107**

GOD IS GOOD

OUR PSALMIST recounts some of God's many mercies: re-deeming, v. 2; gathering them as the congregation of the Lord, v. 3; leading them by the right way, v. 7; satisfying the longing soul, v. 9; delivering them out of bondage and dark-ness, v. 14; saving them from the storm-tossed sea of despair into His peace, vv. 23-30, and turning the dry ground into watersprings, v. 35.

Are these not enough to bring forth thanksgiving? Let the reader apply each to its respective spiritual analogy. Truly the Lord *is* good, v. 1, and we should say so, v. 2, and also say it in the congregation, v. 32. Moreover, we should make the thanksgiving a sacrifice freely offered and of a fragrant odour to the Lord, v. 22.

Of old, the peace offering was used as a thankoffering, Lev. 7. 12. Psalm 100 was a psalm especially "for the thank offer-ing", R.V. marg. "Enter into his gates with thanksgiving...be thankful unto him" was the fitting exhortation, 100. 4.

With that offering, vows were recalled, Lev. 7. 12-16, in such words as, "thy vows are upon me, O God: I will render thankofferings unto thee", Psa. 56. 12 R.V. So now our thankful hearts will soon sense the obligation upon them when recalling how in the past God's goodness had evoked either spoken or unspoken promises to Him.

Hebrews 13. 15-16 is an echo of the praise offering of Leviticus 7 in a New Testament setting, "By him therefore let us offer the sacrifice of praise to God continually, that is, the fruit of our lips giving thanks to his name". Another ele-ment in the praise offering was sharing with others, Lev. 7. 31-32; Psa. 22. 26. Therefore Hebrews 13. 16 continues, "to do good and to communicate forget not: for with such sacrifices God is well pleased".

Among the many blessings for which we should more particularly give thanks continually is "his unspeakable gift (the Lord Jesus)", 2 Cor. 9. 15, including the remembrance of His holiness vindicated at the cross, Psa. 30. 4, and the coming final victory over death through our Lord Jesus Christ, 1 Cor. 15. 57.

"Thanks be to God, which giveth us the victory through our Lord Jesus Christ", 1 Cor. 15. 57.

31

January 23rd

READING: **Psalm 47**

GOD IS GONE UP WITH A SHOUT

WHEN DAVID escorted the ark of the Lord up to mount Zion, he wrote a psalm for the occasion, 1 Chron. 16. 7-36; Psa. 105. 1-15; Psa. 96; Psa. 106. 47-48. The first part of Psalm 105 is quoted in the record of that event in 1 Chronicles 16. Psalms 47 and 48 have the same event as their background. As a prophet, David the seer perceived the occasion as having more than local significance.

The ark of the covenant symbolized the presence of God among His people, and its instalment in Zion implied the establishment of the kingdom. The voice of triumph is heard, Psa. 47. 1. The "shout" of acclamation and the trumpet-sound assert God's kingship, v. 6, and His kingdom, vv. 7-8.

He who was mocked with the robes of Jewish and Roman royalty, and crowned with thorns, uttered the triumphant, loud cry, "Finished", Matt. 27. 28; Luke 23. 11; John 19. 30. The strong one was overcome by the Stronger, and his "goods" that he had held so securely were taken as spoils of complete victory, Luke 11. 21; Isa. 53. 12. By His cross, Christ "spoiled principalities and powers ... triumphing over them in it", Col. 2. 15. It is the Lamb of sacrifice that alone is worthy to take the kingly rule, Rev. 5. 7.

In His resurrection and ascension, He is exalted and made very high, Isa. 52. 13. He went up with a shout, Psa. 47. 5. Ephesians 4. 8 quotes Psalm 68 (which had reference to the ark): "he ascended up on high, he led captivity captive, and gave gifts unto men". The "sure mercies of David" are Christ's, Acts 13. 34. We are in the kingdom of God's dear Son, Col. 1. 13.

By faith we know His goings in the sanctuary as High Priest, Psa. 68. 24, with all power and full sympathy, Heb. 4. 14, 15. Thus even now, before His public assertion of kingly rule, we should "say among the heathen that the Lord reigneth", Psa. 96. 10, as we are led along in triumph in Christ, 2 Cor. 2. 14, in the heralding of the gospel.

In view of this triumph, we are to be steadfast, immoveable, always abounding in the work of the Lord, 1 Cor. 15. 57-58, and "Sing praises ... sing praises unto our King", Psa. 47. 6-7, thereby owning His regal rights.

32

READING: **Psalm 94**

GOD TO WHOM VENGEANCE BELONGS

OUR PSALMIST is perplexed by the triumph of the wicked. He sees them prospering in their pride and in the oppression of the people of the land. It has been so throughout history, especially Christian history. Only those who have felt the consternation that it brings can fully sympathize with the suffering saints.

"How long?" is the question wrung out of the sufferers, vv. 3-4. So it will be in a future day, Rev. 6. 10. They are persuaded that the Judge of all the earth will do right, Psa. 94. 2; Gen. 18. 25.

The wicked act as if the Lord ignores the oppression, and as if He were deaf to the cries of His people, v. 7. But surely He that planted the ear hears, and He that formed the eye sees?, vv. 9-10.

Even an unjust judge eventually must respond to the importunate pleading of the sorely tried. Shall not God avenge His own elect, though He postpone His wrath? "I tell you that He will avenge them", says the Lord, Luke 18. 1-8. "Vengeance is mine; I will repay, saith the Lord", Rom. 12. 19. This springs from judgment which is holy and right, without vindictiveness, Rev. 16. 7; 19. 2.

God is called upon to show Himself, to render a recompense to the enemy, so that He can be justified in all His ways, and to plead His own cause, Psa. 94. 1-2.

When He shall do so, the saints in glory will acquiesce in shouts of "Hallelujah", for He will come and not keep silence for ever, Rev. 19. 6; Psa. 104. 35; 50. 3. Even grace on the lips of the King Eternal will not cancel the instruments of His sore judgments, Psa. 45. 2-5. It will be found that God has never had any fellowship with the evil, Psa. 94. 20.

At present, we are in the "patience of Jesus", Rev. 1. 9; unless this is kept before the soul, the foot may slip, Psa. 94. 18, and the heart become vindictive, being overcome by the prevailing evil, Rom. 12. 19, 21. The Lord is our Example, "Father, forgive them", Luke 23. 34; 1 Pet. 2. 21-23, while Stephen the first martyr showed the same grace, Acts 7. 60. *"Love your enemies ... that ye may be the children of your Father"*, Matt. 5. 44-45.

READING: **Psalm 136. 10-26**

GOD THE REDEEMER

THE WRITERS of the Old Testament Scriptures delighted to consider the blessed truth that God is a Redeeming God. The psalmists had a similar delight, as is evident by their frequent references.

Redemption is by Power: "With a strong hand, and with a stretched out arm", God delivered His people out of Egypt, Psa. 136. 10-12. He declared His strength among the people, and with His own arm redeemed them, 77. 14. Their own arm did not save them, but "thy right hand, and thine arm", 44. 3. Thus was His promise fulfilled, for He had said, "I will redeem you with a stretched out arm, and with great judgments", Exod. 6. 6. On the basis of this redemption by power, Nehemiah could plead with God concerning the remnant in his day, Neh. 1. 10.

As to ourselves, it was "when we were yet without strength, in due time Christ died for the ungodly", Rom. 5. 6. Through the gospel, we experience nothing less than the power of God, 1 Cor. 1. 24. The gospel came to us "in demonstration of the Spirit and of power", 2. 4, and this *effectually* works in those that believe, 1 Thess. 2. 13.

Redemption is by the Pity of God: God has a favour unto sinners, Psa. 44. 3, for His mercy endures for ever, 136. 10; it was "in his love and in his pity he redeemed them", Isa. 63. 9. "Thou in thy *mercy* hast led forth the people which thou hast redeemed", Exod. 15. 13.

Redemption is with a Great Price: "thy congregation, which thou hast purchased of old ... which thou hast redeemed", Psa. 74. 2. We confess that "Christ our passover is sacrificed for us", 1 Cor. 5. 7, for He came to give His life a ransom for many, Matt. 20. 28. In glory we shall boast that "thou ... hast redeemed us to God by thy blood", Rev. 5. 9, for "the redemption of their soul is costly", Psa. 49. 8 R.V.

The Purpose of Redemption is to deliver from the pit, Job 33. 24, from the curse of the law, Gal. 3. 13, from the grave, Job 19. 25-26; Eph. 1. 14; 4. 30. Surely it is plenteous redemption, Psa. 130. 7!

We were redeemed from our vain (empty) manner of life, 1 Pet. 1. 18, to live as those who are His alone, Isa. 43. 1. Let us "subscribe" to this truth by heart and action, Isa. 44. 5.

January 26

READING: **Psalms 18. 2, 29-39; 42. 9; 62. 2**

GOD MY ROCK

IN A WORLD of uncertainty and instability, nothing can be more precious than knowing and believing that God is one's Rock. He *only* is the Rock, Psa. 18. 31; 62. 2. No other foundation is laid, 1 Cor. 3. 11, for our souls' salvation, and for faith to build upon, Matt. 7. 24.

The world has its bogus rock-foundations, but "their rock is not as our Rock"; eventually this will be admitted by our enemies, Deut. 32. 31. On their rock is the subtle serpent who can persuade his dupes that incohesive sand is solid rock, Prov. 30. 19, but God will lay bare such a foundation, Mic. 1. 6.

Our Rock is our fortress, saving us from the assults of our enemies, Psa. 18. 2-3, and causing us to stand upon the Rock while He makes all His goodness panoramically to pass before our souls, Exod. 33. 19-23. This is mercy from first to last.

In the fearsome gales, we hide in the cleft of the rock, His hand covering us with warmth and tenderness, Exod. 33. 22.

In perplexity, it is well to utter our questionings to God, who is the Rock higher than we, Psa. 42. 9; 61. 2. Then our hearts will confess, "He only is my Rock ... I shall not be greatly moved", 62. 2.

Paul sees the Rock smitten in the wilderness as prefiguring Christ: "that Rock was Christ", 1 Cor. 10. 4; Exod. 17. 6. It was consequent on the Lord's being smitten for our sins, and being glorified, that the streams of the Spirit's blessing came to us, John 7. 39. Of the wilderness rock it is testified that "He opened the rock, and waters gushed out" as streams, Psa. 105. 41; 78. 16. Of the Spirit's effusion, it is asserted that He was *poured* forth, Acts 2. 17-18, 33; 10. 45; Titus 3. 6.

What fruitfulness is brought into the life, when the Spirit is allowed to minister Christ to the heart, Gal. 5. 22. Yea, what sweetness is found in the Rock which is Christ, Psa. 81. 16.

On the Rock, the Son of the living God, confessed by those who believe in Him, His church is founded, Matt. 16. 16-18, so *"Unto you therefore which believe he (the Stone) is precious"*, 1 Pet. 2. 7.

READING: **Psalm 145**

HOW GREAT THOU ART!

THE MUSICAL background and cadence of the poetical construction of the Psalms assume that God's people are in tune with Him. He has put a new song in their mouths, even praise to His name, Psa. 40. 3. They have discovered Christ, in whom all true concord and harmony are found.

In Psalm 145, they extol (uplift) Him, by giving Him the pre-eminence in all things, v. 1; they bless Him (speak well of Him and desire His glory). This they wish to do for ever and ever, not only in eternity, but day by day, varied as those days may be, v. 2. In this they abundantly utter (bubble over in speaking) His great goodness, v. 7.

God's greatness is in the mighty acts of His redeeming works, v. 4, in His awe-inspiring acts which show His righteousness, v. 6, in His great and tender mercies, vv. 8-9. His people speak together of those things that pertain to His kingdom, and they make them known to others, for the power and goodness of the gospel is to do with His counsels and kingdom, v. 12; Acts 20. 24-25. When the Lord is so magnified, man finds his true stature; but when man is wrapped up in himself, he makes a small parcel, Isa. 21. 17 R.V.

The might and glory of all these acts of our Great God assures support for those who fall and for those bent under heavy burdens, v. 14; Matt. 11. 28; Luke 13. 11. Better still, the Lord will enlarge our steps under us, if we are willing, so that we do not slip, Psa. 18. 36. Those who are restored fear Him, call upon Him, and love Him, 145. 18-20.

Moreover, they have spiritual desires implanted in their hearts by His supportive hand, and these He will fulfil, for they supremely desire His will alone, vv. 19-20. They would concur with the Scripture that states, "this is the confidence that we have in him, that, if we ask any thing according to his will, he heareth us", 1 John 5. 14.

All flesh shall yet bless His holy name, for at the name of Jesus every knee shall bow, Psa. 145. 21; Phil. 2. 10-11, because His is the kingdom, and the power, and the glory, for ever, 1 Chron. 29. 11; Matt. 6. 13.

But *now "My mouth shall speak the praise of the Lord"*, Psa. 145. 21; Rom. 15. 6.

READING: **Psalm 19. 1-6**

THE VOICE OF THE LORD

By DAY and night creation bears constant witness to the wisdom and power of God. Its message leaves man without excuse, for creation is a visible evidence of the invisible God, Rom. 1. 20.

In the regular operation of the laws governing the universe, God is operative, and He is not shut out by His own laws! He holds it together as surely as He initiated it, Col. 1. 17; Heb. 1. 3. He can intervene in miracle or in judgment.

One of the greatest interventions was the conception of Jesus by the virgin mother. In His ministry the Lord intervened to turn water into wine, to walk on the sea, to still a violent storm, to ride an unbroken colt, etc.

He who has made heaven and earth, Acts 4. 24, can declare the prophetic word concerning His Son, v. 25, and can overrule the actions of many persons so as to bring that word to pass, vv. 26-28.

It is the *Creator* to whom we confess, "there is nothing too hard for thee", Jer. 32. 17; Gen. 18. 14. It is because He numbers and names the (to us) innumerable heavenly bodies, that we are assured that *He* cannot ignore our state and weariness, Isa. 40. 26-31.

The Spirit of inspiration gave Paul to see a further meaning to "their voice ... is gone out through all the earth, and their words to the end of the world" : it is the gospel that has gone out to Jew and Gentile. "The same Lord over all is rich unto all that call upon him". How beautiful are the feet of those who preach peace and bring glad tidings into all the earth, Rom. 10. 12, 15, 18.

When the Lord's fiat went out, "Go ye into all the world", it began its course. Paul could state that it *was* preached to every creature which is under heaven, for he perceived that it inherently had its own worldwide fulfilment, as surely as the sun completes its course, Psa. 19. 6. Have we a burden to share in its progress until there is no speech or language where it is not heard?, v. 3.

Pray that the Lord of the harvest will thrust forth labourers into His harvest. He sends, for it is His harvest. *"The fields ... are white already to harvest"*, John 4. 35.

READING: **Psalm 33. 12-22**

THE GOD OF HOPE

IN THE world's vocabulary, "hope" is a very tentative word; sometimes it is founded upon mere sentiment, and thus it is illusory. Scripture asserts that the unsaved, however optimistic they may be, are without God and hope in the world, Eph. 2. 12. If in this life hope is limited to what is seen, we are most miserable, 1 Cor. 15. 19.

But for believers, "faith is the substantiating of things hoped for, the conviction of things not seen", Heb. 11. 1 J.N.D. The saints of old set their hope in God, Psa. 78. 7, whose promise formed the foundation of their hope for the circumstances of their lives, and for the coming of Messiah. "We hoped that it was he" was the sad confession of two who knew not the One who walked with them on His resurrection day, Luke 24. 21 R.V.

"Our hope is lost", said Israel in dismay at their sad condition, Ezek. 37. 11. But they could hope in God's mercy, Psa. 33. 18, for the door through which hope could be regained was the "valley of Achor", that is, the place of repentance, Hos. 2. 15; Josh. 7. 26. Even if they were prisoners by their own sins, they were prisoners of hope. They could turn to the Stronghold for mercy, Zech. 9. 12. "Let Israel hope in the Lord: for with the Lord there is mercy, and with him is plenteous redemption", Psa. 130. 7. All this can speak to a backsliding believer.

In New Testament language, we rejoice in hope of the glory of God, because we stand in grace. This hope "putteth not to shame", Rom. 5. 2-5 R.V., because the love of God has been shed abroad in our hearts. This is the hope of the gospel, Col. 1. 23; of our calling, Eph. 1. 18; of our justification, Gal. 5. 5; and of our glory, Col. 1. 27. Because of this hope, faith and love to all saints are produced, Col. 1. 4-5 R.V.

This hope must be kept alive in the heart continually, and it must be centred in God our hope and not in present circumstances, Psa. 71. 14-15. Thus we shall ever be ready to give the reason for our hope in quiet testimony, 1 Pet. 3. 15.

"Now the God of hope fill you with all joy and peace in believing, that ye may abound in hope, through the power of the Holy Spirit", Rom. 15. 13.

READING: **Psalm 19. 7-14**

THE MEDITATION OF MY HEART

"THE WORDS of wise men are heard in quiet", Eccles. 9. 17; this is true in all study, but especially when reading the words of Him "who of God is made unto us wisdom", 1 Cor. 1. 30.

Diligence in the daily task and in the Lord's service is expected from all who belong to Him who untiringly served others in His holy sojourn on earth. But He often withdrew from the crowds, and even from most or all of His disciples so as to be alone in prayer, Matt. 14. 23. He often taught them by calling them to be alone with Him, Matt. 13. 36; Mark 6. 31.

There is no substitute for the quiet time. Without it, there will be impoverishment of spirit, for which no spiritual activity can be a substitute.

It was while the dew was on the ground that the bread from heaven was to be gathered daily, Exod. 16. 21. David, the sweet psalmist of Israel, knew the value of sitting before the Lord, 1 Chron. 17. 16. Daniel had valuable companions in testimony, but he alone saw the vision, Dan. 10. 7. Isaac went out into the field to meditate, Gen. 24. 63.

In Psalm 1, it is the meditation in the Word that causes roots to deepen, leaves to be unfading, and fruit to abide. And whatsoever the godly man does in his activities prospers. Joshua is personally urged to meditate in the Book, for then, as leader, he shall have good success, Josh. 1. 8.

The Shepherd leads by the still (quiet) waters, so that the sheep may both enjoy the green pastures and ruminate, Psa. 23. 2. The fiery prophet needed the still small voice to quieten his soul, 1 Kings 19. 12. "Commune with your own heart ... be still" is the psalmist's advice, Psa. 4. 4, so that he could add, "I have ... quieted myself", 131. 2.

This quiet time is not a mindless vacuum, but an active consideration of our beloved Lord, Heb. 3. 1; 12. 3. It is a sitting at His feet, like Mary. Afterwards, she joined Martha in useful service, but "that good part" of quietly listening shall not be taken away. In fact, it enhanced her service, Luke 10. 39-42. Mary would agree with the psalmist when he affirmed, "my meditation of him shall be sweet", Psa. 104. 34.

Accompanying the meditation of the heart, the words of the mouth will express worship and prayer, Psa. 19. 14.

READING: **Psalm 67**

THIS GOD IS OUR GOD

THIS GOD, some of whose names and ways we have considered for the last thirty days, *this* God is *our* God, Psa. 48. 14. His diverse revelations and many graces can meet all the differing circumstances of each of His children.

In Revelation 1, the varied glories and graces of our God and Saviour Jesus Christ are seen. In chapters 2-3, certain of these characteristics are chosen suitably to meet the diverse needs of each assembly addressed. Such an High Priest became us (i.e., fitted us, and was perfectly adapted to our need), Heb. 7. 26. We cannot have a need, at any time and under any circumstances, that is not appropriately met by Him.

This God is "our God", "even our own God", and "my God", Psa. 67. 6; 18. 2; 68. 20. We are not lost in the multitude of His children. The twelve tribes had their separate names on differing precious stones, each of which was secured on the breastplate upon the heart of the high priest. Individually the Shepherd has called us by name, John 10. 3, and indelibly written each name in the Lamb's book of life, Luke 10. 20; Heb. 12. 23; Rev. 3. 5; 13. 8. In resurrection, the Lord addressed His own by their personal names, "Simon", "Mary".

Little wonder that Paul, although his heart was all-encompassing, could often speak of "my God", as if he had God to himself!, Rom. 1. 8; Phil. 1. 3; 4. 19. The Lord Jesus used this title "My God" personally in Matthew 27. 46 and John 20. 17, but in this latter verse He shared Him with others, "my God, and your God". See Rev. 3. 12.

This Saviour God who is both the Alpha and Omega, is the One who will guide even unto (and over) death, Psa. 48. 14. We can join with others to exclaim, "Lo, *this* is our God; we have waited for him, and He will save us ... we will ... rejoice in His salvation", Isa. 25. 9. We will be met by this same Jesus, and not another, Acts 1. 11. This same Redeemer "I shall see for myself ... and not another", Job 19. 27.

> There no stranger-God shall meet thee,
>> Stranger thou in courts above,
> He, who to His rest shall greet thee,
>> Greets thee with a well-known love. (J.N.D.)

40

What is Man?

THE PSALTER has been described as a very human book. No doubt the writer meant that its contents revealed an awareness of human needs and situations. This is true. It is to be noted that the book opens with the blessedness of man and closes with the praise of God. How fitting this is! If man is truly blessed, then God's praise is inevitable. Yet if God is truly praised, then man's highest blessing is bound to follow. In this is the meaning of life and living.

It is good to notice the way in which the Psalms trace the course of man in his relationships with God Himself. We note his *dominion* as the cornerstone of God's creation: made perfect, God's viceregent, made to rule; e.g., Psa. 8. But we also see his *downfall*, his *defilement* and *degradation* as the result of the fall. Man's sinfulness is nowhere more emphasized then in the Psalms; e.g., Psas. 14 & 53. So man's *destitution* is inevitable, robbed of those virtues which true righteousness gives. We note the contrast between the wicked and the righteous. The sad result is told out in the *distance* that separates man from his God. How shall he approach, what shall he bring?, e.g., Psa. 15.

But perhaps the beauty of the Psalms is enhanced by the story told of God's *deliverance* in answer to man's deep *desires* for forgiveness and reconciliation. The longings are deep; e.g., Psas. 42 & 84. But the readiness of God to save and deliver is told out in the beautiful songs of deliverance; e.g., Psa. 40. How precious is the assurance we find of God's pardon for true penitence in such Psalms as 32, 51 & 130.

The frailty of man and his *dependence* upon God is a vital truth in the songs of the Psalter. This makes an encouraging study; e.g., Psas. 37 & 90. And the total understanding and involvement of God in the life of the godly is recorded in masterpieces of poetry such as Psalm 139. God is the Rock and Refuge, the Shield and Strength of those who rely upon Him; e.g., Psas. 46 & 91. Man's *destiny* is reflected in the utterances of hope in the mercy and compassion of God; e.g., Psas. 16; 17. 15.

As we daily consider the theme of man, we remember that God had one Man in His mind, one only, His well-beloved Son, the Man of His right hand, Psa. 80. 17. He shall not fail.

February 1st

READING: **Psalm 8**

DIGNITY AND DOMINION

DURING HIS shepherd days, David had plenty of time to consider the wonders of creation. We notice that he joins the glories of the heavens to the excellence of Jehovah's Name, v. 1. In God's Name, we find enshrined His nature and character. The glory of created things displays His excellence. His Name is Wonderful (Secret), Jud. 13. 18; Isa. 9. 6. Yet His glory is revealed. The psalmist, in an interesting way, links earth and heaven together in extolling the majesty of God.

Because God is great and His Name excellent, His sovereignty is evident in the means that He can use to declare His strength or praise. Here is a thought of beauty. Strength is ordained out of infant mouths to still or silence the voice of the enemies of God. Note how the Lord Jesus used this psalm in Luke 19. 39-40. Such was His appreciation of the praise of "babes and sucklings", that to silence them was to invite praise from the very stones.

Against the backcloth of the glory of creation, the question is asked, "What is man?". Why should God consider frail man, son of the earth-born? Insignificant in size and attraction, he is so valued in the divine purpose, that he is given the dignity of dominion over all God's works. The theory of evolution provides no satisfactory answer to the uniqueness of man. The Bible revelation sets man in his right place in the creation of God. Unfallen, man reflected the perfect image of God.

We pause today to reflect that man was the crown of a perfect creation, with delegated authority to control it. Verses 5-8 describe the extent of man's dominion; cf. Gen. 1. 26-31. When Adam fell, his rights to dominion were forfeited and Satan usurped the power. Thus he is "the god of this world", 2 Cor. 4. 4; "the whole world lieth in the evil one", 1 John 5. 19 R.V. We do not see these evidences of authority today—rather the reverse. Such is the tragedy of sin. Yet God's purpose is that in the Second Man, the Last Adam, man's dignity and dominion will be recovered and restored. The Lord Jesus, the Son of man, is the centre of God's purpose for man's redemption. By faith we see Him crowned with glory and honour, Heb. 2. 9. How good to realize that He will never fail.

Let us reflect today, *"we shall be like him"*, 1 John 3. 1-2.

February 2nd

READING: **Psalms 139. 13-24; 22. 9-10**

FEARFULLY AND WONDERFULLY MADE

THE HUMAN BODY is a miracle of construction. It is a manifestation of the creative power and beauty of God. The words that we have read make us realize that in no way can we accept the theory of spontaneous generation. Note the context: God's all-knowing, ever present character is outlined. The psalmist states that every feature of his life is an open book to God. A perception that lays everything bare and an all-pervading presence that is inescapable, lead him to exclaim, "Such knowledge is too wonderful for me; it is high, I cannot attain unto it", Psa. 139. 6.

Then comes the amazing realization of the dominating power of God. "Thou hast possessed my reins (my inmost being): thou hast covered me in my mother's womb", v. 13. Here we touch on the *sacredness* of life. We are taught that from its conception, it is given by, and belongs to God. Many current ideas are challenged by this truth. The demands for abortion need to be brought to this description of the origin of a human life. This word of the psalmist assails its validity. "Fearfully" means "made with distinctiveness, different from other orders of life". "Wonderfully" suggests the miracle of life as conceived in the womb. We dare not disregard the sanctity of life.

We touch also on the *secret* of life. "My substance was not hid from thee, when I was made in secret", v. 15. Here life was curiously wrought, intricately fashioned, moulded in secret. Unseen by human eyes, all is seen and known by God. Human personality is recognized in the womb prior to birth, v. 16; this is strange but true. There is a record kept of all our members, such is God's value of them. Let us think well on these things, for here is the ground of human accountability to the Creator. David goes on to state that life given by God is *sustained* by Him. He is conscious of the preciousness of God's thoughts for him and his well-being, vv. 17-18. They are numberless. He could sleep in peace, and awake in the companionship of his God. Are not these thoughts encouraging to us today? Note how the Lord Jesus amplified these values in Matthew 6. 25-34.

In the consciousness of such wise and unfailing care, the psalmist opens his inmost being without fear. Note his closing words, "*Search me ... know my heart ... try me ... lead me*".

READING: **Psalms 14 & 53**

NO ONE SEEKING GOD

IN READING these psalms, we may well ask the question "What, is the greatest tragedy in the history of the world?". In the light of history, the student of the Bible is bound to say that it is the fall of man in Eden's garden. Desire for the forbidden thing brought disobedience to God the Creator. The sad climax is seen in God's banishment of man from His presence, Gen. 3. 24. What tragic results have followed! Man without God—God without man! Think how much God lost in the fall. Surely the hurt was felt more in heaven than on earth.

In these writings, we can see something of the extent of the conditions that sin has produced. There is the folly of the man who says, "no God", v. 1; not necessarily a denial of the existence of a divine Being, but "no God for me", or "hands off my life". Here is an arrogant refusal to submit to God's right to own and control. The pride of man will not seek God, Psa. 10. 4. Rebellious independence shuts God out and He becomes a stranger. But we reflect that conversion reverses this; the saved sinner is glad to own Jesus as Lord. How vitally different!

Verses 2-3 give a vivid picture of the absence of God in a world of evil. "The Lord looked down", v. 2, is an interesting statement. In the examination of the human race by the All-knowing God, we get a true picture of the ruin made by sin: all lost and defiled, with none doing good, v. 3; absolute hopelessness. Every evangelist needs to keep this picture firmly in mind. Paul declares the total depravity of man without God in Romans 3, before presenting the power of the gospel as he displays the glorious truths of justification and redemption.

Violence, oppression, degradation and nameless fears are bound to follow. Current events prove this only too clearly. No wonder we get the expression of longing for salvation, v. 6. The psalmist recognized, as we must do, that only in God is there hope. The Lord who looked down, came down to save, John 3. 17, and the Lord who came down laid down His life for man's salvation, 10. 11. We can also praise God that, when He had completed this tremendous work on the cross, He sat down at God's right hand, Heb. 10. 12.

Reflecting on these things, how foolish it is to shut God out of our lives. Are we willing to surrender to Him?, Rev. 3. 20.

February 4th

READING: **Psalm 15**

SEEKING GOD—ASSOCIATIONS

WHEN ADAM sinned, he lost the greatest blessing of nearness to God. "So he (God) drove out the man", Gen. 3. 24. Just think again of this tragedy: made by God, for God, yet turned away by God. Humanly speaking the distance was irrevocable; there was no return. Yet ever since that event, man has been searching for a return to God. One thing that human beings can never altogether lose is a hunger for God. So Job cried out, "Oh that I knew where I might find him", Job 23. 3.

With this in mind, we look at the opening words of Psalm 15, "who shall abide ... who shall dwell?". This question does not just concern a visit to divine dwellings, but a permanent enjoyment of the company of the Lord. How often we are content just to think of a visit instead of an abiding enjoyment of God's presence. The answer in this psalm of David is most important. Fitness to enter and abide is a priority. Four matters to which we must give our attention are outlined.

1. *Walk*. "He that walketh uprightly", v. 2. No slipshod approach to spiritual values will fit in with the presence of God. Only a careful choice of the path that we tread will fit us for fellowship with God; Enoch knew this, Gen. 5. 22-24.

2. *Works*. "And worketh righteousness", v. 2. The behaviour patterns of a Christian must be right if associations with a righteous God are to be enjoyed. God is righteous, and in His grace He declares believing ones righteous in Christ. How necessary that our actions do not clash with values belonging to the holiness of God. We do not practice sin, 1 John 1. 5-9.

3. *Words*. "Speaketh the truth in his heart ... backbiteth not with his tongue", vv. 2-3. The speech of those who draw near to God is important. In dealing with the unruliness of the tongue, James writes of blessing God and cursing men with the same member, James 3. 9. The mainspring of true speech is the heart. Yet how often the manifestation of speech is in words that reveal a wrong inward state. We need to watch our words as we enter God's presence, Eccl. 5. 1-2.

4. *Ways*. The associations of those who are godly are important. Those who would abide in God's presence must have a blameless testimony before men. Thus our privilege in enjoying communion with God is great; it must not be taken for granted.

Febuary 5th

READING: **Psalm 24. 1-6**

SEEKING GOD—THE ASCENT

TODAY WE take another look at the matter of approaching God. Experience often proves the truth of Augustine's words that human hearts are restless until they find rest in God. As we consider that it is gloriously possible for the redeemed to enjoy this rest in God's presence, a question rises within as to how man can rise to the holiness of God. Never for one moment can we think that God will lower His standards. Yet it is true that to enjoy God's presence means an experience that lifts us higher—we enter the holiest of all, Heb. 10. 19-20.

We notice the *place* in question, "the hill of the Lord ... his holy place", v. 3. The place is holy because of the Person who occupies it. Therefore for those who would enter His presence the road must be upward. He is "the high and lofty One that inhabiteth eternity", Isa. 57. 15; cf. 6. 1. It is therefore so necessary to pay attention to reverence as we come into the presence of the Lord.

We notice also the *purity* demanded in those who would ascend. Undefiled hands, unsoiled heart and sincerity of spirit are the requirements that the psalmist states befits those who draw near to God, v. 4. Self-examination proves to us that, humanly speaking, these qualities do not belong to us. The uncleanness of sin shuts the door on enjoyment of His presence. Thank God today for the reconciling work of the Lord Jesus. In the positive values of the sacrifice of the cross, peace has been made, and now we have our access through Him by one Spirit unto the Father, Eph. 2. 12, 18. Read this lovely scripture again.

So it is that this section ends with a wonderful *promise* for those who enjoy the privilege of drawing near, "blessing from the Lord", v. 5. We can almost see the picture in the psalmist's mind of priestly hands uplifted in blessing, Num. 6. 22-27. We never leave the presence of our Lord without carrying away a sense of the glorious spiritual blessings that are ours in Him. "And righteousness from the God of his salvation", Psa. 24. 5; here is the basis of peace, that realization that none shall lay anything to the charge of God's elect, Rom. 8. 33-34. How lovely is the consciousness for the believer of acceptance in the Beloved One. Do we avail ourselves of the privilege of the ascent into His holy place?

46

February 6th

READING: **Psalm 90**

MAN AND HIS DAYS

THE WORDS of this psalm, attributed to Moses, express some fine truths. It is thought that this could be the oldest of all the psalms. It is a meditation on the eternity of God, and also on the frailty of man. Verses 1-6 tell us three facts concerning the existence of God. First, that before created things came into being, God was there; He was before all His works. The second fact is He will "out-date" all His works, "from everlasting to everlasting, thou art God", v. 2. The third great fact is that, though He is eternal, He is involved in the affairs of time, "the span of existence between the eternities", v. 4. He far exceeds the limitations of time and space. It is into this context that we place the incarnation, 1 Tim. 3. 16. We see its mystery and its miracle.

Let us notice what is said about man and his days. Often we remark that we live a day at a time. In verses 5-6, we see how transient this time is; as grass, we flourish and then wither. Because of our sinfulness known to God, we pass our days under the wrath of God. By wrath, we are not so much thinking of His *dealings* with sin, but of His *disposition* towards it because He is God. This is a solemn thought. So it is that we spend our days as a tale that is told, v. 9. Note just how limited time is. There is an allotted span, 70 years. Many outlive this today, but prove how true verse 10 is. A doctor was told by one of his aged patients that we are prevented from dying, but we are not helped to live.

It is in relation to this that verse 12 has great relevance for us today. "So teach us to number our days, that we may apply our hearts unto wisdom." Time is given to us as a precious endowment. To waste it is a sin. Each day matters to a Christian and it is necessary to seek wisdom as to how to use it. As we are able to find timely satisfaction in His mercy, we can fill our days with rejoicing, v. 14. We can turn our hearts to God in days of affliction, when perhaps depression and despair threaten, and we can ask Him to make us glad, v. 15. Most of all we can seek that our days may be useful in His work and for His glory, vv. 16-17. Think on Ephesians 5. 15-16:

"See then that ye walk circumspectly (with thoughtful wisdom), redeeming the time, because the days are evil".

February 7th

READING: Psalm 144

MAN—VANITY YET VALUE

THE QUESTION "What is man?" is asked twice in the psalms. Each time a different answer is given. In Psalm 8. 4-9, the dignity and dominion of man are considered. In today's psalm, we are faced with the frailty and transience of his being. "Man is like to vanity: his days are as a shadow that passeth away", vv. 3-4. If we read the context of these verses, they could seem isolated from the rest of the contents. Verses 1-2 are an affirmation of confidence in the strength and power of the Lord who teaches the writer victory. Then follows a cry for intervention to overthrow the enemy, vv. 5-8. Yet pausing to reflect, where would man be, even we ourselves, in our frailty, if the Lord did not "Bow thy heavens ... and come down"?, v. 5.

It is to the blessing of every Christian to realize that the Lord does not despise the weakness and failure of our humanity; note Psalm 103. 14, "he knoweth our frame; he remembereth that we are dust". So it is that He condescends to our low estate, that through the work of salvation He might lift us up, even to heaven itself. We can join with the psalmist in verse 9, as we sing even a better "new song" than he knew, "It is he that giveth salvation". The true dignity of the man portrayed in Psalm 8 can only be regained and revealed, as in grace the Lord takes frail and fallen man, in Christ bringing him to glory. Let us consider all the implications of this today.

It is interesting to read the rest of the psalm, and to consider the possibilities of blessing for those people who know God as their God, v. 15. Verses 11-14 give a picture of the earthly blessing and prosperity of God's people when they are delivered from their enemies, v. 11. There is a healthy and happy family life, v. 12. Garners are full and livestock are productive; there is no falling away and no complaining, v. 14. We look at the nation naturally and say that this is but the fulfilment of promise and godliness. Over against this, put the desire of John in 3 John 2, "Beloved, I wish above all things that thou mayest prosper and be in health, even as thy soul prospereth". Frailty yet fulness—what does this mean?

Let us ask today, "If our material, physical well-being depend on our spiritual health, how would we be?". May we find our true strength and fulfilment in communion with God.

48

February 8th

READING: **Psalms 88 & 6**

DRAWING NEAR TO DEATH

WE HAVE read today one of the most gloomy of all the psalms; three words seem to sum it all up—depression, despair, death. Yet gloomy though it is, we realize how relevant to life and experience the psalms are. Problems of life are not just swept under the carpet. Neither are we only shown the light and cheerful side of life. In no way do the psalmists tell us that trust in God is an insurance policy against the ills of life. We can be thankful for this, for we can find help and comfort in the uncertainties and troubles of life today.

Verse 3 expresses the heart of the matter. Here we find one who is full of troubles and who is drawing near to the grave; people count him as one who is finished, v. 4. In verses 6-7, the depths are plumbed: "the lowest pit ... darkness ... the deeps". God's wrath lies upon him, he is afflicted with all God's waves. Could any soul descend lower—can we imagine a case more desperate and hopeless?

It is interesting to study what the O.T. as a whole, and the Book of Psalms in particular, say about death. Words such as Sheol, the pit, the grave, are used, and all give the impression of a place of nothingness where the good and evil are found. Note verse 10, "Wilt thou show wonders to the dead? shall the dead arise and praise thee?". So verses 11-12 intensify this sense of emptiness and loss. This is true regarding the mentions of the grave. "In death there is no remembrance of thee: in the grave who shall give thee thanks?", Psa. 6. 5; cf. 49. 14; 89. 48. Dimly the godly could see light beyond the grave, but a solid hope of immortality was waiting for a fuller revelation and greater light.

Thank God we know that this hope awaited the resurrection of our Lord Jesus Christ. Daniel 12. 2 epitomizes the Jewish hope of a general resurrection of the dead. In the Lord Jesus we are confronted with resurrection *from among* the dead. In this, He was the Firstborn, Col. 1. 18; Rev. 1. 5. We can triumphantly meet the gloom of Psalm 88 with the words, "our Saviour Jesus Christ, who hath abolished death, and hath brought life and immortality to light through the gospel", 2 Tim. 1. 10.

Death is now a defeated foe, John 11. 25-26. Depression and despair give place to joy; He lives: we shall live also!

49

February 9th

READING: **Psalm 38**

TROUBLES

"MAN IS BORN unto trouble, as the sparks fly upward", Job. 5. 7. So spake one who many centuries ago endured indescribable suffering. Job could say in reality, "Man that is born of a woman is of few days, and full of trouble", 14. 1. A reading of today's psalm reveals a sense of despair because of an avalanche of adversity that had assailed the psalmist. When examined, it reveals troubles that are only too common in the experiences of life.

We notice how much the writer's physical frame is affected: "my flesh ... my bones", v. 3; "mine head", v. 4; "my wounds", v. 5; "my loins", v. 7; "my heart ... mine eyes", v. 10. The psalmist was conscious of a loathsome disease that clung to him, making his presence offensive, v. 5. So he suffered, enduring painful physical effects. As we look deeper into these words, we feel that suffering and sin are linked together, vv. 4, 18; cf. 32. 3-4; 51. 8. It is well to note that this is one of the seven "penitential" psalms (6; 32; 38; 51; 102; 130; 143), all of which have to do with a sense and confession of sin. They make an interesting study of the pressures that a consciousness of sin can bring into life, and also the relief that is brought through confession and cleansing of these sins.

Let us learn that, when our lives are out of gear with God, when sin mars the way we live, physical and mental well-being are often affected. Notice the dark picture that the psalmist had of life. Not only is the Lord's hand against him, v. 2, but his friends have forsaken him, v. 11, and his enemies are arrayed against him, vv. 12, 19, 20; he is oppressed and burdened within himself, vv. 13-14. There seems no light in the dark tunnel, no way out of the maze of trouble and distress.

What light can we bring into this picture? Let us never say that sickness and disease are a direct result of a person's sin. But the Christian can take comfort in the fact that trouble does not indicate God's lack of love and care. If the Lord does chasten, v. 1, the believer can be sure it is in love, Heb. 12. 10. The hope of the Christian, often born out of despair, must be in the Lord Himself, Psa. 38. 15. He measures our longings, v. 9, and hears every cry of despair, vv. 21-22.

Reflect: trouble, turned into trust in God, brings triumph!

50

February 10th

READING: **Psalm 129**

AFFLICTED BUT NOT ABANDONED

THE MEMORY of days of affliction were indeed a reality to a nation such as Israel. The history of the chosen people was filled with instances of tragedy and trouble. There were, of course, times when they celebrated great victories, Exod. 15. 1, but how many bitter memories there were of oppression and exile. Yet if we take the time of youth, Psa. 129. 1, this would take us back to Egypt's slavery; when Israel was a child (youth), it was out of Egypt that he was called, Hos. 11. 1. Many periods of suffering were permitted by God—often the results of their waywardness and sin. Verse 3 suggests that stripes were laid heavily upon the nation, deep furrows in their back. And still the nation suffers today.

The force of the psalmist's words lies in verse 2: "yet they have not prevailed against me". Here is a testimony to the amazing fact of Israel's preservation through all their trials and troubles. They survive! They are oppressed but not overcome! This preservation did not rest in what they were or achieved; it was the result of the actions of their God. "The Lord is righteous", v. 4. The sovereign activity of the God of Israel, often mysterious, showed that He would never allow His own people, whom He loved, to be finally defeated. Verses 5-8 tell of God's dealings with their oppressors.

This has a great lesson for us today. It is good to consider the apostle Paul's approach to tribulations and trials. Note 2 Corinthians 4. 8-9, "troubled on every side, yet not distressed ... perplexed, but not in despair". He is "persecuted, but not forsaken; cast down, but not destroyed". What great words these are. Perhaps we can remember times of great affliction, when there seemed to be no light in the dark sky. We were battered and bruised, utterly cast down. Yet with the apostle we can look away and say, "The Lord shall deliver me from every evil work, and will preserve me unto his heavenly kingdom, to whom be glory", 2 Tim. 4. 17-18. Let us lay hold upon this.

As we view the meaning of affliction in the life of a believer, it is good to fall back on the unerring wisdom of God. He knows how much we can take—He knows when to lift the burden and give relief. He is a faithful God, and with the temptation or trial, He will make a way of escape, 1 Cor. 10. 13.

51

February 11th

READING: **Psalm 83**

COPING WITH GOD'S SILENCE

THERE IS a perversity in man's reactions to God's activity; when He speaks, in rebellion man refuses to listen. Yet so often when God seems indifferent and silent, man cries out, "Why does God keep silent?". The Lord Jesus was especially conscious of man's perversity as He sought to meet their needs. Often, the Christian has to learn a difficult lesson. It is that every action of God is relevant to each demand of experience. He is never silent when He should speak. He never speaks unless it is necessary for His voice to be heard. Those who live nearest to Him are most conscious of this.

The psalmist is baffled by the silence of his God. We also note this dilemma in Psalm 28. 1; 35. 22. The enemies of the Lord are noisy, make a tumult, arrogantly lift up their heads, 83. 2. In cunning they plan to destroy God's people, to act in confederation to cut off the name of Israel, the chosen nation, vv. 3-5. It would seem from verses 6-11 that Judah is surrounded by hostile nations, all of whom are noted as thorns in the flesh of God's people. These are vocal in their demand to take over God's heritage, the possession of His people, v. 12.

"Keep not thou silence, O God: hold not thy peace." What a cry is this! Think of what it implies as to God's relations with His own. Is He turning His back on the ones He loves? Is He deaf to their cries? Will He desert His loved ones in their hour of crisis? Can it be that His heart is not touched by the plight of those in trouble? Surely we can say a resounding "No" to all these questions. And there are times, we are sure, when His silence is more eloquent than speech.

What shall we say then? We can think of the silence of heaven when Christ suffered in the hours of darkness on the cross. As one has said regarding this, "A silent heaven is the mystery of the universe". The anguish of the words of Psalm 22. 1, used by Jesus on the cross, are an expression of utter loneliness. No voice of sympathy, no intervention of power, as He put away sin by the sacrifice of Himself, Heb. 9. 26. Yet how eloquent to lost sinners is the work of the cross, 1 Cor. 1. 18.

"Be still, and know that I am God", Psa. 46. 10, are vital words; though the reverses of life create a tumult within, it is good to sit still in submission, for in acceptance comes peace.

February 12th

READING: **Psalms 64. 1-6; 140**

DEFINING THE WICKED

BOTH OF THE psalms for today describe in clear terms something of the character of wickedness. We see this, not just as an abstract force, but as involved with man's personality and actions. This is one of the great human values of the Psalms. They often pin-point in unmistakable ways what wickedness really is. This surely is essential if we are to apply them to contemporary experience. Evil is not an abstraction, a nebulous quality, abroad in the world in a vague indefinite way. Sin is intrinsic in human personality, and is worked out in people's behaviour. In a day of lax moral thinking, we do well to keep this in mind.

Psalm 64 begins with a prayer for deliverance from a wicked enemy. This "enemy" seems to be a company of those who secretly plot against the psalmist, vv. 2-4. The point worth noting is that these are men whose wickedness is deeply hidden in the heart, v. 6. It makes us realize that the seat of evil is not in outward acts, but in the depth of man's being. The Scriptures confirm this time and time again; cf. Jer. 17. 9-10. So it must be, that in any definition of the meaning of wickedness, the emphasis must be on its inward source.

Psalm 140 is interesting in that it defines more clearly the outward acts of evil. Again it begins with a cry for deliverance from the evil man, v. 1. It also speaks of those who imagine mischief in their hearts, v. 2. Notice the features of wickedness: the "evil man", "violent man", "the proud" who hide a snare for the psalmist, and the wicked who plan the downfall of the righteous. We look at these descriptions from the writer's own experience, and because we know people today, we can identify the reality of the evils expressed.

As we consider our disturbed and violent society, seeing the increasing trends of opposition to that which is of God and the gospel, we do well to measure the meaning of the times in which we live. "Evil men ... shall wax worse and worse, deceiving, and being deceived", 2 Tim. 3. 13, wrote Paul as he described the character of the last days. Note Psalm 140. 6-7; "I said unto the Lord" is a *personal* appeal to the Lord. "Hear ... my supplication" is *prevailing prayer*. "The strength of my salvation" is *power*. We need not fear wickedness!

53

February 13th

READING: **Psalm 55**

THE TRAGEDY OF TREACHERY

THE BURDEN of this psalm, attributed to David, is that of one who in the agony of his experience is driven to extremity. If we consider the tone of verses 1-8, we must be impressed with the sense of desperation that is there. Here is one who mourns loudly in his complaint. The voice of the enemy, the oppression of the wicked, torment him. He has no defence; he desires to escape and flee from his circumstances, v. 6. He feels hemmed in completely by his enemies, v. 10. Some commentators relate these words to the time when David experienced the uprising of Absalom against him, 2 Sam. 15; Ahithophel, his counsellor, went over to the other side, a bitter blow to the king. This could well be the background of this psalm.

How important that we learn from this psalm the need of loyalty in friendship, and the terrible perils that lie in the misuse of the tongue. Note the pathos in verses 12-14. A friend counted as equal, a guide and acquaintance, one who was a companion indeed, "it was thou", v. 13. Verses 20-21 extend the idea. Covenant was broken, soft spoken words were mere cover-ups for war in the heart. "Drawn swords" describe them.

It will do us good quietly to think through the meaning of the hurt that such treachery brings. We think of the treachery of Judas as he betrayed the Lord Jesus. He walked with Jesus, was one of His companions, sat at table with Him, John 13. 26-28. How bitter must have been the knowledge that Jesus had, that the betrayer was with Him, that he would betray Him with a kiss. Note the terrible words that He spoke of him, Matt. 26. 20-25. Of all the evils perpetuated in the events of the cross, this must stand out as the blackest of all.

What lesson can we learn? If maligned by treachery, we can do what David did, "As for me, I will call upon God; and the Lord shall save me", vv. 16-17. If we feel that we have no defence, we can do what the Lord Jesus Himself did: commit our cause to Him who judges in righteousness, 1 Pet. 2. 23. Let us also beware of speaking evil of one another. There is a loyalty that we owe to our fellow-believers that is incumbent upon us who enjoy the faithfulness of God. And let us always remember that the source of an inflamed tongue is hell itself, James 3. 1-12.

February 14th

READING: **Psalm 49**

THE MATERIALIST'S MISTAKE

THIS PSALM for the sons of Korah exposes the mistaken confidence that is often displayed in earthly wealth and possessions. Verses 12-20 must be carefully noted. These give great importance to the psalmist's concern: man is like the beasts that perish! Yet man is in honour! It would seem very clear from these repeated statements, vv. 12, 20, that the wrong attitude to wealth and prosperity robs man of his dignity, and degrades him to the level of beasts. Think on this.

"They that trust in their wealth", v. 6. Is such *confidence* wise? We notice the mistakes made in such trust: there are limits to its purchasing power. Even in regard to material things this is true, but when it comes to the deeper demands of the soul, wealth has no relevance. "None ... can by any means redeem his brother", v. 7. There are surely things that money cannot buy. Again, wealth is related to the temporal and transient, v. 11. Materialists would like to stamp their posterity with permanence. Death steals all; such reckoning is folly, v. 13. This is the *course* of the worshipper of wealth. How vital the truth in verse 14. Wise and foolish, rich and poor, all are levelled together in the grave. Finally, how mistaken is the idea that wealth has value for the life beyond the grave, vv. 17-19. The *consummation* of life is like its beginning; nothing is brought in, and nothing is taken out. This is true for all. How slow men are to learn this lesson. A man's life does not consist in the things that he possesses, Luke 12. 15.

In verse 15, how much did David, in his day, know about the higher spiritual values which belong to the realm of the soul? "God will redeem my soul from the power of the grave: for he shall receive me"; what price did the psalmist have in mind as he spoke of redemption? As an Israelite, the great pattern of redemption for him would be linked to the Passover and the blood of the lamb slain. May we remember the precious blood of Christ providing for the believer's spiritual wealth, 1 Pet. 1. 18-20.

"What shall a man give in exchange for his soul?", Mark 8. 36-37, asked the Saviour as He dealt with the need of distinguishing the priorities of life in following Him. Let us heed Paul's words when we are tempted to make the mistake of the materialist, "God who giveth ... richly", 1 Tim. 6. 17.

READING: **Psalms 40. 11-17; 34. 1-10**

POOR YET PRECIOUS

PERHAPS ONE of the greatest dividing factors among men is that between those who are rich and affluent, and those who are poor and destitute. So often wealth means influence and power; poverty is linked with obscurity. This subject is found in the Psalms, with their occupation with all aspects of human experience, including much that speaks of the rich and the poor. The rich are often castigated for their wrong approach to wealth; the cause of the poor receives sympathetic consideration, but the Lord is on the side of those who are poor.

"I am poor and needy; yet the Lord thinketh upon me", 40. 17; the context of this reflection is the psalmist's sense of the pressures of evil around him. Innumerable evils compassed him about; his own sins had gripped him as in a vice, and shame tormented him, v. 12. So he cries to the Lord to deliver him from his enemies, v. 13, with desolations for those who seek his hurt, vv. 14-15, and delight for those who seek the Lord, v. 16. Then he pauses to reflect that, though poor and needy, perhaps obscure and unnoticed, yet he was the object of divine thoughtfulness, v. 17. In all our needs today, how lovely for us to realize that the divine thoughts that are higher than ours, and that will miss none of our needs, are towards us for our comfort and blessing. Note in Psalm 139. 17-18 the preciousness and plenitude of God's thoughts towards His own.

"This poor man cried, and the Lord heard him, and saved him out of all his troubles", Psa. 34. 6. Human poverty is not only the subject of divine thought but of divine action as well. "This poor man"! The emphasis here is on a personal experience of destitution. It is in the context where one is recounting the goodness of the Lord, vv. 4-5. Such goodness calls for praise to the Lord's Name, v. 3. There is also the invitation to taste and see that the Lord is truly good, v. 8. It is good to realize that to enjoy the goodness of the Lord is not an experiment but a glorious experience.

We remember the involvement of the Lord Jesus with the cause of the poor, Luke 4. 18; 2 Cor. 8. 9. Our greatest poverty was measured when, as bankrupt sinners, we came to Him and He forgave us all, Luke 7. 41-42. It is in the sacrifice of the cross that we learn that, though poor, we are precious to Him.

READING: **Psalm 114**

WHEN GOD ACTS!

THE LANGUAGE of this brief song is dramatic. It begins with the impact made by God's power in action. It ends with the challenge of the impact of His presence. When the human is confronted with the divine, there is bound to be a reaction. Mere finite man can never grasp the dimensions of the ways of the infinite God. It is interesting to notice Job's reaction as the Lord unfolded His wisdom and power to him; he is found in dust and ashes, Job 42. 1-6.

The writer of this psalm re-creates from memory the sensation caused by the deliverance of the nation of Israel from Egypt, and their establishment as His possession, vv. 1-2. His *power* delivered them, His *presence* sanctified them, and His *purpose* controlled them. Pause and reflect today on these ways of God with His people, and especially apply them to the church. Every member has been delivered from sin's slavery by His redemptive power, Col. 1. 12-14. Each member, whether Jew or Gentile, has been built into the church, being made a habitation of God through the Spirit; we are His dwelling place, Eph. 2. 19-22. And as we recognize the Lordship of Christ, and know Him as the Head of the body, we move under His dominion, 4. 11-16. Could anything be more glorious?

From the *experience* of the nation, the psalmist tells of the *effects* upon the people round about. He uses similies of the disturbances among the elements; he gives a picture of fear first of all, then of gladness. "What ailed thee, O thou sea, that thou fleddest? ... Ye mountains, that ye skipped like rams; and ye little hills, like lambs?", vv. 5-6. What power could stand before such a God as this? All creation reacts and rejoices when God puts forth His glorious power. It is good to think that, in the last analysis, when the effects of redemption are seen in their ultimate realization, all creation will cease its groaning and rejoice, Rom. 8. 19-23.

"Tremble, thou earth, at the presence of the Lord, at the presence of the God of Jacob", v. 7. What awe-inspiring majesty is associated with the divine presence. For the unregenerate to be confronted with such a manifestation is fear and death. Note in closing Revelation 6. 14-17; 20. 11-15; a terrible day!

READING: **Psalms 25. 1-14; 112. 1-3**

THOSE THAT FEAR THE LORD

WE HAVE seen that one of the greatest privileges of the godly is to have access to God. Yet is there not a danger that such a privilege can be taken for granted? Such high favour, granted to us on the grounds of free grace, could cause an undue familiarity in drawing near to God. Such considerations lead us to think on the meaning of the fear of the Lord.

The Psalms always emphasize the necessity of reverence and godly fear. This was built into every feature of the Jews' religion. "I the Lord am holy" is repeated many times. There is a significant word in Psalm 34. 11, "Come, ye children, hearken unto me: I will teach you the fear of the Lord". That we have to learn what fear means suggests that it is not natural for men to give reverence and fear to God. When we speak of fear, we are not speaking of terror, dread, servility; we mean that the character of God demands that we tread reverently, as the lesser would approach the greatest, the lower to the highest, even the sinful to the purest and the holiest of all. We have much to learn in this school, and in our irreverent and blasphemous age, it can only be for our good.

Let us consider three great blessings which the psalmist links with the fear of the Lord.

1. There is *intimacy*. "The secret of the Lord is with them that fear him", 25. 14. This opens up to us the lovely possibilities of communion with the Lord. He shares the counsels of His mind with those who reverence His presence. We can remember Abraham, as the Lord was about to destroy Sodom, Gen. 18. 17-19. God was ready to reveal His purpose to this man, the friend of God. He will unfold His covenant, those sacred ties that bind the godly to the Lord; cf. John 15. 14-15.

2. There is *instruction*. "What man is he that feareth the Lord? him shall he teach in the way that he shall choose", 25. 12. A reverent approach to the Lord lays the foundation for a safe walk with Him—the blessing of a guided path. Each command from the Lord is treasured as a word from the Highest.

3. There is *intelligence*. "The fear of the Lord is the beginning of wisdom", 111. 10. The mind that reverences most in God will learn most from Him. There is an intelligence that is born alone of the Spirit of God; we need it, 1 Cor. 2. 16.

February 18th

READING: **Psalm 128**

A GOD-FEARING HOME

THIS PSALM presents a beautiful picture of a home that is marked by the fear of the Lord. The man of the house is happy because he sets the pattern of life in godly fear. One quaint translation of verse 2 is, "O well is thee and happy shalt thou be". How relevant are the expressions of this Song of Degrees to conditions of today. In everyday life, the family is threatened. We are told that one out of every three marriages end in the divorce court. We cannot help wondering what hope there is for the future, and we certainly cannot blame many young people for their scepticism in regard to married life.

A home where God is honoured, where the atmosphere is governed by the fear of the Lord, is bound to be happy. Look at the picture painted by the psalmist. The man is industrious, not idle. He eats because he works and his family enjoys the benefit, v. 2. Remember that godliness never sanctions idleness; note 2 Thess. 3. 7-13. The wife is as a fruitful vine, v. 3. She is not the slave, exploited by the rest of the household (often the case), but in the innermost parts of the house she provides satisfying qualities that establish a contented home life. Note Titus 2. 3-5. In spite of much that is said today, it is no disgrace for a woman to be keeping things together at home. And children are like olive plants or branches round the table, v. 4. This gives a lovely touch to the picture. Meal times in a happy, God-fearing home can be wonderful occasions, not only for feeding physically, but for enjoying the spiritual food of the Word of God. What about "the family altar"?

The family is essentially the foundation for the fruitful development of human life. Notice that the affairs of the nation are linked with the affairs of the home, vv. 5-6. Note how this patriot writes of blessing "out of Zion", "the good of Jerusalem", "peace upon Israel". All that was precious to the chosen people of God is matched to His favour in the home.

The Lord Jesus valued homes as He was here on earth. There was a special place for Him in the home at Bethany, John 12. 1-2. It is interesting to note that when Paul moved into the western world with the gospel, it was a home of a woman "whose heart the Lord opened" that was opened to him and his friends, Acts 16. 14-15. Where He is feared, others are welcome!

READING: **Psalm 87**

IS MY NAME THERE?

FROM THE earliest days of man's civilization, rank and privilege have been reckoned as greatly important. To belong to the right place and to be regarded among the right people are vital. In studying the ways of man in the Bible, it is interesting to note where things began. It was Cain who built the first city, Gen. 4. 17. Among the many cities that were built after that, the pride of Judah was the city of Zion. This was God's dwelling place where He placed His Name. It was a bulwark of strength and a centre of beauty, Psa. 48. 1-2. According to the prophecies that relate to the future of Israel, it will be the metropolis of the earth, to which all nations will make their way, and into which they will pour their wealth; cf. Mic. 4. 1-5. It is the place from which Christ will reign as King of kings during His millennial reign.

Following the thoughts of the dwelling place of God in Zion, verses 4-6 speak of the citizens of the city, and the privilege that comes from its birthright. Some commentators suggest that this is a psalm that illustrates the energies of Jewish proselytism—the wish that all should come under the polity of the city. So "The Lord shall count" indicates a register of those who had found their way under its shadow and protection; "this man was born there". The franchise of the city was of great importance and a great blessing.

What can we learn from this? For the Christian today, there is privilege greater than citizenship in even the greatest of earth's cities. When the disciples came back to the Lord Jesus and told Him that they saw the effects of their preaching and teaching, even to demons being subject to them, He answered them in a strange way. He told them not to rejoice so much that these things had happened. We can be sure that He was as pleased as they were. But "rather rejoice", said He, that "your names are written in heaven", Luke 10. 17-20. So it is that all believers have their names written in the Lamb's book of life. They are granted the franchise of heaven, Rev. 20. 15.

Thus it is that citizenship in heaven belongs to every redeemed soul. How lovely to know that He reckons us in this way. This man, this woman—the dignity and privilege of it! Not a colony of Rome, but a colony of heaven!, Phil. 3. 20.

February 20th

READING: **Psalm 101**

WISE BEHAVIOUR

THIS PSALM has an important lesson for us all. It expresses the intention of one who is determined to abstain from evil. Sin is contagious, a disease that will rapidly spread, and its infection will sadly defile and degrade. We notice that the wrongs to be avoided are clearly labelled. "Wicked thing", v. 3; "A froward heart", v. 4; slander and pride, v. 5; "deceit ... lies", v. 7. If we look at these carefully, we must recognize them as some of the evils in life today. Perhaps we call them social evils—they are this and much worse.

The choice of association is obviously very important for the psalmist. From verse 1 it is clear that he felt indebted to the Lord for His mercy and justice. He could sing about these things. Blessings that brought joy were his. Yet how vital to notice that he linked *blessing* to *behaviour*; response to the Lord's work for him must lead to regard the Lord's will in his life; "I will behave myself wisely". But one look at these verses, and we must realize that living for God in a godless environment demands that life should be treated carefully. And there must be a sober commitment to good things, strengthened by a deliberate avoidance of evil. We must "Abstain from all appearance of evil", 1 Thess. 5. 22; Psa. 1. 1-3. Contrast 2 Peter 2. 6-8.

It is interesting to relate this psalm to the life of David; three times we are told in 1 Samuel 18 that he "behaved himself wisely", vv. 5, 14, 30. He had just received the expression of Jonathan's love and the call to Saul's service. Because of his victory over Goliath, he was very much in the public eye. How essential it was that the behaviour patterns of Israel's future monarch should be without blame. So these activities and avoidances were essential to such a man. And as we examine the principles behind these verses, we realize that some of the foundation pillars of Christian morality are here.

Our society is corrupted today by easy-going ways of life that deny God's principles of holiness. Let us ensure that we are in the right company, Psa. 119. 63, and that by avoiding the wrong values of life, we walk in ways that honour and glorify our Lord Jesus. "Be ye holy; for I am holy", 1 Pet. 1. 15-16. Blamelessness is not sinlessness—but it is essential!

February 21st

READING: **Psalm 32**

THE HAPPINESS OF THE FORGIVEN

THERE IS a special dimension of blessedness for those who experience the forgiving love of God. This is surely because there is no human misery to be compared with that sense of the awfulness of sin before God. Who can measure the inward agony of a soul tormented by the guilt of unforgiven sin?

"Blessed is he whose transgression is forgiven, whose sin is covered", v. 1. This is an utterance of spontaneous gladness that gives expression to sheer relief. Each word used to describe the wrong in the psalmist's life reveals his evaluation of it. *Transgression*—rebellion, cutting across God's ways, breaking away from God. *Sin*—wandering from the way, missing the mark. *Iniquity*—depravity, moral distortion, careless unconcern. Thus have these words been interpreted. Having said all this, how can we ever say all that sin really is? Only God knows! The deep consciousness of evil rendered the psalmist sick in body and mind. Silence tore him apart, and he felt the hand of the Lord upon him, vv. 2-4. Such was the *consciousness* of sin.

We notice that the extremities of *conviction* brought him to *confession*, vv. 5-6. The effects of sin on the human mind and the physical frame can be disastrous. A deep sense of inward guilt concerning committed evil, maybe years ago, can cause disabilities that have no seeming connection with that sin. Many Christian doctors and counsellors have found this as they have sought to deal with the problems of those who seek their help. Yet in confession there is release, and the pathway to blessedness in forgiveness, v. 5.

What shall we learn from the writer's experience? It is good to know that *repentance* brought *remission*, "thou forgavest the iniquity of my sin". Like the paralytic in Luke 5. 16-26, and the sinful woman in 7. 47-50, the Lord speaks the word, of forgiveness—music to the soul indeed! Instead of the fear of *retribution*, God becomes a *refuge* to the soul, vv. 6-7. A *regulated* pathway is possible, "I will instruct thee and teach thee in the way", vv. 8-9. Thus the psalm ends with *rejoicing*. The justified have joy; remission brings rejoicing, Rom. 5. 1; Eph. 1. 7. Let us realize today that all sin's distortions can be answered in God's forgiveness.

February 22nd

READING: **Psalm 37. 23-40**

ORDERED STEPS AND PEACEFUL ENDS

This is one of the most interesting and most practical of all the psalms. It deals basically with the effect that the ways of the wicked can have upon the thinking of the righteous. But it also shows that experience can be enriched and ennobled through fellowship with God. To trust, delight, commit, wait for, and to rest in the Lord gives stability and strength in the face of the imbalance so often seen in life. That the main thrust of the conclusions arrived at have to do with Jewish life and thought is apparent from the earthly character of the blessings promised, vv. 3, 9, 11, 19, etc. Yet there is a spiritual atmosphere which makes the underlying principles relevant to the Christian life today.

We notice two verses which have to do with *direction* and *destiny* in relation to the life that knows God's blessing.

1. "The steps of a good man are ordered by the Lord: and he delighteth in his way." The message is quite clear—when the Lord delights in one of His own people, He gives direction to move along in His way. In the context of the psalm, there is always the danger that confusion and anxiety will always come from viewing life from the wrong perspective. Things just look wrong!; cf. v. 1. To see wickedness progress, and the evil man prosper, seems to belie the pursuit of goodness. Why bother to walk with God, when the advantage lies with evil? Note what is said about the wicked in verses 2, 9, 12-13, 14-15, etc. But we can be assured that to walk with God is to walk in a divinely ordered pathway. Think of the great worthies of old, Enoch, Noah, Abraham. How wonderfully God showed His pleasure by guiding them aright. There was a vast difference in the way that God evaluated the paths of Abraham and Lot.

2. "Mark the perfect man, and behold the upright: for the end of that man is peace", v. 37. *Destiny* lies in the pathway of every man. The end is in the beginning. Compare the words of the Lord in Matthew 7. 24-29. There is a future for a man who loves peace. How good to reflect that those who have been made right with God through faith in the Lord Jesus have peace with Him now and the hope of a glorious future, Rom. 5. 1-3. Guided by His counsel, we shall be received up to glory. Thus our perspectives and prospects are right in Him.

February 23rd

READING: **Psalms 31. 7-16; 59. 10-17**

MAN AND GOD'S MERCY

SOMEONE HAS described mercy as the main characteristic of God's dealing with man. The Hebrew word *"chesed"* is often used, and in' the A.V. is rendered by kindness, mercy, pity, favour, goodness and lovingkindness. It is often found united with righteousness, faithfulness, truth, compassion and other divine qualities. As we study its many uses in the psalms, we feel that we are touching the very tenderness of the heart of God who knows the very worst about sinful man, yet cannot leave him altogether to the deserts of his own wrong doings. We are sure that there is a deep longing in God's heart that evils should be remedied, and it is God in His mercy who finds the way.

1. "I will be glad and rejoice in thy mercy", 31. 7; 89. 1; 101. 1. Note the professions of trust in the Lord, 31. 1. To him God is both rock and fortress, v. 3. The context suggests that he trusts the Lord with a desire for protection and guidance, vv. 2-3. So it is that as he senses his security, he breaks into song. The subject is the mercy of God, and we note how he describes the character of this attitude of his God: "thou hast considered my trouble". Here is the essence, the mainspring of mercy— divine consideration for human need and weakness. Human exposure to trouble, and the deep feeling the writer had of being hemmed in by enemy action, brought forth suitable sympathy to act, and the liberating hand of God brought him into a large room, v. 8. The quality of God's mercy answers the character of man's need; cf. Heb. 4. 16.

2. "Have mercy on me, O Lord", v. 9; 51. 1; 85. 7. The *cry* of the psalmist is for just this consideration which has sympathy for need. Note how desperate is the psalmist's need, revealing depths of weakness that left him helpless, vv. 9-13. Can mercy meet it all? "There's a wideness in God's mercy: Vaster, broader than the sea." Note v. 14: "I trusted in thee, O Lord: I said, Thou art my God".

3. "God is my defence, and the God of my mercy", 59. 17; cf. 52. 8. As so often with the psalmist, he looks away from the attribute, the values of mercy which he enjoys, to the God who is at its source: "God of *my* mercy". We look at the suitability of His mercy, because He is the God that He is. Only this answers the need, and in this we rejoice.

READING: **Psalm 77**

PRECIOUS MEMORIES

THIS IS a very full psalm, with many strands of thought in it. The writer is speaking of days of trouble, even of a time which he could call "the day of my trouble", v. 2. It may be that it was some circumstance of special tragedy, worse than many others. "My soul refused to be comforted", v. 2. Note the extremity of verse 4; then the questions of verses 7-9. There seems to be no break in the clouds of sorrow. "Hath God forgotten to be gracious?", v. 9, is a desperate question. Trouble often isolates, leaves the soul alone, takes away the sense of companionship. Maybe some of us have echoed this question; we have felt forgotten. Over against the sense of God's forgetfulness (a mistaken concept), the psalmist speaks of the exercise of his own memory. Reflect—is it feasible that, if humans can remember, God can forget? Cf. Isa. 49. 15.

"I remembered ... I call to remembrance ... I will remember", vv. 3, 6, 11. Let us consider something of the value of memory for those who know the Lord. There must be experiences of God that we have had, that we shall never forget. Moses exhorted the people, as he recounted the words of God, that they should remember the ways, works and words of their God, Deut. 8. 2-4. This exercise of memory was to be a corrective and a consolation in their later life as a nation. Is it any less important for us, that we should always call Him to remembrance?

Note that in the psalmist's *sorrow* he calls to remembrance his *song* in the night, v. 6. Under the cloud of sorrow, so troubled that he could not speak, suddenly he breaks loose and sings. Memories of a song—sung at midnight! We can be sure that Paul and Silas remembered many times their song in the Philippian gaol, their backs bleeding and sore, Acts 16. 22-26. Precious memories!

Then the psalmist in his weakness remembers the *strength* of the years of the unchanging most High God, v. 10. They were years of His right hand of power. Precious memory! When our hands are weak and feeble, His hand is strong to keep and sustain. So he remembers the *works* and *wonders* of his God, v. 14. We know today, that those who prove God most will have most to remember about Him.

READING: **Psalm 37**

CONTRAST THE RIGHTEOUS!

IN STUDYING the psalms in relation to man, it is noticeable how differently the righteous and the wicked are seen. Often expression is given to concern, even puzzlement, as the prosperity of the wicked is seen. They spread themselves like a great tree—overshadowing the righteous in their rapid advancement in worldly wealth and status; cf. Psa. 73. 3. Yet there is no doubt where heaven's approval lies, and also the quality of the life that pleases God. "The Lord knoweth the way of the righteous", 1. 6; "The eyes of the Lord are upon the righteous, and his ears are open unto their cry", 34. 15.

Our psalm for today can be used to illustrate several themes, but one theme for our meditation is that of the contrast drawn between the righteous and the wicked. There is encouragement in this study, because without doubt it emphasizes the worth of right living. Remember as you read "righteous" that the believer's only righteousness is in Christ. It is imputed on the grounds of the blood shed at Calvary. It is accepted by faith. How true that "the just shall live by his faith", Hab. 2. 4. Let us look briefly at four contrasts.

1. "A little that a righteous man hath is better than the riches of many wicked", v. 16. *Possessions* are measured, not by quantity, but by quality. Not that the righteous are foolish in the matters of material things; rather their priorities are right, with the best values of wealth, treasure in heaven, and spiritual blessings in the heavenlies, Eph. 1. 3.

2. "The arms of the wicked shall be broken: but the Lord upholdeth the righteous", v. 17. *Power* in the hands of the wicked is self-centred, often despotic, cruel and vulnerable. The strength of the righteous lies in Jehovah, the Lord of hosts. In this there is no failure or defeat, but the assurance of victory.

3. "The wicked borroweth, and payeth not again: but the righteous showeth mercy, and giveth", v. 21. The *perspective* of the wicked is all take and no give, a selfish grasp on gain; the righteous is generous, ready to give, and in compassion to share his possessions. Unselfish giving is the right way.

4. "The transgressors shall be destroyed ... But the salvation of the righteous is of the Lord", vv. 38-40. Here is the climax of all contrasts: the righteous are safe—*preserved.*

February 26th

READING: **Psalm 116**

I WILL

IT IS interesting to notice throughout the psalms the way in which man's response to God is portrayed. The utterances in poetry, which were expressed in song, often tell the sense of indebtedness felt by hearts in tune with God. "Give unto the Lord" is an expression often used, Psa. 29. 1-2; 96. 7-8. We feel the energy and enthusiasm behind the dedication and worship of those who celebrated God's greatness and goodness.

It has been said that "the New Testament itself could hardly give a better glimpse than this of heaven's grace and man's response, all in the simplest most direct terms" (D. Kidner). Today we shall look at some "I will's" in this psalm which express such response of one who loves his God. Note the beauty of verse 1, "I love the Lord, because ...". Affection has been drawn out by God's gracious dealings with the soul.

1. "I will take the cup of salvation, and call upon the name of the Lord", v. 13. "What shall I render ... I will take", vv. 12-13. Rendering by receiving. Man's greatest answer to God's saving grace is to receive with open hand the fulness of life in Christ. Here is expressed penitence and gratitude. In such a response, God is glorified; cf. Rom. 10. 9-13.

2. "I will offer to thee the sacrifice of thanksgiving, and will call upon the name of the Lord", v. 17; "I am thy servant", v. 16. The psalmist is enjoying the sense of freedom that comes as his bonds are loosed. Freedom inspires thanksgiving and devoted service—a paradox! But in the service of the Lord there is the highest freedom; cf. Col. 1. 12-13.

3. "I will pay my vows unto the Lord now in the presence of all his people", vv. 18-19. It is interesting to remember that, added to the compulsory offerings of Israel, there were "vows" and voluntary offerings which expressed devotion and gratitude to the Lord, Lev. 7. 16. Compare the Nazarite vow in Numbers 6. Vows must be honoured as a token of devotion to the Lord; cf. Eccles. 5. 1-5.

4. "I will walk before the Lord in the land of the living", v. 9. No mere lip service will satisfy the claims of the Lord upon our lives. The true response of devotion can only be seen in the walk that pleases God.

"Walk worthy of the Lord unto all pleasing", Col. 1. 10.

READING: **Psalm 84**

HIGHWAYS IN THE HEART

THIS PSALM expresses the longing for the enjoyment of the place where the Lord dwells. We can outline it thus: *desire*, vv. 1-4; *direction*, vv. 5-8; *destiny*, vv. 9-12. It is one of those gems of the Psalter which has been called the pearl of psalms. It vividly describes the attraction of the presence of God for the one who feels at a distance. Note the intensity of verse 2 and the pathos of verse 3. Can we identify ourselves with the psalmist in his deep affection for the place where God is found?; cf. Psa. 42.

We centre our thoughts today on verses 5-8. These are words of pilgrimage. They describe the pathway of those who are on the way to the house of God. We can pick up some helpful thoughts as we look more closely on the passage.

The *happiness* of the pilgrim lies in the strength desired from the God who is sought. Here is enablement in anticipation of the fulfiment of desire. Surely the way is shortened with such enjoyment, and weary feet are encouraged.

The *heart* of the pilgrim has within it the very highways of Zion. This is a beautiful touch. The feet move in the right direction because the ways of the journey are in the heart. Is it not true that the intrepid climber, who would conquer the heights, must surely have the rugged way deeply set in his heart and mind as he climbs. When difficulties arise, this will nerve him to pursue the summit. So with the pilgrim on the road to the divine dwellings. The upward way is set in his heart, and thus inspiration is achieved; cf. Heb. 11. 9-10, 14-16.

Verses 6-7 describe the *health* of the pilgrim as he journeys. The vale of tears, the place of depression, is turned into a well of refreshment. And those who dwell in Zion shall go from strength to strength. The aspiration is fulfilled as they appear before God.

Let us learn today that no sincere longing for God's presence will ever go unanswered. The home of man's soul is in God Himself. The believer today has the privilege of closer and more continued fellowship with the Lord than the psalmists knew. Let us carry the sanctuary in our hearts, "Christ in you, the hope of glory", Col. 1. 27; Eph. 3. 14-19.

As one has said, "Heaven in the heart—the heart in heaven".

READING: **Psalm 18. 31-50**

THE GOD OF VICTORY

THE READER of the psalms is confronted many times by the uncompromising and often cruel attitude of the writers to their enemies. There are measures of revenge which are sought and executed that are literally offensive to our thinking. We recoil from them. Yet the incentives for battle were focused on the fact that the psalmists' enemies were the enemies of God. They were the wicked, representing antagonism towards divine laws and divine ways. The relentless fight was essential as giving expression to the divine cause. All enemies must be destroyed; the psalmists fought for the Lord of hosts, the God of armies.

We look today at some of the ways in which the psalmist expresses the ability he has through the power of God, successfully to do battle and gain the victory.

We note the *training*, "It is God that girdeth me with strength", v. 32; "He teacheth my hands to war", v. 34; cf. v. 39. He was a trained soldier, but he attributed to the Lord that skill which he had acquired. As David went to meet Goliath, we notice how this fact is illustrated. Saul's armoury had nothing to offer. He could defy the sword of the Philistine, for it was in the name of the Lord of hosts. He came and overcame, 1 Sam. 17. 45-47. The battle is the Lord's: cf. 1 Chron. 12. 8. So Paul could speak of the fitness of the soldier in 2 Timothy 2. 4. God's warrior must be skilled to do battle.

We notice also the *triumph* of the psalmist. He had pursued his enemies; he wounded them until they fell, vv. 35-42; these are expressive of complete triumph. Yet not to himself the glory, but to the God who enabled him; "he is a buckler to all those that trust in him", vv. 30-31; cf. 115. 1. It is good for us as Christians to learn the secret of victory in the warfare against evil. It is only in Christ that we can overcome, Rom. 8. 35-37; Eph. 6. 10-11.

The psalm ends on a note of *testimony*, vv. 49-50, thanksgiving for deliverance, mercy to His anointed. Great deliverance calls for great praise. Among the nations it is good to proclaim the triumphs of the Lord. It was when Israel left Egypt and went through the sea that they sang, Exod. 15; every victory over Satan and his hosts must be proclaimed, and will be in a day yet to come: cf. Rev. 19. 1-6.

February 29th

READING: **Psalms 1. 1-3; 2. 1-6**

FAVOUR AND FURY

OUR FIRST daily study this month concerned the dignity and dominion of man in God's creation, Psa. 8. He was given control over all created things that God made man to rule. But we noted also the tragedy of the fall and the rebellion that followed as man cried "no God", Psa. 14. Throughout we have noted the strands of truth which relate to human life and experience; much more there is to be enjoyed. We also see in the psalms the evidence that man is quite prepared to live without God. Yet in His compassion and care, God does not easily give up His involvement with man. The two psalms for today will present two vital truths regarding humanity with which to end our thoughts.

1. *Secret of Blessing*, 1. 1. "Blessed is the man"; here is a spontaneous exclamation which comes from observation, "Oh the happiness of the man". The deportment of the man, as walking, standing and sitting, is right! In his movements, he avoids the wrong, acting positively in that which pleases God. Day and night, the law of God is his delight, v. 2; therefore he abundantly prospers. Here is manhood as God intends it should be. And upon such a life which is in accord with Himself He pours His favour. The basis of such a life is surely the possession of the divine Word. Paul was able to remind Timothy, a man of God, that from earliest childhood he had known the Scriptures, 2 Tim. 3. 15-17. So he encouraged him to meditate in these things, giving himself wholly to them that all might see his profiting, 1 Tim. 4. 15-16.

2. *Sequel to Rebellion*. Psalm 2. 1-6 shows man and the nations in their worst light, open hostility to God and to His anointed. "Why do the heathen rage?". Man without God is lawless, and has within him the seeds of his own destruction. God laughs, mocks, when his calamity comes, v. 4; Prov. 1. 24-27. But God has His Man, the Last Adam, His King set on Zion. No rebellion of man will thwart God's eternal purpose; cf. Eph. 1. 9-10.

The man of sin, the lawless one, will be the final expression of man's rebellion. It will precede the final overthrow of all that is against God, 2 Thess. 2. 3-12. "Kiss the Son", Psa. 2. 12; thank God we can bow the knee before Him.

We shall escape His *fury*; we can enjoy His *favour*.

Prayer, Trust, Confidence in God

THE BOOK of psalms was the temple song book. It contained "prayer songs" and "praise songs". An example of the former is Psalm 17, where the title reads, "A Prayer of David", and of the latter, Psalm 145, where the title reads, "David's Psalm of praise". Many fine hymns that we sing today are prayers. Prayer psalms are made up of the following:

Prayers for deliverance. There are many psalms where David is seen in distress, danger or despair. In times of extreme adversity, he found a safe retreat in prayer. There is, however, a prophetic aspect to these psalms which reflects the distress of the godly Jewish remnant in the future time of "Jacob's trouble", Jer. 30. 7. David was a type of Messiah of whom it is written, "In all their affliction he was afflicted", Isa. 63. 9. This fact will be a comfort in that day.

Imprecatory prayers. Under law, it was "eye for an eye"; the cries for judgment upon enemies, found in some psalms, were therefore consistent with that age of law in which they were written. Remembering the prophetic nature of the psalms, it will be seen how appropriate such language will be on the lips of the harassed remnant in the tribulation, as they wait for the Messiah to come in judgment on their persecutors. Under grace, the opposite applies. James and John were rebuked for wishing judgment on the Samaritans, Luke 9. 55; Peter, too, for using the sword, Matt. 26. 52. Other relevant scriptures are, Matt. 5. 1-11, 38-39; John 18. 36; Rom. 12. 17-21.

Penitential prayers. Psalm 51 stands out in this class; there are many others where confession of sin is made and forgiveness sought. These, again, have an application to the future, when God's wrath will lie hard upon His people, Psa. 88. 7. Then there will be acknowledgement of sin and a looking to the One whom they pierced, Isa. 53. 5; Zech. 12. 10.

Devotional prayers. Many psalms express deep longings for God and for zeal of His house. Psalm 42, is an example. May God deepen our spiritual desire and devotion to Himself.

Prayers of confidence and trust. God is referred to by the various writers as their "fortress", "refuge", "defence", etc. If He were not all these and more, our prayers would be in vain. Confidence in His power and wisdom glorifies Him.

March 1st

READING: **Psalm 13**

HOW LONG WILT THOU FORGET ME?

THIS PSALM is one of the many in which the psalmist is tested to the extreme. It also provides an example of the fact that God does not always immediately answer the cries of the distressed. The repeated sigh, "How long?", vv. 1-2, indicates that there was delay in answering David's prayer.

The depth of his distress and despair is expressed in the questions which commence the psalm. The cause of his anxiety appears to be relentless persecution from enemies, vv. 2, 4. The experience affected him physically and brought him near to death, v. 3. His trust in God's mercy and the resulting relief from the distress is recorded in vv. 5-6.

Delays in answering petitions do not mean that God has forgotten us or that He has hidden His face from us. These are intended to test and strengthen our faith and trust. The trial of faith is precious, 1 Pet. 1. 7; Job 23. 10.

There is always a tendency to resort to one's own counsels when prayers are not answered quickly. There are numerous examples of this in Scripture. Abraham and Jacob stand out in this respect. In times of testing and delay, instead of waiting, they employed methods of their own. These proved to be futile and a hindrance to faith. The psalmist, in his protracted conflict, seems to reflect this in the words, "How long shall I take counsel in my soul?", v. 2. In view of the hopelessness of his own means to solve his problems, he appeals to God to *consider* him, rather than to hide His face from him; to *answer* him, rather than to forget him, v. 3.

God will not forget His people. A woman may forget her suckling child and lack compassion on her offspring, yet He assures that He will never forget His own. They are graven upon the palms of His hands, Isa. 49. 15-16. In his despair, David asked, "Wilt thou forget me for ever?". The reality is, however, that He will not forget at all. He has said, "I will never leave thee, nor forsake thee", Heb. 13. 5.

Prayer changes things. David's sorrow is turned to joy; his sighs to song; his despair to hope and trust, vv. 5-6.

"Are not five sparrows sold for two farthings, and not one of them is forgotten before God? . . . ye are of more value than many sparrows", Luke 12. 6-7.

READING: **Psalm 25**

THE SECRET OF THE LORD IS WITH THEM THAT FEAR HIM

INTIMACY WITH God and knowledge of His ways are the portion of those who fear Him. He does not reveal His mind and ways to those who live at a distance from Him. Joseph, Daniel and Paul are outstanding examples of this fact, Gen. 40. 8; Dan. 9. 22-23; 2 Cor. 12. 1-4.

Prayer must be spiritual and sincere if it is to be heard. James writes of the selfish, materialistic prayers which go unanswered, "Ye ask, and receive not, because ye ask amiss", James 4. 3. The spiritual character of the psalmist's prayer is seen in the holy desires that it expresses, and in the suppliant attitude of heart with which it is made, "Unto thee . . . do I lift up my soul", v. 1. David's sincerity is marked by the requests that he makes, "Show me thy ways"; "teach me thy paths"; "Lead me in thy truth", vv. 4-5. The language used resembles that spoken by Moses, "show me now thy way, that I may know thee", Exod. 33. 13. We are informed in Psalm 103. 7 that God did, in fact, make known His ways to Moses in contrast to the Israelites who only saw His acts.

David had a teachable spirit, and was also willing to be led in the truth that he had been taught. It is an important principle, which has always been applicable, that God does not communicate His ways of truth, unless there is a resolve on our part to be responsive thereto.

When there are desires after holiness, there will inevitably be a consciousness of sin. This fact is evident in verses 7, 11, 18. Recalling God's past graciousness, v. 6, David is reminded of his own past, "the sins of my youth", v. 7. With respect to the keeping of the covenant, he is aware of great failure and appeals for pardon, vv. 10-11. Even Paul had to cry, "O wretched man that I am", Rom. 7. 24; the prophet, "Woe is me", Isa. 6. 5; and Job, "I abhor myself", Job 42. 6. The lines of a well-known hymn sum this up:

"And they who fain would serve Thee best
Are conscious most of wrong within."

The submission, confession and contrition exhibited in this psalm are features that mark the prayers of the godly, and are prerequisites if we are to learn the secrets of God.

"Draw nigh to God, and he will draw nigh to you", James 4. 8.

March 3rd

READING: **Psalm 27**

WAIT, I SAY, UPON THE LORD

THE THOUGHTFUL reader will observe a contrast between the first and second parts of this psalm. In vv. 1-6, David is brimful of confidence, whereas in vv. 7-13 he is in a different mood, namely, one of anxiety, in which he appeals to God for help. In the first part, he could face all forces arrayed against him without fear, because of confidence in his God. In the second part, he fears being forsaken, v. 9, and the falseness and cruelty of his enemies, v. 12. The final verse, however, indicates a return again to confidence.

David, being human, was subject to contrasting moods—delight and assurance at one time; depression and care at another. We are no exceptions to this natural weakness. We get our mountain top and also our valley experiences. Paul knew what it was to be "cast down", and to have fears within, 2 Cor. 4. 9; 7. 5. Yet he exhorts us to "Rejoice in the Lord alway", Phil. 4. 4. Elijah was a man subject to like passions as ourselves. His prayer brought drought for three and a half years, yet he also fled from the threats of Jezebel, and sank into despondency, James 5. 17-18; 1 Kings 19. 2-4. The Lord Himself, in His real and sinless humanity, knew times of joy and of sadness. Coming from the deep sorrows of the garden, He nevertheless faced His enemies with calmness and confidence, knowing that His hour had arrived.

David's confidence sprang from knowing God as his "light", "salvation", and "strength" or "stronghold", v. 1. He speaks of his darkness having been lightened, Psa. 18. 28; 2 Sam. 22. 29. In the many situations of danger that he encountered, he also proved that God was his salvation and stronghold, 2 Sam. 22. 36, 47; Isa. 37. 39.

The Lord Jesus has become these things to us in a far more wonderful way. He is our Light, John 8. 12; our Salvation, Luke 2. 30; and our Refuge, Heb. 6. 18-20.

Like David, we too may have our dejected spirits lifted and our confidence restored, by waiting upon the Lord, v. 14; Isa. 40. 31. Moses, when confronted with the Red Sea ahead and pursued by the Egyptians behind, said, "Fear ye not, stand still, and see the salvation of the Lord", Exod. 14. 13.

"If God be for us, who can be against us?", Rom. 8. 31.

74

READING: **Psalm 31**

INTO THY HAND I COMMIT MY SPIRIT

THE TEXT which heads today's reading is one which speaks of submission to the will of God. The same spirit is also seen in verse 15, "My times are in thy hands". Similar words were spoken by Stephen when he was stoned to death, Acts 7. 59. At a ceremony of degradation, a bishop said to John Huss the reformer, "and now we commit thy soul to the devil". To this the martyr replied, "I commend my spirit, which Thou hast redeemed, into Thy hands O Lord Jesus Christ". He was then burned to death.

On the cross, the Lord took up these words of David, Luke 23. 46. However, He imparted a new meaning into the words which could not apply in David's case. The Lord committed His spirit by an act of His own free will.

There are many references in the psalms to the hand of the Lord. The two occurrences here, vv. 5, 15, are set against two mentions of the hand of David's enemies, vv. 8, 15, which were of no match in comparison. This is always so. Sennacherib, through his spokesman Rabshakeh, boasted that his hand was greater than God's. He taunted Hezekiah and his men with the words, "that your God should be able to deliver you out of mine hand?". God took up the challenge, and slew his mighty men so that he with shame of face returned to his own land, 2 Chron. 32. 11-15, 21.

The hand of the Lord is not only strong, Psa. 89. 13, but it is also a shepherding hand, 95. 7. David, the shepherd king, knew the reality of this, 23. 1-2. We, too, have a Shepherd, out of whose hand none can pluck us, John 10. 28.

In the thick of trouble, adversity, conspiracy and slander, vv. 7, 9, 13, David was sorely distressed, vv. 9-13, and bewildered, v. 22. In Psalm 30. 6, we have the danger of prosperity; here, the danger is adversity. In circumstances like these, to whom could he appeal except to the Lord? Three times his trust in Him is stated, vv. 1, 6, 14. This was not in vain. Instead of being put to shame, he testifies of God's great goodness, v. 19, which filled his mouth with praise, v. 21, and inspired him to encourage others, vv. 23-24.

God "*comforteth us in all our tribulation, that we may be able to comfort them which are in any trouble*", 2 Cor. 1. 4.

March 5th

READING: **Psalm 35. 1-10**

LORD, WHO IS LIKE UNTO THEE?

THIS IS ONE of the imprecatory psalms about which mention has been made in the Introduction to this month's readings. To this the reader is referred. At this point, therefore, it is sufficient to say that David lived in a different dispensation to ours. We who live in this church-age of grace, who are indwelt by the Spirit, and who are members of Christ's Body, are to love our enemies, not to avenge ourselves, and to pray for our persecutors, Matt 5. 44; Rom. 12. 19.

By contrast, however, it is a fact that God in His providential ways does sometimes act in judgment on evil men, even though the day of His judicial vengeance does not begin until this age of grace has run its course. There have been cases of divine intervention during the course of this dispensation. In apostolic times, Herod is a case in point, Acts 12. 21-23. There must be many others.

Eventually, the day of the Lord will come as a thief in the night, 1 Thess. 5. 2; 2 Pet. 3. 10, when the ungodly will be taken completely by surprise. In this connection, verse 8 of this psalm is instructive.

David, a man after God's own heart, Acts 13. 22, had many enemies who conspired against him. In his prayer, he refers to them as those "that strive with me", "that fight against me", "that persecute me", "that seek after my soul", "that devise my hurt", vv. 1-4. Writing figuratively, in verses 7-8 he refers to a net concealed by hunters in a pit, dug to trap the unsuspecting prey. In this descriptive way, he speaks of the intrigues of those who pursued him.

In this situation, David displays a complete absence of self-confidence. He acknowledges his weakness in his appeals to the Lord, "stand up for mine help", "say unto my soul, I am thy salvation", vv. 2-3. Some lines from Luther's fine hymn are worth quoting in this context:

"Did we in our own strength confide,
Our striving would be losing."

The secret of strength lies in the confession of weakness and reliance upon the Lord. Paul learned this and wrote, *"when I am weak, then am I strong"*, 2 Cor. 12. 9-10; *"be strong in the Lord"*, Eph. 6. 10.

March 6th

READING: **Psalm 40**

THE MAN THAT MAKES THE LORD HIS TRUST

THIS IS ONE of the psalms that we are more familiar with, and which we often quote in prayer. This is because verses 1-3 aptly illustrate our deliverance from the pit of sin, and because verses 6-8 obviously refer to Christ, Heb. 10. 5-9.

There is a predictive and a historical character to many psalms, of which this is one. It is the historical aspect with which we are concerned here.

The psalm falls into two parts: (i) vv. 1-10, (ii) vv. 11-17. The first part recalls a past experience, "I waited"; "he inclined . . . and heard"; "He brought me up"; "set my feet"; "established my goings", vv. 1-2. The second part records a present experience. The three petitions, vv. 11, 13, 17, reflect a pressing need at the time.

Man's extremity is God's opportunity. David proved this in the variety of experiences through which he passed. In this psalm, he refers to a dreadful experience which he metaphorically describes as a boggy pit from which the Lord rescued him. In his extremity, he "waited patiently for the Lord", an attitude that displayed the trust of his soul.

Experiences of divine intervention leave deep impressions on those who have had them. This was so in David's case. Firstly, his mouth was filled with a song of praise that magnified the Lord and testified to others to make the Lord their trust also, vv. 3-5. What a different effect his sin had on those around, 2 Sam. 12. 14. It was a *new* song based on a new experience of deliverance. Secondly, his heart is filled with a desire to obey out of his own will and not in the mere ritual of sacrifice and offering, vv. 6-8. David's greater Son fulfilled these verses to perfection.

In the second part of the psalm, David makes his appeals on the ground of the deliverance recorded in the first part. His pleas are marked by *confession*, "mine iniquities have taken hold upon me", v. 12; by *urgency*, "make haste to help me", v. 13; by *humility*, "I am poor and needy", v. 17.

"His love in time past, forbids me to think
He'll leave me at last in trouble to sink."

"Who delivered us from so great a death, and doth deliver: in whom we trust that he will yet deliver us", 2 Cor. 1. 10.

READING: **Psalm 51**

A BROKEN AND A CONTRITE HEART

GOD LOVES to see repentance. He hates sin, but longs to show mercy. If this were not so, then David's case would have been hopeless, and so would ours. "But God, who is rich in mercy", Eph. 2. 4, saves the penitent from despair. David sought forgiveness in the multitude of His tender mercies.

God took the initiative towards David's repentance. The title of this psalm and the record of Nathan's visit to the king, 2 Sam. 12. 1-14, show that it was then that David was smitten with conviction. God did not allow him to cover up his sins which he contrived to do; see Prov. 28. 13.

David's crime was great; so was his contrition. In Psalm 32, he reflects the happiness of being forgiven; in Psalm 51, the heartache of conviction of sins. 2 Samuel 12. 14 shows the effect of his sin on those around; in Psalm 51, we see the effect upon himself. Heart-broken and in anguish he cries, "Have mercy upon me", "Wash me"; "Cleanse me"; "Purge me". The reference to *hyssop*, v. 7, shows the sense of defilement that he felt (see Num. 19. 18; Lev. 14. 4). In his confession, as a proof of true repentance, he did not just admit his sin, but acknowledged that he understood its serious nature, using the words, "sin", "iniquity", and "transgressions" to describe it. He had broken the sixth, seventh and tenth commandments. These applied to one's neighbour, yet he was convicted of the Godward aspect of his guilt, "Against thee, thee only, have I sinned", v. 4. He was also aware that he had an inherent sinful nature, v. 5.

In his prayer for restoration, vv. 10-12, David pleads, "take not thy holy spirit from me". He knew that this had happened to Saul his predecessor, who had been rejected from being king, 1 Sam. 15. 23-30; 16. 14.

Such a request would be inappropriate from our lips today. We are permanently indwelt by the Spirit, John 14. 16-17. Furthermore, "we have an advocate with the Father", 1 John 2.1. We have been cleansed from all sin, once and for all, 1. 7, but we need the continual "washing of water by the word", Eph. 5. 26.

"For godly sorrow worketh repentance to salvation not to be repented of", 2 Cor. 7. 10.

READING: **Psalm 54**

SAVE ME, O GOD, BY THY NAME

THE TITLE given to this psalm directs us back to 1 Sam. 23. 19; 26. 1, where there are recorded the circumstances of the psalmist which form the background. The whole of chapter 23 should be read, because it throws much light on the psalm. David is a fugitive, hunted by Saul who sought his life. He had been made aware by God of the treachery of the men of Keilah, 1 Sam. 23. 12, and then the Ziphims inform Saul of his hideout.

Note how David addresses his prayer, "Save me, O God, by thy name". The Name involved is "Elohim" (The Triune God), used four times in verses 1-4. He also uses two other titles, "Adonai" (Sovereign Lord), v. 4, and "Jehovah" (The Ever Existing One), v. 6. Both appear as "Lord" in the A.V. In his prayer for direction, 1 Sam. 23. 10-11, David combined both "Elohim" and "Jehovah" in his address, "O Lord God of Israel". Knowledge of the many facets of God's character conveyed in His Names gave David confidence in the direst of situations. For other interesting references to His Name, see Psa. 20. 1, 5, 7; 33. 21; 44. 5.

David's trust in God incited the hostility of his enemies. Unlike him, "they have not set God before them", v. 3; cf. Psa. 53. Because of this, he regarded them as "strangers" both to God and to himself, possibly because of his trust in God about which he was not ashamed to testify, "God is mine helper", v. 4. Even Saul had to admit to him, "Thou art more righteous than I", 1 Sam. 24. 17.

David's cry was answered in a remarkable way, 1 Sam. 23. 27-28. Either after the deliverance or in confident anticipation of it, he says in gratitude, "I will praise thy name, O Lord (Jehovah)", v. 6. In using the title "Jehovah", he testifies to God's trustworthiness.

Our Lord in His prayer, John 17, refers to the Name of His Father, vv. 6, 26, which He had revealed to His own. This was something new—a revelation of God as Father which was not known in O.T. times. It is as sons of the Father that we have great boldness in prayer:

"Whatsoever ye shall ask the Father in my name, he will give it you", John 16. 23.

READING: **Psalm 55**

CAST THY BURDEN UPON THE LORD

As in many other psalms, David begins this one with a cry of despair, but ends it on a note of confidence. This is yet another proof of the effect that prayer has upon the weary heart. It is true that through prayer:

"In seasons of distress and grief,
My soul has often found relief."

God allows burdens to come upon us, but He does not expect us to bear them alone. David learned this, and encouraged others to cast them upon the Lord. What comfort saints of all ages have drawn from the psalms of David!

David's burden on this occasion was a grievous one. "Pained", "terrors", "fearfulness", "trembling", "horror", are the words employed to describe his state from which he longed to fly away with wings like a dove. The dove, which depicted his state of soul, is a bird of peace, tenderness, harmlessness, sorrow and innocence; see Gen. 8. 9; Matt. 10. 16; Isa. 38. 14; 59. 11; Hos. 7. 11.

The cause of his sorrow was the treachery of a former acquaintance and guide whom he called "mine equal", v. 13. They had worshipped together, v. 14, but David had been deceived by his falseness, vv. 20-21. Open hostility from enemies was easier to bear than this, v. 12. In Psa. 54, David knew the treachery of his own countrymen; here, of one who had been a close companion. We are not told who this person was, but it seems very likely that Ahithophel was the man, 2 Sam. 15. 12-14; 16. 16-23. The rebellion of his own son Absalom; the perfidy of Ahithophel; the defection of friends and the resulting lawlessness in the city, vv. 10-11, brought David down to the depths of despondency.

The Lord Jesus is the supreme Example of one who was betrayed. He was "troubled in spirit" by the presence of the traitor. Yet He gave Judas the sop—an act of friendship, John 13. 21, 26. Later in the garden, Jesus still called him "friend", Matt. 26. 50. The Lord's character was dove-like to perfection, unlike that of David's, whose mood changed to one of indignation in verse 15 of the psalm.

Jesus said, *"Take my yoke upon you ... For my yoke is easy, and my burden is light"*, Matt. 11. 29-30.

READING: **Psalm 59**

FOR GOD IS MY DEFENCE

FROM THE TITLE given to this psalm, we learn that David wrote it during the time "when Saul sent, and they watched the house to kill him", 1 Sam. 19. 11-12. There appears to be confirmation of this in verse 3, "For, lo, they lie in wait for my soul: the mighty are gathered against me". On that occasion, his escape was assisted by Michal his wife, who proved herself to be less devoted to him at a later period, 2 Sam. 6. 20.

David does not attribute his deliverance here to his wife but to God who, he claims, was his defence (high tower, *marg.*), vv. 9, 16. The variety of divine titles that he employed is proof of where his confidence lay. The mighty men who were gathered together against him made him look to the One who was mightier. In the song of praise which ends the psalm, he says, "Unto thee, O my strength, will I sing", vv. 16-17.

There was no legitimate reason why Saul should have sought David's life. There was no "transgression", "sin", or "fault" which deserved it, vv. 3-4. It was because Saul was jealous of him, 1 Sam. 18. 7-9. The psalmist was hated without cause, just as the Lord was, John 15. 25; Psa. 35. 19; 69. 4. Jealousy is "cruel as the grave", Song 8. 6. The cruelty of Saul towards David betrayed his envy.

The Lord Jesus said to His disciples, "If the world hate you, ye know that it hated me before it hated you", and "because ye are not of the world, but I have chosen you out of the world, therefore the world hateth you", John 15. 18-19. Like their Lord, they also would be hated without cause.

In poetic style, David ascended his high tower of defence and surveyed his assailants. He describes them as undomesticated, half-starved dogs that roamed the city, returning at evening with appetites unsatisfied, v. 6. His faith in "Jehovah God of hosts", v. 5, assured him that since He was his defence, no harm could befall him, vv. 9-10. What folly on their part to leave God out of their reckoning, v. 7, or to imagine that their counsels could succeed against Him "that ruleth in Jacob", v. 13. We may boldly say, "*The Lord is my helper, and I will not fear what man shall do unto me*", Heb. 13. 6.

March 11th

READING: **Psalm 61**

THE ROCK THAT IS HIGHER THAN I

As we have seen, many of David's psalms were composed either when he was in flight from the hand of Saul, or when he was in exile during the time of Absalom's rebellion, 2 Sam. 15. This psalm appears to have been inspired at the time of the latter. The words "From the end of the earth (land) will I cry unto thee", v. 2, indicate that David was not then in the land. According to 2 Sam. 17. 24, he was at Mahanaim beyond Jordan, considered by an ardent Jew to be a foreign part. Then again, the words "Thou wilt prolong the king's life", v. 6, imply that he had been established as king in Israel which was not the case in the days of Saul.

When we consider the manifold trials and sorrows which David endured, we wonder why he did not break down under the strain. What was the secret? Surely, that his prayers had been heard and attended to, and that he had been led to the rock that was higher than himself. Time and again, he was overwhelmed with adversity, yet he survived going under by retaining his trust and confidence in God his Helper. In the prayer "lead me to the rock that is higher than I", David expressed his longing to get above the circumstances which threatened to engulf him. He also confessed a sense of helplessness in the realization that the rock was out of his reach without divine assistance; hence his plea "lead me".

His reference to the tabernacle and, possibly, to the wings covering the mercy seat in the words "the covert of thy wings", v. 4, shows his deep attachment to the sanctuary. If cut off from Zion, he was not, however, cut off from his God. He affirms his desire and resolve to abide in His presence. His trust is based on past experiences of protection, "thou hast been a shelter for me, and a strong tower from the enemy", v. 3.

Our Rock is Christ, 1 Cor. 10. 4. He has been "made higher than the heavens", Heb. 7. 26. He has entered the heavenly sanctuary "which the Lord pitched", Heb. 8. 2. "Let us therefore come boldly unto the throne of grace ... and find grace to help in time of need", 4. 16.

"Lead to the shadow of the Rock Eternal, my heart opprest;
There in the secret of Thy holy presence, calm shall I rest."

READING: **Psalm 62**

TRUST IN HIM AT ALL TIMES

In Psalm 61, David was depressed and desired to reach the "higher rock". In this psalm, he is in a mood of confidence, having risen to that higher plane above his circumstances.

God is everything to David, "My salvation", vv. 1, 2, 6, 7; "my rock" and "the rock of my strength", vv. 2, 6, 7; "my defence", vv. 2, 6; "my glory", v. 7; "my refuge" and "a refuge for us", vv. 7, 8. Consequently, God is his one and *only* trust. Note the repetition of the word "only" in vv.2, 4, 5, 6; also the words "truly" and "surely" in vv. 1, 9, both of which may be rendered by the same word "only". As seen before, Psa. 40. 4, David, out of his own experience of God, encourages others to trust Him at all times, v. 8.

"We may trust Him fully all for us to do;
They who trust Him wholly find Him wholly true."

Trust in God is seen in different aspects: either in "silently waiting", for this is the meaning in vv. 1, 5; or in "pouring out the heart", v. 8. In Psalm 46. 10, the writer said, "Be still, and know that I am God". It was in the "still small voice" that God spoke to Elijah, 1 Kings 19. 12. Our Lord is the highest Example of the aspect of "pouring out the heart", Heb. 5. 7. Is it not true that sometimes we are too busy or in a too agitated state of mind and soul to wait in silence upon God; and at other times, too reticent to unburden our hearts before Him?

David ascribed "power" and "mercy" (loving kindness) to God, vv. 11-12. It has been said, "Power without Love is brutality, and Love without Power is weakness. Power is the strong foundation of Love, and Love is the beauty and crown of Power". In the knowledge of the perfection of God's character, David warns against putting trust in men of whatever rank, for they are "lighter than vanity", or in wealth obtained through violence, greed or otherwise, v. 10. We are likewise warned by Paul not to "trust in uncertain riches, but in the living God", 1 Tim. 6. 17.

Paul prayed that we might know "the exceeding greatness of his power", Eph. 1. 19.

"Now unto him that is able to do exceeding adundantly above all that we ask or think, according to the power that worketh in us", 3. 20.

March 13th

READING: **Psalm 70**

BUT I AM POOR AND NEEDY

THE TITLE of this psalm reads, "A psalm of David to bring to remembrance". The same applies to Psalm 38. The meaning appears to be, either a memorial of his suffering and deliverance, or "to bring him into remembrance with God". Possibly the latter is the right one. If this is so, it does not mean that God needs to be reminded about matters. He knows everything, but He expects to see persistence in the holy exercise of prayer. Paul reminds us of the same, "in every thing by prayer and supplication ... let your requests be made known unto God", Phil. 4. 6.

Except for a few variations, this psalm is a repeat of the last part of Psalm 40 (vv. 13-17). It is not a needless repetition, however. It forms a fitting sequel to Psalm 69, in which the psalmist was the object of reproach, shame and ridicule. The imprecatory nature of the prayers in both of the psalms is understandable when considered against such a background. Nevertheless, it is important to remember that many psalms have a predictive character, pointing to future tribulation days when the godly, under great harassment, will rightly cry for vengeance upon their persecutors, Rev. 6. 10. David's prayer, "Let them be ... confounded", did not spring from a spirit of revenge, but from a devout desire that God should be magnified, v. 4.

David's lowliness and humility are reflected in the phrase, "But I am poor and needy". He frequently employed it, Psa. 35. 10; 37. 14; 40. 17; 86. 1. It is an attitude that God approves as confirmed by Scripture, "God resisteth the proud, but giveth grace to the humble", James 4. 6; 1 Pet. 5. 5. If David's estimation of himself was small, then his estimation of his God was great, "Let God be magnified". He who thinks highly of Him will inevitably think less of self, John 3. 30.

The Lord was "meek and lowly", Matt. 11. 29; He was the object of shame and contempt, but He prayed, "Father, forgive them", Luke 23. 34. He who took a lowly guise amongst men has been "highly exalted", Phil. 2. 9, and will ultimately come in judgment upon His enemies.

"Humble yourselves therefore under the mighty hand of God, that he may exalt you in due time", 1 Pet. 5. 6.

READING: **Psalm 71. 1-14**

CAST ME NOT OFF IN THE TIME OF OLD AGE

THIS PSALM begins with the cry, "let me never be put to confusion". This might be rendered, "let me never be ashamed" (J.N.D.). In this plea, the psalmist expressed, not so much a fear of being let down, but rather his desire to trust in Jehovah *forever*. Those who trust Him will never be let down. Of Israel's fathers it is recorded, "they trusted in thee, and were not confounded", Psa. 22. 5. Paul also quotes, "whosoever believeth on him shall not be confounded", Rom. 9. 33 marg., being a reference to Isaiah 28. 16 LXX. The psalmist's trust was not only sincere but long-standing, "from my youth", v. 5. His dependence upon Jehovah is portrayed in v. 6, "By thee have I been holden up from the womb". As a helpless babe is held in the strong and loving hands of its father, so he had rested in Jehovah's strength. After a life of trust and experience of God's faithfulness, it would be unthinkable that at the onset of old age and failing strength, God could cast him off, v. 9. This would be putting him to confusion.

In God's economy, no one is made redundant or considered too old. "They shall still bring forth fruit in old age", Psa. 92. 14. When one hundred years old, Abraham "considered not his own body now dead", Rom. 4. 19; it was in later life that he had his richest experience of God. Daniel, a youth when he went into captivity, grew up in Babylon to become a powerful influence there. He must have been at least eighty years old when cast to the lions. Despite advancing years, God's secrets were still revealed to him. These noble characters caught the admiration as well as the hostility of some. So it was with our psalmist who said, "I am as a wonder unto many", v. 7.

"Thou hast given *commandment* to save me", v. 3, is of interest regarding the means employed in answering prayers; cf. Psa. 44. 4. God commands angels, Dan. 9. 23; 10. 12; 2 Chron. 32. 21-22; men, as in the case of Cyrus the Persian monarch, 2 Chron. 36. 22; Ezra 1. 1; and sometimes the forces of nature, Psa. 107. 25-29.

"We faint not; but though our outward man perish, yet the inward man is renewed day by day", 2 Cor. 4. 16.

March 15th

READING: **Psalm 88**

WHY HIDEST THOU THY FACE FROM ME?

THERE IS no certainty as to the identity of the author of this psalm. Many suggestions have been made, but none is conclusive. There is an affinity in language with that of Job. Some think that he was the writer, but this is not decisive, for similar language is employed by others, Psa. 6. 5-6; 30. 3; Isa. 38. 10-11. In the introduction, the chief musician is instructed to sing the psalm "upon Mahalath Leannoth", i.e. in a mournful tone. It is considered to be the gloomiest psalm in the psalter. It reflects the utter despair of the composer, e.g. "my life draweth nigh unto the grave", v. 3.; "Thy wrath lieth hard upon me", v. 7; "Mine eye mourneth by reason of affliction", v. 9; "Lover and friend hast thou put far from me", v. 18. It ends in darkness without a ray of hope. The only glimmer of light amidst the gloom is in verse 1, where he mentions that the Lord God was his salvation.

We also observe that this psalm is a "Maschil psalm", i.e. a psalm giving instruction—not just to the precentor, but to us as well. What can we learn from such a sorrowful psalm? Firstly, that we must cling to God in times of inexplicable gloom. The prophet wrote, "Who ... walketh in darkness, and hath no light? let him trust in the name of the Lord, and stay upon his God", Isa. 50. 10. Job said, "Though he slay me, yet will I trust in him", Job 13. 15. However hard, it is better to walk *with* God in the dark, than to walk *alone* in the light. Secondly, that times of affliction drive us to earnest prayer. What a formality prayer sometimes can be! Trial produces reality. The psalmist pours out his soul plaintively, "I have cried day and night before thee"; "I have called daily upon thee"; "why hidest thou thy face from me?", vv. 1, 9, 14.

However dark our path, we who live in this age have more light than the psalmist. God's wrath no longer rests upon us; death's sting is gone; we know that nothing can separate us from His love. This, and much more, is because He *spared* not His own Son, who in the darkness endured sin's penalty, John 3. 36; 1 Cor. 15. 55; Matt. 27. 45; Rom. 8. 32, 39.

"My God, my God, why hast thou forsaken me?", Matt. 27. 46.

March 16th

READING: **Psalm 94. 12-23**

JUDGMENT SHALL RETURN UNTO RIGHTEOUSNESS

THE FIRST part of this psalm, vv. 1-13, is taken up with the miscarriage of justice by the wicked. This made the psalmist cry to the Judge of the earth to whom vengeance belongs, "how long shall the wicked triumph?". God's apparent silence and inactivity in this respect have been a mystery to the godly of all times. This mystery of God will come to an end, Rev. 10. 7. He will intervene in human affairs. The same theme is present in the second part, but the psalmist is now confident that "judgment shall return unto righteousness", v. 15, and that "the throne of iniquity" can never be approved by God, v. 20.

The man who is chastened (instructed) by Jehovah is a happy man. In the midst of adversity, he is given peace in the knowledge that all misrule will eventually be dealt with. In the meanwhile, God will not forsake His earthly inheritance, i.e. Israel. We are His heavenly inheritance, that of the saints in light, Eph. 1. 18; Col. 1. 12.

Authorities, set up by God, Rom. 13. 1, often abuse their power and afflict the righteous. The psalmist appears to have been afflicted almost to the silence of the grave, but the Lord was his help, comfort and delight, vv. 16-19. He was also his defence and refuge, v. 22.

Paul was called to stand before Nero; no man stood with him, but he wrote, "Notwithstanding the Lord stood with me ...and I was delivered out of the mouth of the lion". This gave him confidence, for he adds, "And the Lord shall deliver me from every evil work", 2 Tim. 4. 17-18.

Worldly powers pass sentence, but often without righteousness. Pilate passed judgment on the Lord, even though He was faultless—an outstanding miscarriage of justice.

We live in a world of anarchy, repression and corruption. With the psalmist, we look to the future with certainty, to the time when the Lord will sit upon the throne of David in righteousness, Isa. 11. 5; 32. 1; Prov. 16. 12. Meanwhile, we have a responsibility to pray for, and to be subject to ruling authorities, 1 Tim. 2. 1-2; 1 Pet. 2. 13-14.

"Thy throne, O God, is for ever and ever: a sceptre of righteousness is the sceptre of thy kingdom", Heb. 1. 8.

87

March 17th

READING: **Psalm 107. 1-9**

O GIVE THANKS UNTO THE LORD

IT IS GOOD to give thanks to the Lord, Psa. 92. 1. It is good, because *He* is good. His goodness is seen in manifold ways of providence. Examples are given in this psalm of travellers, rebels, the foolish and mariners who, in dire peril, cry to the Lord and are delivered. These providential acts of mercy call for thanksgivings, vv. 8, 15, 21, 31.

These are not always forthcoming. Men are guilty of ingratitude, Rom. 1. 21; Luke 17. 17. Nebuchadnezzar, restored from insanity, and Jonah, vomited alive out of the fish, are recorded exceptions, Dan. 4. 34-37; Jonah 2. 9. Winston Churchill, in his book *My Early Years*, recounts that on escaping from Pretoria, he found himself in such straits out of which only the help of God could extricate him. Fearing recapture, he cried to God. Circumstances turned out so unexpectedly for his deliverance, that he could only attribute them to the hand of God.

God's goodness extends to all men in the essentials of life, Matt. 5. 45; Acts 14. 17. These are often taken for granted, without any thought of the Giver. The believer should be thankful for everything, 1 Thess. 5. 18.

Israel experienced the goodness of God and saw His wonderful works. It seems that this psalm was written at the time of the return from Babylon. Yet the nation was guilty of ingratitude before and after the exile; see Psa. 106. According to many prophecies, there is to be a future return out of all lands. In that day, Israel will give thanks unto his holy name and triumph in his praise, Psa. 106. 47. God's goodness in the sphere of redemption calls for even greater thanksgiving. Thankfulness is a mark of the filling of the Spirit, Eph. 5. 20. It is also an important part of prayer. We should always thank the Father for our salvation, Col. 1. 12-14; also for reports of the conversion and progress of others, Col. 1. 3-4; 1 Thess. 1. 2-3; 2. 13. All our requests should be accompanied by thanksgiving, Phil. 4. 6. God is unlikely to grant further requests if He sees no gratitude for what He has already bestowed.

"Whatsoever ye do ... do all in the name of the Lord Jesus, giving thanks to God and the Father", Col. 3. 17.

March 18th

READING: **Psalm 109. 21-31**

HE SHALL STAND AT THE RIGHT HAND

THE ACCUSER in a trial stood at the right hand of the accused; cf. v. 6 with Zech. 3. 1. David, to whom this psalm is ascribed, had been accused by a "lying tongue" with "words of hatred", vv. 2-3, and abused additionally with curses, vv. 17-18. Among his adversaries, there was one who stood out in particular, vv. 6-19. Understandably, David was deeply wounded. He felt like a declining shadow at evening, like a detested locust shaken out of a garment. He was also the object of ridicule, vv. 22-26.

For practical purposes, Shimei might be considered as typical of David's adversary, 2 Sam. 16. 5-8. He hurled accusations and invectives at David when the latter was fleeing from Jerusalem. Abishai asked to take off Shimei's head, but David refused him, manifesting a meekness of spirit that was quite the reverse of the strong imprecations spoken at other times. Compare "so let him curse", 2 Sam. 16. 10, with verse 28 of this psalm "Let them curse, but bless thou". Balaam, hired by Balak to curse Israel, found it impossible, and had to admit "he hath blessed; and I cannot reverse it", Num. 23. 20. A curse pronounced upon God's people is like the swallow which swoops but never lights upon them. We who are so richly blessed, Eph. 1. 3, must never forget that the Lord bore the curse for us, Gal. 3. 13.

The prayer for deliverance, vv. 21, 26, was motivated by the desire that deliverance should be seen to be by the hand of the Lord, v. 27. Our Lord was falsely accused by men but was exalted by God. Of Him it is said, "this is the Lord's doing, and it is marvellous in our eyes", Matt. 21. 42.

Should any of us pass through an experience like David's, let us remember the Lord's example: He "committed himself to him that judgeth righteously", 1 Pet. 2. 23.

David ends with confidence and with his mouth full of praise, vv. 30-31. Jehovah, his Advocate, was at his right hand to defend him against the accusation of his adversary, as He defended Joshua the high priest in Zechariah 3. 1-5 referred to at the beginning.

"Who shall lay any thing to the charge of God's elect? it is God that justifieth", Rom. 8. 33.

89

March 19th

READING: Psalm 115

NOT UNTO US, UNTO THY NAME GIVE GLORY

IT IS HARD to understand how Israel, who knew the only God and saw His wonderful works, could have turned to idolatry. It happened, however, and consequently the nation went into captivity amongst the nations whose idolatrous practices they had followed, Jer. 2. 17; 44. 16-18. The seventy years captivity almost cured the nation's proneness to idols, Hos. 3. 4. Though a veil of blindness still remains upon the hearts of its people, there has been no return to idolatry.

The psalm expresses the deep concern within the hearts of the returned exiles that God *only* should be glorified, cf. Isa. 42. 8; 48. 11. The idolatry witnessed in Babylon was still fresh in their minds. The answer to the taunt of the heathen, "Where is now their God?", is answered by "our God is in the heavens", v. 3. Moreover, He was sovereign: "he hath done whatsoever he hath pleased". By contrast, the idols of the nations, though of gold and silver, were but works of men. Israel's God, if invisible, was uncreated and therefore eternal. The title "Jehovah" (the Ever-Existing One) is used ten times, and "Jah" (the Eternal) twice (New Trans., J.N.D.). Their idols looked like men, but were lifeless. The psalmist adds, "They that make them are like unto them", vv. 5-8. Paul makes the same observation, Rom. 1. 21-23. Conversely, Jehovah was Israel's help and shield, and could be trusted implicitly. What confidence this inspired in the psalmist. It should inspire us too, for He is our God, John 20. 17.

The psalmist began with a confession of unworthiness, "Not unto us". How differently the Pharisee began his prayer in Luke 18. 10-12; he went on as he began, drawing attention to himself as if God was obligated to him. The disciples were warned against this attitude, Matt. 6. 5. Paul rebuked the Corinthians for glorying in men. In discounting himself and Apollos, and attributing the work at Corinth to God who gave the increase, he was virtually saying, "Not unto us ... but unto thy name give glory", 1 Cor. 3. 5-6, 21. The Lord did not seek His own glory, John 8. 50; 12. 28.

"Now unto the King eternal, incorruptible, invisible, the only God ... be glory for ever and ever", 1 Tim. 1. 17 R.V.

READING: **Psalm 120**

I AM FOR PEACE

RECORDING A PAST experience, the psalmist testified that he had cried unto the Lord and had been answered, v. 1 R.V. In the strength of this, he entreats the Lord again. The prayers of the righteous are not only "heard" but "answered" also. They may not be answered in the way requested. The answer may be "yes", or it may be "no", and often it may be "wait" —but answered they are. He will not turn a deaf ear to the cries of the sincere.

The man of prayer will be a man of peace, and the man of peace will not be guilty of the misuse of the tongue. The psalmist was a man of peace who suffered from the lies and deceit of those among whom he sojourned. Their tongues were as sharp as arrows and as coals of fire. It was as if he lived among the savage, warlike tribes of Meshech in the north, and of Kedar to the south of the land. Meshech was a descendant of Japheth, along with Tubal and Magog, Gen. 10. 2; Kedar was the son of Ishmael, 25. 13.

The misuse of the tongue often leads to conflict between nations and, regrettably, among the Lord's people. James, in his Epistle, goes into great detail in describing the tongue, and shows how damaging it can be when not controlled. He uses graphic illustrations to show the devastating effects its misuse can have: a forest fire ignited by a spark, and "a world of iniquity among our members", James 3. 5-6 R.V.

Like the psalmist, we need to pray earnestly that we may maintain a peaceable spirit when assailed by the tongues of others. We ought to pray more earnestly still that our own tongues should be kept under tight control. Our prayers will not be heard if we fail in this area of life where self-control is so vital. The link between answered prayer and the control of the tongue, along with the pursuit of peace, is seen in Psalm 34. 12-16 and 1 Peter 3. 10-12. Of course, there is a time to speak out. We are often guilty of silence when we should be speaking; cf. Psa. 39. 1-3; Eccl. 3. 7; Jer. 20. 8. Our blessed Lord, in whose mouth there was no guile, perfectly displayed this before Pilate.

"If it be possible, as much as lieth in you, live peaceably with all men", Rom. 12. 18.

March 21st

READING: **Psalm 121**

THE LORD IS THY KEEPER

THE THEME of this psalm is the *keeping* power of Jehovah. Six times the word *keep* is used. The word *preserve*, vv. 7-8, is the same word, and is given as *keep* in the margin. None should ever doubt God's ability to keep. He is the Creator of heaven and earth, v. 2. He not only made the universe with its intricate system, but sustains it so that it never gets out of hand. The heavenly bodies are kept in their orbits. The earth rotates on its axis at an angle that brings the seasons with unfailing regularity, Gen. 8. 22. The atmospheric pressure, causing a force that bears down on the earth, never exceeds a prescribed limit, up or down; if it did, no one would survive. This, and much more beyond our finite capacities, display His omnipotence and omniscience. What is more, He never suffers from fatigue, nor is He ever off duty, for He neither slumbers nor sleeps. "Hast thou not heard, that the everlasting God ... the Creator of the ends of the earth, fainteth not, neither is weary?", Isa. 40. 28. In view of this, how can we doubt God's ability or His readiness to cope with the circumstances of our lives?

Elijah mocked the prophets of Baal who cried in vain to their god to answer them. How caustic were his remarks in suggesting that perhaps Baal was asleep and needed to be aroused, or was too preoccupied to hear them, 1 Kings 18. 27.

Consider the case of Peter, Acts 12. 4-10. Four soldiers at a time were charged to *keep* him in prison. What follows proves that the Lord was Peter's Keeper not the soldiers. The same was true of Paul and Silas, 16. 23, 27.

Israel was the object of God's providential care as was Jacob, Gen. 28. 15. That care extends to us. This does not mean that we, any more than they, will be always *kept from* trial. There have been many imprisoned who never had the miraculous deliverance that Peter and Paul had. If our *Keeper* allows us to endure trials, He will *keep* us *through* them. In this age we are *kept* spiritually, "preserved (kept) in Jesus Christ", Jude 1. We should pray to be kept from evil, 2 Thess. 3. 3; "preserved (kept) faultless", 1 Thess. 5. 23; "to keep you from falling", Jude 24. Confidently we affirm, *"kept by the power of God"*, 1 Pet. 1. 5.

March 22nd

READING: **Psalm 123**

UNTO THEE LIFT I UP MINE EYES

WITH THE ABOVE words, the psalmist expressed his implicit trust in the Lord. He looked neither *within* nor *around*, but *above*. He and the people for whom he pleaded were surrounded by scoffers who contemptuously derided them.

The psalm is very applicable to the time of Nehemiah, when the returned exiles began picking up the pieces of their disrupted national life. As they built the wall, they were mocked and laughed at by enemies. Nehemiah was not put off by this, but resorted to prayer, and the work of the building of the wall proceeded, Neh. 2. 19; 4. 1-5.

God spoke to the exiles in captivity through Ezekiel, impressing upon them that they had become the objects of scorn and derision because they had forgotten Him. God, however, promised that the situation would be completely reversed, cf. Ezek. 23. 32, 35; 36. 3-7. See also Psa. 2. 4. This must have given hope and confidence to the remnant.

The eyes of slaves and maidens in servitude looked up to their masters; we lift up ours with hope and expectation. In these last days, we are surrounded by scoffers as predicted by Peter, 2 Pet. 3. 3. Our confidence will not be shaken by these if we keep looking up. We ought not to be surprised if, in school, office, factory, the street or even in the home, we are taunted, derided and laughed at. These have been the portion of the godly, especially when engaged in doing a work for God. Timothy was reminded that "all that will live godly in Christ Jesus shall suffer persecution", 2 Tim. 3. 12. Paul became a "spectacle", and was "reviled" and "defamed", 1 Cor. 4. 9, 12, 13. Preachers, like Whitfield who travelled the country preaching the gospel, were pelted with stones, ridiculed and sometimes spat upon.

Our sinless Lord was the object of mockery and contempt in His lifetime as well as in His death. Nothing could deter Him from the path of trust and obedience to His Father. Twice it is recorded that He lifted up His eyes heavenward, John 11. 41; 17. 1, but the whole of His life was lived out in the conscious presence of His Father.

"Consider him that endured such contradiction of sinners ... lest ye be wearied and faint in your minds", Heb. 12. 3.

March 23rd

READING: Psalm 4

WHO WILL SHOW US ANY GOOD?

VERSES 6 and 8 of this psalm are very similar to verses 2 and 5 of Psalm 3. This leads to the view that both psalms were written about the same time, namely during Absalom's rebellion (see the title of Psalm 3). That unhappy episode in the life of David is recorded in 2 Samuel 15-18. Whether the psalm belongs to that period or not, it is applicable to the psalmist's circumstances at the time.

The question asked, "Who will show us any good?", reflects the outlook of men who walked by sight and not by faith. Their happiness lay in the possession of earthly things. Those who raised the question may have been the companions of David in distress. Let us guard against lack of faith.

In contrast, David was enlarged by distress, v. 1. He had a gladness which exceeded that of those who reaped a good harvest, v. 7; cf. Hab. 3. 17-19.

Absalom "stole the hearts of the men of Israel" ; he also offered sacrifices, either in pretence or as an appeal to God to bless the revolt, 2 Sam. 15. 6-12. Let us beware of following men and of asking God to bless what is not right.

David made his appeal to God on the ground of righteousness, and admonished the people that the sacrifices of righteousness were the only ones acceptable to God, vv. 1, 5.

Absalom's beauty attracted a following, 2 Sam. 14. 25. His hair, however, was his downfall. "Favour is deceitful, and beauty is vain", Prov. 31. 30. He was praised for his beauty, but not for fear of the Lord. With David, the countenance of God was more to be desired. "Absalom" means "father of peace", but he instigated revolution, not peace. David, for his part, knew an inward peace, v. 8.

David's response to the unbelief of some was to look to heaven, and claim the blessing that Aaron was instructed to pronounce upon Israel, v. 6; cf. Num. 6. 24-26. That he was able both to lie down and sleep, despite the danger that he was in, reflected a peace and sense of safety, showing that he was in the good of the blessing he sought.

Jesus fell asleep in the boat, in the midst of a tempest. He was at peace; there was no tempest in His soul.

"He said unto them, Where is your faith?", Luke 8. 25.

March 24th

READING: **Psalm 5**

I WILL DIRECT MY PRAYER UNTO THEE

"PRAYER is the Christian's vital breath" are words from a hymn often sung at prayer meetings. We all agree that they are true. Notwithstanding, this vital exercise is sadly neglected, both in our private and collective lives. During the Jewish day, three times were set aside for prayer: morning, noon and evening, i.e., nine, twelve and three o'clock. The first and third coincided with the daily morning and evening sacrifices; see Acts 3. 1; 10. 3, 9, 30. Daniel followed this pattern, Dan. 6. 10; and David also, Psa. 55. 17. It would appear, however, that David was in the habit of rising early to pray, Psa. 57. 8; 63. 1; 108. 2. This, of course, was also true of our Lord, Mark 1. 35.

We must at all costs avoid being too busy or too lazy to get up and pray. Like David, we should resolve to start the day with God. We live in a hostile and evil world where dangers and temptations of every kind abound. David requested guidance, v. 8, and to have the joy of divine protection, vv. 11-12. The reason for his prayer is seen in verse 9. Starting the day with prayer will not only be a safeguard, but will lift *us* above mundane and depressing things.

David directed (set in order) his prayer like the priests "set in order" the wood and the parts of the sacrifice on the altar fire, Lev. 1. 7-8 etc. By using the same word, he viewed his morning prayer as a sacrifice rising acceptably to God. Having offered his prayer, he looked up for tokens of acceptance. Fire was sometimes a visible sign of this, Lev. 9. 24; Jud. 6. 21; 1 Kings 18. 38. We do not, any more than David did, expect fire to fall from heaven, but we should look expectantly for answers. Elijah prayed for rain and sent his servant to look no less than seven times before a "little cloud" appeared as proof that God had heard and that rain was on the way. The Lord give *us* more faith in prayer. "Lord, teach us to pray", Luke 11. 1.

"Men ought always to pray", Luke 18. 1, not just in the morning. The Lord, who said this Himself, always prayed. He spent whole nights in prayer, 6. 12.

"And all things, whatsoever ye shall ask in prayer, believing, ye shall receive", Matt. 21. 22.

READING: **Psalm 125**

THEY SHALL BE AS MOUNT ZION

MOUNTAINS symbolize stability and security. Mount Zion, "which cannot be removed", is a picture of stability; Jerusalem, enclosed by mountains, is thus secure. The psalmist uses these pictures to describe those who trust the Lord.

Mount Zion was an impregnable fortress until David took it from the Jebusites, 2 Sam. 5. 6-9. Concerning Zion, the Lord declared, "This is my rest *forever*", Psa 132. 14. In the psalmist's time, Zion and the land were under the power of Persia; he is confident that this could not be *forever*, for he says, "the rod (sceptre) of the wicked shall not rest upon the lot (land) of the righteous", v. 3.

Jerusalem is surrounded by mountains and deep gorges. Consequently, is was difficult to capture. Its real defence, however, was the Lord, not the mountains. It was because Judah forsook Him instead of trusting Him, that the city was ultimately taken and the people led into captivity. The future security of Jerusalem is described in Zechariah 2. 4-5.

The worldly put their trust in wealth, Psa. 49. 6; 52. 7; or in military might, 20. 7; but these give no real security, Luke 12. 16-20; Psa. 33. 16-17; Prov. 21. 31. Even David, when in prosperity, said, "I shall never be moved", Psa. 30. 6. He had a better outlook in Psalm 21. 7; cf. 112. 6; 121. 3.

The psalm is thought to have been written in the time of Nehemiah. He faced many problems in the work of restoration. There were intrigues and threats of intimidation from without. Within, he had to contend with complainers and some who were in league with the enemy, Neh. 4. 10; 6. 2; 13. 4. These are probably in mind in verse 3 of our psalm, "lest the righteous put forth their hands unto iniquity", and in verse 5, "such as turn aside unto their crooked ways". Nehemiah was not moved by these things. He was a man of prayer who trusted in the Lord. Look up the references to his prayers in his book.

"The world lieth in the evil one", 1 John 5. 19 R.V., but not *forever*. In Psalm 2. 6, God will establish His King on Zion; meanwhile, we must expect opposition as we serve. Can we say, "none of these things move me"?, Acts 20. 24.

"We had the sentence of death in ourselves, that we should not trust in ourselves, but in God", 2 Cor. 1. 9.

March 26th

READING: **Psalm 124**

THE LORD IS ON OUR SIDE

THERE IS a correspondence between this psalm and Psalm 121. In that psalm, Jehovah is seen as Israel's Keeper; in this, He is claimed by the psalmist to be "on our side". Therefore, Israel enjoyed not only God's *protection* but His *presence* as well. The nation owes its existence to God alone. The many attempts to exterminate it have always failed. Because the Lord was on Israel's side, they were not swallowed up alive by the Egyptians at the Red Sea, vv. 3-6, nor by the Babylonians, from which nation a remnant had lately returned like birds escaped "out of the snare of the fowlers", v. 7.

David went out to meet Goliath in the confidence that God was on his side, 1 Sam. 17. 45-46; Elisha assured his panic-stricken servant of the same, 2 Kings 6. 16-17; Nehemiah rallied his fellow-workers likewise, Neh. 4. 20; Moses confirmed the same fact to Israel, Deut. 20. 1-4. See also Num. 14. 9; Josh. 5'. 13-15; 2 Chron. 13. 12.

Israel was delivered from an earthly bondage; we, from a spiritual bondage, Col. 1. 13-14. Their conflict was against flesh and blood; ours, against principalities and powers, Eph. 6. 12. Furthermore, "the weapons of our warfare are not carnal", 2 Cor. 10. 4. As we travel the wilderness of this world, we are exposed to the attacks of our adversary, the devil. He is depicted as a roaring lion, ready to devour, or to swallow up the believer, 1 Pet. 5. 8. On our own, we are no match for him, but the Lord is on our side. He is our Captain, leading us to glory, Heb. 2. 10. If this were not so, we would be easy prey for Satan. John encourages us with these words, "greater is he that is in you, than he that is in the world", 1 John 4. 4. Christ, the great Overcomer, dwelling within us by the power of the Spirit, makes us "more than conquerors", John 16. 33; Rom. 8. 37.

Notwithstanding, we must be vigilant. Paul exhorts us not only to "be strong in the Lord", but also stresses the need to put on "the whole armour of God". Perseverance in prayer and supplication in the Spirit are seen to be vital accessories to the Christian's panoply, Eph. 6. 13-18.

"But thanks be to God, which giveth us the victory through our Lord Jesus Christ", 1 Cor. 15. 57.

READING: **Psalm 46**

A VERY PRESENT HELP IN TROUBLE

THE ABOVE might be rendered, "A help readily found in trouble". The psalmist, whoever he was and whenever he wrote, had historical proof that this was true. Long before, Moses had said, "what nation is there so great, who hath God so nigh unto them, as the Lord our God is in all things that we call upon him for?". In his final blessing upon the people, he also said, "The eternal God is thy refuge, and underneath are the everlasting arms", Deut. 4. 7; 33. 27.

In Jehoshaphat's reign, Moab and Ammon declared war on Judah. He "feared, and set himself to seek the Lord", saying, "If ... we ... cry unto thee in our affliction (trouble), then thou wilt hear and help". The Lord responded, "Ye shall not need to fight in this battle ... stand ye still, and see the salvation of the Lord", 2 Chron. 20. 3, 9, 17. At a later period, when Jerusalem was besieged by the Assyrian armies, Hezekiah besought the Lord saying, "This day is a day of trouble". God answered, "Be not afraid". Shortly after, the siege was lifted and the enemy withdrew his forces, 2 Kings 19. 3, 6, 7. The Lord not only "maketh wars to cease", Psa. 46. 9, but is also able to prevent them.

The knowledge of divine help readily available filled the psalmist with confidence. Despite catastrophies, natural or political, he says, "Therefore will we not fear", vv. 1-3. We live in a time of political instability and international tension. Men are fearful and kingdoms are moved, v. 6, but we belong to "a kingdom which cannot be moved", Heb. 12. 28, and should not fear. God is still on the throne.

His help in trouble applies individually as well as nationally. David said, "This poor man cried, and the Lord heard him, and saved him out of all his troubles", Psa. 34. 6; and again, "Though I walk in the midst of trouble, thou wilt revive me", 138. 7. He encouraged others, "The Lord hear thee in the day of trouble ... send thee help from the sanctuary", 20. 1-2. Of the Lord it is recorded, "Be not far from me; for trouble is near; for there is none to help", 22. 11. God says, "call upon me in the day of trouble: I will deliver thee", 50. 15.

"Let us therefore come boldly unto the throne of grace ... and find grace to help in time of need", Heb. 4. 16.

March 28th

READING: **Psalm 17**

THOU HAST PROVED MINE HEART

THE LORD warned against the "leaven of the Pharisees, which is hypocrisy", Luke 12. 1. The prayers of the Pharisees were a pretence; they loved to be seen by men. They honoured God with their lips only; their heart was far from Him. The Lord severely condemned these self-righteous hypocrites, Matt. 6. 5; 15. 8; 23. 27-28; Luke 18. 9.

David's prayer was both righteous and sincere. It came "not out of feigned lips", v. 1. In asserting the righteousness of his cause, vv. 2-4, he was not guilty of self-righteousness like the Pharisee in the parable, Luke 18. 10. He was attesting his honesty of heart and stedfastness of purpose. The words, "thou hast tried me, and findest nothing", v. 3 R.V., were not a boastful claim to faultlessness. His appeal for help lest his feet should slip, v. 5, and the requests that he makes in verses 6-8, are proof of this.

David's confidence in prayer sprang from self-examination in the presence of God. In the stillness of the night when the conscience is not easily silenced, he exposed himself to Him who searched his heart, v. 3; cf. Psa. 139. 1, 23, 24. He knew that if he regarded iniquity in his heart, the Lord would not hear his prayer, Psa. 66. 18. Out of his own personal experience, David passed on this wise counsel to his son Solomon, 1 Chron. 28. 9.

We, no less than David, need to pray, "Search me, O God"; when we sing the following lines, do we really mean them?

"Search all my thoughts, the secret springs,
  The motives that control;
The chambers where polluted things
  Hold empire o'er the soul."

Our prayers will be more effective if we submit to the discipline of self-examination before Him who searches the heart, Jer. 17. 10; 1 Cor. 11. 28, 31. The two-edged sword of the Word of God is the means the Spirit uses to search us. It pierces, cuts, judges and exposes us before "him with whom we have to do", Heb. 4. 12-13. When we awake in Christ's likeness, Psa. 17. 15, heart-searching will no longer be needed.

"Beloved, if our heart condemn us not, then have we confidence toward God", 1 John 3. 21.

March 29th

READING: **Psalm 56**

WHEN I AM AFRAID, I WILL TRUST IN THEE

THERE WERE times when David was afraid and did not trust in the Lord. The courage he displayed before Goliath was lacking when he fled from Saul. Having been anointed king by Samuel, he should have left matters in the hands of God, but in fear he resorted to his own devices. Going to Nob, the site of the tabernacle, he lied to the high priest there in order to obtain food and a sword. Having obtained these, he fled to the Philistines, Israel's long-standing enemies, and to Gath, where Goliath had lived, of all places. His presence there was suspect by some, on account of his past successes against them. In fear, he stooped to feigning madness and escaped; see 1 Sam. 21. 2, 8-9, 10-15. After his final encounter with Saul, David was still afraid, and fled yet again to the Philistines among whom he was guilty of further deceit; see 1 Sam. 26. 25; 27. 1, 10-12.

The title of this psalm refers it to the time when David was among the Philistines. Yet, later on, he fled in fear of his life from his son Absalom, and this became a talking point throughout Israel, 2 Sam. 15. 14; 19. 9. This shows that he failed at times to practice lessons previously learned and is a salutary reminder of the weakness of the flesh.

Let us be warned. Resorting to dishonesty in times of fear can lead into greater danger. Only by divine intervention were Abraham and Isaac delivered from the predicaments that their lies got them into, Gen. 12. 12-20; 26. 7-10. David almost got caught up in a war against his own nation through his involvement with the Philistines, 1 Sam. 28. 1; 29. 4.

Fear is common to us all. It can un-man the bravest. It is inherent in human nature, and is the legacy of sin. There are many things that make us afraid, sickness, poverty, loneliness, reproach; but there are also many "Fear not's" in the Scriptures to allay fear. David found strength in the Word of God, vv. 4, 10. It is the fear of man, however, which the psalm reflects, and which beset the psalmist so often. Let us remember that "The fear of man bringeth a snare: but whoso putteth his trust in the Lord shall be safe", Prov. 29. 25.

"Ye fearful saints, fresh courage take." "Let not your heart be troubled, neither let it be afraid", John 14. 27.

March 30th

READING: **Psalm 91**

THE SECRET PLACE OF THE MOST HIGH

THE PSALM opens with a rich range of divine titles: "most High", "Almighty", "LORD", "God", vv. 1-2. The title "most High" first appears in Genesis 14. 19, 22, where it is twice recorded that God is "possessor of heaven and earth". The title therefore denotes *universal supremacy*. "Almighty" appears first in Genesis 17. 1, where the context shows that it denotes God's *all-sufficiency*. Though Abraham was 99 years old, God would fulfil His pledge to him concerning a son. God said to him, "walk before me". Abraham had just walked according to Sarah's carnal policy to obtain seed of Hagar, and this had bitter consequences. The title "Jehovah", usually translated "LORD", occurs more frequently than the others; it conveys *eternal changelessness*. "Elohim", translated "God", denotes *divine power*.

The psalm closes with a bunch of divine "I will's", vv. 14-16. These precious promises apply to those who set their love upon Him and know His Name, v. 14. To know His Name means to know Him personally. Knowing about Him is not the same as knowing Him intimately. In order to know Him thus, we must dwell in His presence. This is the "secret place", where there is security from every kind of danger, and an all-sufficiency for every need, vv. 3-13.

The divine Names are a manifestation of God's Person and character. The fullest revelation of Himself, of course, was made in the Son, John 1. 18; Heb. 1. 1-3. In His prayer to the Father, the Lord said, "I have manifested thy name", John 17. 6. He was referring to the revelation of God as Father—an aspect of Him not known by the psalmist. God as revealed in the N.T. is *our* God and *Father*, John 20. 17. Our unique relationship gives us an even greater sense of security. No difficulties can befall us apart from the Father's will.

"Precious thought—my Father knoweth! in His Love I rest;
For whate're my Father doeth must be always best."

To "abide (pass the night) under the shadow of the Almighty" gives comfort, not only to those who fear the night, but also to us all who look for the Morning Star to end our sojourn in this scene of moral and spiritual night.

"The night is far spent, the day is at hand", Rom. 13. 12.

101

March 31st

READING: **Psalm 141**

LET MY PRAYER BE AS INCENSE

THE REFERENCES to "incense" and "evening sacrifice", v. 2, imply that David had in mind the daily sacrifices which were offered morning and evening. They were accompanied by a gift offering of flour mingled with oil. Closely associated were the incense offerings, performed every morning and evening at the altar of incense situated within the holy place, Exod. 29. 38-42; 30. 7-8. The incense offered by the priest consisted of a compound of sweet spices. One of these was frankincense which also formed an essential part of the gift offering, Lev. 2. 2. The sacrifice to which David refers in verse 2 is the gift offering (see margin).

Incense is a symbol of prayer, Rev. 5. 8; 8. 3. David desired the lifting up of his hands in prayer to be as incense giving pleasure to God. He was therefore concerned that his life should be consistent with his prayer. Even if righteous rebuke was necessary, he was ready to accept it gladly, so that nothing should prevent the acceptance of his prayer, Psa. 141. 3-5. If David had his desire in his day, how much more should we with greater privileges seek to bring pleasure to our Father by "lifting up holy hands" in prayer, 1 Tim. 2. 8.

Daniel's prayer, made at the time of the evening gift offering, must have ascended as incense. The visit of Gabriel to him was proof that his prayer was accepted. Similarly with Cornelius; his prayers and almsgiving went up as "a memorial before God", Dan. 9. 21; Acts 10. 4.

The Holy Spirit has given us a knowledge of the Levitical sacrifices not possessed by David. We understand that the flour and the oil of the gift offering are typical of the holy and perfect humanity of Christ. The added frankincense speaks of the fragrance, which His life here below yielded to the heart of the Father. The golden altar, where the incense was presented, typifies Him exalted as our High Priest engaged in the work of intercession for us. These things should encourage *us* to a deeper sincerity in prayer, because

"To all our prayers and praises
Christ adds His sweet perfume."

"By Him therefore let us offer the sacrifice of praise to God continually ... the fruit of our lips", Heb. 13. 15.

Righteousness, Justice, Judgment

GOD IS THE Righteous God, and He demands like character in those who follow Him. The description "the righteous" is therefore frequently found in the psalms. God knows the way of the righteous, Psa. 1. 6; He upholds them, Psa. 37. 17; He will bless the righteous, Psa. 5. 12, etc. In all, there are nearly fifty references to "the righteous". Of God it is said, "Righteous art thou, O Lord, and upright are thy judgments", Psa. 119. 137. "The upright" is another description frequently found. God saves the upright in heart, Psa. 7. 10, and He knows the days of the upright, Psa. 37. 18. With an upright man, God shows Himself upright, Psa. 18. 25. Likeness of character is again seen, for "Good and upright is the Lord", Psa. 25. 8.

Sometimes the psalmist calls upon the Lord to "judge" him, Psa. 7. 8; 26. 1; 35. 24; 43. 1; 54. 1. What he is saying is, "Do me justice", "vindicate me". The grounds of such vindication are then given. The claims that the psalmist subsequently makes are no Pharisaic assertion of self-righteousness, or that he feels superior to the rest of the world. Indeed, he is not aware of the peril of sin; cf. Psa. 26. 4, 5, 9, 10. He does feel innocent of false charges made against him; e.g., Psa. 7. He is conscious of rectitude of walk; see Acts 23. 1. He is demonstrating the spirit of simple faith and childlike trust which throw themselves unreservedly upon God.

There are occasions when the psalmist calls for vengeance on his foes, and this is very evident in the Imprecatory Psalms; thus words like those found in Psalm 137. 7-9 may startle the reader by their vehemence. Yet here the psalmist is re-echoing the words of an earlier prophet; cf. Isa. 13. 16. Further, the justice of the inevitability of retribution must be recognized. Sin carries its consequences alike in kind and degree.

The psalmist sees the Sovereign God on His eternal throne as the Judge of the universe, and an appeal for vindication is made away to the Righteous Judge from earthly judges and rulers who may manipulate their office unjustly, Psa. 18. 6; 11. 4, 5. He who is righteous in Himself cannot but approve of righteousness in others, and an appeal to Him is not in vain. He has pledged Himself to save those who put their trust in Him, and He cannot deny Himself, for He loves righteousness, Psa. 45. 7.

April 1st

READING: **Psalm 92**

THE RIGHTEOUS SHALL FLOURISH

THIS PSALM was sung on the second day of the feast of tabernacles. Its theme is the faithfulness and truth of God as displayed in His righteous administration of the universe, and as
vindicated by the ultimate destiny both of the righteous and of
the wicked. The psalmist commences by declaring the seemli-
ness of praise, vv. 1-4. The reasons for praise are then given,
vv. 4-15. Praise is good, both as the first exercise of the day
and also as the last: the sense of all the provision made for us
as we face the conflicts and responsibilities of the day; for faithfulness at night, with the conviction that the Lord has been
true to His covenant through all the hours of need. The psalm
ends with a gracious description of the growth and perennial
freshness of the righteous.

Two figures are used in verse 12: the palm tree and the
cedar. Here the tree is set forth as an image of the Christian
spared to "old age", flourishing like a palm tree, or as a cedar
in Lebanon. In old age, when others fade, he shall bring forth
the fruits of peace and righteousness. He is an evergreen, like
the palm tree, rejoicing in the sun, casting a pleasant shadow
over the weary and the needy, producing sustaining fruit, and
even at the end, beautiful and attractive as in former days.

How great the contrast between the lasting fruit of the
righteous and that of the ungodly. The contrast is pictured in
the grass which soon perishes, vv. 7, 9, and the palm tree and
cedar, v. 12. The one is quickly up and soon away, but the
fruitful palm and fragrant cedar are evergreen. The soil into
which the righteous are planted is His holy temple, v. 13, and
they find there their chief nutriment. There they stand in
sacred ground which conveys to them ever new vital power.

It is there that they put forth growth, produce fruit and preserve a verdant freshness and vitality, even in old age. This is
not because they are anything in themselves, but "to show that
the Lord is upright; he is my rock, and there is no unrighteousness in him", v. 15. They witness by their fruitfulness to the
faithfulness and justice of the Lord. The world will form its
opinion of God from what it sees of Him in His servants. May it
not be disappointed!

READING: **Psalm 106. 29-48**

PHINEHAS—COUNTED FOR RIGHTEOUSNESS

A LONG recapitulation of the history of Israel, in which the sins of God's people are humbly acknowledged, forms this psalm. All the failures written into that history are recognized, and the righteous chastisement which the sin of the nation merited is recorded. One of the dominant thoughts of the O.T. is that success and failure are linked with loyalty to God. The last twenty verses of the psalm develop this theme. In this section Phinehas and his loyalty to God are found. Of him, verse 3 is true, similar in thought to "Blessed is the man" in Psalm 1. 1; this too was true of Phinehas. God has His champions left in the worst times, and they will stand up when the need arises. So it was with Phinehas.

The background to these verses 30-31 is found in Numbers 25. Phinehas was zealous for his God, Num. 25. 13. He could not fold his arms and see God's law insulted, His rule defied. The servant's heart moved in one blaze of godly indignation. He must be up to vindicate God; he "stood up".

This is a picture of one zealous man rising up from the midst of the inactive multitude who sit still and make no effort. It is more, for it brings echoes from an earlier scene when again sin had reared its head in the camp, and Aaron stood and the plague was stayed, Num 16. 48. Phinehas stood up from the rest, and presented himself before the people, assuming the office and discharging the duty from which the regular, official leaders seemed to shrink. His bold resolve feared nothing in a righteous cause. The offender, Zimri, was a prince, but this did not matter; he was not spared. His companion was a princess of the house of Midian, but no fear of reprisal held Phinehas back. Are we as courageous and zealous for the honour of God?

"So the plague was stayed"; cf. Num. 25. 8-11, and God said that Phinehas "hath turned my wrath away", because he acted with zeal for God's glory and for Israel's good. The zeal of Phinehas was a true act of faith. It was counted as a righteous act, for ever memorable. He was a true son of Abraham, of whom similar words are written in Genesis 15. 6. There faith, here an act springing from faith—both are counted for righteousness. His reward was "the covenant of an everlasting priesthood", Num. 25. 12-13. God honours those who honour Him.

April 3rd

READING: **Psalm 141**

THE REPROOF OF THE RIGHTEOUS

THE PSALMIST had felt the attraction of worldly luxuries, the "dainties" of verse 4, and it seems that ungodly men had been trying to persuade him to throw in his lot with them. He prays to be kept from "the snares" and "the gins" of the wicked, v. 9; that he may be kept from sin in word and thought and deed, vv. 3, 4. At the same time, he had experienced the reproof of the godly, possibly such reproof not always being received with love. He therefore prays that he might welcome correction as kindness, and reproof as ointment and perfume which rejoice the heart, v. 5. "Ointment and perfume rejoice the heart: so doth the sweetness of a man's friend by hearty counsel", Prov. 27. 9. He declares that he would prefer to be severely handled by the righteous, rather than to be subtly pampered by the wicked.

Reproof is something that is trying to flesh and blood. The terms here are strong. The smiting is used as that of a hammer, Jud. 5. 26, or of an anvil, Isa. 41. 7. It is translated "beaten", Prov. 23. 35, and "broken down", Isa. 16. 8. The reproof included rebuke and correction. The psalmist knows that his frailties often need reproof. He needs to have his attention called to them and to be told of them. But by whom? "It is a question whether it is more difficult to accept reproof from those who know better than we, or from those who are not so good. The former should carry more weight; but the latter often carry more sting." Well-meaning reproof should be acceptable and spiritually profitable to him. If the righteous reprove him, he is not to be proud and resistant, but to take their action as a kindness, as choice oil on his head intended for his welfare. Proverbs constantly insists on the value of reproof which the wise man welcomes and the fool resists; cf. 3. 11; 13. 18; 15. 5, 31, 32; 28. 23.

But what of those who administer the rebuke? They must not be those who see the mote in their brother's eye, but have a plank in their own, Matt. 7. 4-5. Their rebuke must be done in the spirit of love, for "Faithful are the wounds of a friend", Prov. 27. 6. They must be characterized by humility. Let none who is unspiritual attempt such work, and when it is done, let it be done in a spirit of meekness, Gal. 6. 1.

April 4th

READING: Psalm 142

THE COMFORT OF THE RIGHTEOUS

THIS IS one of the eight psalms assigned by inspiration to the time of the persecution of David by Saul, and to the fugitive days of David when in the cave of Adullam. The first four verses are a *Cry in Danger*. Twice the word "cried" is used, vv. 1, 5. The nature of David's cry is found in the word "supplication", which here means a prayer for grace or mercy. He gives two reasons for his calling upon God.

The *first* of these is his distress—his spirit was overwhelmed within him. For him it is an hour of great dejection. In the second half of the psalm, he will say, "refuge failed me; no man cared for my soul ... I am brought very low", vv. 4-6. Such dejection has been the experience of many Christians; take courage, there is deliverance. The *second* reason is his trust in the divine omniscience—"thou knewest my path", v. 3. Nothing of this is hidden from God's loving eye.

The second half of the psalm is a *Cry for Deliverance*, vv. 5-7. This man will triumph. Already he has set over against his despondency the fact that the Lord knows his path. He has claimed that no man cared for his soul, so he calls on God for his refuge. Brought low, he says to God, "deliver me". In these dark days, we should set over against our problems and perplexities the sure and certain facts about our God.

So the song ends in triumph, and he finds himself surrounded by the righteous. The opposite picture is found in Habakkuk 1. 4. There, where justice is not executed, where corruption is prevalent, and strife and violence abound, "the wicked doth compass about the righteous". The existing low moral and spiritual state of Habakkuk's nation would bring the "bitter and hasty nation", the Chaldeans, into their land to take them into captivity. A similarly hostile use of the word is found in Psalm 22. 12. There the Sufferer looks out on His enemies by whom He is surrounded. "Many bulls have compassed me", He says. Their hatred shown to Him was vividly described: "They gaped upon me with their mouths, as a ravening and a roaring lion", v. 13. Here, however, in Psalm 142 the psalmist is compassed by the righteous who sympathize with his cause. An excellent N.T. illustration is found in 1 Corinthians 12. 26.

April 5th

READING: **Psalms 11; 7. 10-12**

TO FLEE OR NOT TO FLEE!

PSALM 11 commences with a statement of faith, "In the Lord put I my trust". Then follows a question, "how say ye to my soul?". These were things being suggested to David, and particularly so that he might flee. The reasons why he should do so were also given to him.

The *first* reason was that his enemies were out to destroy him; indeed, their arrows were already fitted to the bow, v. 2, and as they "loved darkness rather than light, because their deeds were evil", John 3. 19, they aimed at him under cover of night. So the advice of his friends seemed justified by the peril that he was in. The *second* reason given for his flight is that the foundations of society were being destroyed, v. 3. The administration of justice had at that time fallen into total confusion. What, then, could the righteous do? Surely flight was the answer?

Looking at the circumstances by which he was surrounded, it seemed a correct solution. But remember how David started the psalm. Having sought and found shelter in God Himself, how absurd that he should listen to this advice and flee. The advice of fear in verses 2-3 has significant omissions—the Name and thought of God are absent. The peril is paramount; there is nothing to do but flee. Yet the vision of faith is that of the Lord enthroned, v. 4; He also sees the peril. The enemy may have fitted his arrow to the string, but there is Another whose bow is bent and whose arrow will fly before his; cf. Psalm 7. 12. Furthermore, do not measure things by the circumstances of the hour—look up, the throne is filled. Self-preservation is not a man's first duty; flight is his last. Better to be noble, standing fast, staying at our post, though we fall there. Better far to toil on, even when toil seems vain and results few, than to keep a whole skin at the expense of a wounded conscience, or to throw up the work in despair because the going is hard and the results imperceptible.

So David rejects the counsel of his friends to save his life by flight. Similarly the friends of Nehemiah came under guise of friendship, and hoped to trap him by advising him to escape for his life, Neh. 6. 11. "Should such a man as I flee?", he asked. Faith will do more for us than flight.

April 6th

READING: **Psalms 11; 18. 1-6**

THE LORD IS IN HIS HOLY TEMPLE

"IF THE FOUNDATIONS be destroyed." The psalmist raises his eyes on high, for that is where his foundations are fixed. He sees, as did the prophet Habakkuk, the Lord in His holy temple, Hab. 2. 20. No matter that the Chaldean, "that bitter and hasty nation", was coming to devastate his land; all was under the control of the Sovereign of the universe. He sees, as did Isaiah, the Lord upon His throne, Isa. 6. 1. No matter that the good king Uzziah had died, the Lord was still on the throne. The earthly throne may be empty, but the heavenly throne was, and is, eternally filled. This foundation has not changed; circumstances may seem unpropitious, but God has not changed. He has not vacated His throne; He remains faithful.

David's friends looked to earth alone; he looked up to heaven. They judged by the circumstances of the time; his faith beheld the righteous Governor of the world exercising His sovereignty. On earth, justice may not be executed, but the Eternal Judge never quits His throne in heaven. This throne, this temple, is the place whence comes the ultimate decision of all earthly things. The Lord sitting there is the All-Seeing and the All-Knowing One. Appeal can be made to Him in time of trouble. "In my distress I called upon the Lord ... he heard my voice out of his temple, and my cry came before him", Psa. 18. 6. "In his temple doth every one speak of his glory", 29. 9. It is from His temple that Micah sees the Lord hold inquiry over the sins of His people, Mic. 1. 2.

It is His "holy temple" —"holy" in contrast to earth. The confusion and mistakes of earth cannot enter there. To the eyes that have seen that vision, before which eyes it ever burns, all earthly sorrows and dangers seem small indeed.

For the Christian, that throne has become a "throne of grace". The Lamb, as newly slain, is in the midst of it, Rev. 5. 6, and this fact constitutes it a throne of grace. Therefore, in time of need we can approach that throne, "that we may obtain mercy, and find grace to help in time of need", Heb. 4. 16.

Here, then, is faith. The man who fears is one who measures things by the circumstances of the hour. The man who sees the Lord enthroned, and governing, has no panic.

April 7th

READING: **Psalm 11**

THE RIGHTEOUS LORD

THE LORD enthroned is the true refuge of the hunted soul. But He is not only enthroned; He is active. He also sees the peril. Do the wicked watch the righteous? But the Lord watches the wicked. Are the righteous tried in the process? The Lord presides over the trial. Are the wicked going to shoot? So is the Lord, "snares ... and brimstone". God is seen not only as enthroned, but as scrutinizing all men's acts with a keen, discriminating gaze. As a man partly closes his eyes in a concentrated gaze, so the Lord scrutinizes men. He tries them, as a Refiner, distinguishing between the dross and the gold. He tries the righteous, v. 5, seeing into the inmost depths of his soul. The Lord subjects him to many a test to prove him, to show him what he is; to stir him up to watchfulness and trust; to make him strong in His strength.

If all things were made easy for us; if no cloud ever crossed our horizon, if no danger ever crossed our path, the mettle of our character would not be formed. Trials are all ordered for our good. It is thus that faith is tested, sincerity is discerned, the walk becoming more close with our God, more wary and circumspect. These probings are among our blessings. The wicked He judges, but the righteous He protects.

He loves righteousness; He is the righteous Lord, v. 7. That is His character. What He approves are righteous deeds. The "For" at the beginning of verse 7 suggests the close connection between God's judgment on the wicked and His favour on the righteous. The nature of God determines His judgment and acts. He who is righteous in Himself cannot but approve of righteousness in others. "Jehovah is righteous" is the rock foundation of the indomitable faith of the psalmist in the certain, ultimate triumph of patient righteousness. He would deny Himself if He did not defend the just. The character of the Lord is the ground of His judgment in verse 6 and His reward in verse 7. The wicked are banished and destroyed, but the upright are admitted to His presence and they gaze upon His face, Matt 5. 8; 1 John 3. 2: Rev. 22. 4. God looks on the upright and the upright gaze on Him here and now in the communion of that faith which is a better kind of sight, and also hereafter in glory, Psa. 17. 15.

READING: **Psalm 50**

THE UNIVERSAL JUDGE

THERE IS a solemnity about this psalm. God puts Israel on trial in the presence of all nature, v. 4, as He also does in Isaiah and in Micah 6. 1. He is at once Plaintiff and Judge, Psa. 50. 6-7. The introduction to the psalm presents the Judge in great splendour, vv. 1-6. He rebukes the formalism of the people. They had not failed in their outward worship—the sacrifices had been daily offered, v. 8, but there had been no true approach to Him with their hearts. They had treated Him as if He, the Creator of all things, needed their offerings, Acts 17. 24-25, and were supplying His hunger, Psa. 50. 9-13. What He asked of them was the sacrifice of thanksgiving, v. 14; Heb. 13. 15, the payment of their vows (all that they had promised to give Him), and finally, believing prayer, v.15. He rebukes the hypocrisy of His people, vv. 16-21. They declared His statutes, but did not keep them. They said, and did not. The conclusion of the matter is in verses 22-23.

The solemnity of the occasion is set by the impressive introduction to the psalm. The opening phrase, "the mighty God, even the Lord", is intended to evoke the solemnity and the awe proper to the psalmist's theme of a great assize. Here three of the divine Names are grouped together. The only other place where this occurs is in Joshua 22. 22, on the occasion of another solemn inquest. There it is repeated twice by the people on the other side of the Jordan in an earnest appeal to Him who knows all things, and therefore knew their intention to remain faithful to the covenant.

Here, the character of the Judge is being set forth. The use of the three divine Names is intended to enhance the grandeur and solemnity of the scene as setting forth the titles of the Judge and Sovereign. "El" comes from a root meaning "power", and is often coupled with other words, e.g., El Elyon—the Most High God; El Shaddai—the Almighty God. "Elohim" is the God who is reverenced and worshipped. The word is sometimes used for heathen deities, and sometimes for human judges, Psa. 82. 1, 6. "Jehovah" is God's personal Name, distinguishing Him from all other beings in heaven and on earth, Isa. 42. 8. It expresses eternal being, underived existence, omnipresence, One who is ever present. Such a God is ours.

April 9th

READING: **Psalm 58**

UNJUST MEN AND A JUST GOD

HERE IS a protest against those who were supposed to administer justice fairly, but who themselves were the worst offenders. The psalmist expresses wonder, as if it were scarcely credible that those whose office it was to speak for God and against the sins of men were silent, v. 1. This was the passive side of their guilt; the active side was that they were guilty of positive injustice, v. 2. If any seat should be recognized for its honest equity, it is a tribunal of justice. Too often the cause of God has called for righteous judgment, but injustice has seen to it that it has never been executed.

So it was with the Jewish Sanhedrin and the vacillating Pilate who administered the Roman law. When the spotless and innocent One stood before them, righteous judgment was strangely lacking. No guilt was found; the judge recognized that freedom from any shadow of blame existed, yet the sentence was, "Let him be crucified". Paul had stood before another unjust tribunal, looking beyond this scene to the day when he would stand before "the Lord, the righteous Judge" to receive from Him a crown of righteousness, 2 Tim. 4. 8, 16. Happy are those who look to that righteous Judge, and to the throne where the plea "Christ died for me" cannot be argued in vain; this ensures acquittal and, beyond that, exaltation to glory.

The psalmist appeals to God to sweep away these false judges, vv. 6-9. There follows a double result to this judgment. Firstly, the righteous, now freed from their oppressors, will rejoice. The rejoicing of the righteous is at the judgment that God has executed upon those who have wilfully and obstinately resisted every effort to touch their hearts and consciences, vv. 4-5. The righteous cannot but rejoice over a triumph of good over evil. At the same time, it can never be right for the Christian to cherish a spirit of vengeance, Matt. 5. 44-45. Yet again, the righteous can never believe it to be right and just that the wicked should escape. But also, if it is right for God to destroy, then it cannot be wrong for His servants to rejoice in what He does; this introduces the second result. It proves that God is true to His revealed character as a just Judge and a Sovereign Ruler, and men in general acknowledge His moral government of the world, Psa. 58. 11.

April 10th

READING: **Psalm 82**

JUDGES IN THE DOCK!

THE COURT is packed, the judges are present, but they are in the dock! God is on His own judgment seat; He has summoned before Him the rulers of Israel, and is about to deal with their evil ways. A similar scene is found in Isaiah 3. 13-15, "The Lord standeth up to plead, and standeth to judge the people". Again, the rulers of the people are in the dock because of their wicked ways; the charge is made against them in verse 2. They abused their privilege; they would fail to observe the injunctions of Jehoshaphat to the judges that he established in his kingdom, 2 Chron. 19. 5-7. "There is no respect of persons with God", Rom. 2. 11. Paul also identifies other principles according to which God exercises judgment; it is "according to truth", v. 2, "according to deeds", v. 6; it is, writes Paul, the judgment of the secrets of men's hearts "according to my gospel", v. 16. Now it is possible to have respect of persons in church life, James 2. 1-9, but we are told not to have "the faith of our Lord Jesus Christ, the Lord of glory, with respect of persons". If we do become partial in ourselves, we are judges with unsound ideas.

The exhortation of the psalmist which appears in verse 3 is a continuation of the charge against them. This command is an inverted way of telling them what they ought to have done, but have not. They have held the office and title, but have not done the work; indeed, they have done the opposite to what they were appointed to do. Are there not sadly those occasions in church life when office and title are sought without respect to the spiritual qualifications required and to the nature of the task entered upon? These judges were ignoring the poor and needy. God had desired to develop a merciful spirit in His people. The Israelites were commanded to care for the poor and strangers within their gates, Deut. 15. 7-11; 24. 19. The same thought of care is continued in the N.T., James 1. 27; 2. 5. In the feast of weeks, Deut. 16. 10, when the freewill offering was brought to God, provision was also made for the poor, Lev. 23. 20, 22; 19. 9, 10; Deut. 24. 19. A similar combination of giving of thanks to God and of providing for the needy is found in Hebrews 13. 15, 16. "Go, and do thou likewise", Luke 10. 37.

READING: **Psalm 82**

"YE ARE GODS"

GOD HAS taken the judges and rulers to task because of their unjust exercise of their office. The charge has been made against them, vv. 2-4. They had shown partiality, and had not defended the poor, needy and fatherless. The fatherless are continually spoken of as the proper objects of both mercy and of justice. They had received neither from these rulers. The charges laid against the rulers do not seem to have affected them in the way of remorse and repentance for their evil doings. The divine protest is unavailing. They have hardened their hearts against God, v. 5. Those who should have been the defenders of the poor were in fact their persecutors.

So the Lord passes sentence on them, vv. 6-7. He describes them as "gods". The word is "elohim", the very same word as is so often used for God Himself; in fact, it is the same word as used for God in verse 1. These earthly judges are called "elohim" because the office that they hold and the judgment that they should give are really God's. They were intended to be the mouthpiece and representatives of God, but instead they sought their own interests and preferment. Their sin consisted in abusing the authority granted to them, and in imagining that it relieved them of responsibility, whereas it really increased it. They were God's representatives, but for this very reason they were called upon to be pre-eminently just and faithful.

The psalmist saw what the judges did not see—God Himself standing in the midst of His people, judging them Himself and judging the judges, v. 1. So, finally, he appeals to God to judge and exercise His righteous rule over all the earth, v. 8. Since the delegate judges have proved so unfaithful, the psalmist petitions that God should appear in Person and reclaim the powers which had been so wickedly abused.

The prayer in verse 8 is already answered, Acts 17. 31.

Verse 6 of this psalm is found in John 10. 34-38. The Pharisees had charged the Lord with blasphemy in claiming to be the Son of God. He refers to their judges being called "gods". They were unrighteous judges while He was the One whom the Father had sanctified and sent into the world, and whose work was a witness to His righteousness. He was in His Person and character divine.

April 12th

READING: **Psalm 33**

THE WORD AND THE WORKS OF THE LORD

THIS PSALM presents a devout, calm contemplation of the creative power and providential government of God. In verses 1-3, the righteous are called upon to praise the Lord. His creative and providential work in the world, vv. 4-11, and in Israel, vv. 12-19, are then celebrated. The psalm concludes with the righteous expressing trust and prayer, vv. 20-22.

A call to rejoice opens the psalm. We cannot rejoice in ourselves, but we may rejoice in the Lord, Phil. 3. 1; 4. 4; Hab. 3. 18. Such an exercise is eminently befitting those who owe to Him all they are and all they hope for. They can sing unto the Lord "a new song", v. 3; Psa. 96. 1; 98. 1; 149. 1; Isa. 42. 10; Rev. 5. 9. They can praise Him for the power of His words, "By the word of the Lord were the heavens made", vv. 6-7; for the wonder of His works, vv. 7-8; for the wisdom of His thoughts, v. 11. They can rejoice because He has His eye upon them, "he beholdeth", v. 13; because He has His hand upon them, "He fashioneth", v. 15; and because He has set His mind on them, "he considereth", v. 15. There is also in verse 1 the clear recognition of purity as the condition of access to God. The "righteous", whose lives conform to the divine will, alone are they who can shout aloud their joy in Jehovah. Praise fits and adorns the lips of the upright.

The immediate reasons for rejoicing and praise are given in verses 4-5. The moral attributes of the Lord are emphasized in verse 4 and His principles of government in verse 5. His word is "upright", morally perfect, uttered in sincerity, and with a full determination to redeem it; cf. Num. 22. 18-19; Psa. 19. 8; 105. 42. The word of the Lord underlies His works. The "word" here means "word of promise" ; "work" is its performance or fulfilment. The acts which flow from His word are in "faithfulness". Word and work include all the expressions of the will of Him who is always consistent with Himself, James 1. 17. There is no lie in God's word, and no sham in His works. The perfect word and works have for source the deep heart of God who loves "righteousness and judgment", and therefore speaks and acts in accordance with these. For the psalmist, there is but One omnipotent will at work everywhere, and that is a will whose law for itself is righteousness and truth.

115

April 13th

READING: **Psalm 71**

THY RIGHTEOUSNESS

FIVE TIMES the psalmist makes reference to "thy righteousness", vv. 2, 15, 16, 19, 24. His plea is for deliverance "in thy righteousness", which is "very high". He will make mention of it; his mouth will show it forth, nay, more, he will talk of it all the day long. This psalm is the utterance of a faith which has proved the goodness of God in a life of many trials, and trusts to experience it to the end.

In the midst of danger, he put his trust in God, v. 1. So he prayed for deliverance, v. 2. "In thy righteousness" comes emphatically at the beginning of the sentence in Hebrew. He loves to dwell on the thought of the righteousness of God, who must be true to His promise, and who cannot desert His servant. The psalmist is impressed by the elevation of that righteousness, v. 19; it reaches unto the height of heaven. Who can reach the summit of God's faithful dealings, of His righteous acts? The Lord is incomparable for power and goodness; we take note, and can humbly adore. Past mercies become the ground of hope for deliverance in the present. His mouth will unceasingly declare "thy righteousness", the attribute on which all hope of salvation depends.

Salvation is coupled with righteousness inasmuch as one is the outward and visible manifestation of the other. God's salvation stands to His righteousness in the same relation as the effect does to the cause. God has pledged Himself to save those who put their trust in Him, and as a righteous God He cannot deny Himself. The demonstrations of divine righteousness and salvation are in themselves endless, and hence the matter for praise that they offer is inexhaustible. The psalmist will declare those things which cannot be counted up, v. 15; God's mercies are an inexhaustible theme. His righteousness and His salvation are infinitely above all man's power to calculate or to repeat. The effect on the psalmist was to resolve that his lips would never cease to give due praise: "all the day". He will mention "thy righteousness ... thine alone", v. 16, not his own, nor that of any other creature. He has been a lifelong disciple in the school of God; he delights to declare His marvellous works, v. 17. Indeed, lips and tongue, song and speech, shall conspire together to praise God, vv. 23-24.

116

READING: **Psalm 119. 7, 62, 75, 106, 160, 164**

THY RIGHTEOUS JUDGMENTS

THERE ARE words which recur often in this "Psalm of the Law", e.g., "word" (23 times); "law" (25 times); "saying, sayings" (19 times); commandments" (22 times); "statutes" (21 times); "testimony" (22 times); "precepts" or "injunctions" (21 times); "judgments" or "ordinances" (23 times). Six times the judgments are referred to as "righteous judgments". In verse 7, the psalmist knows that he has not yet attained to a complete knowledge of God's will, but he gives thanks for every advance; the will to obey, "to keep thy statutes", v. 5, is the condition of progress. It is those who do His will who shall know of the doctrine, John 7. 17.

Throughout the psalm, he prays repeatedly for teaching and direction. The learning of God's righteous dealings leads to praise, but begins with a teachableness of spirit. The psalmist will praise at midnight, v. 62. There were others who did this, and did so when they were in the most uncongenial of circumstances, Acts 16. 5. Far from forgetting God's law, he will interrupt sleep with thanksgiving, and again the ground of his praise is God's righteous dealings. It is when we allow the voice of praise to be silent that we give Satan the victory.

There were times when the psalmist experienced chastisement in accordance with God's righteous dealings, v. 75. "Thy judgments are righteous" R.V.; (literally, "righteousness"). All God's laws are in conformity with the perfect standard of His righteousness; faithfulness to His covenant leads God to use the discipline of chastisement to teach men obedience to these laws.

The visitations of God are right, whether we know it or not; but it is well for us if we know it. Recognizing the Source of such affliction, v. 107, the psalmist pledges himself to keep God's righteous judgments, v. 106. When we make solemn promises such as these, they should be speedily performed.

God is true to His word, v. 160. If the psalmist reckons up all God's words of commandment or promise, their sum total is truth, and His righteous dealings are forever. Not morning and evening only, but again and again each day the psalmist thanks God for His righteous guidance, which is a fountain of peace inexhaustible, vv. 164, 165.

April 15th

READING: **Psalm 45**

THOU LOVEST RIGHTEOUSNESS

THE PRAYER with which Psalm 44 ends, "rise for our help", receives its answer here in verses 3-5. The song is said to be "A song of loves", a very refreshing thing in a world of lusts. Much is called love which should be very differently described. Verses 6-7 are quoted in Hebrews 1. 8-9 as applying to Christ. The mighty king of the previous verses of the psalm is now adored as God, and both psalm and Epistle concur in this. The words apply directly to the Lord Jesus, and declare His Deity and the eternal nature of His kingdom. In "Thy throne, O God", He is acknowledged as the living and true God; the Epistle quotes the verses so as to set forth the unapproachable glory of Him who is the express image of God in His own Person. "O God" asserts His Deity, but "thy fellows" indicates His Humanity. Here we have the twofold nature of the same Blessed Person. Further, here Christ is man's Fellow; in Zechariah 13. 7 He is God's Fellow.

Then the words declare the eternal nature of His kingdom. Whatever may be shaken by storms, the foundation of that throne stands fast. It is God's throne, and therefore righteous altogether. What a mercy for us that our Saviour is God, for who but God could execute the work of salvation? What comfort there is in the fact that He reigns on the throne which will never pass away. Could Christ cease to reign, we should cease to be blessed; were He not God and therefore eternal, this must be the case. His royalty is a royalty of righteousness, "the sceptre of thy kingdom is a right sceptre". He is the lawful Monarch of all things that exist. His rule is founded in right, "Thou lovest righteousness, and hatest iniquity".

Righteousness is the very basis and animating principle of His rule. He is not neutral in the great conflict between right and wrong. He loves righteousness, and His protection is over all those who love it and seek after it. He hates wickedness, and therefore He is against it wherever it is found. What qualifications for a Sovereign! To be like Christ, we must love righteousness as He loved it, and hate wickedness as He hated it. The dominion of perennial righteousness is also that of unparalleled gladness, v. 7. His gladness flows from His righteousness.

April 16th

READING: **Psalm 97**

THE LORD REIGNETH

THAT "The Lord reigneth" should cause us to rejoice. The psalmist certainly sees it as a solid reason for joy. If God reigns, the earth should rejoice. In this fact there is rest and hope. We may not always understand His ways, for "Clouds and darkness are round about him". We are looking at the methods of God's judgment, and the phrase indicates that they are mysterious. "Clouds and darkness" do not belong to the divine nature, but are characteristic of divine movements: "God is light, and in him is no darkness at all" ; "Thy way is in the sea, and thy path in the great waters, and thy footsteps are not known", Psa. 77. 19.

Then, again, His methods are founded upon the strictest justice: "righteousness and judgment are the habitation of his throne", i.e., the foundation of His throne. "Righteousness" and "judgment" are related as the attribute is to the act. Righteousness is the essential perfection of the divine Being; it is His nature. If there had been no creatures for Him to govern, He would still have had an unchangeable and invincible love of rectitude. Judgment is the application of the principle of righteousness in His government of His creatures and their actions. Every aspect of divine conduct is just, regulated rectitude, while judgment cannot err.

It is the consolation of His people to know that His rule is founded on righteousness. Fearful we need not be, for righteousness and judgment are the foundation of His throne. He does not depart from righteousness nor deviate from justice, and in this we can take confidence even in the darkest hour. The psalmist tells us further that God's methods are powerful, "A fire goeth before him", v. 3. The effects of His judgment are declared: enemies are destroyed, His glory revealed, His people filled with joy. The underlying reason for this is His holiness; all wickedness is hateful to Him because of the harm it works among His people. Therefore let us learn the lessons and "hate evil", v. 10. The result will be "light" and "gladness", v. 11; "Light is sown for the righteous", i.e., strewn upon his life and way so that he goes forward step by step in the light. Since joy is the portion of the righteous, let them accept it, and make use of it, v. 12. Joy is united with praise of God, v. 12.

April 17th

READING: **Psalm 75**

THE APPOINTED TIME

THE MESSAGE of this psalm is that God is Sovereign in His own world. It celebrates the righteous judgment of God; it speaks of a great act of judgment by which God has condemned the proud pretensions of some boastful enemy, vv. 4-5. The people address God with thanksgiving for the recent manifestation of His power on their behalf. The voice of God Himself from heaven is heard declaring His righteousness, v. 2, announcing to the world that He is not regardless of wrong and suffering. He only waits for the moment which is best according to His infinite wisdom, so that He might punish the wrongdoers.

The phrase "When I shall receive the congregation" is better read as "when I reach the appointed time". The "appointed time" is the proper moment foreordained in the divine counsel and known to God. The same word, indicating a "set time", is found in Psalm 102. 13, where the psalmist looks ahead for the appointed time of deliverance for Zion. It is also found in Habakkuk 2. 3, where the vision given to the prophet was for a set time. This scripture is taken up in Hebrews 10. 37, where we read of the promise of the certainty of the Lord's coming, "he that shall come will come, and will not tarry". Gabriel used the same words when he spoke to Daniel of the Medo-Persian and Grecian empires, and beyond of the rise of a sinister individual who will stand up against "the Prince of princes", Dan. 8. 19, 25. The same words are used again in the context of the end times, 11. 27, 35.

The picture which comes through is of a God who is in control, and who had appointed the events of history and prophesy according to His foreordained plan. So always, at a fitting moment, God intervenes. There may be times when the pillars and framework of life appear shaken, and when stable situations disappear, but God assures His people that He maintains the order that He has established in the world, v. 3, though all may seem to be confusion. God is ever the righteous Judge who acts, not according to man's impatient expectations, but at the moment chosen. He can afford to wait, but His seeming delays should not cause saints to despair or sinners to presume. Sometimes His delay may seem hard on the righteous and favourable to wickedness, but in truth it never is.

April 18th

READING: **Psalm 72. 1-11**

A GREATER THAN SOLOMON IS HERE

THE TITLE of this psalm should read "of Solomon", yet the events pictured in this psalm were never truly fulfilled in either Solomon or his father David.

The psalm describes an ideal Monarch who is exercising universal rule. It looks ahead to a time still future when God's kingdom on earth will be perfect and universal. It is a perfect order which has never yet been realized. Here is the kingdom, for which the creation still waits, and for which the church still prays "Thy kingdom come". A human monarch stands in the foreground, but the aspirations expressed go far beyond anything that he is or can be; they reach out beyond their immediate occasion to the King, "the greater than Solomon".

There are five stanzas in the psalm, and each emphasizes a particular feature of the King's reign. The first stanza emphasizes its righteousness, which is the foundation of His kingdom. There can be no abiding peace where a kingdom is not based on righteousness. God is the Source of all justice, v. 1; just judgment is the constant characteristic of the ideal King. "The king" and "the king's son" in verse 1 are One and the same Person. It is not the King and His heir, but a King who is a King's Son.

In His reign, all oppression will be put down, the destroyer and destruction will be destroyed. The King will champion the cause of the wronged and distressed, v. 2. His sceptre is a right sceptre. All events regulated by Him will bring peace and comfort to those who receive Him as their Lord and King. Peace will be associated with righteousness, v. 3, since peace is always represented in Scripture as the fruit of righteousness, the one the fruit, and the other the root.

Melchizedek was first King of righteousness, then King of peace, Heb. 7. 2. There can be no abiding peace where the kingdom is not based on righteousness. The peace promised, then, is the fruit of righteous government, Isa. 9. 7; Mic. 4. 3. The King will judge the poor, Psa. 72. 4, that is, He will do them justice, redeem their wrongs, vindicate their rights. Here is the gracious exercise of wise authority. That Blessed One, who called Himself "a greater than Solomon", is surely here, Matt 12. 42; cf. Isa. 32. 1-3.

April 19th

READING: **Psalm 35**

A MAN IN DANGER

THE PSALMIST'S life is in danger. He is the victim of an ungrateful hatred, and accused of crimes of which he knew nothing. There is, therefore, a sob and an agony in the song, and what makes his misery more acute is that he is shown cruelty and oppression by those whom he has befriended in the past. His enemies are relentless. Their hostility is groundless, and its maliciousness is aggravated by their ingratitude. Their methods are those used by many cruel interrogators who persecute the innocent: "They ask me of things that I know not", v. 11 R.V. The idea is that of enemies trying to elicit by questions some ground for accusation, Mark 14. 55; Luke 11. 53-54; John 18. 19.

The psalm dates from the period when David was being hunted by Saul. Each of the divisions of the psalm (vv. 1-10, 11-18, 19-28) raises a cry for deliverance, and closes in the assurance that it will be granted. Each of the divisions ends with praise, vv. 9, 18, 28.

There are verses in the psalm which call for vengeance upon David's enemies. How do we account for these imprecations from the mouth of the psalmist? That David was capable of such passion is seen from his treatment of Nabal, 1 Sam. 25, but his conscience could also be gently stirred to turn from it, 1 Sam. 25. 32ff.

The psalms truly reflect O.T. piety, and it does not seem possible that the unholy fires of personal passion should mar the holy flame of love to God. Rather, the imprecations flow from the pure spring of unselfish jealousy for God's honour. Here, where it appears as David's jealousy for his own person, it is because he stands over against Saul, the king who had alienated himself from God. David was the divinely appointed king, in whom the cause of God and the future of Israel coincide. His prayer for judgment on his foes was no expression of secret malice against Saul, for had he not spared his life? It is a plea for the visible demonstration of essential righteousness.

Compare this with the teaching of the N.T. and this age of grace, Luke 9. 51-56. For the Christian it is a comfort to be able to appeal to the bar of God from the judgments of men, 2 Cor. 5. 11.

READING: **Psalm 37. 27-40**

HE SHALL DELIVER ME

THE UNDERLYING problem in this psalm is the prosperity of evil men. Such prosperity is shortlived, and meanwhile the righteous are to "trust in the Lord", v. 3, "delight in the Lord", v. 4, commit their way to the Lord, v. 5, "rest in the Lord", v. 7, "wait ... for him", v. 7. At the same time, to be fretful is unnecessary.

In verses 27-40, the whole psalm is summarized. The lots of the wicked and of the righteous are contrasted; righteousness and wickedness are irreconcilable. On the one hand the wicked succeed and prosper; on the other, the righteous are often in distress. The ends, however, are different—for the wicked, destruction; for the righteous, peace, vv. 36-37. The reason for this is that the Lord is for the righteous and against the wicked, so in this life God manifests His righteousness.

The righteous are to "Depart from evil", v. 27. As evil includes all that is morally wrong, so good includes all that is morally right, and to "do good" is to act rightly. The Lord loves the doing of justice, v. 28; as a natural result of this He will not forsake the objects of His grace, v. 28. Those whom He once favours, He will never forsake. So certain is this, that David appears to look back upon the future as already past, saying that the saints are preserved for ever. Secure is the realm wherein they dwell; eternity is the measure of their happiness, v. 29.

The righteous are distinguished by the test of character. Their words are wise and just, v. 30. The law of God is in their heart, and that is the foundation on which permanence is built. God's law, treasured in the heart, regulates all their conduct. Without wavering or variation, they pursue the path of light. Men may condemn them, but God acquits, v. 33. Here, as in 1 Cor. 4. 3, the righteous judgment of God is opposed to the inadequacies of human judgment.

The second thing that the righteous are told to do is to "Wait on the Lord", v. 34. Despite the prosperity of the wicked, salvation is possessed by the righteous, v. 39. It is a gift of grace; God wills it, He achieves it, and He bestows it. It is a gift without recall, for He calls His saints to heaven, and to heaven they attain.

April 21st

READING: **Psalm 4**

THE GOD OF MY RIGHTEOUSNESS

A CALL to God for deliverance from present trouble is how the psalmist opens this psalm. "Hear me", he pleads; that is, hear and answer me. His plea is based on two facts: on the Name of God given here, and on His past acts.

He appeals to God as "God of my righteousness". It is only here in the Scriptures that God is so addressed. Another beautiful title of God is found in Psalm 59. 10, "the God of my mercy". David calls this God of righteousness his, for the righteousness that he has, he has in Him, and the righteousness that he looks for, he looks for from Him. Similarly, what righteousness we have, we have in Christ. The believer stands pardoned through grace and richly robed in Christ's merits. One with Christ, he appears as free from guilt as God's own Son.

Since God is the Source of the psalmist's righteousness, He may be expected to vindicate it by answering prayer by deliverance. It is as if the psalmist was saying, "Thou who maintainest my right and my cause, asserting my righteousness against the slanders of my enemies ... ". He who feels that all good in himself comes only from God may be quite sure that, sooner or later, and by some means or other, God will witness to His work. To the psalmist, nothing was so incredible that God should not take care of what He had planted.

His appeal to God as the God of righteousness implies the justice of David's cause, and shows that he asks nothing inconsistent with God's holiness. The same rule should govern our prayers—we should not ask God to deny Himself.

The second ground for his appeal relates to God's acts in the past. Many of the prayers of the great men of the Bible are prayers which remind God of what He has done in the past, and believe that He can do the same again. So here, past mercies become the pledge of present and future blessing. The mercy of deliverance which the psalmist asks for here is no new favour; it is because he has experienced it before that he dares to ask it now. "Thou hast set me at large", v. 1 R.V., he says, namely, liberated me, set me free. That was "when I was in distress", he says, "Now do it again, Lord; be merciful unto me". What God has done in the past, we are assured that He is perfectly able to do again; cf. Rom. 8. 31-39.

April 22nd

READING: **Psalm 9**

THOU HAST MAINTAINED MY RIGHT

THIS IS the first of the acrostic or alphabetical psalms, of which there are nine (Psalms 9, 10, 25, 34, 37, 111, 112, 119, 145). It is a psalm of thanksgiving for the Lord's righteous rule by which He overcame the enemies of His chosen people. There runs through the psalm a note of praise, vv. 1-5, 11, 12, 14. Such praise must not be with a divided heart, v. 1. The remembrance of past deliverance, vv. 1-5, is excellent fuel for praise. The Lord has indeed rebuked our arch-enemy, vv. 5-6, as in Zechariah 3. 1-2, and his strongholds are now laid waste, 2 Cor. 10. 4; Col. 2. 15. Any present deliverance is an earnest of coming triumph. A day draws near when our Lord will sit on His glorious throne, a throne which is based on righteousness, Psa. 9. 4. From it all righteous judgment will go forth. For the present, however, the psalmist sees in the defeat of his enemies God's judicial intervention on his behalf. God has pronounced and exacted sentence in his favour.

There also runs through the psalm an element of trust, vv. 7-12, 18. The oppressed, the humble, the needy and the poor have strong encouragement. The poor are those who know their need, and are utterly dependent upon God. They are "the poor in spirit", of whose happiness the Saviour spoke, Matt. 5. 3. When we know our weakness and spiritual poverty, we have the best claim to be remembered by Him. Calamity drives us to God and makes us familiar with the secrets of His character. The more we know of God, the more we trust Him. Doubt is born of ignorance.

The psalm also sets forth the government of the enthroned Lord among the nations, a government based on righteousness, vv. 5-8, 12, 16, 17, 19. The eternal nature of God's sovereignty is contrasted with the destruction of His enemies, the righteousness of His rule with the injustice of the wicked, vv. 6-7. In the next verse, there is an emphasis on the word "he". Because it is He, and not any human judge, the world shall yet see a rule of righteousness. Whatever earthly courts may do, heaven's throne ministers judgment in uprightness. The administration will be one of perfect justice and equity. It will be universal. The psalmist has been vindicated, v. 4, this being the promise of justice that will embrace the whole world.

READING: **Psalm 51**

AGAINST THEE ONLY

THIS IS the greatest of the penitential psalms. Its background in found in 2 Samuel 11-12, where the record of David's adultery with Bathsheba and the arranged killing of Uriah, her husband, is given. Here also we have Nathan's accusation of David's guilt, and his conviction of it in his own heart. David acknowledges his transgressions and his sin; he emphasizes the fact of his own acknowledgement: "I acknowledge", and his "I" is emphatic. His sins had always been known to God, but now he has come to know them himself; they are ever present to his conscience. Such consciousness of sin is the first step towards the repentance and confession which are indispensable conditions of forgiveness.

Then he says, "Against thee, thee only, have I sinned", v. 4; but were they not sins against others? Against Bathsheba, whom he had tempted; against Uriah, whom he had had killed; against his own family, whom he had polluted; against his kingdom, which he had weakened? Yet he says, "Against thee, thee only, have I sinned". This is because of his deep conviction of his sin. He must confess to, and be forgiven by God, before he could ever think of the wrong done to his neighbours. Then again, all sin is, and must be, against God, 1 Cor. 8. 12. All sin, even that by which man is most grievously injured, is in its ultimate nature sin against God, a breach of His holy law.

The real character of sin is rebellion against God. This constitutes its essence, its enormity, its malignity. The blow is aimed at God's supremacy. What does David mean, then, when he says, "that thou mightest be justified ... when thou judgest"? Is it not that "Thy righteousness and Thy holiness may be declared and vindicated when Thou dost pronounce sentence on my sin"? Man's sin brings into clearer light the justice and holiness of God. This poses a problem. Does it mean that because this is so, sin ceases to be sinful, and that man ceases to be responsible for it? No!, for the O.T. firmly asserts the truth of man's responsibility, and Paul refutes the suggestion that God is responsible for sin which He overrules to His glory, Rom. 3. 4ff. David confesses his guilt unreservedly, so as to admit the justice of whatever sentence God may pronounce. This is the true essence of penitence.

April 24th

READING: **Psalm 118**

THE GATES OF RIGHTEOUSNESS

THIS IS the last of the Hallel Psalms. This group of psalms comprises Psalms 113-118, and were repeated by the Jews at their festivals. It also formed part of the prayer for the Passover night. It was therefore most probably repeated by the Lord Jesus and His disciples at the inauguration of the Lord's Supper, "when they had sung an hymn, they went out into the mount of Olives", Matt. 26. 30. His voice must have been strong to sing, "This is the day which the Lord hath made; we will rejoice and be glad in it", Psa. 118. 24, though it was to be the day of His infinite sufferings and untold sorrow. He was the Sacrifice bound with cords of divine love to Calvary's altar, v. 27. Beyond that cross lay the exalted position, "the head stone of the corner", v. 22-23, though this had been rejected by the builders, Mark 12. 10-11.

The psalm celebrates a great deliverance which can be no other than the return from Babylon. It was also written for use in temple worship, vv. 19-20, 26, and was the fullest expression of jubilant thanksgiving. It was intended to be sung by the procession of worshippers on their way to the temple in a time of national rejoicing. Verses 1-4 were sung by the procession as it started on its way. The words of verses 5-18 rang out as the pilgrims made their way to the temple. When they reached its gates, the procession sang the challenge of verse 19. The following verse gives the response of priests within the gates. The gates open, and the procession sings on entering the temple courts, vv. 21-25. There follows the granting of blessing by the priests, v. 26, and the psalm ends with a final chorus from the procession's singers, vv. 27-29.

On reaching the gate, the procession had described them as "the gates of righteousness". This was so because they had come to the abode of the righteous God, Jer. 31. 23, from whence He manifested His righteousness in the salvation of the people, sending "help from the sanctuary", Psa. 20. 2. A voice from within then reminded them of the conditions of entry, v. 20. The emphasis is on the word "righteous"; those who would enter must be righteous like Him who dwells there. Evil cannot dwell with Him, Psa. 5. 4, but the description of those who do is not left to conjecture. It is clearly stated in Psalms 15. 2-5; 24. 4.

April 25th

READING: **Psalm 15**

WHO ARE THE LORD'S GUESTS?

THIS PSALM was probably composed with Psalm 24 to celebrate the bringing of the ark up mount Zion. The form of the psalm is very simple. There is first a question, v. 1, and then an answer to the question, vv. 2-5.

All through the psalms, David states his longing for fellowship with the living God, Psa. 61. 4. Thus he asks the question here. It is for the Master of the house to say on what terms He extends hospitality to guests, and a sense of the glory of God and of the holiness which becomes His presence causes the psalmist to ask the question. The desire behind the question is for intimate communion with God. The psalmist recognizes that the character of the Host determines the character of the guest, and therefore only the man of upright life can be the guest of God.

God wants approved character in His guests—the fundamental requirement is righteousness; the self-righteous man cannot stand here. It is in the presence of God that the psalmist draws his portrait of the godly man. He describes what he is positively, vv. 2, 4, and also what he is not, vv. 3, 5. So practical righteousness consists of what a man does not do, as well as what he does. He "walketh uprightly"; this contains the idea of wholehearted devotion to God, and complete integrity in dealing with men, Gen. 17. 1. Walking is of far more importance than talking! A man's life carries more weight with others than his speech.

Then he also "worketh righteousness". A man must first be righteous before he can work righteousness in life. "He that doeth righteousness is righteous, even as he is righteous", 1 John 3. 7. The tree makes the fruit, and not the fruit the tree; therefore the tree must be good before the fruit can be good, Matt. 7. 18. A righteous man can do a righteous work, but no work of an unrighteous man can make him righteous. We become righteous only by faith. He also "speaketh the truth", and his whole heart goes along with it. Here is a man who has a blameless life—by doing right and speaking truth. It is very needful that we watch our work, walk and talk, if we would have fellowship with God. Those who would walk with God must be like Him, 1 John 2. 29; Phil. 1. 10-11.

April 26th

READING: **Psalm 26**

INTEGRITY

INTEGRITY is uprightness of purpose and rectitude of dealing. The psalmist begins with a claim, "I have walked in mine integrity", v. 1, and he ends with a resolve, "as for me, I will walk in mine integrity", v. 11. Here is the appeal of a conscious integrity for recognition and vindication, "Judge me" ("Do me justice"), v. 1. Consciously to claim integrity, as the psalmist does here, may be something that we may well shrink from doing. Yet the psalmist is not unaware of the peril of sin, vv. 4, 5, 9, 10, of the danger of association, or of the need for deliverance and mercy, v. 11. He knows that God is the only Object of trust, v. 1, and that all goodness flows from Him, v. 3. Conscious of these things, he calls upon God to do him justice, pleading the integrity of his life and offering himself to the searching scrutiny of the All-knowing One, upon whose loving kindness and faithfulness he bases his confidence. He does not claim a sinless life, but asserts a sincere and constant endeavour to walk uprightly. Sincerity of purpose and single-heartedness of devotion have been the rule of his life. He has not only walked in his integrity, but also in God's truth, v. 3.

This is a remarkable testimony, and is offered to the Searcher of hearts, a claim of utter honesty of life and purpose. Happy the man who, knowing what God requires of him, can confidently and without fear advance the same appeal. It has not been achieved in his own strength; he has "trusted also in the Lord", v. 1. His prayer not only makes a claim of integrity; it also expresses his desire that if anything of evil remains, it might be purged away, v. 2.

Two words are used to describe the thoroughness of the scrutiny that he calls for. "Examine me", he says, inviting a test that brings him into circumstances that will demonstrate the reality of his faith. "Try me", he says, as the refiner smelts gold to get rid of any remaining dross. He desires to keep nothing back; he will submit himself to the searching flame of the great Refiner. His "reins", the seat of affections, and his "heart", the seat of thought and will, are open to scrutiny. The process may be painful, but he has no fear for the result, since He knows God's lovingkindness and faithfulness, v. 3.

April 27th

READING: **Psalm 7**

ACCORDING TO MINE INTEGRITY

THE INSCRIPTION to this psalm is a help to us in understanding it. It refers to Cush the Benjamite. He was possibly a supporter of the house of Saul, for he came from the same tribe, and would therefore be an enemy of David. He had made charges against David. It appears that he charged him with having iniquity in his hands, v. 3, but that David had returned good for the evil shown him, v. 4.

There was no truth in the charges, and David appeals to God to do him justice: "judge me" (to vindicate him), v. 8, asking for a judgment favourable to himself, the petitioner. Verses 6-10 constitute a cry for the coming of the divine Judge, and four times he dwells on the thought of God as Judge, vv. 6, 8, 9, 11.

David has a clear conscience, and he pleads for justice to be secured him by God, a plea which he bases on his own innocence and integrity, v. 8. When he desires to be judged according to his righteousness and his integrity, when he professes his innocence, it is not that he is betraying a spirit of self-satisfaction and self-righteousness. It is not that he would claim to be perfect and sinless. It does not indicate that he feels that he is superior to the rest of the world, as did the Pharisee who claimed to be "not as other men", and certainly not as "this publican", Luke 18. 9-12. It indicates that David is conscious of freedom from guilt with reference to the particular charge laid against him. It indicates that he takes his place alongside Paul in his consciousness of rectitude, Acts 20. 26ff, 23. 1. It indicates the spirit of simple faith and childlike trust which throws itself unreservedly on God.

David asks for a true judgment on the wicked and those who seek his life, on the ground that all evil-doing must be revealed as bringing about its own destruction. The wicked person has fallen into the ditch that he himself has made, and the mischief rebounds on his own head, vv. 15-16. God, in His justice, has ordained it so.

It is blessed to be able to stand before God with a conscience void of offence towards God and towards men, bringing praise to God and giving men no cause to blaspheme.

READING: **Psalm 26**

SO WILL I COMPASS THINE ALTAR

THE PSALMIST has appealed for vindication, v. 1, and based his petition on his relation to God. He affirms complete freedom from sinful intention, and that he has always trusted in the Lord. It is no case of self-righteously claiming perfection; he appeals only to the deepest aim of his heart, as being absolutely turned to God. He has invited God to examine, try and prove him, v. 2. Thus God proved Abraham, Gen. 22. 1, and Israel, Deut. 8. 2, 16. The purpose of such heart searching is "to give every man according to his ways", Jer. 17. 10, to purge out the dross, and to demonstrate trust and faithfulness.

The psalmist then provides reasons why he should not be involved in the fate of the ungodly. Firstly, he refers to his conduct in the past and his resolve for the future, vv. 4-7; note the verbs "I have not ... neither will I ... I have ...and will not ... I will ... so will I". Secondly, he points to his concern for God's house, vv. 8-12, "the place where thine honour dwelleth", and where "in the congregations" he can praise the Lord. Central to the psalm is his statement, "so will I compass thine altar, O Lord", v. 6.

Conditions of personal life precede this statement. He speaks of separation from evil ways and evil persons, vv. 4, 5, 9, 10. "Vain persons" is a general term for the ungodly; the word "vain" passes judgment on the way of life which is content with the world, its transient pleasures, its tinsel attraction, and its blindness to the truth. One who loves the habitation of God's house, and who walks in the truth, is not going to sit in an easy association, nor "go" with those who have no such desires. In the daily routine of living, association with such men is necessary, but it is impossible for one whose heart is truly in touch with God not to feel ill at ease in the company of those who do not share his deepest feelings. His longings instinctively turn to his heart's home, the sanctuary. The more a man feels out of sympathy with a godless world, the more longingly will he seek communion with his God. The Christian must note and practice such separation. His joy should be in the company of God's people, vv. 8, 12, and only then does he stand secure, v. 12. Fellowship with the Lord is only possible when there is no fellowship with evil, 1 John 1. 6-7.

April 29th

READING: **Psalm 18. 20-36**

ARE YOUR HANDS CLEAN?

THIS PSALM is recorded twice, here and in 2 Samuel 22. David commences by praising God for His wonderful deliverances, vv. 1-3. These deliverances he then proceeds to describe in strong poetical figures, vv. 4-19. These deliverances have not only been acts of mercy, he states, but acts of righteousness, vv. 20-24. These reasons for his deliverances are based upon the character of God and the principles of His moral government. These verses must have been written before David's sad fall, Psa. 51. After this fall, the tone is different, yet then, too, there is the acknowledgement of the dread power of sin, so that the psalmist prays to be kept from his iniquity; he recognizes an inward tendency to sin, an inherent sinfulness, but he kept himself on guard against it.

Twice in verses 20-24 the psalmist refers to "the cleanness of my hands". The Lord rewarded him, i.e., dealt with him on this basis. He repeats the claim in verse 24. The hands are instruments of action. The hands of some were "full of blood", Isa. 1. 15, but the Lord would not hear such men, 59. 1-3. By cleanness of hands, he means the innocence of his conduct. It is the person who has clean hands who ascends into the hill of the Lord, and who stands in His holy place, Psa. 24. 3-4. Those who compass the altar are those who have washed their hands in innocency, Psa. 26. 6. The substantiation of the psalmist's claim comes in verses 20-23.

The righteousness claimed in verse 24 is not an absolute perfection or an entire exemption from all sinful infirmity, but with a faith in God's mercy, and with a sincere controlling desire to do His will. It is no vainglorious boasting of his own merits, but a testimony to the faithfulness of God to guard and reward His faithful servants. He does not claim perfection, but a single-hearted sincerity in his devotion to God: compare his own testimony, 1 Sam. 26. 23, God's testimony, 1 Kings 14. 8, and the testimony of history, 1 Kings 11. 4; 15. 5, to his essential integrity.

God deals with His servants according to their righteousness, in that sin that is cherished separates from Him, and forces His love to leave cries for help unanswered. This is permitted, so His people may have a wholesome fear of straying from Himself.

132

READING: **Psalm 17**

TO BEHOLD HIS FACE IN RIGHTEOUSNESS

THE PSALM commences with the psalmist's prayer to God to "Hear the right", i.e., his righteous cause, v. 1. He boldly asks for his sentence from the divine presence, v. 2, and the ground of that petition is that He beholds equity, R.V.

The question arises as to whether the psalmist was being Pharisaic in his bold protestations of innocence. No; he is asking for God's vindication of his innocence in the matters charged against him. In protesting the cleanness of his heart and his outward obedience, v. 3, he is not so much denying his sin, but is stating his sincere devotion and his obedience to God's law. These things are not the same as the complacency of the Pharisee. The psalmist continues to paint the contrast between the desires of the worldly man and his own spiritual aspirations. He does not complain of their prosperity—his blessings are far greater than theirs could ever be. They culminate in his triumphant assertion in verse 15. Here, he expresses the deepest longings of his heart—to behold the face of the Lord in righteousness, and to be conformed to the divine likeness. Is not that our supreme desire too?

The satisfaction of worldly men is in their wealth and family honours; that of the psalmist is in the sunshine of God's presence and the vision of His righteousness. Their portion is in this life, and they leave their substance behind them when they die, but to the Christian, whose portion is God, it means the fuller possession of all that he loves and desires. The psalmist's "I" is emphatic, for it is in contrast to those described in the preceding verse 14.

It must be in righteousness that he would gaze upon His face. The condition of beholding the Holy One is holiness. The condition of holiness is trust in Christ. The contrast throughout is between the false life and the true life in the present world, and therefore the word "awake" could have the immediate meaning of the psalmist's desire for the continuation of communion with his God each waking day.

Yet, of course, the concept of eternal life cannot be far away from the words. Communion begun with God down here will not be terminated by death. The N.T. has a richer fulfilment, 2 Cor. 3. 18; Phil. 3. 21; 1 John 3. 2; Rev. 22. 4.

The Blessings of Mercy, Lovingkindness and Compassion

THE READINGS and meditations from selected psalms during the month of May will have as their dominant theme those attributes of God upon which we depend so heavily as guilty sinners and as failing believers, i.e. His mercy, lovingkindness, compassion and forgiveness. That these features are indeed characteristic of the God of Israel is demonstrated abundantly by the psalms. There is a wealth of evidence from which supporting evidence can be drawn, as any reader can confirm by using a good concordance. It is very encouraging to discover that there is no shortage of material upon which to base this series of studies. No Christian would be surprised to find that these attributes of God are unfolded most fully and in greatest detail in the N.T. Scriptures. But we may well be surprised to learn how frequently they feature in the psalms. This demonstrates, despite claims often made to the contrary, that the revelation of God in the O.T. is perfectly consistent with that contained in the N.T.

The character of God has been unchanging through the centuries of human history, and will ever be so through all eternity. There are writers and preachers who teach that the God of the O.T. is a God of wrath and of judgment, totally intolerant of human sin and weakness, whilst the God of the N.T., especially as revealed in the life and ministry of the Lord Jesus, is by contrast a God of love, ready to pardon sin and to make allowance for human frailty; those who teach such things reveal their ignorance both of God and of His Word. His great love for fallen humanity is repeatedly in evidence in the O.T., and His righteous wrath and indignation against sin is as frequently taught in the N.T.

The balance of truth thus established in the Scriptures is well illustrated in Psalm 130. 3, 4, 7, 8:

> If thou, Lord, shouldest mark iniquities,
>> O Lord, who shall stand?
> But there is forgiveness with thee,
>> that thou mayest be feared.
> ... with the Lord there is mercy,
>> and with him is plenteous redemption.
> And he shall redeem Israel
>> from all his iniquities.

READING: **Psalm 17**

SHOW THY MARVELLOUS LOVINGKINDNESS

THIS PHRASE, v. 7, begins an urgent prayer of David, written at a time of intense pressure. He cries for protection from "the wicked that oppress me, from my deadly enemies, who compass me about", v. 9. He precedes the appeal by earnestly protesting his freedom from guilt—"give ear unto my prayer, that goeth not out of feigned lips", v. 1. We should cultivate similar sincerity, knowing that God always expects "unfeigned faith" in Himself, 2 Tim. 1. 5, and "unfeigned love of the brethren", 1 Pet. 1. 22.

We may be surprised by the strength of David's claim in the early verses, especially in verse 3, "Thou that hast proved mine heart; thou that hast visited me in the night; thou hast tried me, and shalt find nothing" (or "thou hast found nothing" J.N.D.). Moreover, verse 5 is not a request (as the A.V. suggests) but a claim, "My steps have held fast to thy paths, my feet have not slipped" R.V. If the psalm belongs to David's outlaw life, it pre-dates his tragic lapses involving Bathsheba and Uriah. We are not invited to sit in judgment on David, however (or on any other believer!). Rather, it will be our wisdom to keep in mind Paul's warning, "let him that thinketh he standeth take heed lest he fall", 1 Cor. 10. 12. And let us note with approval the secret of David's upright walk at the time he wrote this psalm, "Concerning the works of men, by *the word of my lips* I have kept me from the paths of the destroyer", Psa. 17. 4.

A remarkable feature of this prayer is its extended description of the God to whom it is offered, "Show thy marvellous lovingkindness, O thou that savest by thy right hand them which put their trust in thee from those that rise up against them". David was urging the Lord simply to act consistently with His character as revealed by His past deliverances. There lay the foundation of his confidence. Since we possess in the Scriptures a much fuller record of divine activity over the centuries, and have experienced a mightier deliverance than David ever knew, we have no excuse for lacking confidence in God today.

"Cast not away therefore your confidence, which hath great recompense of reward", Heb. 10. 35.

May 2nd

READING: **Psalm 25**

TENDER MERCIES AND LOVINGKINDNESS

THREE TIMES in verses 6-7 David makes requests concerning the remembrance of God. The first and third urge God to remember, and the second urges Him to "Remember not".

(i) "Remember, O Lord, thy tender mercies and loving-kindnesses; for they have ever been of old", v. 6. "Mercies" translates a Hebrew word whose meanings include "womb", "compassion", "tender love" and "pity". The word in the plural expresses, as here, the affective aspect of love, its compassion and pity. "Lovingkindness" is the same word as used in Psalm 17. 7. David is pleading with the Lord to maintain towards himself those tender and loving attributes which have characterized His dealings with men from their earliest history. But he is keenly conscious that he does not merit such divine treatment; he says:

(ii) "Remember not the sins of my youth, nor my transgressions", v. 7. This plaintive appeal returns twice later in the psalm in a more specific form, "For thy name's sake, O Lord, pardon mine iniquity; for it is great", v. 11; and "Look upon mine affliction and my pain; and forgive all my sins", v. 18. Many generations after David, God sent Jeremiah to the depleted and idolatrous kingdom of Judah as it declined into defeat and exile following the Babylonian conquest. But the weeping prophet announced the amazing terms of the future convenant which God was to make with His people: "I will forgive their iniquity, and I will remember their sin no more", Jer. 31. 34, also quoted in Hebrews 10. 17 as a blessing to all those who believe the gospel.

(iii) "According to thy mercy remember thou me for thy goodness' sake, O Lord", v. 7. David dreaded being ignored by God. This request (faintly anticipating that of the repentant thief), appealing both to divine mercy and to divine goodness, shows his longing to be remembered with a view to divine blessing. We who live in the full-orbed blessings of the gospel have access to promises and blessings which David never knew. For example, we may ever appropriate the matchless words of 1 John 1. 9, "If we confess our sins, he is faithful and just to forgive us our sins".

"Remember Jesus Christ raised from among the dead, of the seed of David, according to my glad tidings", 2 Tim. 2. 8 J.N.D.

READING: **Psalm 25**

MERCY AND TRUTH

TODAY WE catch further glimpses of God's mercy in this precious psalm, this time by linking a general promise, v. 10, with a personal appeal, v. 16. "All the paths of the Lord are mercy and truth unto such as keep his covenant and his testimonies", v. 10. By "the paths of the Lord", David means the path along which the Lord is willing to lead His people. He had just written, "The meek will he guide in judgment: and the meek will he teach his way", v. 9. Meekness implies a readiness to be led by the Lord, to be dependent on and sensitive to His guidance in daily life. "He leadeth me in the paths of righteousness for his name's sake", Psa. 23. 3. Those who tread those paths will experience both mercy and truth at God's hands, proving Him to be both kind and trustworthy in His dealings with them. They will be those who "keep his covenant and his testimonies", fulfilling His requirements and obeying His Word. These are abiding principles, as relevant for us as they were for David. He knew these things to be true from his own experience as well as from his observation of others. Verses 12-14 strike a similar note.

But as in so many of his psalms, David was writing under severe adversity. He felt the need of the personal enjoyment of these blessings. So his general reflections give way to renewed longing: "Mine eyes are ever toward the Lord; for he shall pluck my feet out of the net", v. 15. It is good to cultivate a heavenward gaze, "Looking unto Jesus the author and finisher of our faith ... at the right hand of the throne of God", Heb. 12. 2. Then comes the urgent appeal, "Turn thee unto me, and have mercy upon me; for I am desolate and afflicted", v. 16. David's boldness here is born of troubles and distress, v. 17, affliction and pain, v. 18, and the cruel hatred of his enemies, v. 19.

He cries to the almighty God of the universe: "Turn thee unto *me*", v. 16. He feels neglected and vulnerable, as though God were "busy elsewhere" in the hour of his acute distress. David longed for a consciousness of the Lord's nearness.

Prosperity rarely creates such longings. "Before I was afflicted I went astray: but now have I kept thy word", Psa. 119. 67. Let us remember that He is never far away.

"I will never leave thee, nor forsake thee", Heb. 13. 5.

May 4th

READING: Psalm 31. 19-24

HIS MARVELLOUS KINDNESS

THE EARLIER verses of this psalm tell of the harrowing circumstances under which it was written: "Pull me out of the net that they have laid privily for me", v. 4; "thou hast considered my trouble; thou hast known my soul in adversities", v. 7; "I am in trouble; mine eye is consumed with grief", v. 9; "my life is spent with grief, and my years with sighing: my strength faileth because of mine iniquity, and my bones are consumed", v. 10. Read also verses 12-13.

What a vivid portrayal of distress and adversity! Yet it throws into relief the triumphant note of our closing passage, vv. 19-24. How did David scale such heights of assurance from such depths of despair? By reminding himself of the source of all comfort, "Thou shalt hide them (that fear thee) in the secret of thy presence from the pride of man: thou shalt keep them secretly in a pavilion from the strife of tongues", v. 20. These words remind us of the sublime statement in Psalm 91. 1, "He that dwelleth in the secret place of the most High shall abide under the shadow of the Almighty". Believers today have direct access into that same secret place, for the Lord Jesus taught His disciples, "But thou, when thou prayest, enter into thy closet, and when thou hast shut thy door, pray to thy Father which is in secret; and thy Father which seeth in secret shall reward thee openly", Matt. 6. 6.

Which of us has not felt at times as David did, when he wrote, "Oh that I had wings like a dove! for then would I fly away, and be at rest", Psa. 55. 6. It is very tempting to run away from our problems, to leave the sphere of present heartache (the assembly, the neighbourhood, the place of work, the town, the school or college). But even the world knows the dangers of stepping "out of the frying pan into the fire".

If we must retreat, let it always be into the presence of God. There we shall get things back into perspective and gain new resources of peace, assurance and strength. Expositors suggest that Keilah, 1 Sam. 23. 1, is the "strong city" of verse 21; then David is saying that even in such a hazardous scene God had shown to him "his marvellous kindness".

"Peace I leave with you, my peace I give unto you ... Let not your heart be troubled", John 14. 27.

138

May 5th

READING: **Psalm 32**

REJOICING IN FORGIVENESS

THIS PSALM (according to A. Maclaren) records David's experience in the dark time when, for a whole year, he lived impenitent after his great sin, and then was broken down by Nathan's message and restored to peace through pardon following swiftly on penitence. As David gives sweet expression to the relief of forgiveness and the recovery of fellowship with God, he speaks for all of us. Verses 1 and 2 alone are sufficient evidence that in O.T. days God had shed enough spiritual light for His people to enjoy both His pardon and the peace flowing from it. The process begins (as it always must) with confession, for verse 5 records, "I acknowledged my sin unto thee, and mine iniquity have I not hid. I said, I will confess my transgressions unto the Lord; and thou forgavest the iniquity of my sin".

Confession is a humbling task but vital to recovery and the resumption of spiritual progress. W. Graham Scroggie, in his book *Method in Prayer*, wrote these weighty words, "Oh how difficult it is to give expression in words to the sorrow of our hearts for sin; they are upon our lips as burning coals; and the sound of them fills us with shame".

David received God's forgiveness for crimes which merited the severest judgment. But a review of his subsequent experiences (from 2 Samuel 13 onwards) makes it clear that his sins caused enduring sorrows for himself and the royal family. May we conclude, then, that God's pardon was only partial after all? Certainly not; it is thorough and unreserved, in anticipation of Christ's redemptive work at Calvary. It remains true, however, that God's people cannot escape the earthly consequences of their sins, for Paul stated an abiding principle when he wrote, "Be not deceived; God is not mocked: for whatsoever a man soweth, that shall he also reap", Gal. 6. 7.

1 John 1 deals with the issues of sin, forgiveness and cleansing; John then writes, "My little children, these things write I unto you, that ye sin not", 2. 1. We shall never be perfect down here, but we ought to be making constant progress towards that goal.

"But grow in grace, and in the knowledge of our Lord and Saviour Jesus Christ", 2 Pet. 3. 18.

May 6th

READING: **Psalm 32**

COMPASSED ABOUT BY MERCY

THIS PENITENTIAL psalm concludes on a triumphant note, vv. 10, 11, showing the completeness of David's restoration. He had proved by his own lapses the truth of his words, "Many sorrows shall be to the wicked", v. 10.

Let us consider this. Appearances often seem to belie these words, as Asaph wrote, "I was envious at the foolish, when I saw the prosperity of the wicked ... They are not in trouble as other men; neither are they plagued like other men ... they have more than heart could wish", Psa. 73. 3, 5, 7. This seemed like gross injustice to Asaph, until he recovered a true perspective, "When I thought to know this, it was too painful for me; until I went into the sanctuary of God; then understood I their end. Surely thou didst set them in slippery places: thou castedst them down into destruction", vv. 16-19. This corrected view of things convicted Asaph, "Thus my heart was grieved, and I was pricked in my reins. So foolish was I, and ignorant: I was as a beast before thee", vv. 21-22.

Read David's wise counsel in Psalm 37. 1-2.

Again in verse 10, "but he that trusteth in the Lord, mercy shall compass him about". Since God is trustworthy, His people should trust Him! *When* should we trust Him? "Trust in him *at all times*; ye people, pour out your heart before him: God is a refuge for us", Psa. 62. 8. *How* should we trust Him? "Trust in the Lord *with all thine heart*; and ' an not unto thine own understanding", Prov. 3. 5. And *why* should we trust Him? Because (as our verse says) mercy will then compass us about. The psalms declare that it is folly to trust in chariots and in horses, Psa. 20. 7, in bows and swords, 44. 6, in wealth, 49. 6, or in oppression and robbery, 62. 10.

Let us savour the closing words of verse 10 in various renderings: "mercy shall compass him about" A.V.; "lovingkindness shall encompass him" J.N.D.; "stedfast love surrounds him" R.S.V.; "with lovingkindness he will encircle him" MACLAREN. What security and comfort are available to the trusting heart! The disciples in the boat could have spared themselves their panic (and the Lord could have benefited from further sleep) had they only learned this lesson, Mark 6. 45-51.

"*Where is your faith?*", Luke 8. 25.

May 7th

READING: **Psalm 34. 1-10**

MAGNIFYING THE LORD

THE PSALMIST makes three appeals in these verses: "O magnify the Lord with me", v. 3; "O taste and see that the Lord is good", v. 8; "O fear the Lord, ye his saints", v. 9.

In verses 4 to 7, he justifies his appeals by rehearsing the Lord's blessings. Verses 4 and 6 describe personal blessings, and verses 5 and 7 describe collective blessings. We shall review verse 4 as representative of the others.

"I sought the Lord, and he heard me, and delivered me from all my fears", v. 4. The heading of the psalm places it in the days when David, a fugitive during the reign of Saul, fled to the Philistines. The repeated hazards and stresses of the preceding days had so preyed on David's mind that, shortly before he fled to Gath, he said to Jonathan the son of Saul, "truly as the Lord liveth, and as thy soul liveth, there is but a step between me and death", 1 Sam. 20. 3. He had lost the assurance of God's protecting care and (very understandably) had succumbed to intense fears. But the resulting defection to enemy territory led him into a path of compromise and deceit which, but for the Lord's intervention, would have resulted in his fighting with the Philistines against the army of Israel.

He reached the depths of despair when, on being sent back to Ziklag by Achish of Gath, he and his men found that the city had been burnt down, and their loved ones captured and removed by the Amalekites. His own followers threatened to stone him: and then we read these inspiring words, "but David encouraged himself in the Lord his God", 1 Sam. 30. 6. He and his men pursued and routed the Amalekite invaders, and rescued all their loved ones. Truly he "sought the Lord" and was delivered from all his fears. Soon afterwards he ascended the throne of Judah, and finally became king of all Israel.

If we allow the pressures of adversity to undermine our trust in the Lord, there is no limit to the problems which we may bring upon ourselves. But recovery is always possible, for the Lord never abandons us, nor loses patience with us. "There hath no temptation taken you but such as is common to man: but God is faithful, who will not suffer you to be tempted above that ye are able; but will with the temptation also make a way to escape, that ye may be able to bear it", 1 Cor. 10. 13.

141

READING: **Psalm 34. 11-22**

THE NEARNESS OF THE LORD

A CENTRAL LESSON of these verses is that all men, righteous and unrighteous, live beneath the all-searching scrutiny of God. "The eyes of the Lord are upon the righteous", v. 15; "The face of the Lord is against them that do evil", v. 16. We may conceal our faults from others, even from our nearest and dearest on earth. But God misses nothing. This writer was sitting an external examination some years ago, and was incensed to observe that competing candidates were cheating and were either undetected or unreproved. The divine Invigilator sees everything! "Thou hast set our iniquities before thee, our secret sins in the light of thy countenance", Psa. 90. 8.

These things should solemnize us but need not terrify us. "The Lord is nigh unto them that are of a broken heart; and saveth such as be of a contrite spirit", v. 18. Contrition and brokenness are undervalued qualities today. The sense of personal failure, the keen awareness of unholy thoughts and tendencies, the conscious inadequacy of our devotion to the Lord, should make us all mourn and grieve. Many an embattled Christian knows what this means. Certainly it is good to rejoice in the Lord, but unalloyed happiness is scarcely possible in this groaning creation in which we also groan, Rom. 8. 22-23. The promise before us is that God draws near to brokenhearted saints, "I dwell in the high and holy place, with him also that is of a contrite and humble spirit", Isa. 57. 15.

Before leaving this precious psalm, we should notice verse 19: "Many are the afflictions of the righteous: but the Lord delivereth him out of them all". Persecuted Christians in some countries are better qualified to speak of afflictions than we are in our home country. Isolated Christians in non-Christian homes or workplaces, however, can face fierce hostility at times. They may be sure that God has not forgotten them and will never desert them: "Fear not ... When thou passest through the waters, I will be with thee; and through the rivers, they shall not overflow thee: when thou walkest through the fire, thou shalt not be burned; neither shall the flame kindle upon thee", Isa. 43. 1-2.

"Our light affliction ... worketh for us a far more exceeding and eternal weight of glory", 2 Cor. 4. 16-17.

May 9th

READING: **Psalm 36**

HOW EXCELLENT IS THY LOVINGKINDNESS

THE FIRST four verses contain a devastating description of wicked men enjoying their sin. (Verse 1 is obscure in the A.V., R.V. and J.N.D., but is clarified in the N.I.V. thus: "An oracle is within my heart concerning the sinfulness of the wicked: There is no fear of God before his eyes".) Then follows a sublime review of certain attributes of God, i.e. His mercy, faithfulness, righteousness, judgments and lovingkindness, vv. 5-7(a). Verses 7(b)-10 depict God's people in the enjoyment of divine resources, and verses 11-12 provide a final glimpse of the fate of the wicked.

David likens God's attributes to His creation: "Thy mercy, O Lord, is in the heavens; and thy faithfulness reacheth unto the clouds. Thy righteousness is like the great mountains; thy judgments are a great deep", vv. 5-6. Thus God's ways are seen to possess the grandeur, the majesty and the awesomeness of His universe; enduring in its strength, abiding in its beauty, vast in its scope. If we feel diminished by these lofty and inspiring glimpses of the God of creation, so much the better. Human nature too readily exalts itself, but we are tiny creatures, insignificant in stature and even superfluous, in the sense that the everlasting God does not *need* us either to further His plans or to complete His joy. If (as Scripture amazingly teaches) He has chosen to confer value and dignity upon us by redeeming us from sin and making us His children, we should remember that these blessings are bestowed but not deserved.

David makes it clear that it is God's lovingkindness, His steadfast love, which will encourage us to draw near to Him, however conscious we may rightly be of our sinfulness and our smallness: "How excellent is thy lovingkindness, O God! *therefore* the children of men put their trust under the shadow of thy wings", v. 7. These tender words remind us of the plaintive sorrow of the Lord Jesus, "how often would I have gathered thy children together, as a hen doth gather her brood under her wings, and ye would not!", Luke 13. 34. Men may refuse to approach Him, but those who do "shall be abundantly satisfied with the fatness of thy house; and thou shalt make them drink of the river of thy pleasures", v. 8.

"He that cometh to me shall never hunger", John 6. 35.

143

READING: **Psalm 51**

A CRY FOR MERCY

THIS IS the most famous of the penitential psalms. The heading states that it was the result of Nathan's accusation of David after the king's sin with Bathsheba and Uriah, 2 Sam. 11 & 12. Psalm 32 is attributed to the same period (see pages 139, 140), where David rejoices in the assurance of forgiveness, vv. 1-2, a note of gladness absent from Psalm 51.

David's guilt was great and inexcusable. It has been said to originate from one of life's unguarded moments, 2 Sam. 11. 1-2, his lapse occurring during a period "when kings go forth to battle", but when "David tarried still at Jerusalem". He would have been safer in the thick of the battle than in the idleness of his palace. Let us keep busy in Christian service, for it will help us avoid the sins of lethargy, and will also further the Lord's work. David's lustful glance led to adultery, and his attempt to conceal his guilt led to murder. Sadder still, it was murder by proxy, for he put the onus on Joab to arrange for Uriah's death. Uriah's own integrity led to his death, for he refused to spend a night with his wife in Jerusalem when his colleagues were camping on the battle field. His words must have burned into David's conscience by high-lighting his own unusual idleness, 2 Sam. 11. 11.

We are neither qualified nor authorized to judge David, though we should learn from his downfall. We need to cultivate godly habits of daily Bible study and prayer, and to develop an increasing sense of dependence on the Lord.

David begins Psalm 51 by casting himself upon God's mercy, v. 1. The tax collector did the same, "the publican, standing afar off, would not lift up so much as his eyes unto heaven, but smote upon his breast, saying, God be merciful to me a sinner", Luke 18. 13. We should notice (i) his humble deference in keeping away from the Pharisee, (ii) his conscious unfitness to look up to God, and (iii) the self-loathing with which he smote himself. The Lord added that he went home that day justified. Let us enter into the joy of the prophet Micah, "God ... that pardoneth iniquity ... he retaineth not his anger for ever, because *he delighteth in mercy*", Mic. 7. 18.

"But God, who is rich in mercy ... hath quickened us together with Christ, (by grace are ye saved)", Eph. 2. 4-5.

May 11th

READING: **Psalm 51**

LOVINGKINDNESS AND TENDER MERCIES

THE EARNEST cry in David's opening words, "Have mercy upon me, O God" is based on an appeal to two divine attributes, (i) "according to thy lovingkindness", (ii) "according unto the multitude of thy tender mercies". Lovingkindness means steadfast love. David's appeal may have been encouraged by his knowledge of the revelation which God gave of Himself in answer to Moses' request, "I beseech thee, show me thy glory", Exod. 33. 18. We read that, "the Lord passed by before him, and proclaimed, The Lord, The Lord God, merciful and gracious, longsuffering, and abundant in goodness and truth, keeping mercy for thousands, forgiving iniquity and transgression and sin", 34. 6-7.

If God kept mercy for thousands, could not He spare some for David? If He was a forgiving God, might He not forgive David? The king was thus claiming a personal share in the blessings which God Himself declared to be part of His attributes.

"Mercy" and "mercies", v. 1, translate two different Hebrew words, the first of which means, "the gracious favour of the superior to the inferior, all undeserved", while the second involves love's "compassion and pity". We should notice also the three pairs of words by which David describes his evil conduct, and by which he pleads with God to remove his guilt, vv. 1-2. Maclaren distinguishes the first three words thus: "Transgression" is literally rebellion; "iniquity", that which is twisted or bent; "sin", missing a mark. A. G. Clarke is especially helpful: Sin is here regarded as (a) a blotted record to be expunged; (b) a polluted robe to be washed; (c) a fatal disease to be cured. It is "transgression" = law violated; "iniquity" = morals perverted; "sin" = mark missed.

Notice the intensely personal note in these verses, for David is having dealings with God about his own guilt; thus he speaks of "*my* transgressions", "*mine* iniquity", "*my* sin".

Verse 4 is surprising at first, "Against thee, thee only, have I sinned". Not against Bathsheba, Uriah and Joab. In a secondary sense, certainly; but primarily all sin is against God our Maker, to whom men are finally accountable.

"The blood of Jesus Christ his Son cleanseth us from all sin", 1 John 1. 7.

145

May 12th

READING: **Psalm 57**

THE SHADOW OF THY WINGS

THE HEADING of this psalm places it in David's outlaw days, "when he fled from Saul in the cave"; it is connected with the event recorded in 1 Samuel 24. 1-8. The urgent repetition in verse 1 of the phrase, "Be merciful unto me", discloses the stress and tension under which David was living. His high destiny as the future king of Israel was being hindered and even threatened by the implacable hatred of Saul. To his enduring credit, David refused every opportunity to slay the king. The temptation must have been strong at times, and could have been justified by arguing that "if it is decreed that Saul must forfeit the throne and that I must succeed him, surely he deserves to die in the interests of the people". But David awaited God's time, and refused to touch the Lord's anointed; as John Gillespie once beautifully remarked, "it was a greater thing to let Saul live than to slay Goliath".

In the meantime, how would David endure the recurring dangers of his fugitive days? Verse 1 contains the secret, "my soul trusteth in thee: yea, in the shadow of thy wings will I make my refuge, until these calamities be overpast". The expression "the shadow of thy wings" takes us back to Psalm 36. 7. It suggests a place of warmth, security and protection, in marked contrast to the physical conditions of David's days in exile. He and his men lived roughly, always ready to make a swift retreat, with food and supplies sometimes low, and always unpredictable. Faith was constantly challenged, doubtless by God's deliberate policy. For those men were being trained for warfare after David ascended the throne.

These are abiding principles. Present experiences are meant to equip us for future trials. God would not have us settle down and stagnate behind the front line. Our homes and our assemblies should be God's outposts, garrisons from which spiritual warfare is waged against Satan and his followers.

Mark the closing words of verse 1, "until these calamities be overpast". For David and his men, their calamities would be relieved, but would give way to later and more demanding ones. And so for us; hence let us get used to it!

"The sufferings of this present time are not worthy to be compared with the glory which shall be revealed", Rom. 8. 18.

146

READING: **Psalm 57**

PRAISE IN THE MIDST OF AFFLICTION

A REMARKABLE feature of this psalm is that David did not allow his trials to silence his praises. He was certainly living through dark and dangerous days, "My soul is among lions: and I lie even among them that are set on fire, even the sons of men, whose teeth are spears and arrows, and their tongue a sharp sword", v. 4. "They have prepared a net for my steps; my soul is bowed down: they have digged a pit before me, into the midst whereof they are fallen themselves", v. 6.

His reaction was to turn his gaze heavenward rather than earthward, that he might draw fresh inspiration and courage. Surely this was exemplary, "I will cry unto God most high; unto God that performeth all things for me", v. 2. And he asserts his confidence in God in the teeth of all dangers, "He shall send from heaven, and save me from the reproach of him that would swallow me up. Selah. God shall send forth his mercy and his truth", v. 3.

How impressive is David's emphatic resolve to maintain a spirit of praise and thanksgiving, "My heart is fixed, O God, my heart is fixed: I will sing and give praise", v. 7. He will allow nothing to deflect him from the high praises of God. He rouses himself, and stirs up his mind and heart, "Awake up, my glory; awake, psaltery and harp: I myself will awake early. I will praise thee, O Lord, among the people: I will sing unto thee among the nations", vv. 8-9.

David strikes an unfamiliar note here (at least, for this writer!). Are not praise and thanksgiving simply our spontaneous response to the Lord, depending very much on our appreciation of His blessings at the time? David would reject that view. For he reveals in these rousing verses a determination to praise God come what may, a commitment to maintain a thankful and worshipping attitude by an exercise of the will. "*I will* cry unto God", v. 2; "*I will* sing and give praise", v. 7; "*I myself will* awake early", v. 8; "*I will* praise thee, O Lord ... I *will* sing unto thee", v. 9.

If David's resolve was so firm and enthusiastic in all adversity, what should ours be in the light of Calvary?

"*By him therefore let us offer the sacrifice of praise to God continually ... the fruit of our lips*", Heb. 13. 15.

May 14th

READING: **Psalm 63**

LOVINGKINDNESS BETTER THAN LIFE

WHAT EXACTLY did David mean by these words? He meant that nothing that life consists of in ordinary earthly experience, however enriched by the joys of family and social life, by wealth and travel, by power and influence, by art and recreation, by ability and achievements; none of these things could compare with the bliss of experiencing the lovingkindness, the steadfast love of God. Now it is one thing to know this, but another to prove it.

How may we prove the truth of David's words? Initially, by following his example. The striking words in verses 1-2 describe how he had sought the knowledge of God, "O God, thou art my God; early will I seek thee: my soul thirsteth for thee, my flesh longeth for thee in a dry and thirsty land, where no water is". David reveals his commitment to pursue after God, and we must take up that pursuit. Each day (preferably in the early morning) we must make time for unhurried communion with God in prayer and for the thoughtful reading of His Word. Achieving this will justify any sacrifice.

David's inspiration was the vision of God, as he writes in verse 2, "I have seen thee in the sanctuary". Not literally, of course, for "no man hath seen God at any time", John 1. 18. It is He "which no man can approach unto; whom no man hath seen, nor can see", 1 Tim. 6. 16. But David was looking back to occasions in the sanctuary when the unseen God had become visible to faith's vision. Those glimpses, however transient, had so enraptured him that he thirsted and longed for more. And he would be satisfied with nothing less.

For us, the glory of God is revealed in the face of Jesus Christ, 2 Cor. 4. 6. That glory will dawn upon us increasingly as we saturate our minds in the Word of God, and especially in the Gospels. There we may see Him at close quarters, and hear His matchless teachings. The Son of God on earth, growing through infancy, boyhood and youth into manhood and ministry, compassion personified as He eagerly spread His blessings abroad and met every form of human need—He should eclipse and surpass any competing interest in our daily lives.

"That I may know him, and the power of his resurrection, and the fellowship of his sufferings", Phil. 3. 10.

148

May 15th

READING: **Psalm 77**

GOD'S WAY IN THE SANCTUARY

COMMENTATORS differ as to the occasion of this psalm; some suggest the time of the Chaldean invasion, while others suggest the time of the Babylonian exile. The psalm certainly emerged from the writer's great distress; see v. 2, which the R.V. renders as "In the day of my trouble I sought the Lord; *my hand was stretched out in the night, and slacked not*".

His distress became so acute that he suddenly uttered a succession of anguished questions, vv. 7-9. Only those who have themselves been in the depths of despair are likely to sympathize or even to understand. Verse 9 is plaintive beyond measure, "Hath God forgotten to be gracious? hath he in anger shut up his tender mercies?".

The psalmist was being transparently sincere. In this he has much to teach us. At times of overwhelming grief, when faith is bruised and doubt looms large, it is better to pour out our hearts in God's presence than to nurse our sorrows. He will not chide us for being honest and for voicing our griefs plainly and earnestly. Once the psalmist had got his doubts "out of his system", his thoughts clarified and faith returned. Verse 10 has given commentators some difficulty, but after discussing the Hebrews words and their alternative possibilities, Maclaren concludes that its meaning is, "This my affliction is sent from God, and I must bear it with resignation. I will remember the time when the right hand of Jehovah had the pre-eminence".

The remaining verses are bright with recovered confidence in God even while adversity continues. There is resolve in the repeated phrase "I will remember ... I will remember", v. 11. In the closing verses, vv. 16-19, he recalls the mighty deliverance of his forefathers at the Red Sea. Maclaren's brilliant comment on verse 19 is that it refers "to the path through the sea, whose waters returned and covered God's footprints from human eyes". So the psalmist's final comfort is in recalling God's mightiest redemptive work by which the nation was brought into liberty from Egyptian tyranny. This teaches us how to deal with despair today. Let us remember Calvary, and our conquering Redeemer who wrought His mighty victory there, of which we are among the eternal beneficiaries.

"This do in remembrance of me", 1 Cor. 11. 24-25.

May 16th

READING: **Psalm 79**

POUR OUT ... PURGE AWAY ...

OBSERVE THE contrast between these two requests in verses 6, 9. The psalm (along with Psalm 74) has been dated at the time of the destruction of Jerusalem by the Chaldeans (cf. v. 1 with 2 Kings 25. 9). The writer recognizes his own and his nation's guilt as having brought down God's judgment upon them. He appeals to the Lord, "Remember not against us the iniquities of our forefathers; let thy tender mercies speedily come to meet us: for we are brought very low", v. 8 J.N.D. In that prayer he puts the blame for their distress on earlier generations of Israelites. In the following verse, however, he confesses to sharing their guilt, and prays, "Help us, O God of our salvation, for the glory of thy name: and deliver us, and *purge away our sins*, for thy name's sake".

All Christians should feel the appropriateness of that plea. Confession of sins secures the promise of forgiveness and cleansing, 1 John 1. 9; this should swiftly follow conviction, to gain prompt recovery of fellowship with our Father.

But how are we to view the other request referred to in our title, as fully stated in verse 6, "Pour out thy wrath upon the heathen that have not known thee, and upon the kingdoms that have not called upon thy name"? The same desire for revenge recurs later, "Wherefore should the heathen say, Where is their God? let him be known among the heathen in our sight by the revenging of the blood of thy servants which is shed", v. 10; see also verse 12. Undoubtedly the psalmist had witnessed appalling carnage by Israel's enemies (verses 2-3 make horrific reading). Does that justify his thirst for revenge? His law could have taught him otherwise, "Thou shalt not hate thy brother in thy heart ... Thou shalt not avenge, nor bear any grudge against the children of thy people, but thou shalt love thy neighbour as thyself", Lev. 19. 17-18; Rom. 12. 20.

There are two lessons for the Christian here: (i) "Father, forgive" is our Saviour's response to human provocation; (ii) C. S. Lewis writes "we must avoid so maltreating people as to provoke in them an ugly thirst for revenge even if only a pale reflection of that expressed here".

"Christ also suffered for us, leaving us an example, that ye should follow his steps", 1 Pet. 2. 21.

May 17th

READING: **Psalm 85. 1-7**

WILT THOU NOT REVIVE US AGAIN?

THE SECOND clause in verse 1, "thou hast brought back the captivity of Jacob", seems to refer to the return of the captivity from Babylon. From the note of thanksgiving for that release in verses 1-3, the psalmist immediately appeals for further deliverance in verses 4-7. Then in verses 8-13 he expresses his confidence that the Lord will ultimately bless His people. Psalm 126 possesses a similar structure.

This distinction between the enjoyment of an earlier deliverance and the longing for a further one, explains the apparent conflict between "thou hast turned thyself from the fierceness of thine anger", v. 3, and "cause thine anger toward us to cease", v. 4. God had forgiven His people for the backsliding and idolatry which had led to their captivity in Babylon. But now that some were back in the land, they had again lost their zeal for the Lord and so were incurring further judgment.

Christian experience has its counterparts to these dealings of God with His earthly people. By believing the gospel we learn the joyful meaning of verses 2-3, "Thou hast forgiven the iniquity of thy people, thou hast covered all their sin ... thou hast turned thyself from the fierceness of thine anger". But if we later deviate by neglecting daily prayer and Bible study, and by becoming careless about Christian living and fellowship, we rapidly succumb to further bondage to sin and failure. Paul wrote of this dilemma in Romans 7. 24, "O wretched man that I am! Who shall deliver me from the body of this death?".

If we persist in the course of backsliding, the Lord reserves the right to deal with us severely until we return to Him and cry, "Wilt thou not revive us again: that thy people may rejoice in thee?", v. 6. Revival ever leads to rejoicing. Only victorious Christians can rejoice! They are often taxed by conflict. They face discouragement and perplexity. The way is never easy and always upward. But still they rejoice, for they keep right with God, drawing on His resources, supported by His strength and trusting His unfailing presence.

"Show us thy mercy, O Lord", v. 7. Mercy is for saints as well as for sinners, *"Let us therefore come boldly unto the throne of grace, that we may obtain mercy"*, Heb. 4. 16.

May 18th

READING: **Psalm 85. 8-13**

MERCY AND TRUTH ARE MET TOGETHER

THIS PORTION of the psalm begins with a wise resolve which all believers should make: "I will hear what God the Lord will speak". Centuries earlier, Moses had written, "And he (the Lord) humbled thee, and suffered thee to hunger, and fed thee with manna, which thou knewest not, neither did thy fathers know; that he might make thee know that man doth not live by bread only, but by every word that proceedeth out of the mouth of the Lord doth man live", Deut. 8. 3. Eli's advice to young Samuel is always valid, "thou shalt say, Speak, Lord; for thy servant heareth", 1 Sam. 3. 9. God speaks to us today through the Scriptures, which should therefore be read prayerfully, diligently, systematically and expectantly. And surely we ought to plan our reading so as to cover all 66 books of the Bible at least once yearly, quite apart from pursuing a detailed study of selected books or themes. We must not neglect whole portions of His Word and merely read what we enjoy!

"For he will speak peace unto his people, and to his saints: but let them not turn again to folly", v. 8. Habitual exposure to God's Word makes for peace and serenity in the Christian. Do we not regularly find that a season of prolonged Bible reading has a cleansing and stabilising effect on mind and heart, irrespective of the portion being read? "But let them not turn again to folly": for God's Word is meant to be corrective as well as informative. It should modify our behaviour as well as enlightening our minds. If we "turn again to folly", if we close our Bibles and resume frivolous or disobedient living, we must expect discipline. "Be ye doers of the word, and not hearers only, deceiving your own selves", James 1. 22.

We conclude with part of J. G. Bellett's fragrant comments on verses 10-11 in *"Meditations on the Psalms"* : "Truth, which required death, Gen. 2. 17, and mercy which can think of nothing but life and blessing, are here together. Death is endured according to truth, and the culprit given life and liberty according to mercy. Righteousness also kisses peace and peace kisses righteousness. Instead of being offended at each other's presence, they welcome each other".

"By the obedience of one shall many be made righteous", Rom. 5. 19.

May 19th

READING: **Psalm 86**

UNITE MY HEART TO FEAR THY NAME

A. G. CLARKE points out that this is the only psalm in Book III (73 to 89) ascribed to David, and suggests that it may belong either to the time of David's exile among the Philistines or to the period of Absalom's rebellion.

Among the various appeals and requests scattered throughout the psalm, there are three statements concerning the attributes of God: "For thou, Lord, art *good*, and ready to forgive; and plenteous in mercy unto all them that call upon thee", v. 5; "For thou art *great*, and doest wondrous things: thou art God alone", v. 10; "But thou, O Lord, art a God full of compassion, and *gracious*, longsuffering, and plenteous in mercy and truth", v. 15.

(i) *The Lord is good*, v. 5. This takes us straight to the person of Christ. Nathanael asked Philip, "Can there *any good thing* come out of Nazareth?", John 1. 46; and he later became a follower of *the good Shepherd*, 10. 11. Peter told Cornelius and his friends how "God anointed Jesus of Nazareth ... *who went about doing good*", Acts 10. 38. The Lord's goodness was unique in that it never varied. He never deviated from His own standards, for He was goodness personified. His goodness was absolute, not progressive; perfect, not partial.

(ii) *The Lord is great*, v. 10. The angel Gabriel said to Mary, "thou shalt conceive in thy womb, and bring forth a son, and shalt call his name Jesus. *He shall be great*, and shall be called the Son of the highest", Luke 1. 31-32. He did *great things*, Mark 3. 8; 5. 20; He wrought *a great salvation*, Heb. 2. 3; He was raised as *the great Shepherd*, 13. 20; and is now our *great High Priest*, 4. 14.

(iii) *The Lord is gracious*, v. 15. This is obviously linked with the other attributes referred to in our verses. He is "ready to forgive", v. 5, not reluctant; "plenteous in mercy", v. 5, not meagre; "full of compassion", v. 15, not half-hearted; "longsuffering", v. 15, not impatient. All these things were eminently true of the Lord Jesus, who was full of *grace* and truth, John 1. 17, and at whose *gracious words* men wondered, Luke 4. 22.

"For in him dwelleth all the fulness of the Godhead bodily. And ye are complete in him", Col. 2. 9-10.

May 20th

READING: Psalm 103

RANSOMED, HEALED, RESTORED, FORGIVEN

HERE IS a psalm of abiding beauty and timeless relevance, spanning the centuries and appropriate to any dispensation. It is a personal act of worship, and should be read thoughtfully in the secret place so as to inspire our praises.

The psalmist begins and ends by urging himself, "Bless the Lord O my soul", vv. 1, 22. His mind ranges alternately over the revealed character of God, vv. 8, 11, 13, 17-18, and over His dealings with His people, vv. 3-7, 9-10, 12, 14. It all adds fuel to the sacrifice of praise. Moreover, as the Lord looms ever larger in the writer's thoughts, so man is diminished and seen in his frailty and littleness, vv. 14-16.

Let us consider some of these treasures.

(i) *He removes our transgressions*, v. 12. There are two negative statements, "He hath not dealt with us after our sins; nor rewarded us according to our iniquities", v. 10, and the positive statement, "Who forgiveth all thine iniquities", v. 3. The psalmist does not say "as far as the north is from the south (which is measurable), but "as far as the east is from the west" (which is immeasurable).

(ii) *He redeems our lives*, v. 4. Before we were redeemed our lives were empty and meaningless. But Peter teaches us that we have been redeemed from "our vain conversation", i.e. our "vain manner of life", 1 Pet. 1. 18 R.V.

(iii) *He renews our youth*, v. 5. Isaiah wrote, "Even the youths shall faint ... But they that wait upon the Lord shall renew their strength ... they shall run, and not be weary", Isa. 40. 30-31. Thus God rejuvenates His people, as in the cases of Moses and Caleb.

(iv) *He remembers our frailty*, v. 14. This is linked with verse 13, "Like as a father pitieth his children, so the Lord pitieth them that fear him".

(v) *He reckons us righteous*, v. 17. Admittedly it is unlikely that the doctrine of imputed righteousness was in the psalmist's mind when he wrote of "his righteousness" being "unto children's children", but his words irresistibly remind us of our unmerited standing before God.

(vi) *He rules the universe*, v. 19. "His kingdom ruleth over all", so how infinitely favoured are His subjects.

READING: **Psalm 108**

THE STEADFAST HEART

THIS PSALM consists of parts of two earlier ones (57 and 60) probably brought together in this form when Judah's exiles returned from Babylon (A. G. Clarke). Divine blessings are celebrated, vv. 7-9, and further blessings are sought, vv. 6, 10-13. But the psalmist begins with worship, vv. 1-5, and the opening words are a striking expression of his resolve to maintain a spirit of constant praise, "O God, my heart is fixed". In Psalm 57. 7-9 this resolve is emphasized by the words, "I will sing ... I will awake ... I will praise".

It is easy to pour out our praises to God when we have obvious reasons for doing so, e.g., when our prayers are answered, or good health returns after illness, or rain gives way to sunshine, or examination results are favourable. But our psalmist clearly regarded praise as resulting from a deliberate choice, a conscious resolve, a matter of the will as well as of the heart. He rouses himself, stirs himself, challenges himself. A vital phrase occurs at the end of verse 2, "I myself will awake early" ("I will wake the dawn" J.N.D.). Repeatedly in the psalms we meet the call to commune with God in the morning, "My voice shalt thou hear *in the morning*, O Lord; *in the morning* will I direct my prayer unto thee, and will look up", 5. 2-3; see 59. 16; 63. 1; 92. 1-2.

In verse 4, the psalmist indicates the reasons for his praises, "For thy mercy is great above the heavens: and thy truth reacheth unto the clouds". The recognition of God's mercy and truth, as revealed in His law and as experienced in life, motivates the psalmist's praises. And since those divine attributes never vary, nor should the praises of His people. We should be prepared to "wake the dawn". And to be very practical, this may demand a judicious use of the alarm clock.

A formative influence in this writer's early Christian life was the classic I.V.F. booklet, "*The Quiet Time*". One contributor gives this terse advice, "Go to bed in time. Late nights are the relentless enemy of the morning watch. The devil will fight us here. He must be fought back. Pray the night before about your getting up the next morning".

"*Rising up a great while before day, he went out ... and there prayed*", Mark 1. 35.

May 22nd

READING: **Psalm 113**

FROM THE RISING OF THE SUN

THIS COMPACT little psalm of nine verses begins and ends with the command, "Praise ye the Lord". Between these two edicts is to be found ample reason to justify this response. The psalmist furnishes us with answers to four questions:

(i) By whom is the Lord to be praised?: "ye servants of the Lord", v. 1.

(ii) When is he to be praised?: "from this time forth and for evermore", v. 2.

(iii) Where is He to be praised?: "From the rising of the sun unto the going down of the same", v. 3.

(iv) Why is He to be praised?: because of His supremacy, vv. 4-5; His humility, v. 6; His mercy, vv. 7-8; His pity, v. 9.

His Supremacy. "The Lord is high above all nations, and his glory above the heavens ... who dwelleth on high", vv. 4-5, statements that help us to gain exalted thoughts of God. He is the almighty and everlasting One, supreme over the universe of which He is the Maker and Upholder.

His Humility. "Who humbleth himself to behold the things that are in heaven, and in the earth", v. 6. For Him to behold His universe, and us who are His fallen creatures, is evidence of His humility. The hallowed and sweet fellowship existing between the Members of the Godhead is so complete that it needs no enhancement from any external source. But we know what was hidden from the psalmist, that He who humbled Himself to behold us, would humble Himself far more to redeem us, Phil. 2. 8.

His Mercy. "He raiseth up the poor out of the dust, and lifteth the needy out of the dunghill; that he may set him with ... the princes of his people", vv. 7-8. The Lord who stooped to behold us, and who descended to redeem us, has been pleased to exalt us. "God ... hath raised us up together and made us sit together in Christ Jesus", Eph. 2. 4-6.

His Pity. "He maketh the barren woman to keep house, and to be a joyful mother of children", v. 9. This has been fulfilled spiritually for many devoted sisters in Christ who, though missing the joys of marriage and motherhood, have served the Lord faithfully at home or abroad, leading souls to the Lord and finding great joy in caring for them.

"Blessed ... with all spiritual blessings", Eph. 1. 3.

READING: **Psalm 116**

RETURNING TO REST

THE PSALMIST speaks to himself in verse 7, counselling himself very wisely, "Return unto thy rest, O my soul; for the Lord hath dealt bountifully with thee". This illustrates an important feature of the psalms. Frequently we find a writer exhorting himself, challenging himself, rebuking himself—in fact, talking to himself! We have already encounted examples of this, including the famous words in Psalm 103. 1, "Bless the Lord, O my soul: and all that is within me, bless his holy name". The psalmist is there harnessing his energies and rousing his faculties for engagement in the praises of God.

In verse 7, the psalmist urges himself to return to his rest. This implies that he had been doing otherwise. He had been turning from his rest. He had allowed trial and adversity to distract him, to divert his thoughts away from God. He had become anxious and fearful. This was understandable, for he had been grappling with danger and the threat of death: "The sorrows of death compassed me, and the pains of hell gat hold upon me: I found trouble and sorrow", v. 3. But these hazards had driven him to his knees, and God had heard and answered him wonderfully. His gratitude for answered prayer appears to have promoted him to write this psalm, "I love the Lord, because he hath heard my voice and my supplications. Because he hath inclined his ear unto me, therefore will I call upon him as long as I live", vv. 1-2. Moreover, his experience had given him a fresh, threefold appreciation of the Lord, "*Gracious* is the Lord, and *righteous*; yea, our God is *merciful*", v. 5. It is not that the psalmist had been ignorant of these divine attributes previously, but that he had now experienced their activity in his own circumstances.

There is no substitute for experience. That is how theoretical knowledge becomes proven reality. And it is good when we have the wisdom to return to our rest, recovering tranquillity in the calm assurance of our Father's care. It is better still, of course, never to depart from it and from its Author.

"*Peace I leave with you, my peace I give unto you: not as the world giveth, give I unto you. Let not your heart be troubled, neither let it be afraid*", John 14. 27.

May 24th

READING: Psalm 126

REAPING FOLLOWS WEEPING

THIS PSALM celebrates one deliverance, v. 1, and pleads for another, v. 4. It involves the emotions: blissful incredulity, v. 1; laughter and singing, v. 2; gladness, v. 3; tears and rejoicing, vv. 5-6. Its structure is as follows:

(a) Enjoyment of past blessings, vv. 1-3.

(b) Entreaty for further deliverance, v. 4.

(c) Encouragement for zealous toil, vv. 5-6.

The release of the first group of Jewish captives in Babylon to return to the promised land overwhelmed the exiles with bliss and amazement. They were like them that dream, unable at first to grasp that it was really happening. And when the glad truth dawned, they were filled with laughter and singing.

Their pagan neighbours were equally staggered. They could think of only one conceivable explanation. The God of Israel must have intervened on behalf of His people. No other explanation was adequate or tenable. "Then said they among the heathen, The Lord hath done great things for them". These pagans were not predisposed to reach such a conclusion; they worshipped their own gods. But the sheer improbability of the decree of Cyrus which led to the release compelled them (rightly) to attribute events to the living God. To which the liberated Jews agreed, "The Lord *hath* done great things for us; whereof we are glad", v. 3.

But once back home, the exiles encountered persecution and problems as well as joy and encouragement. They were led to pray, "Turn again our captivity, O Lord, as the streams in the south". Verses 5-6 contain God's rather unexpected answer, "They that sow in tears shall reap in joy". It is as though God said to His people, "There is work to be done. Get on with it, whatever the cost".

And so must we. God's answer to any barrenness we feel today, especially in our witness to the lost, is that we commit ourselves to earnest sowing of the seed of the gospel. "He that goeth forth and weepeth, bearing precious seed, shall doubtless come again with rejoicing, bringing his sheaves with him", v. 6. We have to learn how to weep for the lost if we are ever likely to lead them to Christ, Acts 20. 19.

"The fields ... are white already to harvest", John 4. 35.

READING: **Psalm 130**

PLENTEOUS REDEMPTION

AFTER REQUESTING that his prayer might be heard, vv. 1-2, the psalmist recalls the one barrier to all communion with God, "If thou, Lord, shouldest mark iniquities, O Lord, who shall stand?", v. 3. The word here rendered "mark" is used twice in verse 6, where it is translated "watch". The American Berkeley Version renders it by the phrase "keep-in-mind", and a footnote amplifies this to mean, "strictly watch, and keep in memory in order to punish". "Who shall stand?" means "stand before God in judgment and maintain innocence" (A. G. Clarke).

The question is rhetorical, i.e., the answer is self-evident; "No man could sustain that righteous judgment. He must go down before it like a flimsy hut before a whirlwind, or a weak enemy before a fiery charge" (Maclaren).

Having recalled man's guilt, however, the psalmist recalls God's grace, "But there is forgiveness with thee, that thou mayest be feared". Amazingly, God is not disposed to keep our iniquities in mind with a view to judgment. There is forgiveness with Him; He would rather pardon than punish! This truth gripped the prophet Micah, "Who is a God like unto thee, that pardoneth iniquity, and passeth by the transgression of the remnant of his heritage? he retaineth not his anger for ever, because he delighteth in mercy", Mic. 7. 18.

We who live in the gospel era know the secret of the divine pardon. We have been to Calvary and have learnt that forgiveness is based on sacrifice. It is the Lord Jesus "in whom we have redemption through his blood, the forgiveness of sins".

We conclude by noting that forgiveness leads to fear! "There is forgiveness with thee, *that thou mayest be feared*", v. 4. The psalmist does not envisage a craven fear, a dread that God may change His mind, a lurking terror that judgment may yet overtake us after all. For the believer, the thunders of Sinai are silenced for ever. No, the psalmist means a pious fear, a reverent fear of grieving our pardoning God, a sensitive concern to live holy lives, a fear of dishonouring in any way the Lord who bought us.

"*Having therefore these promises, dearly beloved, let us cleanse ourselves from all filthiness of the flesh and spirit, perfecting holiness in the fear of God*", 2 Cor. 7. 1.

May 26th

READING: Psalm 136

HIS MERCY ENDURETH FOR EVER

THIS IS a unique psalm. It is distinguished from all the others by the fact that each verse ends with "for his mercy endureth for ever". Each of the first three verses begins with "O give thanks", followed respectively by "unto the Lord", v. 1, "unto the God of gods", v. 2, and "unto the Lord of lords", v. 3. The "great wonders", v. 4, are then identified in chronological order, namely, the creation, vv. 5-9; the deliverance of the Hebrew slaves from their Egyptian bondage, vv. 10-12; the crossing of the Red Sea, vv. 13-15; and the journey to the borders of the promised land, vv. 16-25. Verse 26 closes with a final appeal, "O give thanks unto the God of heaven: for his mercy endureth for ever".

The psalm was "almost certainly intended for liturgical use in the second temple. (It) is based on Psalm 135 and is antiphonal, the first part of the verse being recited by the precentor and the second part—the refrain—the response by the people" (A. G. Clarke). The recurring refrain emphasizes that all the activities which the psalmist celebrates were motivated by the mercy (the "steadfast love") of God. Creation itself is seen here as a product of that mercy. "The psalm looks at the story of Creation from an original point of view ... that its motive lay in the eternal lovingkindness of Jehovah ... That is the deepest truth concerning all things visible. They are the witnesses, as they are the result, of lovingkindness which endures for ever" (Maclaren).

We should remember this when pondering the beauties of creation, when the rain falls as well as when the sun shines. Consider the Saviour's words, "for he (your Father) maketh his sun to rise on the evil and on the good, and sendeth rain on the just and on the unjust", Matt. 5. 45. Observe God's perfect impartiality there, for the Lord gives priority to "the evil" in the first statement, and to "the just" in the second. This supplements verse 44 R.V., "Love your enemies, and pray for them that persecute you". We are required to surround our enemies with love, and to pray down the showers of divine blessing into their parched and thirsty lives.

"Be ye therefore perfect, even as your Father which is in heaven is perfect", Matt. 5. 48.

READING: **Psalm 138**

THE PERFECTING WORK OF GOD

THIS PSALM of David, like so many others, was written during a period of pressure, "Though I walk in the midst of trouble, thou wilt revive me: thou shalt stretch forth thine hand against the wrath of mine enemies, and thy right hand shall save me", v. 7. These words remind us of the more famous ones, "though I walk through the valley of the shadow of death, I will fear no evil: for thou art with me", Psa. 23. 4.

Verse 1 implies that David was in the company of pagan idolaters, "before the gods will I sing praise unto thee". An idolater could not sing praises, for "Dead gods have dumb devotees" (Maclaren).

Twice in the psalm we find distinct prophecies, one concerning the world, and the other concerning David.

(i) "All the kings of the earth shall praise thee, O Lord, when they hear the words of thy mouth. Yea, they shall sing in the ways of the Lord: for great is the glory of the Lord", vv. 4-5. This prediction has stood for many centuries, but its fulfilment is not in doubt; see also Psalm 72. 11. The millennial reign of the Lord Jesus Christ will witness the literal realization of these and similar promises.

(ii) "The Lord will perfect that which concerneth me: thy mercy, O Lord, endureth for ever", v. 8. Paul supplies three N.T. counterparts of this prediction in his letter to the Philippians: "Being confident of this very thing, that he which hath begun a good work in you will perform it until the day of Jesus Christ", 1. 6; "For it is God which worketh in you both to will and to do of his good pleasure", 2. 13; "The Lord Jesus Christ ... shall change our vile body, that it may be fashioned like unto his glorious body, according to the working whereby he is able even to subdue all things unto himself", 3. 20-21.

There is a doctrine of perfection in the Scriptures, for we read of *the gift of perfection*, Heb. 10. 14, *the thirst for perfection*, Phil. 3. 12, and *the call to perfection*, Matt. 5. 48. God is at work in our lives, moulding us and fashioning us into the likeness of Christ.

"For we are his workmanship, created in Christ Jesus unto good works, which God hath before ordained that we should walk in them", Eph. 2. 10.

May 28th

READING: **Psalm 143**

LEARNING FROM THE PAST

A. G. CLARKE fittingly calls this psalm "A Cry in a Crisis". At the time of writing, David's spirit was overwhelmed within him; his heart within him was desolate, v. 4. His spirit was failing, v. 7. His enemy had persecuted his soul, smitten his life down to the ground, and made him dwell in darkness, v. 3. He felt urgently the need of guidance as to his movements and his conduct, "cause me to know the way wherein I should walk ... Teach me to do thy will ... lead me into the land of uprightness ... bring my soul out of trouble", vv. 8, 10, 11.

His present distress caused him to recall earlier and happier days, and to learn from them, "I remember the days of old; I meditate on all thy works; I muse on the work of thy hands", v. 5. There was wisdom in this, for David was pondering the past without becoming immersed in it. His musings rekindled his desires after God, "I stretch forth my hands unto thee: my soul thirsteth after thee, as a thirsty land", v. 6.

We too can learn from the past provided we do not dwell in it. And we must avoid like the plague any tendency to regret past sacrifices, concentrating instead on future glory, as Paul did in his inspiring words, "forgetting those things which are behind (i.e. the things which he had counted loss for Christ, v. 7, and all things of which he had suffered the loss, v. 8), and reaching forth unto those things which are before, I press toward the mark for the prize of the high calling of God in Christ Jesus", Phil. 3. 13-14.

The value of David's backward look lay in reviewing God's dealings with him in the past, "I meditate on *all thy works*; I muse on *the work of thy hands*". It is always profitable to recall God's past dealings with us, both in salvation and in providence. In particular, we are meant to learn from our trials, as Paul taught in Romans 5. 3-4, "we glory in tribulations also: knowing that tribulation worketh patience; and patience, experience, and experience, hope". Such a cycle of events can only be discerned by musing on God's dealings with us.

"And we know that all things work together for good to them that love God, to them who are the called according to his purpose", Rom. 8. 28.

READING: **Psalm 145**

GREAT IS THE LORD

THIS IS surely one of David's most sublime psalms, dominated throughout by the note of praise. Fresh causes of thanksgiving keep occurring to the psalmist as he writes. These can be identified as seven statements describing different attributes of the Lord, namely,

"Great is the Lord", v. 3; "The Lord is gracious", v. 8; "The Lord is good", v. 9; "The Lord upholdeth", v. 14; "The Lord is righteous", v. 17; "The Lord is nigh", v. 18; "The Lord preserveth", v. 20.

Some of these statements were based on David's observation and some on his experience. They prove both that he knew a great deal about the Lord from the law, and that he had learned very much also from the Lord Himself. This should be true for all of us. "Learn of me", Matt. 11. 29 A.V., R.V., is rendered "learn from me" by J.N.D. This amendment is important. It is obviously possible to learn of a man without learning from him. The first phrase suggests the acquisition of knowledge without any acquaintance with the person concerned. But we can only learn *from* someone by being in his company. That the Lord was thinking of such personal learning is proved by the surrounding context, "Take my yoke upon you, and learn from me ... my yoke is easy, and my burden is light". As we are yoked to Christ, walking in fellowship with Him, we may learn from Him. Correspondence course students often encounter problems because they cannot consult their tutor directly; when he is remote from his students, they will struggle. It is often said that the ideal teaching situation is "one-to-one"; this is what the Lord Jesus offers when He says, "learn from me".

It is good to learn about Him in the Scriptures. We should all be enthusiastic Bible students. Prayerful Scripture-reading is always profitable, and is vital to spiritual growth. But what we learn in God's Book we must prove in our lives. Head knowledge alone may produce legalism and pride. Heart knowledge gleaned in communion with the Lord will enrich us spiritually and result in increasing likeness to Christ.

"*But ye have not so learned Christ; if so be that ye have heard him, and have been taught by him, as the truth is in Jesus*", Eph. 4. 20-21.

May 30th

READING: Psalm 145

EVERY DAY WILL I BLESS THEE

Verses 1 and 2 both conclude with the psalmist's long-term resolve to go on praising God throughout the remainder of his earthly life and the eternity beyond, "I will praise thy name for ever and ever", v. 2. The opening words in verse 2 reveal the consequent short-time resolve to which the psalmist commits himself, "*Every day* will I bless thee". This emphasizes an aspect of praise which we have encountered before, that praise should not ebb and flow according to our experiences or feelings, taken up with cares, griefs or disappointments.

We are unlikely to feel like singing all the time, but should resolve to praise the Lord despite any disinclination we may experience. Let us find fuel with which to feed the flames of our worship by meditating on the powerful words, "*Great is the Lord, and greatly to be praised*", v. 3.

Living as we do in the full-orbed glories of the gospel era, we can identify how the greatness of God characterizes every aspect of His saving work. Referring to the incarnation, Paul wrote, "*great is the mystery of godliness*: God was manifest in the flesh", 1 Tim. 3. 16. The angel of the Lord told Mary of the coming One, "*He shall be great*, and shall be called the Son of the Highest", Luke 1. 32. Referring to His arrival in Galilee, Matthew wrote, "The people which sat in darkness saw *great light*", Matt 4. 16. Mark wrote that "the wind ceased, and there was *a great calm*", Mark 4. 39. The healed demoniac published in Gadara "how *great things* Jesus had done for him", 5. 20. In a parable, the Lord hinted at the cost of our redemption by referring to "one pearl of *great price*", Matt. 13. 46. As He prayed in Gethsemane, "his sweat was as it were *great drops of blood* falling down to the ground", Luke 22. 44. We also read of "*great salvation*", Heb. 2. 3; of the "*great Shepherd*", 13. 20; of our "*great high priest*", 4. 14; and of "*great and precious promises*", 2 Pet. 1. 4.

Surely we should endorse from our hearts, "Bless the Lord, O my soul. *O Lord my God, thou art very great*; thou art clothed with honour and majesty", Psa. 104. 1.

"*God ... is rich in mercy, for* his great love *wherewith he loved us*", Eph. 2. 4.

READING: **Psalm 145**

UPHELD AND PRESERVED

TWO DAYS ago, we noticed seven statements in this psalm which describe divine attributes and which inspired the gratitude and worship of the writer. These statements are of two kinds, the first five telling us *what the Lord is*, and the other two *what the Lord does*. We now consider these other two statements, what He does on behalf of His people.

(i) "The Lord upholdeth all that fall, and raiseth up all those that be bowed down", v. 14. As members of a fallen race, believers are liable to stumble on the Christian pathway. There are various reasons for this. One Christian may put "a stumblingblock or an occasion to fall in his brother's way", Rom. 14. 13. A novice may be given recognition as an elder in a local church prematurely, causing him to be lifted up with pride and so "fall into the condemnation of the devil", 1 Tim. 3. 6. A believer who becomes covetous of riches may "fall into temptation and a snare", 6. 9. A Christian whose speech is not scrupulously honest may "fall into condemnation", James 5. 12. And perhaps our greatest danger is self-confidence, referred to by Paul when he wrote, "Wherefore let him that thinketh he standeth take heed lest he fall", 1 Cor. 10. 12.

(ii) "The Lord preserveth all them that love him: but all the wicked will he destroy", v. 20. The word "preserve" translates a Hebrew word whose root-meaning is "to hedge about", i.e. to guard, protect. Believers are under the protection of the Almighty God of the universe. This accounts for Paul's majestic statement of assurance, "For I am persuaded, that neither death, nor life, nor angels, nor principalities, nor powers, nor things present, nor things to come, nor height, nor depth, nor any other creature, shall be able to separate us from the love of God, which is in Christ Jesus our Lord", Rom. 8. 38-39.

Taking these two verses together, it is clear that our liability to stumble and fall should keep us humble and trusting as we tread life's pathway, but that our final and eternal security in Christ is unassailable.

"Now unto him that is able to keep you from falling, and to present you faultless before the presence of his glory with exceeding joy, to the only wise God our Saviour, be glory and majesty, dominion and power, both now and ever", Jude 24-25.

Glory

GLORY IS THE public expression of greatness, Gen. 31. 1; 45.
13. Paul's Epistle to the Romans gives us a short history of the
glory of God. In chapter 1, he notes that there was a time when
man knew God, but "they glorified him not as God ... Professing themselves to be wise, they became fools, and changed
the glory of ... God", vv. 21-23. Ever since, man has consistently "come short of the glory of God", 3. 23. This latter
expression tells us than man's aim and target in life should be
the glory of God. However, all his efforts fall short of this
standard, just as an arrow or a javelin falls short of a target
because the sportsman involved has insufficient strength,
however good his aim may be.

What man in the flesh is not able to do, the man saved by
faith can do. The example is Abraham, who according to
Romans 4. 20, "staggered not at the promise of God through
unbelief; but was strong in faith, giving glory of God". God's
purposes extended further, and Abraham's descendants were
called to a privileged position, for "Israelites ... to whom
pertained the glory", 9. 4. Indeed, the first mention of the
glory of God is with respect to Israel; see Exod. 16. 10.

Spiritual men in Israel always realized their great privilege,
as related to Isaiah, "But now thus saith the Lord that created
thee, O Jacob, and he that formed thee, O Israel, Fear not: for
I have redeemed thee, I have called thee by thy name; thou art
mine ... for I have created him for my glory", Isa. 43. 1, 7.

God's glory (expressed as a bright, supernatural light) was
associated with the tabernacle, Exod. 40. 34, and later with the
temple, 1 Kings 8. 11. Eventually however, the glory departed
because of the nation's sin; see 1 Sam. 4. 21 and Ezek. 39. 21.
One day, however, it is yet to return to a restored Israel, Ezek.
43. 2.

Moses besought God to show him His glory, Exod. 33. 18;
he was granted his desire, and the vision left its mark on him
for some time, 34. 29. Here in the Psalms, David and the other
psalmists, representing often only a minority in Israel, sought
to extol the greatness of God, and to glorify Him.

Today, we too have the privilege of glorifying God. Paul
goes on in Romans to state our position, "that ye may with one
mind and one mouth glorify God, even the Father of our Lord
Jesus Christ ... that the Gentiles might glorify God for his
mercy", Rom. 15. 6, 9.

READING: **Psalm 8**

GLORY ABOVE THE HEAVENS

DAVID, the faithful Israelite, begins this psalm by linking three things: God's covenant people (seen in the word "our" in v. 1); His glory set above the heavens, and His Name exalted in all the earth. This expanding thought (Israel, the earth, the heavens) takes in the great sweep of David's appreciation of his God. Immediately following, however, comes his realization that things are not as they should be, for God has to take unusual steps to establish His purposes. The simple, unaffected words of a two-or-three year old illustrate God's use of "foolish things ... to confound the wise" and "things which are not, to bring to nought things that are", 1 Cor. 1. 26-29. God's enemies are overcome by His power displayed in weak things; David's experience with Goliath is an example of this.

Turning his eyes heavenward, David contemplates the grandeur of the night sky, noting the detail that God has worked into the moon and the stars. He cannot but wonder again at the great condescension of God in thinking and caring for frail mortal men, who are only the descendants of Adam. Adam's original privileges made him king of the natural world; crowned with the glory and honour of being God's representative on earth. Sin, however, snatched the crown away and stripped him of his glory, leaving him without his spiritual crown and covering. Man was expelled from Eden, having lost his dominion; hence David had to fight off a lion and a bear.

When the writer to the Hebrews takes up the subject of dominion in "the world to come" (the millennium), 2. 5, he too notes that in the present world man does not have dominion. Like David, however, he looks to heaven, not now seeing the stars, but looking beyond he sees "Jesus ... crowned with glory and honour", v. 9. The Lord Jesus Christ, though rejected down here, is honoured in heaven. Because of His death, the Father is able to bring many sons to glory, not now as sons of Adam who had lost his glory, but as those on their way to share glory with the Captain of their salvation. Let us therefore look up into heaven, seeing there the spiritual equivalent of David's "glory above the heavens", that is, seeing "the glory of God in the face of Jesus Christ", 2 Cor. 4. 6, and seeing Him "let us run with patience the race that is set before us", Heb. 12. 1-3.

June 2nd

READING: **Psalm 19**

THE HEAVENS DECLARE THE GLORY OF GOD

IN THE FIRST four verses of this psalm, David adds to his statement of Psalm 8 that God has set His glory above the heavens by telling us that the heavens themselves demonstrate this fact. They declare or show and utter God's existence and His power. The language of the heavens is universal, being able to communicate equally to all men, irrespective of their spoken language, in a voice that is everywhere heard, v. 3.

The N.T. bears out this same truth. The apostle Paul explains in Romans 1 that "the invisible things of him ... are clearly seen, being understood by the things that are made, even his eternal power and Godhead"; however, "when they knew God, they glorified him not as God ... and changed the glory of ... God into an image", 1. 19-23. The images were of earthly things, because they refused the message from the heavens. The truth of God was changed "into a lie, and (they) worshipped and served the creature more than the Creator", vv. 24-25.

Although man can know about God's existence and power through creation, and although his conscience will tell him that he is a sinner, Rom. 2. 15, he can know no more, and in particular he has no means of finding his way back to God. The latter half of our psalm shows that God's Word is the only source of such knowledge, for "the law of God is perfect, converting the soul", v. 7. The Word of God brings the will of God before us in different ways as expressed in the different words used to describe it; i.e., law, testimony, precepts, commandments, judgments, etc. These are amplified in Psalm 119, of which the latter half of Psalm 19 is a miniature.

The Word of God brings about a change in people: it makes them wise; it rejoices the heart and enlightens the (spiritual) eyes. The child of God today should desire His Word more than he or she would desire the most valuable things (much fine gold, v. 10), or the sweetest things obtainable (the droppings of the honeycomb). Peter tells us similarly that we should "desire the sincere (i.e., unadulterated) milk of the word", 1 Pet. 2. 2. This milk is unaffected by the contamination in the world. Proper use of the Bible warns the servant of God down here, and gives him the assurance of reward in a day to come. Note verses 11-14 of this psalm.

READING: **Psalm 24**

WHO IS THE KING OF GLORY?

WE START today by looking, not now at the heavens, but at the world around us. David informs us that the earth, its fulness and its dwellers, all belong to God. However, in this vast earth, there was only one place where God had placed His name, Deut. 26. 2; then it was within Jerusalem where His ark was to rest, that is, mount Zion. In this psalm, David is very probably referring to "the inauguration of the newly captured fortress of Zion as the final resting-place of the ark, Jehovah's earthly throne"; cf. 2 Sam. 5. 7; 6. 16.

Practical holiness is always necessary for those approaching God (see vv. 3-4, and also Matt. 5. 8). As we saw yesterday, the Word of God rightly used can bring about the right condition of heart and life. Approach brings blessing from the Lord, v. 5. Seeking Him should have been Jacob's (that is, the nation of Israel by the grace of God) occupation, v. 6 R.V.

The words of verse 7 tell us that either in a physical or a moral sense the gates and ancient doors of Zion were too low for the triumphal procession bringing in the ark. God, who dwelt between the cherubim upon the ark, 2 Kings 19. 15, unseen but for the display of His glory seen in the bright light often associated with the ark, was taking up royal residence. He is the King of glory, strong and mighty in battle; He is the Lord of hosts in command of all His earthly and heavenly armies.

The prophetic application of this psalm is the coming back of the Lord Jesus in glory to this earth. He was the rejected King at His first coming, but "he must reign", 1 Cor. 15. 25, claiming His rightful place as Creator of all, Col. 1. 16.

This earth now awaits its King and those who are coming with Him, "For the earnest expectation of the creature (that is, creation) waiteth for the manifestation of the sons of God ... For we know that the whole creation groaneth and travaileth together in pain together until now", Rom. 8. 19, 22. At His coming, creation "shall be delivered from the bondage of corruption into the glorious liberty of the children of God", v. 21. In that day, the mighty King of glory, the Lord Jesus Christ, will liberate creation. He has reconciled all things by His death on the cross, and at His coming will bring into effect the great benefits of His work, Col. 1. 13.

READING: **Psalm 26**

THE TABERNACLE OF THY GLORY

WE HAVE seen that the God who is "higher than the highest", Eccl. 5. 8, and whom the "heaven of heavens cannot contain", 1 Kings 8. 27, has an earthly dwelling place, "thy house, and the tabernacle of thy glory", v. 8 R.V. marg. The godly man will always love such a place, and the spiritual Israelite who already knows that God created the nation for His glory, Isa. 43. 7, will seek the place of God's glory. Although he sees God's glory in the heavens, Psas. 8 & 19, and the earth, Psa. 24, he nevertheless wants to be in the place of the immediate presence of God.

In the presence of God, the state of heart of such a person is examined in this psalm. As far as he is aware, the psalmist's way of life is one of integrity and trust. His confidence that his future life will be lived at the same high level is based solely on his trust in the Lord. Even though as far as he knows his conscience and heart are right with God, nevertheless he wants the benefit of divine examination.

His knowledge of the Word of God assures him of God's lovingkindness, and brings him a knowledge of the truth of God, and like the man in Psalm 1, this knowledge reflects itself in his relationship with those who think otherwise. He does not spend time unnecessarily in their company, neither does he have close relationships with them.

His walk of sincerity and separation makes him suitable for the divine presence, "so will I compass thine altar, O Lord", v. 6. This place of worship also becomes the place of publishing and telling the wondrous works of God. It is also the place of fellowship with the likeminded, as verse 12 says, "in the congregations will I bless the Lord".

Just as the tabernacle was the place where God's glory was seen, so too should the local church show forth His glory today; He has brought us out from the power of darkness into light, Col. 1. 13; Rom. 15. 6. The behaviour of individuals should be like David's; not only should they know how to "behave themselves in the house of God", 1 Tim. 3. 15, but should also have a good testimony outside, being epistles "known and read of all men", 2 Cor. 3. 2. Our walk should be "in wisdom toward them that are without", Col. 4. 5.

READING: **Psalm 29**

IN HIS TEMPLE EVERYTHING SAITH GLORY

DAVID ONCE again sees the glory of God in His creation and in His house, and celebrates it in both, calling upon others to do so also, v. 1 R.V. marg.

Glory and strength are to be given (attributed) to the Lord because it is due to Him. Man's dues as creature are here plainly stated. To display His glory is the clear aim of man, even though he constantly comes short of it, Rom. 3. 23.

Giving this glory and strength leads to worship, that is, expressing to God our appreciation of all that He is and has done. Once again though, we learn that there must be a proper spiritual environment of worship, v. 2. This latter expression is rendered "in his glorious sanctuary" in the A.V. margin, and "in holy array" in the R.V. margin. Putting all these thoughts together, and bearing in mind other scriptural teaching, we see that worship is to be carried out in the right place, and also in the right way. For us today, we remember the words of the Lord Jesus that those who worship the Father must do so in spirit and in truth, John 4. 24.

The greatness and glory of God in creation is seen in this psalm predominantly in the fierce thunder storms that are experienced in the Middle East. To David it was the glory of God that thundered, being "the voice of the Lord ... full of majesty", vv. 3-4. It had powerful effects on the mightiest of trees, the cedars of Lebanon and on the highest mountains, Lebanon and Sirion (i.e., Hermon). It is seen to the west of Israel (the many waters of the Mediterranean), to the east (the wilderness, v. 8), to the south (the wilderness of Kadesh) and to the north (Lebanon and Hermon).

Quite suddenly, David moves his attention to the anticipated temple, where "everything saith, glory", v. 9 R.V. Study of the tabernacle and temple is hence very rewarding! David's mind moves again, this time back to the flood, where the Lord sat as King, v. 10 R.V., and eventually on to peace at the end of the psalm.

Through the cross of the Lord Jesus Christ, peace has been made, Col. 1. 20. He left this peace to His own, John 14. 27, so that amidst the thunder storms of life, they can enjoy peace with God, the One who controls the thunder to His glory.

June 6th

READING: **Psalm 45**

THE KING'S DAUGHTER IS ALL GLORIOUS

THIS PSALM has been called *Messiah's Millennial Marriage*; although its background is a real royal marriage (probably the marriage of Hezekiah to Hephzi-bah, 2 Kings 21. 1), it obviously rises higher and anticipates Messiah's happy reunion with His own who previously had not received Him, John 1. 11. The writer of the psalm, one of the sons of Korah, is a descendant of a rebel, now responding spiritually to the divine purpose. His spiritual enthusiasm with his subject is obvious—he writes readily, using material overflowing from his heart.

The Person in the psalmist's mind is the Lord Jesus Christ preparing to come to earth again. While upon earth, He was known for His gracious words, but when He comes again it will be in power, Rev. 19. 16. He will not ride on the colt of an ass in lowly guise, Mark 11. 7, but will come forth in glory and majesty, and in His Majesty He will ride prosperously, Psa. 45. 3. He will deal with His enemies, and set up His divine everlasting kingdom, "Thy throne, O God, is for ever and ever", v. 6. It will be a time of equity, v. 6 R.V., when He will be anointed as the divine Prophet, Priest and King in that day, v. 7, enjoying universal praise.

In verse 10, we turn to the bride preparing herself for the arrival of the bridegroom. She is beautiful, her attire being inwrought with gold, v. 13. She will be spiritually productive, attracting the attention of all the earth, vv. 16-17.

But now there is another bride in view in the purpose of God. The Church is the bride of Christ, Rev. 21. 2, and she is to expect the soon arrival of the Bridegroom. Until that arrival, she is in a sense preparing her wedding attire herself, this being the righteousnesses of the saints; see Rev. 19. 8. This too, like Israel's future wedding dress, will be beautiful, that is, the King's daughter is all glorious within (the inner part of the palace): her clothing is inwrought with gold. She shall be led unto the King in embroidered work, vv. 13-14 R.V. and margin. What are we contributing to the garment of the bride of Christ?; what righteous acts are we performing that we embroidered in, reflecting in a future day the glory of Christ like the "inwrought gold"?

172

READING: **Psalm 50**

THANKSGIVING GLORIFIETH ME

THE WRITER of this psalm, Asaph (meaning, gatherer) was not very well known in O.T. history; nevertheless, he was quite busy in the service of God. He was one of the leaders of the temple choir, 1 Chron. 15. 17-19; chief minister before the ark, 16. 4-15; a prophet, 2 Chron. 29. 30; and a writer of over a dozen psalms, a poet.

The occasion that initiated this psalm is probably the time when the ark was installed on Zion, when God restated His claim on Israel. At that time, David, in the words of Psalm 105. 1-15, delivered the word of God to Israel, reminding them of their purpose as God's people witnessing for Him in this world.

Here in Psalm 50, Asaph too is used by God to tell Israel His thoughts concerning them and the nations around. First we have a majestic view of God coming as Judge. He is Judge of all the earth in general, Gen. 18. 25, and of His people in particular. The judgment depicted here clearly foreshadows that future day when God will "judge the world ... by that man whom he hath ordained", Acts 17. 31. The scene of judgment here is Zion, which is "the perfection of beauty", from where "God hath shined forth", v. 2 R.V. Verse 3 tells us that the God who had previously been silent, now comes out publicly, being accompanied by fire (itself a type of judgment).

God's dealings with His people are on the basis of the covenant between them, whereas His dealings with the ungodly are on the basis of their works. His people are His saints, the godly or favoured ones; the recipients of His lovingkindness, who in turn exhibit it to others. This, like all the covenants, is based on sacrifice: Noah, Gen. 9. 9; Abraham, 15. 10-18; Moses, Exod. 24. 8; the new covenant, Matt. 26. 27-28.

God is now waiting to be called upon in the day of trouble; then "I will deliver thee, and thou shalt glorify me", v. 15. They will then sacrifice to God, and "whoso offereth the sacrifice of thanksgiving glorifieth me", v. 23 R.V.

For us today the same is true: "By him therefore let us offer the sacrifice of praise to God continually, that is, the fruit of our lips giving thanks to his name", Heb. 13. 15. All prayer should contain thanksgiving, as Paul states many times, Phil. 4. 6; Col. 2. 7; 1 Tim. 4. 3.

June 8th

READING: Psalm 57

LET THY GLORY BE ABOVE THE EARTH

THE HISTORICAL background to this psalm takes us back to the time when David was pursued by Saul, and was in danger of his life. When no human agency could help, David turns naturally to God. He is a refuge, as a mother eagle is to her defenceless chicks; she overshadows them with her wings. The people of God are not immune to the calamities of life, but He keeps them safe "until the calamities be overpast", v. 1.

David's God is "God Most High", v. 2 R.V., who "performeth all things" for him. Abram knew God as "the most high God", Gen. 14. 20, 22. Although this God is in heaven, He can send help all the way down to David's hiding place to save him. Not only will David's life be preserved, but his place in God's plans will be vindicated, for "God shall send forth his mercy and his truth", v. 3, in spite of savage inflamed men.

In the midst of all His personal problems, David turns his eyes to heaven and says, "Be thou exalted, O God, above the heavens; let thy glory be above all the earth", v. 5. Between the sharp sword of verse 4 and the net of verse 6, David rises above all his own troubles to praise God. Eventually, God justifies His persecuted servant, by turning the misfortunes planned for him by his enemies back onto themselves, v. 6.

The confidence that David has in his God means that with repeated confidence he is able to say, "my heart is fixed", v. 7, and again he repeats his wish to sing praises to his God. He especially praises God for His mercy and truth; cf.v. 3 with v. 10. He finishes his praise by asking that God's glory will be above all the earth, v. 11. It is one thing knowing oneself that God's glory is in the heavens and on the earth, but how much greater it is to desire that others will become aware of it for themselves, and to use all one's powers to bring this situation about.

Our knowledge of God through the Lord Jesus Christ is greater than David's, yet how often his appreciation of God in day-to-day things surpasses our own. His ability to rise above his greatest personal trials to praise his God challenges us in our self-centredness. The apostle Paul in his sufferings for Christ looked not for his own ease, but for the thanksgiving of many to redound to the glory of God, 2 Cor. 4. 15.

READING: **Psalm 72**

THE EARTH FILLED WITH HIS GLORY

THIS PRAYER of David for his son Solomon has been prayed many times by parents wanting their children to do better than themselves. David, although a man of war, took no pleasure in it, but for his son requested "abundance of peace". David had suffered many personal injustices, but these had not turned him into a bitter man, rather it made him more sympathetic of others. He had been poor and of a humble background himself, so he knew the disadvantages of poverty in terms of justice being done. He had lived in fear of his life and knew that fear of God alone was desirable.

Interwoven into the psalm are prayers for spiritual, social and material wellbeing. The geographical extent of the kingdom was important, because it was delineated by divine decree.

The ideal king takes a personal interest in his subjects, even the most insignificant, for "precious shall their blood (i.e., life) be in his sight", v. 14.

David's hopes clearly transcend the kingdom of Solomon, and pass on to the kingdom of Messiah the King, the Lord Jesus Christ. Today, we know Him as the perfect Saviour who knows every man, John 2. 24, and more particularly knows His sheep by name, 10. 3. Their lives are so precious to Him that His precious blood was shed for them, 1 Pet. 1. 19. Thus we have the privilege of knowing the character of earth's coming King, who will fulfil the hopes of the psalmist completely. Solomon started well but failed; the Lord Jesus will never fail.

The spiritual conditions of the coming kingdom are set out in the last few verses of the psalm: God's wondrous works will be acknowledged, His glorious name will be known and the end result will be the original purpose of God fulfilled, "Let the whole earth be filled with his glory", v. 19.

David's prayer for peace is reflected in Paul's instructions about the contents of prayers, namely, "prayers ... for kings, and for all that are in authority; that we may lead a quiet and peaceable life in all godliness and honesty", 1 Tim. 2. 1-2. Our prayers can have more influence than the votes of the men of this world, for men cannot guarantee peace in our time, but the "powers that be" are the ministers of God, Rom. 13. 1-7.

June 10th

READING: **Psalm 73**

THOU SHALT RECEIVE ME TO GLORY

WHILE THE previous psalm describes the ideal conditions that will prevail in the coming kingdom, when the glory of God will be universal, the psalmist here looks honestly at the godly and the ungodly and sees the failures of both. The difference between the godly Asaph and the ungodly around him in his day was that Asaph knew where to find a divine remedy, whereas the ungodly did not want to learn anything from God.

Asaph's faith says, "surely God is good to Israel", but his sight sees that the wicked seemed to be able to get away with injustice, and to live and die prosperously. Their ill-gotten gains seem to cushion them from the problems of life, common to others, v. 5, and they seem to be able to scoff at spiritual things with impunity, vv. 8-11.

This had brought initial confusion to Asaph's mind, and he admits "my feet were almost gone; my steps had well nigh slipped", v. 2. His spiritual exercises did not seem to excuse him from problems, vv. 13-14. All was confusion until he went into the sanctuary of God to meet with Him; there he considered the latter end of the wicked. There the whole picture changed: it was now the ungodly in the slippery place. In fact, God cast them down to ruins, v. 18 R.V. marg. The riches of this life were replaced by the ruins of the next.

Asaph frankly admits that his own ignorance had caused his confusion. He had been walking by sight, but he was now walking by faith. His slipping was ended, and he could say, "I am continually with thee: thou hast holden me by my right hand ... Thou shalt guide me with thy counsel", vv. 23-24. If his life was now satisfactory, then equally his future was safe, for afterward God would "receive me to glory ... Whom have I in heaven but thee", vv. 24-25. For Asaph, even if the earth was not yet filled with the glory of God, he was going to the place called "glory". We today are among the many sons who are being brought to glory, Heb. 2. 10. On the way, we might have to experience the chastening hand of God, 12. 6; this might make our lives appear more difficult than those of the ungodly, but the answer is in the sanctuary, and concerns the respective ends of the believer and the unbeliever; indeed, it is a matter of heaven and hell.

June 11th

READING: **Psalm 76**

MORE GLORIOUS THAN THE MOUNTAINS

GOD'S COVENANT people knew His name, His dwelling place, and His power, vv. 1-3. These three sum up all that a man needs to know about his God. "His name" is more than a designation to distinguish the God of Israel from the gods of the nations, for in the Bible a person's name implies his character, in the same way as we speak today of a man's "good name".

God's character is "more glorious than the mountains of prey". If we accept that this psalm was written to commemorate the taking of Jebus, the mountainous stronghold that became mount Zion, then the "mountains of prey" refer to the impregnable fortress hitherto unconquered. God always conquers His dwelling place, taking it from the power of an enemy who relinquishes it unwillingly.

The spoken rebuke from the God of Jacob is enough to stop and render powerless the most formidable foe, v. 6. God acts in grace towards His own (remember Jacob), but in judgment towards His enemies, vv. 7-9. He acts on behalf of "the meek (or lowly) of the earth", v. 9. Whenever the people of God acknowledge their own inadequacy in the face of a superior foe, God is always willing to act for them.

Such is the superiority of God in controlling the affairs of men, then even when in His permissive will He allows "the wrath of man" to manifest itself, even this will eventually praise Him. We have no greater example of this than in the cross; there the wrath of man was allowed its full course, and the Victim was God's own Son. However, Calvary now brings great praise to Him in heaven and on earth. Many times since there have been instances of temporary trouble for the people of God turning eventually to perpetual praise to Him. God is indeed "more glorious and excellent" than all His enemies; although He allows their wrath, He does not allow it to run its full course for the "remainder of wrath shalt thou restrain", v. 10. Although other translations vary slightly in this latter verse, it is nevertheless true that God overrules man's evil will. The Saul who breathed out threatenings and slaughter against the disciples, Acts 9. 1, became Paul the apostle "through the will of God", 1 Cor. 1. 1. Our response is that of the psalmist, "let all ... bring presents unto him", v. 11.

177

READING: **Psalm 78. 1-20, 58-62, 67-72**

HIS GLORY INTO THE ENEMY'S HAND

ASAPH WAS very much aware of his spiritual heritage. He would not have any law, v. 1; words, v. 2; parable, v. 3, or dark saying of old without having heard them or being told, v. 3. He sees also the value of passing them on to "the generation to come". He was conscious that this was not just a good idea, but rather a spiritual obligation, for the Lord had "established a testimony in Jacob, and appointed a law in Israel ... which he commanded our fathers, that they should make them known to their children: that the generation to come might know them", vv. 5-6. Thus there should be continuity of testimony. This was to include the good and the bad: the good things (like "hope in God", v. 7) were to be encouraged, while the bad things (like those seen in their forefathers who "kept not the covenant of God, and refused to walk in his law; and forgat his works, and his wonders that he had showed them", vv. 10-11) were to be forbidden.

In spite of this, the fathers still rebelled, vv. 17-18, and having seen all this they still dared to ask, "Can God furnish a table in the wilderness?", v. 19. The root cause was "because they believed not in God", v. 22. Their later history showed the same sad trend, v. 58. God's longsuffering is meant to lead men to repentance, Rom. 2. 4, but when repentance is wanting, God's anger eventually shows itself.

When this happened, the state religion became a mere sham, and God "forsook the tabernacle of Shiloh, the tent which he placed among men; and delivered his strength into captivity, and his glory into the enemy's hand", vv. 60-61. When the place of testimony became unsuitable, it was removed, even if it had been the place where His glory had been manifested.

The principles on which God operates never change. The need to educate the coming generation in spiritual truths is today entrusted to parents, Sunday School teachers and Bible Class leaders, etc. They have a Bible full of things to pass on: victories and defeats, joys and sorrows, blessings and curses. If this is not done, then local churches of the next generation might experience the ultimate sanction of the Lord upon them, namely, having the testimony removed; cf. vv. 60-62 with Rev. 2. 5.

READING: **Psalm 79**

HELP US FOR THE GLORY OF THY NAME

THE GOD who had conquered Zion, and who had protected Jerusalem for so long, had now allowed it to be captured and the temple defiled. We saw yesterday He is prepared to restrain the wrath of man against His people when they are meek and lowly; nevertheless when they become complacent about sin and haughty about their supposed impregnability, He will not contain His own wrath and His longsuffering becomes exhausted.

The psalmist's world lay in ruins around him, but his faith is still intact. He knew why disaster had struck, v. 5, but still believed that restoration was possible, and he eventually looks forward to a continuing healthy testimony, v. 13.

The basis for any appeal to God is seen in the realization and acknowledgement that everything involved was actually His: "thine inheritance; thy holy temple; thy servants; thy saints; thy people", vv. 1, 2, 10, 13. This resulted in His name being involved, vv. 6, 9. The only recourse now was a display of God's might, "thy wrath; thy power", vv. 6, 11. This would result eventually in "thy praise", v. 13.

The psalmist was concerned for God's good name. True, it had been brought into disrepute by His own people and His anger was against them, v. 5, but the continual disparagement by the surrounding nations was directed not only against them, but also against their God. These nations have not called upon God's name, v. 6, and they say, "Where is their God?". The cry was therefore "Help us, O God of our salvation, for the glory of thy name: and deliver us, and purge away our sins, for thy name's sake", v. 9. The glory of God's name was at stake. Its holiness had been compromised by His own people's sin. This needed to be purged away; but the glory of His name required that He act against "the heathen", v. 10. The end result will be the continual praise to God that He alone merits.

God still acts to preserve the glory of His name. In our own day, He will allow problems and even death to enter, so as to chasten His people if they fail to realize the sanctity of His name. This indeed happened at Corinth, 1 Cor. 11. 29-30. If holiness does not characterize His house, then He will take steps to restore the situation, 1 Pet. 4. 17. He can also move against unbelievers if they violate His house, 2 Tim. 4. 14.

June 14th

READING: **Psalm 84**

THE LORD WILL GIVE GRACE AND GLORY

IF ALL THE people of Israel had the thoughts about God's dwelling place possessed by the writer of this psalm, then Psalm 79 would never have been written. The tabernacles (dwelling places) of the Lord of hosts were thought to be "lovely", v. 1 R.V. marg. The plural refers to the many parts of the one building, namely, the temple. For some reason, the writer is unable for the moment to be at the temple, but his whole being cried out to be there, not for the ritual, but for "the living God", who promised to meet His people there.

The psalm was "of the sons of Korah". Korah had led the rebellion against Moses, God's representative, and consequently Korah came under the judgment of God; see Num. 16. However the grace of God retrieved the situation for Korah's descendants, amongst whom was the writer of this psalm.

He desires for himself the situation enjoyed by the swallow that had nested in the temple. It had constant unhindered access to the temple, and in particular to its altars. The brazen altar was the place where God was completely satisfied with the burnt offering, while the golden altar was the place where He was completely delighted—both speaking of the sacrifice of the Lord Jesus Christ, Eph. 5. 2.

For the writer who did not dwell in the temple, v. 4, even "a day in thy courts is better than a thousand", v. 10. He would rather have the menial task of doorkeeper (or, as some commentators prefer, "a singer standing on the threshold"), than to be something or someone among the wicked.

The reason for this happiness in a lowly position is given in verse 11: "For the Lord God is a sun and shield: the Lord will give grace and glory". Every possible material and spiritual need is catered for by his God. The God of glory will give glory to His people. Indeed, "no good thing will he withhold from them that walk uprightly" ; cf. Phil. 4. 19. Blessed indeed is the man who trusts in Him, v. 12.

Today we too are blessed, but our blessings are spiritual. We are blessed with all spiritual blessings in heavenly places in Christ, Eph. 1. 3. We too enjoy divine protection, "for I am persuaded ... (that nothing) ... shall be able to separate us from the love of God, which is in Christ Jesus", Rom. 8. 38-39.

June 15th

READING: **Psalm 85**

THAT GLORY MAY DWELL IN OUR LAND

LIKE yesterday's psalm, this psalm is of (or for) the sons of Korah. The favourable times promised in the previous psalm have not continued because there had been wilful disobedience and no trust in the Lord of hosts, Psa. 84. 12.

The writer recalls that in the past God had acted favourably to His land and its rebellious people. He had forgiven their iniquity and covered all their sin, vv. 1-2. Now some new sin had distanced the people from their God, who in His indignation had chastened them. However, He is still "the God of our salvation", who was yet able to bring revival to His people, vv. 4, 6. The mercy of God in salvation was longed for, v. 7; God is certain to respond to such a request. When sin and failure are acknowledged, He is swift to return His withdrawn blessings. He is bound to speak, and then with a message of peace. However, along with the blessing comes a warning, "But let them not turn again to folly", v. 8.

The end result of salvation is glory, "salvation ... that glory may dwell in our land". In this favoured state, every blessing is enjoyed; there is complete harmony between things hitherto estranged, v. 10, and then heaven and earth too will be reconciled, v. 11. "Yea, the Lord shall give that which is good; and our land shall yield her increase", v. 12. All this blessing will take place in the millennium.

There must be revival among the people of God before there can be glory in the land. If we are concerned about the state of spiritual things in our land, then we must first look at the state of things in our own hearts. God must deal with His people before He can use them.

When God moves, "righteousness shall go before him; and shall make his footsteps a way to walk in", v. 13 R.V. The word footstep occurs three times in our N.T.: in Romans 4. 12 we are told of those "who also walk in the steps of that faith of our father Abraham"; these are the footsteps of saving faith left firmly implanted in the O.T. Paul's footprints became the guide for Titus' selfless service in 2 Corinthians 12. 18. And those supreme footsteps of the Lord Jesus Christ are plainly seen in 1 Peter 2. 21, showing us the path of suffering for righteousness sake; in them may we plant our own.

June 16th

READING: **Psalm 86**

I WILL GLORIFY THY NAME

ANY MISGIVINGS that a reader of verse 2 of this psalm might have in thinking that David was self-righteous ("I am holy"), are soon dispelled by reading the rest of the psalm. It is a cry for help from one who knows his own failings and his enemies, but more importantly, from one who knows God. Because he knows himself so well, he acknowledges his trust in God, v. 2; his need of mercy, v. 3; and forgiveness, v. 5. He knows his enemies are proud, violent, without fear of God, vv. 14, 17.

David's God was his source of rejoicing; cf. Phil. 4. 4. He is good, v. 5, and is not to be compared with the gods of the surrounding nations, v. 8. David's view of God was not limited to national boundaries. His was no national deity; He had made the world, and He merited universal praise. Thus David anticipated that one day "All nations ... shall come and worship before thee, O Lord; and shall glorify thy name. For thou art great", vv. 9, 10. One day there will be an international anthem of glory to God. Together with "Glory to God in the highest", Luke 2. 14, this praise in Psalm 86 will make up the true universal praise to God.

This great anticipation of David has an immediate practical effect: he asks for help for his everyday life. In particular, he prays that God would "unite my heart to fear thy name", v. 11. He wanted his "whole heart", v. 12 R.V., to praise God. The heart, as the seat of our deepest thoughts and desires, has many conflicting forces within it. For the believer today, this is always true, and we need to have the peace of Christ arbitrating in our hearts, Col. 3. 15 *lit.*, between any interests that seem to be conflicting.

What David was anticipating would happen at some time in the distant future. However, he makes every effort to see it coming about to some extent in his own lifetime, "I will glorify thy name", v. 12. David's hope and ours is tied up in the same Person, the Lord Jesus Christ. As believers, our hope is that soon we shall be like Him, 1 John 3. 2, with bodies like unto his body of glory, Phil. 3. 21. Until then, we are not complacent about our present condition. We want to "put ... on the Lord Jesus Christ", Rom. 13. 14, so that we can glorify God in our bodies and in our spirits which are God's, 1 Cor. 6. 20.

June 17th

READING: **Psalm 89. 1-4, 14-37**

THY GLORY IS THEIR STRENGTH

IN OUR READINGS today, we see the perfect balance between the promises, the warnings and the mercy of God. The promises of God are based on His power, that is, His ability to fulfil them. The warnings of God are based on His holiness, but His mercy is always available to complement them. It is this mercy that we are solely dependent upon.

The character of David's throne was to be derived from that of God's throne, "Justice and judgment are the habitation of thy throne; mercy and truth shall go before thy face", v. 14. The king and people who followed these principles and relied on God for their strength and defence were assured of continued joy and blessing, v. 16. "For thou art the glory of their strength", v. 17. Reliance on God, publicly expressed, brings glory to Him.

The specific blessings promised to David are enumerated in verses 19-29. They culminate in verse 27, where David is made "firstborn, higher than the kings of the earth". We see here an interesting and instructive example of the important word "firstborn", which does not mean born first, but rather to be preeminent in a certain sphere. This is followed by the restatement of God's promised faithfulness to the Davidic dynasty, vv. 28-29.

Human responsibility immediately follows the divine promise, "If his (David's) children forsake my law, and walk not in my judgments; if they break my statutes, and keep not my commandments; then will I visit their transgression with the rod, and their iniquity with stripes", vv. 30-32. However, God goes on to say that "my lovingkindness will I not utterly take from him, nor suffer my faithfulness to fail", v. 33.

Our blessings came about by our association with God's Firstborn, the Lord Jesus Christ. As we have seen, "firstborn" emphasizes supremacy. The Lord Jesus' supremacy over all things arises from His position in relation to creation and resurrection, being firstborn of both, Col. 1. 15, 18.

Our blessings are thus assured because, even if we are unfaithful, "he abideth faithful", 2 Tim. 2. 13. However, like unfaithful Israel, we too can be visited "with the rod", for "whom the Lord loveth he chasteneth, and scourgeth every son whom he receiveth", Heb. 12. 6.

June 18th

READING: **Psalm 90**

LET THY GLORY APPEAR

THIS "prayer of Moses, the man of God" is the oldest psalm of all. Moses' great personal desire was to be shown the glory of God, Exod 33. 18. God placed him in the cleft of the rock, and allowed His glory to pass by, 33. 22. This glory lingered on in his face, although he was unaware of it, 34. 29, and his appearance so alarmed the Israelites that he had to wear a veil until his face returned to its normal condition, 34. 30-35; compare this with the unfading glory in the unveiled face of the Lord Jesus Christ, 2 Cor. 4. 6.

Another of Moses' great desires was that those coming after him would also have a sight of God's glory, v. 16. His own knowledge of God was as the eternal God and Creator, vv. 2-4, to whom time offers no limitation; for example, He is able to compress a thousand years to a day or even a few hours, v. 4; see also 2 Peter 3. 8. Man's time is limited, his "threescore years and ten, or even by reason of strength fourscore years", v. 10 R.V., are "soon gone" and "we bring our years to an end as a tale that is told", v. 9 R.V., "so teach us to number our days, that we may get us an heart of wisdom", v. 12 R.V. The spiritual man thus has a true appreciation of his own life, but also of God's glory as seen by His works, v. 16. Such men can request that the beauty of the Lord our God be upon us".

The Israelites in Moses' day passed their years in wandering in the desert, because of their unbelief. Moses, however, knew that this would not last for ever, but that His glory would eventually be seen; he asked, "how long?", v. 11.

The Christian does not measure his or her days by the fact that death is coming, but that the Lord is coming, 1 Thess. 1. 10; 5. 23; 2 Thess. 2. 1. The Lord Jesus told many parables about those who would not be ready for His coming: not necessarily because they did not believe He would come, but that they had not appreciated the nearness of His coming. The spiritual man is ready for, and welcomes the coming of the Lord, Rev. 22. 20.

For unbelievers, the nearness of eternity is an unwelcome thought. The gospel awakens them to this, and thus "teaches them to number their days". The devil is ever ready to convince them otherwise, and to fill their lives with passing pleasures.

READING: **Psalm 96**

DECLARE HIS GLORY AMONG THE NATIONS

THE PSALM is based on the psalm of David recorded in 1 Chronicles 16. 7-36, when "David delivered first this psalm to thank the Lord into the hand of Asaph and his brethren". It was the occasion when the ark was brought to mount Zion.

The two psalms contain much of the glory of God. First David had a great desire that others should know about his God—"declare his glory among the heathen (nations, R.V.)", v. 3. His statement is backed by two great facts: first that His works are marvellous, and secondly that "all the gods of the peoples are things of nought", v. 5 R.V. marg. The greatness of God in making the heavens, v. 5, and the nothingness of the gods of the nations are to David irrefutable arguments for the superiority of Jehovah, the God of Israel. Thus he says, "give unto the Lord (Jehovah) the glory due unto his name", v. 8.

Israel had a place to meet God and to inquire of Him; this is described in verses 6, 8 as "his sanctuary" and "his courts". Here His character is shown forth as "honour and majesty", "strength and beauty", v. 6. Equally, those who come to worship must do so in the light of His character, and "bring an offering ... in the beauty of holiness", vv. 8-9.

Aaron's holy garments and those of his sons were "for glory and for beauty", Exod. 28. 2. These garments were to "consecrate him", 28. 3, that is, to make them holy, or to set apart for divine service. These garments were made of "gold, and blue, and purple, and scarlet, and fine linen", 28. 5, that is, the same material exactly as the tabernacle interior that surrounded them as they served. Thus Aaron had a beauty not his own, so that he was completely fitted for the place, for "holiness becometh thine house, O Lord, for ever", Psa. 93. 5.

Worship, as always, is followed by testimony, "O worship the Lord", v. 9, "say among the heathen, that the Lord reigneth", v. 10, and "the Lord ... cometh to judge the earth", v. 13.

God's gospel shows forth His glory; it is the "gospel of the glory of the blessed God", 1 Tim. 1. 11 Newberry marg.; see also 2 Cor. 4. 4. We too can worship God and bring our offerings, but we worship "in spirit and in truth", John 4. 24, and we offer "the sacrifice of praise". Our clothing is "the righteousness of God", garments of beauty for priests today.

READING: **Psalm 97**

ALL THE PEOPLES HAVE SEEN HIS GLORY

THE EXPECTATION of Psalm 96 is fulfilled in this psalm. The Coming One has arrived and is reigning. The Messiah, the divine King, is the Lord Jesus Christ who "must reign", 1 Cor. 15. 25, and the nation that had said "We will not have this man to reign over us", Luke 19. 14, has now seen the folly of her ways and gladly acknowledges Him.

In that day "the people" will see His glory and the heavens will "declare his righteousness", v. 6. Some will be ashamed, v. 7, while others will be glad, v. 8. When the Lord comes for us, the same situation will pertain; which group will we be in?

In verse 10, we have the memorable statement "Ye that love the Lord, hate evil". Those that love the Lord are His saints, His favoured ones, whom He preserves. For them, "Light is sown", v. 11. Just as the sower casts his seed, so the sun casts its beams for them. Gladness is sown in their heart and springs up; "Rejoice in the Lord ... and give thanks", v. 12.

The N.T. clearly teaches that believers will be associated with the Lord Jesus when He reigns on earth, 2 Tim. 2. 12; Rev. 5. 10; thus these Messianic psalms have a special interest for us. One of the problems of the Corinthian church was that they assumed such an air of spirituality that they behaved as if the kingdom had already come and they were reigning all on their own, even without the apostle and his coworkers, 1 Cor. 4. 8. Paul indeed looked forward to reigning with them, but for the moment there must be suffering, 4. 9-14. After suffering for Christ, comes reigning with Him, 2 Tim. 2. 12.

A willingness to suffer for Christ now arises from our love for Him which in turn is because of His love to us, 1 John 4. 19. If we, like the psalmist, "love the Lord" (cf. 1 Peter 1. 8), then we should love others also, 1 John 4. 21; Eph. 5. 25.

Love should lead to obedience, as the Lord Jesus said, "If ye love me, keep my commandments", John 14. 15, 23. These commandments are not burdensome, 1 John 5. 3, and thus offer no obstacle to reciprocal love, but rather they give us opportunities to express our appreciation to the One who "preserveth the souls of his saints; he delivereth them out of the hand of the wicked", Psa. 97. 10. May we love the things that He loves, and hate the things which He hates.

June 21st

READING: **Psalm 102**

SUFFERINGS AND GLORY

ACCORDING TO Hebrews 1. 10-12, this psalm has to do with the Lord Jesus Christ, God's Son, particularly as the Unchangeable One, vv. 25-27. Also "ought not Christ to have suffered ... and to enter into his glory?", Luke 24. 26, sufferings as in verses 1-11, and glory as in verses 12-16.

The psalmist's own sufferings and despair at the state of Zion (broken down, v. 14, and in need of divine mercy) will end one day, "the time to favour her ... is come", v. 13.

However, his present state is such that he is about to faint; he uses his last breath to pour out his complaint before the Lord (see the psalm's superscription). His distress is so great that he cannot eat, vv. 4-5, nor sleep, v. 7. He feels like a pelican and an owl (unclean creatures) in a place where there is no sustenance. He feels himself as a national representative, the object of God's indignation and wrath on sin—cast away.

His penitential prayer is heard, and the eternal God comes to his aid, who heard "the groaning of the prisoner; to loose those that are appointed to death", v. 20. The restored Israel will see that "the heathen shall fear the name of the Lord, and all the kings of the earth thy glory. When the Lord shall build up Zion, he shall appear in his glory", vv. 15-16. In that day, "the people ... shall praise the Lord", v. 18.

God does all this that men may "declare the name of the Lord in Zion", v. 21. The eternal nature of the Lord ensures the continuing of "the children of thy servants", v. 28. This reminds us that our position as believers is ensured by the One who "continueth ever ... Wherefore he is able also to save them to the uttermost that come unto God by him, seeing he ever liveth to make intercession for them", Heb. 7. 24-25.

In the direct quotation from this psalm in Hebrews 1. 10-12, we see the superiority of the Son of God over angels, "being made so much better than the angels", primarily because of His name, "a more excellent name than they", Heb. 1. 4. His name is "my Son", v. 5; "God", v. 8; "Lord", v. 10, the One who sits upon the divine throne, v. 13, and whom angels worship, v. 6; this is the One who suffered for sins once, 1 Pet. 3. 18, in order that we might share His glory for ever, 5. 1; Jude 24. "What a wonderful Saviour is Jesus my Lord".

June 22nd

READING: **Psalm 104. 1-5, 23-35**

THE LORD'S GLORY SHALL ENDURE FOR EVER

THE VERY GREATNESS of God, v. 1, arises from the fact that "He has clothed Himself with honour and majesty" (Heb.). Light is His garment, and He sets out earth and the heavens as a patriarch would set up his tent, vv. 2-3, and has the clouds for His chariot, and the wind for His path, v. 3.

We are totally dependant on water, but we can nevertheless be easily overcome by it, v. 9. Under God's hand, it is locally available to all, vv. 10-13. The end result is, "the earth is satisfied with the fruit of thy works". From the availability of water come "the grass ... and herb (vegetables) for the service of man; that he may bring forth food out of the earth; and wine that maketh glad the heart of man", vv. 14-15. He is also able to obtain "oil to make his face to shine (in the intense drying heat of Israel's summer), and bread which strengtheneth man's heart", v. 15. Thus all man's physical needs (bread and wine, water and oil) are divinely satisfied.

The great diversity, intricacy, and richness of His creation bring delight to the saint, v. 24. All aspects of man's present peaceful scientific pursuits are here; the marine biologist for instance would acknowledge "this great and wide sea, wherein are things creeping innumerable, both small and great beasts", v. 25, and in the sea, even man himself is active, for "There go the ships", v. 26.

Out of this great hymn of praise relating to creation comes the cry, "The glory of the Lord shall endure for ever", v. 31, "I will sing unto the Lord as long as I live: I will sing praise to my God while I have my being. My meditation of him shall be sweet", vv. 33-34. The sweet meditation is the same sweetness as that of the acceptable sacrifice which burned wholly away, sending up a sweet savour to God, Exod. 29. 25. The only dark blot on this fair scene "where every prospect pleases" is sin and those sinners ("and only man is vile") who show no interest in getting right with God. When sin is eliminated, v. 35, then comes the great and final "Hallelujah"!

All man's spiritual needs today are met in Christ, who is the Bread of life, John 6. 35, and gives the water of life freely, Rev. 22. 17. Our shining faces and glad hearts come from our sweet meditation of Him, not from anything down here.

READING: **Psalm 106**

THEY CHANGED THEIR GLORY

THIS PSALM records the continual cycle of rebellion and recovery, of sin and salvation, in Israel's history, The first episode, vv. 6-24, shows us the underlying causes, "We have sinned with our fathers, we have committed iniquity, we have done wickedly", v. 6. However, His people's failure did not frustrate God's salvation because His name was involved.

His power was manifested at the Red Sea, when He by the word of His power dried up the sea, led the people safely through, saved and redeemed them, v. 10, destroying the enemy at the same time. This spectacular deliverance meant that "there was not one (of the enemy) left", v. 11. "Then believed they his words; they sang his praise", v. 12. However, "They soon forgat his works", v. 13. They requested things that God did not want them to have, "And he gave them their request; but sent leanness into their soul", v. 15. Material prosperity goes with spiritual poverty, if it is selfishly sought, 1 Tim. 6. 9.

The flesh is not just satisfied with *things, but goes on to seek position*, "They envied Moses ... and Aaron the saint of the Lord", v. 16. Divine judgment follows, vv. 17-18. Still apostasy went on, ending in the worship of the molten calf, v. 19. The result was "Thus they changed their glory", v. 20. God was the glory of Israel; His wonderful works demonstrated His greatness in a very public way, ensuring His glory. However, this was soon forgotten.

Romans 1. 21 shows that Israel's action in "changing their glory" had been predated by the action of the very first idolaters after the flood. They knew God, 1. 21, from His creation, but "they glorified him not as God ... but became vain (empty) in their imaginations (human reasonings) ... Professing themselves to be wise, they became fools, and changed the glory of the uncorruptible God into an image made like to corruptible man, and to birds, and fourfooted beasts, and creeping things", 1. 21-23, changing truth into a lie, v. 25.

Man always wants to change the things of God. God Himself, however, is unchangeable and man's efforts are futile. But as His glory is the public display of His greatness, this sadly can be changed. Our purpose today, therefore, is to do all we can to correct the situation and to glorify God.

June 24th

READING: **Psalm 108**

BE THY GLORY EXALTED ABOVE THE EARTH

THIS PSALM is an amalgam of two earlier psalms, namely, 57 and 60, "revived in this new form probably on the return from Babylon". The psalmist announces that his heart "is fixed"; this is similar to the many times statements like "I shall not be moved" are used in the Psalms, e.g., 16. 8; 62. 6.

The long silent psaltery and harp were called to awaken and, with the psalmist, to give thanks to the Lord, vv. 2-3, and to exalt God and His glory above the earth and the heavens, v. 5.

The great mercy of God had been displayed, but the enemy was still active. The reason for the exaltation of the glory of God was "that thy beloved may be delivered: save with thy right hand, and answer me". The assurance of divine ownership brings rejoicing. God states that "Judah is my lawgiver: Moab is my washpot", vv. 8-9.

The question was asked, "Hast not thou cast us off, O God? And thou goest not forth, O God, with our hosts", v. 11 R.V. The answer is supplied in the N.T., for God "hath not cast away his people", Rom. 11. 2, 26. Down the ages, all those who battle for God and His people, have learned the never-failing battle cry, "Give us help ... for vain is the help of man", v. 12, and can say, "Through God we shall do valiantly: for he it is that shall tread down our enemies", v. 13.

The people of God always have enemies, those who want to see them fail and fall. Today we are under the constant attack of spiritual foes, for we do not war after the flesh: (for the weapons of our warfare are not carnal, but mighty through God to the pulling down of strong holds;) casting down imaginations, and every high thing that exalteth itself against the knowledge of God, and bringing into captivity every thought to the obedience of Christ", 2 Cor. 10. 3-6.

Our chief weapon today is the "sword of the Spirit, which is the word of God", Eph. 6. 17. It is mighty, not through our own intellectual powers, but "through God", and is then effective for attacking Satan's strongholds. Those who are obedient to the Word of God can always be certain that God is with them in the battle, and need not ask the question in Psalm 108. 11. But if we are not relying on divine help and have not learned the emptiness of human help, then it often seems that we are alone.

190

READING: **Psalm 113**

HIS GLORY ABOVE THE HEAVENS

THIS DELIGHTFUL PSALM, the first three verses of which are often sung today as a chorus, was "originally the first part of the 'Hallel' or hymn of praise, which according to Jewish liturgical usage is sung at the three great festivals of Passover, Pentecost and Tabernacles. At the domestic celebration of Passover, Psalms 113 and 114 are sung before the meal, before the second festal cup; 115-118 are sung at the close of the meal when the fourth cup has been filled. These psalms were probably sung by the Lord and His disciples at the Last Supper, Matt. 26. 30 and Mark 14. 26." Therefore our use of these words in praise follows a long tradition, and is but the precursor of the universal praise in a future day.

Although God's throne is in heaven, He nevertheless "humbleth himself to behold the things that are ... in the earth", v. 6. God came down in Genesis ("I will go down ... I will know", Gen. 18. 21) at the time of Sodom, and He saw that this present world was evil. The Lord Jesus Christ, "who, being in the form of God" came down, humbling "himself, and became obedient unto death, even the death of the cross", Phil. 2. 6-8, to save us "from this present evil world", Gal. 1. 4. He came from glory to this world to do the Father's will then returned to glory. Through Him, the Father is now bringing many sons to glory, Heb. 2. 10. They will then have bodies of glory, "like unto his body of glory", Phil 3. 21 Newberry marg., and will afterwards return with Him in glory to this earth, Rom. 8. 19.

As verses 7 and 8 of this psalm say, "He raiseth up the poor out of the dust, and lifteth the needy out of the dunghill; that he may set him with princes, even with the princes of his people". The spiritual equivalent for us today is evident: "the Father ... hath made us meet (fit) to be partakers of the inheritance of the saints in light", Col. 1. 12.

Lastly we note in verse 9 that God is able to make fruitful those who are naturally unfruitful, "He maketh the barren woman ... to be a joyful mother of children". This has been true literally (e.g., Sarah), but how much more has it happened spiritually! As Paul wrote, "the gospel ... bringeth forth fruit", even for those who "were sometime (once) alienated and enemies" in their mind by wicked works, Col. 1. 5-6, 21.

June 26th

READING: **Psalm 115**

UNTO THY NAME GIVE GLORY

THE PSALMIST is emphatic that no glory is due to him or to his nation, it all belongs to the Lord. The reason is twofold: "for thy mercy, and for thy truth's sake". We might imagine that truth, the truth about God, comes first, but so dependent has the nation been on the mercy of God that it comes to mind first. This psalm was probably written after the exile, when God in great mercy had brought back a remnant from Babylon. He had allowed them to go into captivity, not because He was powerless to stop it, but He had a purpose in doing so. In Babylon, the seat of idolatry, Israel was cured of the idolatry that had previously plagued them. God's cure was dramatic, but completely effective.

In this psalm, we have a denunciation of the idolatry of the surrounding nations. The taunt of "Where is now their God?" becomes a wonderful opportunity to demolish the case for idols. "Our God is in the heavens: he hath done whatsoever he hath pleased", v. 3. God is thus sovereign and is the only Person in the universe who has the moral right to please Himself. God is self-existent, but even the best idols (silver and gold, not wood and stone) are only man-made. They have literally all the features of man, but they are lifeless. Those who make and trust them end up in the same state, namely lifeless.

In verses 9-11, there follow a series of statements and responses sung by different parts of the temple choir, emphasizing that trust in the Lord brings help and protection to all in Israel, "both small and great", v. 13.

One of the great needs of the struggling community in Jerusalem at that time was for numerical increase—this was assured to them, v. 14. God is always promising to increase His people, numerically as in the Acts where we have addition, 5. 14, multiplication, 9. 31, and also spiritually. Notice also the many instances in the N.T. where the word "edify" is used.

Man's heritage is the earth, given in trust and responsibility. The believer has been given a trust, particularly the gospel and its associated truths, as Paul wrote of himself, "put in trust", 1 Thess. 2. 4. Much has been entrusted to us by way of truth, talents and things; how well are we using them in the service of, and to the glory of the One who gave them to us?

June 27th

READING: **Psalm 138**

GREAT IS THE GLORY OF THE LORD

IN THE FIRST two verses of this psalm, the depth, direction and discernment of David's worship are clear. It is "with my whole heart ... toward thy holy temple ... for thy lovingkindness and for thy truth", vv. 1-2. In verse 2, we see the correspondence first between the lovingkindness of God and His Word, and secondly between His truth and His name. As with yesterday's study, we note that lovingkindness learned from His Word comes first in our experience since we are sinners.

David's own experience of answered prayer, v. 3, shows that the God who reveals Himself in His Word is also the God who hears and answers prayer. David's witness therefore that "great is the glory of the Lord" is based on his own knowledge of the Word of God, and the ways of God. "Though the Lord be high, yet hath he respect unto the lowly: but the proud he knoweth afar of", v. 6. Mary knew this when she said, "he hath regarded the low estate of his handmaiden ... he that is mighty hath done to me great things ... He hath put down the mighty from their seats, and exalted them of low degree", Luke 1. 48-52.

David's walk in the psalms is distinguished but difficult. It took him away from the counsel of the ungodly, Psa. 1. 1; he walked "in integrity" and "into the house of God in company", 26. 11; 55. 14; but sometimes "through the valley of the shadow of death", 23. 4, and "in the midst of trouble", 138. 7. But in all this he knew that God would save him.

In fact, David knew that God had a plan for his life, and that He would complete His work in him: "The Lord will perfect that which concerneth me", v. 8. His prayer was thus, "forsake not the works of thine own hands". God's plan for David personally gave him confidence in the divine will for his life.

God has a plan for us today. First of all His general plan involving us all: "being confident of this very thing, that he which hath begun a good work in you will perform (perfect) it until the day of Jesus Christ", Phil. 1. 6. Secondly the personal plan, "For we are his workmanship, created in Christ Jesus unto good works, which God hath before ordained (prepared) that we should walk in them", Eph. 2. 10. This means that God has a plan for us composed of particular good works that He wants us to do.

193

June 28th

READING: Psalm 145

THE GLORIOUS HONOUR OF THY MAJESTY

THIS PSALM, entitled "David's Psalm of praise", is his last in the Book, and gives the highest expression of his worship. The second verse forms the chorus of a well known hymn.

David cannot say more about his God and King. He "will extol" and "bless thy name for ever and ever", v. 1, "every day", v. 2. "Great is the Lord, and greatly to be praised; and his greatness is unsearchable", v. 3.

Superlatives alone suffice to speak about God, "I will speak of the glorious honour of thy majesty ... I will declare thy greatness", vv. 5-6. Not only is God's strength extolled, but His moral superiority is to be remembered, "the memory of thy great goodness", v. 7. Then we have His grace and compassion, without which we sinners would be forever lost. We depend on the fact that He is "slow to anger, and of great mercy", v. 8.

God's goodness, however, is not limited to His saints, for "The Lord is good to all: and his tender mercies are over all his works", v. 9. In N.T. language, "God, who is the Saviour of all men, specially of those that believe", 1 Tim. 4. 10, that is to say, He provides the necessities of life to all, as in verse 15 of this psalm. The special nature of divine Saviourhood is the spiritual salvation provided for believers.

The saints' task is to "bless thee", v. 10, and to "speak of the glory of thy kingdom, and talk of thy power", vv. 11-12. So then, the saints have to speak to men about God, and also to speak to God about men, the fallen men of verse 14, for instance, whom "the Lord upholdeth".

Potentially, God can satisfy the need of all. He can satisfy us with his mercy, Psa. 90. 14; good things, 107. 9; His likeness, 17. 15; the goodness of His house, 65. 4, etc. Truly He satisfies the longing soul, 107. 9, but "the doctrines of men" lead only "to the satisfying of the flesh", Col. 2. 23.

The statement in verse 18 that "The Lord is nigh unto all them that call upon him ... in truth" finds its clear parallel in Paul's words to the Athenians, that He is "not far from every one of us", Acts 17. 27. The progression of thought, "them that call upon him ... fear him ... he also will hear ... and will save them ... preserveth all them that love him", Psa. 145. 18-20, is our own experience. We happily concur with king David!

194

June 29th

READING: Psalm 148

HIS GLORY ABOVE THE EARTH AND HEAVEN

THIS PSALM looks forward to the form of worship that will characterize the millennium—the thousand glorious years when the Lord Jesus Christ will rule in righteousness.

The choirmaster assembles his universal choir for the great "Hallelujah Chorus" psalm; this goes beyond Psalm 138 which is occupied with the praise of those on earth to the Saviour God. It looks higher, and includes the heavens and its animate and inanimate occupants, and thereafter collects every phase of earthy life in a great hallelujah!

The heavens and its occupants are to praise the Lord, "for he commanded, and they were created", v. 5. The Lord's creatorial power demands His creatures' praise, equally that of the earth, its strange creatures, and its natural phenomena (fire, hail, snow and vapours, stormy wind fulfilling His word). Prominent geological features (mountains and all hills), vegetable life (fruitful trees and all cedars), and animal life, all are to praise the Lord. Even stones would cry out, Luke 19. 40. The whole groaning creation in that coming day will have finished groaning, Rom. 8. 22, and will be praising Him as it should.

In this vast choir, every kind of human being has his or her part to sing: kings, princes and judges, young men and maidens, old men and children, people of all nations, "let them praise the name of the Lord", v. 13, because "his name alone is excellent; his glory is above the earth and heaven".

The nation of Israel has the most prominent place: "a people near unto him", because they are "his saints"; for them, the Messiah is a horn of salvation.

This universal choir will be in full voice in millennial days, when God's kingdom will have come, and when His will will be done on earth as it is in heaven, Matt. 6. 10.

Today there is a song in heaven and there are "psalms and hymns and spiritual songs" on earth, Eph. 5. 19. The heavenly song is a new song, Rev. 5. 9-10, whose words are "Thou art worthy ... for thou wast slain, and hast redeemed us to God by thy blood out of every kindred, and tongue, and people and nation; and hast made us unto our God kings and priests: and we shall reign on the earth". These redeemed arise from all nations, but they are all of one class, kings and priests.

June 30th

READING: Psalm 149

LET ALL SAINTS BE JOYFUL IN GLORY

THIS PENULTIMATE psalm sounds all the high notes of praise. It is a psalm of victory and joy, it is truly a "new song". The Lord is given the praise due to Him, "Sing unto the Lord a new song, and his praise in the assembly of his saints", v. 1 R.V. The reason is threefold—He is the Maker, the Ruler, v. 2, and the Beautifier of Israel, v. 4. Israel's songs were accompanied by the pipe, the timbrel and the harp, v. 3 marg.; our melody today is "in our hearts", Eph. 5. 19, showing how we must understand Israel's earthly worship compared with ours.

The nation's joy arose from the fact that "the Lord taketh pleasure in his people", v. 4. This pleasure is expressed in the Lord correcting Israel's undesirable appearance in their failure, for "he will beautify the meek with salvation", v. 4. Spiritual beauty is in the eye of the divine Beholder; only what He delights in feasts His eyes. We are made acceptable in the Beloved. Those whom God has beautified are saints, v. 5; they do not need to be beatified (made saints) by men.

The saints have an obligation, "Let the saints be joyful (exult, R.V., rejoice exceedingly) in glory", v.5. The source of their joy is glory, that is, the fact that God has demonstrated His greatness. After all, this is why God created Israel (see our Introduction on page 166), and now in this final mention of glory in the psalms we see spiritual Israel living up to their divinely given responsibility, cf. Rev. 19. 1. This exercise is not just to be in public, but also in private, "let them sing aloud upon their beds", v. 5. Here is no mere public show, but a true joy that echoes through day and night.

Verse 6 breaks the normal parallelism in a striking way; whereas the "high praises (hymns of praise) of God ... (is) in their mouth", a "twoedged sword" is in their hand, v. 6. As well as God's worshippers, they are God's warriors; this is the honour of all His saints, v. 9.

Today we also are worshippers and warriors. We "worship the Father in spirit and in truth", John 4. 23, and "the weapons of our warfare are not carnal, but mighty through God", 2 Cor. 10. 4. Our twoedged sword is the Word of God, Eph. 6. 17; and this is "a discerner of the thoughts and intents of the heart", Heb. 4. 12.

The House of the Lord and Worship

THE MORE poetic the psalm, the more difficult it is to associate it with any particular event in O.T. history, namely in the books of Samuel, Kings and Chronicles. Some psalms can be associated with O.T. events because of the titles given to particular psalms. Again, quite a number of psalms obviously refer to definite events in Israel's history from Exodus to the Babylonian captivity. When such events can be pinpointed, the interpretation of the psalm can rest on a sure basis; its practical lessons can also be drawn from the O.T. event Again, if a psalm is quoted in the N.T., then this can be used to interpret the psalm. A Messianic psalm can be interpreted in the light of its reference to Christ, though such a psalm need not be Messianic in all its verses.

Psalms that contain references to the house of God, to the temple, sanctuary, or tabernacle, are usually easier to interpret, for oftentimes we can pinpoint the O.T. event in the psalmist's experience that gave rise to the psalm. In the selection of psalms that follow, we have sought to pinpoint these events, and to develop the spiritual message of such psalms in the light of their historical associations.

Moses' tabernacle had been moved from Shiloh, to Nob and then to Gibeon, 1 Sam. 1. 3; 21. 1; 2 Chron. 1. 3. Yet David erected another tent or tabernacle on mount Zion to receive the ark of the covenant in Jerusalem, 1 Chron. 15. 1. The most prolific writers of psalms were David (the sweet psalmist of Israel, 2 Sam. 23. 1) and Asaph (one of the chief Levitical singers chosen by David, 1 Chron. 25. 1). They spoke therefore essentially of the tabernacle on Zion, though prophetically their thoughts would extend to Solomon's temple as well.

As far as believers are concerned in the present N.T. era of grace, we must bear in mind that God "dwelleth not in temples made with hands", Acts 7. 49; 17. 24, for both Jews and idolaters loved the materialistic nature of religion, as does non-evangelical Christendom today. We therefore look beyond the material, in order to see for our spiritual profit the antitypes in the local church—its worship and service.

"The house of God, which is the church of the living God" 1 Tim. 3. 15.

July 1st

READING: **Psalm 78. 59-72**

HE FORSOOK THE TABERNACLE OF SHILOH

IN THIS PSALM, Asaph is rehearsing the spiritual and moral history of Israel from the exodus out of Egypt up to the reign of king David, a period of about 450 years. It makes sad reading, for idolatry was rampant, being copied from the nations around. Moses' tabernacle, situated at Shiloh about 20 miles north of Jerusalem, would no longer be recognized by God as His dwelling place amongst men. Consequently, in a battle with the Philistines, God allowed the ark to be taken, 1 Sam. 4. 11, and in its subsequent movements, it was never returned to Shiloh, and God's glory never appeared there again. Asaph recalls this event, "he forsook the tabernacle of Shiloh ... and delivered his strength into captivity, and his glory into the enemy's hand", Psa. 78. 60-61. We shall note later in other psalms what happened to the ark subsequently.

After another 450 years, the moral and spiritual conditions in Jerusalem had declined to the lowest state of idolatry, and through Jeremiah God quoted the example of Shiloh: "go ye now unto my place which was in Shiloh ... and see what I did to it for the wickedness of my people Israel", Jer. 7. 12, since the house had become a "den of robbers"; "I will make this house like Shiloh", 26. 6. And that is what happened a few years later; "the glory of the Lord went up from the midst of the city" to stand on the mount of Olives, Ezek. 11. 23. After God had abandoned the temple, the house of the Lord was burnt with fire, 2 Kings 25. 9.

We find the same thing in the N.T. with regard to Herod's temple. The Lord Jesus "departed from the temple" for the last time, and never returned. He foretold its destruction, Matt. 24. 1-2, and this took place in A.D.70 by the Romans.

A local church or assembly is now a spiritual temple, 1 Cor. 3. 16-17. The Lord is amongst His people, and is seen as walking amongst the golden lampstands, Rev. 1. 13; 2. 1. Even to Ephesus, He said, "I ... will remove thy candlestick out of his place, except thou repent", 2. 5. To the church at Laodicea, representing as some believe Christendom today, He said, "I will spue thee out of my mouth", 3. 16. But this can never happen when faithfulness is displayed.

"I will never leave thee, nor forsake thee", Heb. 13. 5.

READING: Psalm 29

IN HIS TEMPLE ALL SPEAKS OF HIS GLORY

ON A FEW OCCASIONS the word "temple" does not have its usual meaning; we include this psalm to show to the reader this important difference. Usually, the words "tabernacle", "temple", "house" refer to Moses' tabernacle, to David's tabernacle on Zion, to Solomon's temple, and later to Zerubbabel's temple and Herod's temple. The antitypes are, of course, the local church, 1 Cor. 3. 16; the church as the body of Christ, Eph. 2. 21, and the believer's body, 1 Cor. 6. 19. But occasionally it refers to the vast span of the heavens above.

Solomon realized this: he said, "I have surely built thee an house to dwell in ... will God indeed dwell on the earth? behold, the heaven and heaven of heavens cannot contain thee; how much less this house that I have builded?", 1 Kings 8. 13, 27. Thus David implied this in Psalm 11. 4, "The Lord is in his holy temple, the Lord's throne is in heaven". Again, "From the place of his habitation he looketh upon all the inhabitants of the earth", 33. 14; "The Lord on high ...holiness becometh thine house, O Lord, for ever", 93. 4-5. In the book of Revelation, this is also sometimes the obvious meaning, "the temple of God was opened in heaven, and there was seen in his temple the ark of his testament", Rev. 11. 19.

In Psalm 29, David, recalling his experiences as a shepherd, describes the manifestation of God's glory in a fearful phenomenon of nature in the heavens, namely the passing overhead of a thunderstorm. In verses 1-2, we have worship from a mighty one to the Mightiest One. In verses 3-4, we have the oncoming storm—the voice of the Lord is in the firmament. In verses 5-7, the storm is overhead—the voice of the Lord is in the forest. In verses 8-9, the storm is receding—the voice of the Lord is in the wilderness. Hence in verses 10-11, the Mighty Lord gives peace.

Thus "every whit of it speaks of his glory", v. 9. The voice of the Lord is the voice of (what we call) nature. He speaks from His temple to those who have minds capable of recognizing His deeds. Oh that men would recognize these "wonderful works" is the burden of Psalm 107, where many of these powerful works in nature are described. May we also wonder at this glory!

"For thy pleasure they are and were created", Rev. 4. 11.

July 3rd

READING: **Psalm 52**

A GREEN OLIVE TREE IN THE HOUSE OF GOD

THE WORDS "Doeg the Edomite" in the title reveal the nature of the psalm. The Edomites, deriving from Esau, were intimately connected with Israel, and were called "thy brother", Deut. 23. 7. However, they refused to provide a passage for Israel at the end of the forty years; food was also refused, even though money was offered, Deut. 2. 2-8. In other words, mere religious men have nothing for the people of God.

As chief of Saul's herdmen, Doeg was the worst of the lot! Once Doeg was detained before the Lord in Nob where the tabernacle was situated, 1 Sam. 21. 7. David, unknown as the anointed king, in fleeing from Saul, came to the tabernacle and to Ahimelech the high priest. Doeg was a spy, and told Saul that the priest had given David food, 22. 9-10; David knew that this would happen, so escaped to a cave where those in distress came to him, vv. 1-2, 22. Hence Doeg killed 85 priests including Ahimelech. David then wrote Psalm 52.

The status of Doeg was that of a "mighty man", v. 1. The lying of his tongue was his mischevous report to Saul, vv. 2-3. God would destroy him, and being rooted out would bear no fruit, v. 5. He had no thought for God, trusting in his riches and wickedness, v. 7. But David knew he was a complete contrast, being a "green olive tree in the house of God", v. 8.

This has a direct application in the N.T. When the disciples plucked ears of corn on the sabbath, the Lord referred to David at Nob, Matt. 12. 1-4. The Lord had just said, "no man knoweth the Son", 11. 27, as none had known David as king. The disciples were hungry, as was David. The Pharisees were rich in their law, 12. 2, as was Doeg. However, the Lord was "greater than the temple", v. 6, a tree with divine life contrasting with the deadness of the temple ritual—indeed "a green tree", Luke 23. 31. And as Doeg and Saul plotted against David so the Pharisees took counsel how they might destroy Jesus, Matt. 12. 14. As David departed, his followers seeking him, so the Lord withdrew Himself, with great multitudes following Him.

The parallel is complete! We too must be fruitful trees in the local church: "Those that be planted in the house of the Lord shall flourish", Psa. 92. 13-14.

"Filled with the fruits of righteousness", Phil. 1. 11.

READING: **Psalm 68. 1-19**

THOU HAST ASCENDED ON HIGH

IT IS VERY EASY to ascertain the circumstances that gave rise to this psalm of David. In Numbers 10. 35, whenever the ark set forward, Moses said, "Rise up, Lord, and let thine enemies be scattered; and let them that hate thee flee before thee"; in other words, the Lord would be victorious. This is almost identical with verse 1 of Psalm 68. Hence the psalm was sung on an occasion when the ark moved forward triumphantly in David's reign. This only occurred once, namely when David arranged for the ark to be taken from the house of Obed-edom up to mount Zion, 1 Chron. 15. 1, 25.

During this move, there was opposition, shown by verse 16, "Why leap ye, ye high hills? this is the hill which God desireth to dwell in". God's purpose was not thwarted, for the ascent was accomplished, "Thou hast ascended on high ... thou hast received gifts for men", v. 18. Typically, Paul understood this to refer to the ascension of Christ, for this verse is quoted in Ephesians 4. 8. The previous movements of the ark can be correspondingly interpreted. The ark going into the land of the Philistines speaks of the death of Christ. Its return to Kirjath-jearim speaks of His resurrection, 1 Sam. 7. 1. And its ascent to mount Zion speaks of His ascension.

Paul uses verse 18 in a very important context: "unto *every one* of us is given grace according to the measure of the gift of Christ", Eph. 4. 7. It is as ascended that He "gave gifts unto men"—a slight change in wording from Psalm 68. Peter's words in Acts 2. 33 answer directly to the wording of the psalm: "thou hast received gifts", for the apostle states that Christ, as exalted, "*received* of the Father the promise of the Holy Spirit" who was then shed forth. Hence all our spiritual gifts place us in contact with heaven, with the exalted Christ.

Note further that Romans 12. 3 states, as pertaining to these gifts, that "God hath dealt to *every man* the measure of faith", and that 1 Corinthians 12. 7 states that "the manifestation of the Spirit is given to *every man* to profit withal". In other words, the three Persons of the Trinity are involved in giving gifts to *every man*.

"*He gave ... evangelists, pastors, teachers*", Eph. 4. 11.

July 5th

READING: **Psalm 96**

THE BEAUTY OF HOLINESS

WHEN David was made king over all Israel, he had the exercise to bring the ark up to mount Zion, 1 Chron. 13. 3. We have seen in Psalm 68 that this was typical of the Lord's ascension after which He gave gifts to His people, Eph. 4. 8. When this was achieved, David composed a suitable psalm, and gave it to Asaph and his brethren in order to give thanks unto the Lord before the ark, 1 Chron. 16. 7-8. This psalm, vv. 8-36, is really a splicing together of parts of three psalms:

vv. 8-22 = Psalm 105. 1-15, the rest being omitted;
vv. 23-33 = Psalm 96, with minor alterations;
vv. 34-36 = Psalm 106. 1, 47-48, the rest being omitted.

While the omitted parts may be unsuitable for worship under such lofty conditions, nevertheless the whole of Psalm 96 was judged suitable for worship.

There is the recognition that "beauty" was in His sanctuary, v. 6, that glory and an offering were to be brought into His courts, vv. 7-8. Additionally, worship had to be "in the beauty of holiness". What beauty is this?

Certainly Moses' tabernacle was a place of beauty (physically), as were the garments of the priests. But we read of no physical beauty in the plain tent that David erected on mount Zion to receive the ark. What we do read is that the Levites sanctified themselves, 1 Chron. 15. 12, and David and the Levites were "clothed with a robe of fine linen", v. 27. And this answers to the alternative rendering given by Bible expositors to "the beauty of holiness", namely "in holy attire" referring to the Levitical dress for the occasion. God looked beyond the physical whiteness and saw moral excellence granted by Himself.

Thus "the beauty of holiness" or "in holy attire" refers to spiritual standing and not physical position; in Psalm 96 it refers to *worship*, as it also does in Psalm 29. 2. In 2 Chron. 20. 21, the singers went before the army into *warfare*, again in the "beauty of holiness". Finally, under millennial conditions, there is *willingness*, for the people shall be willing "in the beauty of holiness", Psa. 110. 3. This should characterize us in service too.

"Put on the new man", Eph. 4. 24.

202

July 6th

READING: **Psalm 15**

WHO SHALL ABIDE IN THY TABERNACLE?

THERE ARE two questions in verse 1: "who shall abide in thy tabernacle?" and "who shall dwell in thy holy hill?". These should be taken with two further questions: "who shall ascend into the hill of the Lord?" and "who shall stand in his holy place?", Psa. 24. 3. Without doubt, Psalm 24 refers to the occasion when king David brought the ark up mount Zion for the first time, 2 Sam. 6. 12-18. Psalm 15 then refers to the subsequent service of God that took place before the new tabernacle on Zion.

The two psalms reflect upon the essential character and moral qualifications that were necessary for this service. In fact, 1 Chronicles 15. 3-28 provides a long list of those who ascended mount Zion. There were the high priests, Zadok and Abiathar, many Levites (those who carried the ark upon their shoulders, porters, singers, doorkeepers), "all Israel" and king David, with the elders and captains, v. 25. Psalm 68 also refers to this ascent, where we read that "The singers went before (the ark), and the players on instruments followed after", v. 25.

But the Lord was in the midst, "the King of glory shall come in", Psa. 24. 7. Moreover, when the ark was safely established in the tent on mount Zion, David left the singers, players on instruments and porters on the mount, "to minister before the ark continually, as every day's work required", 1 Chron. 16. 37-42. For such holy service, the Levites were sanctified, and were clothed in "fine linen", 15. 14, 27. Moral and spiritual qualifications were necessary, and these are spelt out in verses 2-5 of Psalm 15 and in verse 4 of Psalm 24. Those that "dwell on high" and who "see the king in his beauty" are also described in Isaiah 33. 15-17.

One author has described Psalm 15 as illustrating "Fitness for Fellowship". God is very particular now amongst whom He presences Himself. As citizens of heaven, Phil 3. 20, we have come to mount Zion, Heb. 12. 22-24. The Corinthians, as sanctified and enriched, had been called "unto the fellowship of his Son", 1 Cor. 1. 9, but some were unworthy and had been removed from their mount Zion, 5. 5; 11. 30-32.

"Worship ... in spirit and in truth", John 4. 23.

203

July 7th

READING: **Psalm 40. 1-10**

BURNT OFFERING HAST THOU NOT REQUIRED

THIS IS a Messianic psalm, since verses 6-8 are quoted in Hebrews 10. 5-7. The mention of these sacrifices takes our minds to the brazen altar that Moses made, and that was situated just inside the gate into the tabernacle courts. There was no brazen altar on mount Zion where the ark was placed; the altar remained before Moses' arkless tabernacle that was at Gibeon, and there the priests offered the various sacrifices, 1 Chron. 16. 39-40. Such a distance between ark and altar must have spoken to David's heart—if the ark was of value to God on Zion, then the altar was becoming useless at Gibeon. Later David himself said, "thou desirest not sacrifice; else would I give it: thou delightest not in burnt offering", Psa. 51. 16.

So David expressed the same thing in Psalm 40. 6. God confirmed this understanding, saying, "I delight not in the blood of bullocks", Isa. 1. 11. Later Jeremiah recognized this fact, "The Lord hath cast off his altar", Lam. 2. 7. At the end of the O.T. period, God said, "neither will I accept an offering at your hand", Mal. 1. 10.

Thus the ground was being set for the abolishing of the Jewish altar, there being substituted the eternally valuable sacrifice of Christ. Verse 6 in our psalm contains reference to four major Levitical offerings. (i) "Sacrifice" implies the peace offering, the enjoyment of communion because of reconciliation. (ii) "Offering" implies the meal offering, an expression of the perfect life of Christ under trials that led to death. (iii) "Burnt-offering" speaks of the devotion of Christ even unto death; His acceptability to God means that the worshipper is also acceptable. (iv) "Sin-offering" is the means that God used to remove the guilt of sin. Some religions still perpetuate offerings—this means that they discredit Christ as the one true offering.

Note the large number of times the words "thy" and "my" (or "mine") occur in the psalm. Note the number of words used for the voice: "my cry", v. 1; "a new song in my mouth", v. 3; "I would declare and speak", v. 5; "Then said I", v. 7; "I have preached righteousness", v. 9; "I have declared", v. 10.

"How much more shall the blood of Christ ... ?", Heb. 9. 14.

July 8th

READING: Psalm 26

I HAVE LOVED THE HABITATION OF THY HOUSE

THE DIVINE example is, "Christ also loved the church, and gave himself for it", Eph. 5. 25. If there is true affection towards an object, this will dominate one's life. Spasmodic interest proves that there is no real affection.

In David's case, he had to learn the hard way, through deep exercise and repentance. His deep love for Bathsheba led to serious crime. David had to repent with the words of Psalm 51 before he could enter the house of the Lord to worship, 2 Sam. 12. 20. Psalm 26 then shows the necessary state of his mind and heart that enabled him to love God's habitation. He could speak of his integrity, v. 1, and of washing his hands in innocency, v. 6, so great was his appreciation of divine forgiveness. He would then love the habitation of God, seeking there "the beauty of the Lord", Psa. 27. 4.

The altar, to be encompassed, was approached on its east side through the gate of the court; the offering was killed on the north side, v. 11; it was washed on the west side (the side of the laver); it was placed on the altar on its south side (according to Jewish tradition), and finally the ashes were poured out on the east side, v. 16. We too compass our altar, as we gaze upon every aspect of the cross of Christ; else formality spoils our affection for the One who first loved us.

Love for Christ will yield love for His people. For now the house of God is the church of the living God, 1 Tim. 3. 15. This is "a spiritual house", a place for the offering up of "spiritual sacrifices", 1 Pet. 2. 5. In fact, here are the saints, forgiven and so beloved by Himself, gathered together in the Lord's Name. As we love the Lord, so we should be free to love what He loves. Hence we must love the church; this love described in 1 Corinthians 13 is in the context of the local church, in the context of service, of gifts, of edification, of the gatherings of the Lord's people.

David's love developed to the end of his life, when he was preparing the materials for Solomon to build the temple after him. He said, "I have set my affection to the house of my God", 1 Chron. 29. 3. Through love, he thus gave abundantly.

"Walk in love, as Christ also hath loved us, and hath given himself for us an offering and a sacrifice", Eph. 5. 2.

READING: **Psalm 3**

HE HEARD ME OUT OF HIS HOLY HILL

IN Psalm 2. 6, "my holy hill of Zion" refers to the exalted millennial position of the Lord Jesus, but in Psalm 3 "his holy hill" is quite different. (The name "holy hill" also occurs in Psalm 15. 1; 43. 3; 99. 9.) The title given to Psalm 3 shows that this was a psalm of David when he fled from his son Absalom, in particular 2 Samuel 15. The event occurred because of the governmental hand of God upon His servant David, on account of his sin with Bathsheba. God had said through Nathan the prophet, "the sword shall never depart from thine house", 2 Sam. 12. 10.

Although David was forgiven, this sword remained: "for whatsoever a man soweth, that shall he also reap", Gal. 6. 7. Thus David had to flee from Jerusalem because Absalom usurped the throne, for he had stolen "the hearts of the men of Israel", 2 Sam. 15. 6. As he fled, David recognized that those who troubled him were increased, that they mocked him saying, "There is no help for him in God", Psa. 3. 1-2.

The rest of the psalm expressed his confidence in God; this could never be shaken in spite of God's governmental dealings with him. It was thus that he said, "I cried unto the Lord with my voice, and he heard me out of his holy hill", v. 4. The ark of the covenant on mount Zion was the centre of David's religious aspirations; the priests knew this, and so they carried the ark up the mount of Olives as David fled. But the king would not allow this, and ordered the priests to take the ark back to the city, saying, "he will bring me again, and show me both it, and his habitation", 2 Sam. 15. 24-29.

The proper place for the ark was on God's holy hill, and as an exile on the outside David knew this. He was weeping as he went up the mount of Olives, his head covered, and barefoot. Yet Psalm 3 tells us that David by prayer was so in contact with God on His holy hill, that he could sleep in safety, although thousands of enemies were around him. His confidence was that "Salvation belongeth unto the Lord", v. 8, namely that he would be restored as king again in Jerusalem.

Like Peter in Acts 12. 6, we should have confidence to rest in safety, although surrounded by spiritual enemies.

"Prayer was made without ceasing ... for him", v. 5.

READING: **Psalm 4**

THE SACRIFICES OF RIGHTEOUSNESS

IN THIS psalm, David is still in distress, and the subject matter seems to follow on immediately from Psalm 3. This had been a morning hymn, since the psalmist looked back to a night passed with secure sleep, 3. 5. But Psalm 4 is an evening hymn, since in verse 8 he contemplates that the sleep of the coming night will be in safety. So there is a progression in experience between the two psalms, separated perhaps only by the daylight hours of one day in his flight from Absalom.

David was now at some distance from Jerusalem and the ark just returned to mount Zion. Yet guidance was more than ever necessary. The priest may carry the Urim and Thummim that would show God's mind for guidance, Exod. 28. 30; Num. 27. 21; 1 Sam. 28. 6; 30. 7-8. But this was of no use for one far from Jerusalem, so David relied solely upon God lifting up the light of His face upon him, Psa. 4. 6.

David must have known the reason for his trouble, yet in Psalm 51 he had deeply repented, followed in Psalm 32. 2 that the Lord "imputeth not iniquity" to those whom He has forgiven. Hence David recognized that he was "godly", set apart by the Lord for Himself, 4. 3. Being at a distance from the altar, he could no longer offer burnt offerings and bullocks upon it, 51. 19; he had confessed that the sacrifices of God would be "a broken spirit", v. 17. He knew that God would "be pleased with the sacrifices of righteousness", v. 19. Hence David, in his flight, put this into practice, saying "Offer the sacrifices of righteousness", 4. 5. Only one to whom righteousness has been imputed by faith can offer such sacrifices; see Romans 4. 5-8.

In the Christian's experience there are other sacrifices that bring pleasure to the Lord. The gifts sent to Paul were "an odour of a sweet smell, a sacrifice acceptable, wellpleasing to God", Phil. 4. 18; Paul regarded himself as a drink offering poured out on the Philippians' sacrifice and service of faith, 2. 17; the believer's walk in love should be a sacrifice to God, as was Christ's, Eph. 5. 2; the bodies of believers should be "a living sacrifice, holy, acceptable to God", Rom. 12. 1. These are marks of a true priest.

"With such sacrifices God is well pleased", Heb. 13. 16.

READING: **Psalm 42**

I WENT WITH THEM TO THE HOUSE OF GOD

WHEN THIS psalm was written (we suspect by king David), he was still in exile, in the land of Jordan, seemingly far from Jerusalem and the house of God (the tent on Zion). In fleeing from Absalom, David had come to Mahanaim on the east of Jordan, 2 Sam. 17. 24. Mentally, he was "cast down" (repeated twice); twice he recalled the mocking of the enemy, "Where is thy God?" (because David was separated from His dwelling place on mount Zion).

Yet by faith David anticipated better things. He was thirsting after the living God; he expected to be able to praise Him; David's song and prayer would be possible again, even though God's waves and billows had gone over him in the divine governmental dealings with His servant.

And why did David expect to "appear before God" again?, v. 2. Certainly he had said that he would see the ark and "his habitation" again according to God's will, 2 Sam. 15. 25. The reason was that David had experienced the fellowship of the house before, and nothing would stop his experiencing it once again; he said, "I had gone with the multitude, I went with them to the house of God, with the voice of joy and praise, with a multitude that kept holyday". He recalled the happy spiritual experiences over the twenty or so years between the tent being erected on Zion and this flight from Jerusalem. These holydays were the feast days; three times a year all males had to "appear before the Lord thy God in the place which he shall choose"—the feasts of unleavened bread, of weeks (Pentecost), and of tabernacles, Deut. 16. 16.

For believers today, is there a similar desire to gather in the Lord's Name with His people? Not just anywhere, but in local churches or assemblies that gather according to revealed N.T. principles. Do we arrange the positions of our homes, our employment, our holidays, so as to render possible regular attendance? In Acts 20. 6, Paul arranged his time ("seven days") so as to meet with the church at Troas on the first day of the week. In Tyre, he stayed seven days with the disciples evidently, we believe, to pass a Lord's day with them, Acts 21. 4, and the same may be said about Puteoli, 28. 14.

"They assembled themselves with the church", Acts 11. 26.

July 12th

READING: **Psalm 23**

I WILL DWELL IN THE HOUSE OF THE LORD

THIS Psalm has no particular association with any recorded event in David's history. It may represent David's experience over many years of God's faithfulness to him during all his troubles throughout life. It may represent David's psalm of appreciation to God for the provision of refreshment as he fled from Absalom, when they were all "hungry, and weary, and thirsty, in the wilderness", 2 Sam. 17. 27-29. In all this, David preserved a balance; after rehearsing all of God's goodness *to* him, the man after God's own heart had something *for* Him, namely the sweet psalmist would "dwell in the house of the Lord for ever". Not only would David appreciate the goodness of the Lord in the field and by the river, but as dwelling in the house he would "be satisfied with the goodness of thy house", Psa. 65. 4.

Not everyone can dwell in God's house. Joab sought refuge in the tabernacle courts, but there was no safety to be found there, 1 Kings 2. 29; Tobiah the Ammonite lodged in a room "in the courts of the house of God", but was quickly turned out, Neh. 13. 4-9. Similarly in the N.T., the "false prophets" that Peter warned against had no place in the local church, 2 Pet. 2. 1, neither had any spirit of antichrist that John warned against, 1 John 4. 1-3, nor any "false brethren unawares brought in", Gal. 2. 4. Only believers have a permanent place in God's spiritual house, for they are living stones built into this spiritual house; such stones cannot be dislodged by the wiles of men and of Satan.

In Exodus 33. 7-11 there was another tabernacle in use for a short period; there the Lord spoke with Moses, but "Joshua ...a young man, departed not out of the tabernacle". This initial faithfulness led, after 40 years, to his selection by God as Moses' successor. Elsewhere, David expressed the same deep exercise, "That I may dwell in the house of the Lord all the days of my life, to behold the beauty of the Lord, and to inquire in his temple", Psa. 27. 4. An interesting example of this in the N.T. is found in Anna who, with no distraction, "departed not from the temple, but served God with fastings and prayers night and day", Luke 2. 37.

"There shall be one flock, and one shepherd", John 10. 16.

209

July 13th

READING: **Psalm 55. 1-18**

WE WALKED TO THE HOUSE OF GOD IN COMPANY

SOME EXPOSITORS suggest that this psalm represents David's exercises when, upon fleeing from Absalom, he learnt of the treachery of Ahithophel in plotting the king's death, 2 Sam. 17. 1-2, although in the long run this plot was not followed, and he hanged himself, v. 23. (Other expositors pick out certain verses in the psalm that are inconsistent with this suggestion.) Accepting the first suggestion, there are sound reasons why Ahithophel, described by David as "mine equal, my guide, and mine acquaintance", Psa. 55. 13, taking counsel together and walking together to the house, should have changed his attitude to David, even to seeking his death. For it can be traced that Bathsheba was Ahithophel's granddaughter, and David's sin with that woman would cause Ahithophel to change friendship into enmity.

Another case of treachery comes to mind—that of Judas, who was described prophetically as "mine own familiar friend", Psa. 41. 9; but in this case there was no change in the Lord's character that could account for his great sin of betrayal.

But when David said, "We ... walked unto the house of God in company", he was recalling better days in the past. This causes us to ask the question, "With whom do we keep company in the local church and in the Lord's service?". Association with Christ and His church often divides: in Acts 5. 13, believers in the Jerusalem church were so distinct that no one else dare join himself to them. Simon of Samaria attempted to, but Peter would not walk with one in the bond of iniquity, 8. 23. The church at Jerusalem would not walk with Saul as recently converted, until Barnabas explained his conversion and change of life to them, 9. 27. One could not walk to the house of God with a fornicator, or covetous, or a railer, or a drunkard, or an extortioner, 1 Cor. 5. 11. For "what fellowship hath righteousness with unrighteousness?, etc.,", 2 Cor. 6. 14-18. All these quotations are negative. On the positive side, "if we walk in the light, as he is in the light, we have fellowship one with another, and the blood of Jesus Christ his Son cleanseth us from all sin", 1 John 1. 7. We walk with those whom God adds to the church, Acts 2. 47.

"Peter and John went up together", Acts 3. 1.

210

July 14th

READING: **Psalm 5**

I WILL COME INTO THY HOUSE

IT WOULD APPEAR that this psalm follows on from Psalms 3 and 4. David returned to Jerusalem after his flight from Absalom, "David came to his house at Jerusalem", 2 Sam. 20. 3. He found another revolt in progress: "Sheba ... blew a trumpet, and said, We have no part in David ... So every man of Israel went up from after David, and followed Sheba", vv. 1-2. David's exercise in Psalm 5 follows.

The rest of the account in 2 Samuel 20 does not make very pleasant reading. The principal men concerned answer to those in Psalm 5: "workers of iniquity", men of lies and of blood, "their inward part is very wickedness", etc. Yet in verse 7 there appears a perfect gem: "I will come into thy house in the multitude of thy mercy: and in thy fear will I worship toward thy holy temple". (Note the four-fold use of the word "thy" in this verse. David may be surrounded by men seeking their own things, but he knew what pertained to God.) David had said that he would see both the ark and God's habitation again after his flight, 2 Sam. 15. 25, so now that the opportunity presented itself according to God's favour, David immediately comes "into thy house" to "worship toward thy holy temple". When trouble was around, his priority was to seek God's face in His house. This is what Hezekiah did later when the Assyrians surrounded Jerusalem: he "went into the house of the Lord", and spread the enemy's letter before the Lord in the house, 2 Kings 19. 1, 14. Similarly in Acts 4. 23; there was trouble, and the apostles "went to their own company", and they prayed "where they were assembled together", v. 31. There was trouble in Acts 12. 12, so Peter "came to the house of Mary ... where many were gathered together praying".

David knew that there was only one place: "thy house ... thy holy temple". No other place could satisfy his heart; he knew that this was the place that God had chosen out of all the tribes to put His Name there, Deut. 12. 5. In our experience we would say the same thing for believers today. The local church, the house of the living God, is the only place for the Lord's people. Later in the O.T. other places sprung up, 1 Kings 12. 28-33, but no faithful king ever went there.

"They were all with one accord in one place", Acts 2. 1.

July 15th

READING: **Psalm 27**

TO INQUIRE IN HIS TEMPLE

THIS IS another psalm in which David is in trouble; he is surrounded by his enemies. The psalm breathes confidence in God, and the high-point occurs in verse 4 where, as dwelling in the house of the Lord (he refers here to the tent on mount Zion), he desired "to behold the beauty of the Lord, and to inquire in his temple". This last phrase has been rendered by another author as "to look with pleasure upon his temple".

Whereas it is, of course, true that believers today can look for instruction in the local church as they enquire into the pages of Scripture, yet here we shall use this alternative rendering. Our own desires, as members of a local church, must be to gaze (i) upon the Lord, and (ii) His holy temple. The former has the chief priority; He has the pre-eminence.

In the creation, God created man in His image; some of the divine characteristics were passed on to man before the fall. Similarly with the tabernacle and temple; their design and embellishment typified something of the nature of God. And similarly with "the beauty of the Lord". Moses knew this: he said, "let the beauty of the Lord our God be *upon us*", Psa. 90. 17. Speaking through Ezekiel, God implied the same thing with regard to Israel: "thou wast exceeding beautiful ... thy beauty ... was perfect through *my* comeliness, which *I* had put upon thee", Ezek. 16. 13-14. (Though tragedy followed: "thou didst trust in thine *own* beauty", v. 15.)

The implications of this are that first we see the beauty of Christ, and then we see His beauty in our fellow-believers in the local church. Something is seriously wrong if this is not possible. If we have put on Christ, then we are in Him; in an ideal gathering of believers, Christ will be manifest in all and through all. If there are "debates, envyings, wraths, strifes, backbitings, whisperings, swellings, tumults", 2 Cor. 12. 20, then Paul, whose heart was full of Christ whom he had seen in glory, would fail to detect Christ in men who allowed such carnality to exist in a local church. But when things are "true, honest, just, pure, lovely", all is well, Phil. 4. 8.

"Let this mind be in you, which was also in Christ Jesus", Phil. 2. 5.

212

July 16th

READING: **Psalm 134**

NIGHT IN THE HOUSE OF THE LORD

NIGHT AND DAY have followed in regular succession since the original creation. Though darkness may speak of the kingdom of Satan, and light of the kingdom of God, yet the voice of praise is not silent when the Lord's people are as lights shining in a dark place. Thus the Levitical singers were not "nine-to-five" workers, but they also stood by night in the house of the Lord, so that blessing might flow out of Zion.

In the psalms, "the sanctuary" sometimes speaks of the open heavens, while on other occasions it speaks of the dwelling place of God on earth. This refers to the church in its heavenly aspect as the body of Christ, and then to its local aspect, as a gathering of believers in the Lord's Name. But darkness and night exist outside.

(i) We sing of "the night that the Lord passed through", and we read of the Lord's words, "I cry ... in the night season, and am not silent", Psa. 22. 2, corresponding to the hours of darkness when He was on the cross. The scene was set by the words "it was night" when Judas left the upper room, John 13.. 30. We can solemnly contemplate the succession of days and nights as the Lord experienced divine judgment due to sin. Afterwards, we read of the Lord's praise, Psa. 22. 25.

(ii) Spiritually, of course, the Lord's people are "all the children of light ... of the day: we are not of the night, nor of darkness", 1 Thess. 5. 5.

(iii) Positionally, circumstances may be such that "weeping may endure for a night, but joy cometh in the morning", Psa. 30. 5. Thus Anna as a widow served in the temple during the night, Luke 2. 37, while the Lord Himself "continued all night in prayer to God" in the sanctuary of the Father's presence, Luke 6. 12. For ourselves, "The night is far spent", Rom. 13. 12, and we serve and worship "till the day dawn, and the day star arise in your hearts", 2 Pet. 1. 19.

There is worship in the night, Psa. 134. 1; prayer in the night, 130. 6, and doctrine in the night, 63. 6.

Note what comes "out of Zion" : there is blessing out of Zion, Psa. 134. 3; fruitfulness, 128. 5; worship, 135. 21; the blessing of the gospel, 118. 26.

"At midnight Paul ... prayed, and sang", Acts 16. 25.

July 17th

READING: **Psalm 80**

THOU THAT DWELLEST BETWEEN THE CHERUBIM

THE DEEP spiritual desire that the Shepherd of Israel should cause His face to shine is repeated three times in this psalm, vv. 3, 7, 19. The background to this desire must be understood. Only a few men were privileged to see the glory of God. Moses saw this when the tabernacle was first reared up, Exod. 40. 35; Solomon saw it when the temple was dedicated, 1 Kings 8. 11; Isaiah saw it when he was cleansed and sent forth in Isaiah 6; Ezekiel saw it by the river Chebar and when the glory left Jerusalem for the mount of Olives, Ezek. chs. 1, 8-11; Peter, James and John saw the Lord's glory on the mount, Matt. 17. 2, while Paul saw the glory on the Damascus road, Acts 9. 3. But during the time of the judges, this glory was veiled; "there was no open vision", 1 Sam. 3. 1.

Throughout the lives of Samuel and David, this sad state of affairs remained. Asaph was one of the chief singers appointed by David, 1 Chron. 16. 7, and he felt very keenly the lack of the open manifestation of the glory of God. He knew that God dwelt "between the cherubim" upon mount Zion where David had placed the ark, 15. 25-28, so his desire was that God should "shine forth" as in the days of old. The name "Asaph" means "one who gathers", typical of believers gathering as a local church, and his desire reflects upon the Lord's own desire, "that they may behold my glory", John 17. 24.

The three thoughts in verse 3, "saved", "thy face to shine" and "turn us again", reflect upon the three paragraphs that end with this common verse—vv. 3, 7, 19.

(i) Verses 1-3. The prayer is that God should "come and save us", v. 2. Namely, from their enemies that had been the cause of the glory of God withdrawing itself.

(ii) Verses 4-7. God's people had "the bread of tears" to mar their own faces, having "tears to drink", while their enemies' faces were covered with laughter—all in contrast to the shining forth of God's face.

(iii) Verses 8-19. The vine out of Egypt was broken, plucked, wasted and burnt. So they asked God to return to them, and then they would not go back from Him, v. 18. Thus repentance was complete, and glory could shine again.

"We beheld his glory", John 1. 14.

214

READING: **Psalm 122**

LET US GO INTO THE HOUSE OF THE LORD

THE PSALMIST's desire narrowed from the outside of the city Jerusalem, to being within her gates and walls, and then to be in Jerusalem's centre, the house of the Lord. The house came first, and then the city, vv. 1-2; the house came first, leading to the good of the city, v. 9.

It was essential to go into the house of the Lord, to the place "whither the tribes go up ... to give thanks", v. 4. Even before the tabernacle had been built, the command was given, "Three times in the year all thy males shall appear before the Lord God", Exod. 23. 14-17. Forty years later this was defined as "his habitation", and "the place which the Lord your God shall choose", Deut. 12. 5. In David's time, this was to the tent containing the ark on mount Zion; in Solomon's time, this was to mount Moriah on which the temple was built; when the Lord was here, Herod's temple (arkless and disowned by God) was the place of gathering at the usual feasts of the Passover and Pentecost.

In this day of grace, it is not to temples made with hands that believers are glad to enter. The house of God is now the church of the living God, 1 Tim. 3. 15, and believers should be glad to gather in the Lord's Name to serve Him. Thus they were "assembled together" for prayer, Acts 4. 31; they "assembled themselves together with the church" for teaching, 11. 26; they "gathered the church together" for a missionary meeting, 14. 27; the apostles and elders "came together" to discuss and decide an important issue, 15. 6; they "gathered the multitude together" for a Bible Study meeting, 15. 30; and they "came together to break bread", namely to partake of the Lord's Supper, 20. 7. Are we glad to assemble together?

Yet in the O.T. there was weakness. Many in the northern kingdom refused the invitation to come to Jerusalem for the passover; they mocked the messengers with the invitation, 2 Chron. 30. 10. Later, the house of God was forsaken by the Levites, Neh. 13. 11. No wonder there is the exhortation in Hebrews 10. 25, "Not forsaking the assembling of ourselves together, as the manner of some is".

"They continued stedfastly in the apostles' doctrine, fellowship, breaking of bread, prayers", Acts 2. 42.

July 19th

READING: **Psalm 65**

SATISFIED WITH THE GOODNESS OF THY HOUSE

Verses 9-13 of this psalm imply that it was composed to celebrate before God an exceptionally good harvest. David, the sweet psalmist of Israel, while appreciating the good hand of God in providing material blessings, considered first the response of the heart to God's spiritual blessings. The Lord Jesus also preached the same order of priorities when He said, "seek ye first the kingdom of God ... and all these things shall be added unto you", Matt. 6. 33.

David knew that praise and prayer were suitable exercises of heart on mount Zion. Only those who had been forgiven, who had been chosen, were allowed to approach God on mount Zion and even to "dwell in thy courts". No outsider, not knowing the "God of our salvation", could be thus blessed, vv. 1-4.

"The goodness of thy house, even of thy holy temple" were blessings that should give spiritual satisfaction. There can be no duality about this. A man, glorying in worldly attainment and finding satisfaction in worldly pleasures, is not likely to find satisfaction in spiritual things.

In the N.T., being a member of the body of Christ, being a member of a local church or assembly according to the revealed pattern brings blessing and goodness. In the Jerusalem church, even material and financial needs were met, Acts 2. 45; 4. 34-37; 11. 27-30; Rom. 15. 25-27, and this was called "fruit", v. 28. If we were asked, "Count your blessings, name them one by one", would we be able to do so, and would we be surprised at what the Lord has done?

On the highest plane, as members of the body of Christ, a growing holy temple, we have been "blessed ... with all spiritual blessings in heavenly places in Christ", Eph. 1. 3. The goodness of God enables us to continue "stedfastly in the apostles' doctrine and fellowship, and in breaking of bread, and in prayers", Acts 2. 42. The goodness of God provides all believers with spiritual gifts for the edifying of all the churches in many differing ways, 1 Cor. 12. 7, 11. The goodness of God provides ability and opportunity to proclaim the gospel to those on the outside of the church. By these means, we bring forth a fruitful harvest unto God.

"*God gave the increase*", 1 Cor. 3. 6-7.

216

READING: **1 Chron. 29. 10-19**

AFFECTION TO THE HOUSE OF GOD

THOUGH THIS does not appear in the Book of Psalms, we like to think of 1 Chronicles 29. 10-19 as David's greatest psalm of praise, spoken at the end of his life.

Verses 1-5 of the chapter show David's preparation for the house of God. In chapter 28, David the elder had given to Solomon the younger the pattern of the house; now he declares the origin of all the material. Because of his affection to the house of God, he not only supplied material generally, but also of his "own proper good" he supplied gold and silver. Then in verses 6-9, the people reply; by consecrating their service to the Lord, they "offered willingly to the Lord".

David's greatest psalm of praise then follows: he speaks of God's person, vv. 10-11; God's provision, vv. 12-16; God's protection of the heart, vv. 17-19. Note the repetition of the word "all" eleven times in the psalm.

David's recognition of God's person, vv. 10-11, rises to the same most glorious sublime heights attained in the Book of Revelation, where a similar confession is made to the One seated on the throne and to the Lamb, Rev. 5. 12-13. In all our praise and prayer, the recognition of His person as "head above all" must come first.

David had no selfish feelings about his own possessions, vv. 12-16, however materialistic they might have appeared to be. He counted himself very small before the One who possessed all things, saying "all things come of thee, and of thine own have we given thee". All the material was "all thine own". In our own lives and service, we should say the same, realizing that all our material and spiritual blessings are held in trust for the Lord. We should provide "as God hath prospered" us, 1 Cor. 16. 2. Again, "God hath dealt to every man the measure of faith", Rom. 12. 3. We thus return these gifts to Him as we use them faithfully in His service.

Yet the hearts of men are poor, so David prayed that Solomon should have "a perfect heart ... to build", v. 19. Only when we have such a heart can we build with "gold, silver, precious stones", else we build with the material of carnality, "wood, hay, stubble", 1 Cor. 3. 1-3, 11-12.

"Such as I have give I thee", Acts 3. 6.

READING: **Psalm 127**

EXCEPT THE LORD BUILD THE HOUSE

BUILDING ANYTHING for God is a very serious matter, and this applies to material as well as to spiritual things. In particular, in the O.T. there had to be built structures suitable for the dwelling place of God: "let them make me a sanctuary; that I may dwell among them", Exod. 25. 8.

The pattern had to be according to God's will: Moses had to "make all things according to the pattern" shown to him on the mount, Heb. 8. 5. The people who then made the tabernacle by following the pattern had to be chosen by God. Natural expertise had to be superseded by spiritual expertise. Thus God chose Bezaleel, and filled him with wisdom and every ability necessary for the construction, Exod. 31. 1-5. Also in Aholiab and in all those who were wise hearted, God put wisdom "that they may make all that I have commanded thee", v. 6. Thus the work was finished to God's satisfaction, 39. 32.

Similarly with the temple: David gave Solomon the pattern, but confessed that it was "the pattern of all that he had by the spirit", 1 Chron. 28. 12, the Lord having made known the pattern "in writing by his hand upon" David, v. 19. Solomon did not work according to the flesh, but God would be with him until the house of the Lord was finished, v. 20. God would give Solomon "a perfect heart ... to build", 29. 19. Thus it was not in vain that the house was finished, 2 Chron. 5. 1.

Many difficulties were overcome when the second house was built after the captivity, but at last it was finished, Ezra 6. 15. But the same cannot be said about Herod's temple in the N.T. This was a work according to the flesh and unbelief, and even at the beginning of the Lord's ministry it had taken 46 years to build, John 2. 20.

Today, the Lord builds His church directly: "I will build my church", Matt. 16. 18, the Lord adding and not man, Acts 2. 47. Yet He uses His servants who are devoted to Him. Through the grace of God given to him, Paul laid the foundation, 1 Cor. 3. 10; only those with Spirit-given gifts then build upon this foundation which is Jesus Christ. By this grace, Paul laboured more abundantly that the others, 15. 10, doing all things through Christ who strengthened him, Phil. 4. 13.

"Your labour is not in vain in the Lord", 1 Cor. 15. 58.

READING: **Psalm 132**

THE ARK OF THY STRENGTH

WHEN Solomon dedicated the temple, he said at the end of his great prayer, "arise, O Lord God, into thy resting place, thou, and the ark of thy strength", 2 Chron. 6. 41-42. The fact that these two verses are repeated in verses 8-10 of this psalm shows that Psalm 132 was a psalm of Solomon when the ark was brought into the newly completed temple.

In verses 1-7, Solomon recalls his father David's exercises regarding the choice of a place for His habitation. So David placed the ark in a tent on mount Zion, 1 Chron. 16. 1, the ark having been found "in the fields of the wood", Psa. 132. 6, namely Kirjath-jearim, 1 Sam. 7. 1; 1 Chron. 13. 6.

In verses 8-13, we have Solomon's prayer. He was concerned about (i) the priests being clothed with righteousness, v. 9; (ii) the perpetuation of David's royal line, vv. 10-11; (iii) the Lord's desire for mount Zion, v. 13. (This is surprising, since the temple was built on mount Moriah, and the ark had been taken "*out of* ... Zion", 1 Kings 8. 1.

In verses 14-18 we have God's answer. All three points are dealt with. (i) The priests would be clothed with salvation, v. 16. (ii) David's line would bud, v. 17. (iii) God had chosen Zion for His habitation, v. 14.

Here are many lessons for believers today. (i) The lives of all believers as priests in the local church should match their lives as lived in the world. Peter is concerned about this in 1 Peter 2. 1-11; as living stones forming a holy priesthood, we must lay "aside all malice, and all guile, and hypocrisies, and envies, and all evil speakings", abstaining "from fleshly lusts, which war against the soul". (ii) David's line leading to Christ would speak to us of the Lord's divine authority over His people today. For example, in the record of the church at Antioch, the title "Lord" appears five times in Acts 11. 20-26, showing their submission to His authority. (iii) The chosen place for the Lord's presence today is seen in His words, "where two or three are gathered together in my name, there am I in the midst of them", Matt. 18. 20. He does not dwell now "in temples made with hands", Acts 7. 48, but in the hearts of His people by faith, Eph. 3. 17.

"*We will ... make our abode with him*", John 14. 23.

219

July 23rd

READING: **Psalm 84**

I HAD RATHER BE A DOORKEEPER

It is good to faint for the courts of the Lord, v. 2. In Psalm 42. 2, the psalmist's soul was thirsting after the living God, with a desire to "appear before God"; this was his exercise *in the city*. In Psalm 63. 1-2, David was *in the wilderness* thirsting after God, desiring to see His glory in the sanctuary. But in Psalm 84, the desire to come to the courts of the Lord appears to be the exercise of an exile—a Levite *outside Jerusalem*, perhaps when the city was besieged by Sennacherib. Even a sparrow could fly over the besieging army to build a nest on the altar. Yet the exile on the outside found deep spiritual interest in the house, as Paul in prison maintained prayerful interest in the local churches, and John in exile on Patmos could think about the churches in Asia.

There was a supreme blessing to dwell in the Lord's house, v. 4. David desired to dwell there for ever, Psa. 23. 6; in another psalm he wrote, to "dwell in the house of the Lord all the days of my life", 27. 4. Anna put this into practice, for she "departed not from the temple ... night and day", Luke 2. 37. Believers today should appreciate that they are living stones, "built up a spiritual house", 1 Pet. 2. 5, permanently placed there by the Lord who is the chief corner Stone.

The title of the psalm shows that the "sons of Korah" were involved. In Numbers 16. 3, Korah and others tried to usurp the authority of Moses, but they perished when the earth swallowed them up, v. 32, an event recalled in Jude 11 as "the gainsaying of Core". Yet grace prevailed, for "the children of Korah died not", Num. 26. 11, and later became keepers of the gates of the tabernacle, 1 Chron. 9. 19. Grace changes the most unlikely of men into devoted servants of the Lord.

Thus the writer of Psalm 84, no doubt a son of Korah, would not dwell in "the tents of wickedness", v. 10, for such tents had characterized the father's rebellious group, Num. 16. 27, and those of the besieging army. Rather he would be a doorkeeper to keep evil out of the Lord's house, for this was a porter's work, "that none ... unclean ... should enter in", 2 Chron. 23. 19. To such a Levite God would be a sun, contrasting with the glory of judgment that appeared to Korah, Num. 16. 19.

Take heed ... to all the flock, Acts 20. 28.

READING: **Psalm 46**

THE HOLY PLACE OF THE TABERNACLES

THIS IS a psalm of great triumph: the "present help" had triumphed over the roaring waters, over the raging of the heathen, making "wars to cease". In contemplating the reigns of the kings in Jerusalem, we feel that there was only one faithful king who experienced such a divinely-given triumph over surrounding enemy armies—that was Hezekiah with Jerusalem surrounded by the Assyrian armies, 2 Kings 18-19. Such enemies answer to the wicked who are "like the troubled sea, when it cannot rest, whose waters cast up mire and dirt", Isa. 57. 20, for "The waters ... are peoples, and multitudes, and nations", Rev. 17. 15.

In contrast to these Assyrian roaring waters, there is a river with streams of peace in Jerusalem, provided only by the Lord for His people. The Assyrians had no chance of partaking of it. In fact, Hezekiah prevented the enemy from obtaining any water from the fountains outside the city, 2 Chron. 32. 3-4, though he brought water into the city through a conduit, 2 Kings 20. 20; 2 Chron. 32. 30. These purely engineering constructions led the psalmist to view God's spiritual river provided for His people. This was intimately connected with the house of God, "the holy place of the tabernacles of the most High". And this is not surprising, since Ezekiel saw that the waters "issued out of the sanctuary", Ezek. 47. 12. And again, the king associated God's deliverance with the fact that He dwelt between the cherubim in the house of God, 2 Kings 19. 14-16. (The use of "tabernacles" in the plural is explained in Hebrews 9. 2-3, where the holy place and the Holiest of all are viewed as two tabernacles.)

There is a parallel in the N.T. The Lord Jesus referred to His body as "the temple", John 2. 19-21. Then He promised "living water", 4. 10, 13-14, so that those who believe shall never thirst, 6. 35. This water really implied the Holy Spirit that believers should receive, 7. 37-39. And there would be abundance, since from believers themselves, filled with the Spirit, would flow these "rivers of living water" to thirsty men desiring to receive the gospel of eternal peace.

"A pure river ... out of the throne", Rev. 22. 1.

READING: **Psalm 48**

IN THE MIDST OF THY TEMPLE

THIS PSALM, together with the preceding two, form a group, so we may assume that this psalm was composed after the Assyrian enemy had been routed by "the angel of the Lord", when 185,000 of the enemy were slain, 2 Kings 19. 35. For the psalm says, "they were troubled, and hasted away. Fear took hold upon them", vv. 5-6. Immediately after this deliverance, there was death in the house of the Assyrian god, 2 Kings 19. 37, and although Hezekiah was ill, there was promised that on the third day he would "go up unto the house of the Lord", 20. 5. What a contrast! In this temple, there would then be the thought of the loving kindness of God, Psa. 48. 9.

In the psalm, God is praised, not so much for the deliverance, but for the beauty of the city, mount Zion, its palaces and the temple. The city of God was unique. There was no liberty to pick and choose which religion suited one best. The city was "Beautiful for situation, the joy of the whole earth", v. 2. Not that the heathen found it a joy over their cities and temples, rather the psalmist viewed his city as pre-eminent, being "the city of the great King".

There were other buildings around, apart from the temple itself. All had to be considered, the towers, the bulwarks and the palaces. But the temple was not just one of many—it was special in that there God had to be contemplated. And such testimony was not just for the psalmist; the results of the contemplation must be told to "the generation following".

Believers today must not think of the assembly or local church as a formal place of repetitive service week by week. They must view it as bringing joy to the Lord, as being the only place of beauty in a world where Christ is largely passed by and unknown. He would see it as a "chaste virgin", 2 Cor. 11. 2. And our testimony should pass this blessedness on to others being saved. Thus there are those who shall believe "through their word", John 17. 20. The apostle wrote, "That which we have seen and heard declare we unto you", 1 John 1. 3. Paul wrote, "the things that thou hast heard ... commit thou to faithful men, who shall be able to teach others also", 2 Tim. 2. 2. This is the true testimony of Zion.

"For ye are our glory and joy", 1 Thess. 2. 20.

July 26th

READING: **Psalm 74. 1-12**

THEY HAVE CAST FIRE INTO THY SANCTUARY

THE HOUSE of God was sanctified, and yet it could be so mistreated by men. The Messianic psalms were prophetic, as were many psalms speaking of millennial conditions. So were certain psalms that spoke of the house of God in centuries after they were written by the psalmists. Similarly Isaiah prophesied of Messianic and millennial conditions, as well as of events brought about by the Babylonian invasion of Jerusalem: "our adversaries have trodden down thy sanctuary", Isa. 63. 18; "our holy and our beautiful house ... is burned up with fire", 64. 1I.

Thus Asaph (one of David's singers) spoke of dreadful things yet to come: "the perpetual desolations", Psa. 74. 3; "the enemy hath done wickedly in the sanctuary", v. 3; "they break down the carved work", v. 6; "They have cast fire into thy sanctuary, they have defiled ... the dwelling place of thy name to the ground", v. 7. Asaph also said, "the heathen are come into thine inheritance; thy holy temple have they defiled", 79. 1. Such deeds were done both by the kings in Jerusalem and by foreign invaders. Thus Ahaz "cut in pieces the vessels ... and shut up the doors of the house of the Lord", 2 Chron. 28. 24; Manasseh introduced every kind of idolatry into the house and its courts, 33. 3-7; Ezekiel saw men worshipping the sun in the temple courts, Ezek. 8. 16. Finally, the house of the Lord was destroyed by the Babylonians: Nebuzar-adan "burnt the house of the Lord", 2 Kings 25. 9, so Jeremiah cried, "The Lord hath cast off his altar, he hath abhorred his sanctuary", Lam. 2. 7. Later, the Lord Jesus spoke of Herod's temple, "There shall not be left here one stone upon another", Matt. 24. 2.

Viewing the local church as the antitype, we see that the N.T. prophesies of similar dreadful things. This is "the temple of God" and it is holy, but it can be defiled by men, 1 Cor. 3. 17. This can be done by men on the inside or by men coming in from the outside, as Paul warned, Acts 20. 29-30. There can be false brethren, false teachers, false elders, false prophets and false evangelists. As Thyatira and Laodicea, a church can become so worldly that its lampstand can be removed.

"Who hath bewitched you?", Gal. 3. 1.

July 27th

READING: **Psalm 137**

HOW SHALL WE SING THE LORD'S SONG?

HERE IS one of the saddest psalms; because of its sin and idolatry, Jerusalem had been carried away captive into Babylon, and the city and its temple had been destroyed. All its Levitical service established by David had been deserted.

Yet there were some who were spiritual amongst the captives. Originally, the rivers of Babylon had contained nourishment, for they flowed out from Eden, Gen. 2. 10-14, but now the world had changed this, and the rivers merely served the interests of the kingdoms of men. Any source in the world can provide nothing for the Lord's people. Proper nourishment comes only from the rivers of Zion: "There is a river, the streams whereof shall make glad the city of God", Psa. 46. 4. It was necessary to remember Zion from the remote places of the earth, praying to God toward the land, 1 Kings 8. 47-48, as did Daniel when he was a captive, Dan. 6. 10.

But the captives would not allow the "songs of Zion" to appear as mere entertainment so as to satisfy the lust for pleasure by men in the world. Even today, there can be a danger of reducing the proclamation of scriptural truth to the level of entertainment for men in the flesh. This is what Belshazar did with the holy vessels from the temple, Dan. 5. 1-4. Thus the captives would not sing the songs of the Lord in a strange land to satisfy their captors.

It was in Zion that Levites "were instructed in the songs of the Lord", 1 Chron. 25. 7; it was in the temple courts that "the song of the Lord" began at the same time as the burnt offering, 2 Chron. 29. 27. The place that the Lord had chosen was the only place for sacrifice and song. Otherwise, the Lord said of hypocrites, "in vain they do worship", Matt. 15. 9.

Today, only true believers can sing the Lord's song in worship; the world may sometimes try, but this is hypocrisy. It was in the upper room where "they had sung an hymn", Matt. 26. 30; it is "in your hearts" that a spiritual song is made to the Lord, Eph. 5. 19; it is in the local church where one may have a psalm, 1 Cor. 14. 26; it is in heaven where "the new song" is sung, Rev. 5. 9. All this is far from the world's presence, for in the church we are not in a strange land.

"Worship ... in spirit and in truth", John 4. 24.

READING: **Psalm 91**

LEST THOU DASH THY FOOT AGAINST A STONE

WHATEVER ELSE this psalm may speak of, it is clearly prophetical of the lifetime experiences of the Man Christ Jesus when here below. In verse 1, the Spirit speaks of "the secret place of the most High" as the safe dwelling place of Christ. In verse 2, Christ responds—His recognition of Jehovah as the place of safety. In verses 3-8, the Spirit speaks of the preservation of Christ on earth *without any conditions*. In verses 9-13, the Spirit continues to speak of the preservation of Christ *with one condition*, namely in verse 9, "Because thou hast made the Lord...thy habitation". Finally in verses 14-16 the Father speaks—His purpose to set the Son up on high, v. 14.

The words "the secret place", v. 1; "thy habitation", v. 9; "thy dwelling", v. 10, do not refer to any building on earth; the thought is entirely spiritual. In fact, no reference to tabernacle or temple in Jerusalem occurs in the psalm. The angelic ministry in verses 11-12 protected Christ against stumbling-stones (not physical stones) placed before Him by men and Satan. There were twelve legions of angels ready to protect Him, but when on the cross He did not call them.

Yet as we know verses 11-12 were quoted by Satan to the Lord Jesus during the temptation in the wilderness, Matt. 4. 6. Satan's original objective had been to ascend to be like the most High, Isa. 14. 14, though he would be brought down to hell. He could not bear the thought of Christ being set up on high, Psa. 91. 14. So he took the Lord up to "a pinnacle of the temple", namely Herod's temple on mount Moriah, and tempted Him to cast Himself down, quoting Psalm 91. 11-12 to demonstrate the angelic hands that would preserve Him. We doubt whether he believed this psalm; rather the temptation was a plot to kill the Lord so that He could not be raised on high to a position that Satan would like! "It is written", the Lord answered to terminate that particular temptation. "Thou shalt not tempt the Lord thy God" is taken aptly from the O.T. in the context where the people were not to go after other gods, Deut. 6. 14-16. Christ set His love uniquely upon His God, Psa. 91. 14, and Satan was defeated.

"Are they not all ministering spirits?", Heb. 1. 14.

July 29th

READING: **Psalm 69. 1-17**

THE ZEAL OF THINE HOUSE

THIS PSALM, often quoted in the N.T., prophetically and quietly lets us into some of the thoughts of the Lord Jesus as He suffered on the tree. Much is in metaphorical language, though some statements are direct, such as "I was the song of the drinkers of strong drink", v. 12 marg. The song of the Lord in the house of the Lord had given way to the mocking song of the Jewish and Roman onlookers, whose lives were often characterized as being drinkers of strong drink. Today, the song of praise of the Lord's people is completely distinct from the blasphemous songs and utterances of many in the pleasure and entertainment industries.

Another direct statement concerns the Lord's zeal for the house of God, v. 9. In verses 7-9, He speaks of reproach that He sustained for God's sake. Men were reproaching God by their evil deeds and talk; He intervened, taking a stand for His God, and thus their reproach fell upon Him as well.

Such an episode occurred at the beginning of His ministry in John 2. 13-22. Men were reproaching God by using the temple courts for profiteering. When the Lord drove them out, the disciples associated "the zeal of thine house" with the motive governing His act of judgment. But the Lord then went beyond the immediate present, to the destroying of the temple of His body which would be raised again. On the cross, the Lord's zeal would be centred upon His spiritual house that was about to be built on resurrection ground, consisting of Himself as the living Stone and believers as living stones.

Divine zeal is important in Scripture. In 2 Kings 19. 31, a remnant would escape from Judah to be reestablished: "the zeal of the Lord of hosts shall do this". Regarding the child born to be "Wonderful, Counseller, The mighty God", we have the promise, "The zeal of the Lord of hosts will perform this", Isa. 9. 6-7. Regarding divine judgment on Jerusalem, God said, "I the Lord have spoken it in my zeal", Ezek. 5. 13.

And the divine zeal inspires that of others. When Phinehas the priest intervened to save Israel in a time of judgment, God said, "he was zealous with *my zeal*", Num. 25. 11 marg. We too should be "zealous of good works", Titus 2. 14.

"*Epaphras ... hath a great zeal for you*", Col. 4. 12-13.

READING: **Psalm 118**

THE STONE WHICH THE BUILDERS REFUSED

THE STRUCTURE of this psalm is that of a conversation; it recalls the suffering of Christ and the glory that should follow. Verses 1-4 form an introduction by the Spirit, that thanks should be offered to the Lord. Verses 5-21 record the voice of Christ prophetically—profound words that reveal His mind when on the cross surrounded by men likened to a swarm of bees. He anticipated resurrection, vv. 19-21. Verses 22-24 are the voice of the saints, speaking of His exaltation and the Lord's Day. Verse 25 is the voice of Christ, a call for gospel progress (some expositors place this verse in the plural, so it must then be joined to the next verses). Verses 26-27 form the voice of the saints again, a gospel call "out of the house", with worship in the courts before the altar. Verse 28 is the final reply of Christ, joining with the praise of the saints. Finally verse 29 repeats verse 1, a call by the Spirit that thanks should be offered to the Lord.

Verses 22-23 "the stone which the builders refused is become the head stone of the corner. This is the Lord's doing; it is marvellous in our eyes" are quoted by the Lord Jesus after His parable of the vineyard, Matt. 21. 42. The parable left the son dead and the husbandmen destroyed. But Psalm 118. 22 visualizes a building site; an unused stone lay there, and the builders did not know where it should go, so threw it on one side, not realizing that it was the final top-most stone to crown the building. The Pharisees cast the Lord away as One that was unwanted, but they reckoned without His resurrection on the Lord's Day. This was God's marvellous work, testified by the saints. Psalm 118. 23, "This is the Lord's doing", was often quoted publicly by Field Marshal Montgomery at the end of the war in 1945, though in its context believers see that it has a far higher meaning in the resurrection of Christ.

"This is the day which the Lord hath made" refers to the resurrection day, and now we can perceive that it has the meaning of the Lord's Day for us. It is a special day, not the last day of the Jewish week, but the first of the Christian week, a day of rejoicing, gladness and testimony, vv. 26-27.

"In all things he might have the preeminence", Col. 1. 18.

July 31st

READING: **Psalm 99**

WORSHIP AT HIS FOOTSTOOL

WITH THIS psalm, we terminate this theme of the month on "The House of the Lord and Worship". Although they have other applications, Psalms 93-99 are the royal kingdom psalms; they contain thoughts of the throne of God and the fact that He reigns as King, 93. 1; 95. 3; 96. 10; 97. 1; 98. 6; 99. 1. In this sense they are millennial in character, and hence are suitable to terminate the theme.

The psalmist was using tabernacle-temple language with which to describe this higher heavenly scene: "he that sitteth between the cherubim", "worship at his footstool", "priests", "holy hill", and this is extended into Psalm 100, "his gates", "his courts". In the tabernacle, the two cherubim were part of the mercy seat placed upon the ark, but in the temple they were free-standing objects whose wings overshadowed the ark below. Between these cherubim, the presence of God would be found amongst His people. God promised to Moses that there He would meet with him, and would commune with him regarding all His commandments, Exod. 25. 22. It was in the tabernacle that Moses heard "the voice of one speaking unto him from off the mercy seat ... from between the two cherubim", Num. 7. 89. In the temple, king Hezekiah recognized in prayer that God dwelt "between the cherubim", 2 Kings 19. 15. So the cherubim are used in the contexts of worship, prayer and instruction.

We do not have either material ark or cherubim today, but we do have the Lord's presence amongst believers in a local church, where the chief functions are worship (breaking of bread), prayer, and instruction (the apostles' doctrine), Acts 2. 42. These are holy occupations, a fact stressed three times in Psalm 99, "it is holy", v. 3; "he is holy", v. 5, and "the Lord our God is holy", v. 9.

Within the prophetic vision-temple, no reference is made to ark or cherubim in Ezekiel 40-47, but the presence of the Lord, His glory and the place of His throne are evident, Ezek. 43. 4-5. Moreover, all would be "most holy", v. 12.

At that time, the Lamb's wife, holy Jerusalem, shall descend from heaven the glory of God shall be there, but no temple, for God "and the Lamb are the temple of it", Rev. 21. 22.

"The throne of God and of the Lamb", Rev. 22. 1, 3.

228

Hallelujah, Praise and Thanksgiving

"THERE IS no other book", wrote Calvin the great reformer, "in which we are more perfectly taught the right manner of praising God". Certainly whatever other moods characterize the psalms (and there are many), the most pervasive is that of worshipful thanksgiving to Jehovah. Even songs that commence in distress or depression, such as Psalms 22 and 71, conclude on a note of triumphant praise as the very thought of God kindles adoration in the writer's heart.

Over the next month, we shall notice that worship in the Psalter is:

1. *Informed.* The psalmist always rejoices in what he knows of God, and his lips are full of specific examples of divine goodness which, by their very mention, honour the Lord. The better we know the Word the better we shall worship.

2. *Reverent.* In an age of deplorable flippancy, ease and over-familiarity with sacred things, it is challenging to note the godly fear with which David approaches the Lord. The closer we draw to God, the more conscious we shall become of His ineffable holiness and majesty.

3. *Personal.* Although many psalms involve corporate praise, there is always a sense of the individual heart going out to God in deep thankfulness.

4. *Delightful.* It is impossible to read, say, Psalms 146-150 without feeling that the psalmist enjoys praising God. The principle that "God loveth a cheerful giver", 2 Cor. 9. 7, applies to our worship as well as to our financial commitment to the Lord's work.

5. *Continual.* Israel's annual seasons of worship instituted by Jehovah Himself were not meant to be exhaustive. Rather, they brought a spirit of praise to daily life. Finally, all O.T. worship, dare we say it, was incomplete in that it pre-dated Calvary. To restrict ourselves today to the Psalter as a model of God's Word is to ignore the progressive revelation of God's Word, that gradual unveiling of His purpose which finds its climax in Christ, Heb. 1. 1-2. Studied in the full light of N.T. truth, however, this Book is an invaluable aid to our appreciation of our God and Saviour.

August 1st

READING: **Psalm 22. 25-31**

HE HATH DONE IT

PSALM 22 is the song of suffering and glory. It describes in graphic detail the agonies of Calvary, reverently drawing back the veil which the N.T. places over the innermost thoughts of the Saviour. But it does not stop there, for the latter part is an outburst of praise, culminating in our key phrase, "he hath done this". Significantly, on the cross the Lord Jesus quoted not only the first verse of the psalm, expressing His sufferings at the hand of God, Matt. 27. 46, but also the *final* word "done", John 19. 30. And this was no cry of defeat, but a shout of triumph! When we ponder our salvation, it is from first to last a work of God, and should provoke wholehearted thanksgiving.

Consider the character of the work. It is *divine*, for the One who has done it can be none other than the Lord Himself, vv. 28, 30. The Lord Jesus appointed no deputy to take His place at Calvary, for it is His very deity that gives value to His work: "There was no other good enough to pay the price of sin". It is also *perfect*, for can we imagine failure in that which our God does? Scrutinize the cross from every angle, and all is gloriously flawless! Further, it is *complete*, because "he hath done it" admits of no repetition. The once and for all character of Christ's atoning death is the crucial message of Hebrews, "this man ... offered one sacrifice for sins for ever", Heb. 10. 12.

It is a *righteous* work, Psa. 22. 31, because the living God has in no way compromised His holy nature in providing a full salvation to believing sinners; on the contrary. Calvary declares God's righteousness as never before, Rom. 3. 25, in that the full weight of divine wrath against sin was poured out on the Saviour. It is a *proclaimed* work, for those who come into the good of it are indebted to share such glad tidings, and to "declare his righteousness unto a people that shall be born". Do we? It is a *praiseworthy* work, stimulating adoration on the part of its beneficiaries, Psa. 52. 9. Finally, because "he hath done this", it is *eternal*, for "whatsoever God doeth, it shall be for ever", Eccl. 3. 14. Calvary is everlastingly sufficient!

"He hath done all things well", Mark 7. 37.

READING: **Psalm 30**

SAVED TO SING

Do YOU ever wonder why God saved you? Much is shut up in God's wisdom and sovereignty, Rom. 9. 15-16; Deut. 7. 7-8, but at least one suggestive answer is offered in this psalm. We praise because we have been saved, "*for* thou hast lifted me up", v. 1, and we are saved that we might praise, "*to the end that* my glory may sing praise to thee", v. 12.

The first truth is simple but inexhaustible. The psalmist regularly explains the basis of his worship by recounting God's goodness to him. Let us apply the first three verses of this psalm to ourselves. Like David, we have been "delivered", v. 1 J.N.D., from the malicious *desire* of enemies bent on our overthrow. Just as Satan begged the Lord for Peter and the other apostles, Luke 22. 31, so he longs to get hold of us. He is still active as a "roaring lion ... seeking whom he may devour", 1 Pet. 5. 8. Yet by grace we have been safely transferred from his kingdom into that of God's dear Son, Col. 1. 13. And divine property cannot be touched! Further, we have been healed from the *disease* of sin, Psa. 30. 2, for the work of Calvary has provided the effective remedy, 1 Pet. 2. 24. Although physical sickness may still afflict the child of God, ultimate deliverance is promised at "the redemption of the body", Rom. 8. 23 Finally, we have been raised up from *death*, Psa. 30. 3, in that salvation has called us, like Lazarus, from the tomb of this evil world, and made us eternally alive to God, Eph. 2. 1-7. Such deliverance is surely a sufficient reason for worship.

But mark the other truth. Here we enter into God's mind for His people. He, at infinite cost, has brought us from misery into everlasting gladness, v. 11, so that He might receive our praises, v. 12. The Son of man came to seek the lost, Luke 19. 10, but the Father seeks worshippers, John 4. 23. Indeed, the great goal of God's saving activity is His own glory in Christ, Eph. 1. 6, 12, 14. Is God now finding His desire fulfilled in us? Is He receiving the whole-hearted worship that He so richly deserves? Remember, we are saved to sing! Called out of darkness, we show forth His praises, 1 Pet. 2. 9.

"*And they sung a new song, saying, Thou art worthy ... for thou wast slain, and hast redeemed us to God*", Rev. 5. 9.

August 3rd

READING: **Psalm 33**

REJOICING: (1) WHO AND WHY?

TRUE JOY, which is always blended with reverence and godly fear, Psa. 2. 11, is an essential component of scriptural praise. "Rejoice in the Lord, O ye righteous: for praise is comely for the upright", Psa. 33. 1. This implies that the worshipper has personally experienced the goodness of the One whom he adores. Praise is no academic matter. It can neither be taught in a college nor learned by rote. Rather, it is the spontaneous but intelligent response of the heart to God. But what hearts are fit for worship?

Let us observe three characteristics of the people who "exult in the Lord", v. 1 J.N.D. First, they have been constituted righteous, v. 1. Both Scripture and experience teach us that no man is so by nature, but the divine provision is lucidly expounded in Psalm 32. Happiness and joy mark the man "whose transgression is forgiven", v. 1. He alone is equipped to "be glad in the Lord, and rejoice", v. 11, a command which is enacted by Psalm 32 itself as it progresses from "silence", v. 3, through "songs", v. 7, to a "shout for joy", v. 11. Only those who have received His *forgiveness* can rejoice in the Lord. Second, they are described as those who have "trusted in his holy name", Psa. 33. 21. That is, they have exercised *faith* in the living God. Of course, it is through the initial response of faith to God's Word that we receive a righteous standing before Him, Rom. 5. 1-2. But faith is the foundation of the entire Christian life, for "the just shall live by his faith", Hab. 2. 4. Only as we grow in our confidence in God will we acceptably praise Him. Last, those who rejoice in God are those who wait for Him, Psa. 33. 20, and hope in Him, v. 22. They have a glad *future*, for, whatever happens, they rest secure in the hands of an all-seeing, all-powerful God, vv. 18-19.

These precious truths are emphasized at the Lord's Supper where we look back to the crucified Saviour (who purchased our *forgiveness*), up to the crowned Saviour (in whom rests our *faith*), and on the coming Saviour (who is our *future*). Worship there reaches its zenith. Yet our joy in God should scarcely be rationed to one day in the week!

Like Paul, let us *"rejoice in the Lord alway"*, Phil. 4. 4.

READING: **Psalm 33**

REJOICING: (2) WHO AND WHY?

WE LEARNED yesterday that only those who have been saved by sovereign grace have the right to rejoice in the Lord. Today we must consider the reasons for praise.

The psalmist gives a twofold justification for his worship: "for the word of the Lord is right; and all his works are done in truth", v. 4. Consider first God's Word. Can we not delight in the complete infallibility of the Scripture? All around, men seek desperately for answers, and yet they wilfully reject the only source of objective truth, the Word of God. Our God has spoken, and He cannot lie, Titus 1. 2. Further, when we think of God's Word we cannot help but think of God's Son, for He is the Living Word, John 1. 1. And in Him, "the Holy One and the Just", Acts 3. 14, as in the written Word, is nothing but perfection. In a world where so much is wrong we can joy in the God whose Word is right.

"The word of the Lord is right", and His *works* are done in "faithfulness", v. 4 R.V. The psalmist ties the two so tightly together that we cannot disentangle them, vv. 6, 9. Is it not remarkable that when the creative activity of God is mentioned, it is described with such devastating simplicity? "He spake, and it was done", v. 9. God's power is not that of the muscular strongman, straining himself to the very limits of his capacity. On the contrary, God's power is blessedly effortless! He has only to speak the word, Gen. 1. 3.

Each of the divine activities mentioned in Psalm 33 can be illustrated from the divine ministry of the Saviour. Just like Jehovah, the Lord Jesus is the God of *power*, Psa. 33. 6-9; Mark 4. 41; the God of *purpose*, vv. 13-17; John 2. 24-25; and the God of *protection*, vv. 18-19; John 17. 12.

Here is another line of scriptural evidence for the deity of Christ. He could "speak the word only", and a centurion's servant would be healed, Matt. 8. 8, or Lazarus would be raised from the dead, John 11. 43. So why rejoice in the Lord? Because our God is glorious in all He says and all He does, and that glory has been displayed to the full in Christ Jesus our Lord.

"*Born again ... by the word of God*", 1 Pet. 1. 23.

August 5th

READING: **Psalm 48**

THE CHOSEN PLACE OF WORSHIP

WHEN PEOPLE speak of a place of worship, they usually mean a building set aside for religious services. Certainly, in O.T. times, mount Zion was specifically chosen by God to be the site of the temple and the great gathering centre of Judaism, Deut. 12. 10-11; 2 Sam. 5. 7; 1 Chron. 15. 12. Thus Israel was not permitted to worship Jehovah wherever or whenever they pleased, Deut. 12. 13-14; 1 Kings 8. 44-48.

Today, however, our centre of worship is a Person, not a place, for the Lord Jesus has guaranteed His divine presence where two or three are gathered in His Name, Matt. 18. 20. Thus Psalm 48 becomes rich with instruction. Zion is a *dwelling place*, vv. 1-3, for God is there. Whether believers meet in a private house, a hired hall or an open field, the Saviour is assuredly present. Ponder the miracle: He who is gloriously seated at the Father's right hand is also in the midst of His assembled people! But Zion is also a *delightful place*, vv. 2, 9-11, because it is characterized by godly joy. Nothing can thrill the Christian's heart like the knowledge that he worships a Risen Saviour, John 20. 20.

Around us the enemy may threaten and the world mock, but Zion is a *defended place*, vv. 3-7, 12-13. One of the loveliest O.T. promises is that of safety for the loyal worshipper of Jehovah, Exod. 34. 23-24; does not God still honour those who honour Him? There is no place of greater spiritual security than the assembly of God's people. Finally, Zion is a *distinctive place*, vv. 1-2, standing out from all others as the place that God has appointed. However attractive or popular man's traditions may seem, the believer's responsibility is to worship in God's way. Think of the unique simplicity of the Lord's Supper, free from human supervision and ritual, and yet peculiarly marked by godly order and solemnity. There the Christian is most conscious of God's love, v. 9, being most poignantly reminded of Calvary, the place where it was displayed at its greatest.

If we approached our Zion with the reverent joy of the psalmist, would we not equally experience the reality of God's presence?

"*God is among you of a truth*", 1 Cor. 14. 25 R.V.

234

READING: **Psalm 57**

MY HEART IS FIXED

NOTHING OF VALUE can be done for God which does not spring from a steadfast, determined heart. Daniel's separation from evil, Dan. 1. 8; Ruth's dedication to the God of Israel, Ruth 1. 18; the sturdy continuation of the early believers in Jerusalem, Acts 2. 42—all were the result of firm, inward decisions, for from the heart proceed "the issues of life", Prov. 4. 23. It follows, therefore, that worship, the believer's highest occupation, can only rise from a heart fixed upon the Lord and His majesty, Psa. 57. 7.

A fixed heart means absolute *confidence* in God. David's faith was no text-book knowledge, but a real trust in God in the midst of overwhelming difficulties, vv. 1-4. It is precisely in the context of such disasters that true faith flourishes. Thus David seeks mercy from the Lord in whom he found refuge, v. 1. Our hearts will never be steadfast in praise until they are steadfast in trust.

Second, the fixed heart implies *concentration*. David is besieged by distractions, but his focus of attention is still Jehovah, vv. 6-8. Foes without and foes within the believer so often conspire to rob the Lord of His worship. As J. N. Darby wrote, "No infant's changing pleasure, Is like my wandering mind". But the wandering mind cannot worship God. If our prayers of adoration are clichéd, cold, and thoughtlessly repetitive, it is because our hearts are not anchored upon the right object. There is, after all, enough in Him to keep our worship fresh and fragrant for all eternity, Rev. 4. 8. Next time we gather for worship, let us set our minds exclusively on the Saviour, Matt. 17. 8.

Finally, the fixed heart necessitates a *comprehension* of God's great worthiness, vv. 9-11. David recognizes that his God is greater than the nations of the earth, v. 9; Isa. 40. 15-17; greater than the universe, v. 10; Isa. 40. 22; greater indeed than everything, vv. 5, 11. We read of the Lord Jesus that "he that cometh from heaven is above all", John 3. 31, and, by virtue of Calvary, He has now received "a name which is above every name", Phil. 2. 9. May we learn increasingly to fix our hearts upon Him!

"Looking unto Jesus", Heb. 12. 2.

READING: **Psalm 66**

CIRCLES OF WORSHIP

WE SOMETIMES forget that our feeble expressions of praise to God are but a faint foretaste of a coming day of glory. Then the entire universe will become one vast auditorium in which the worship of God and of the Lamb will echo for all eternity.

Psalm 66 introduces us to three circles of worship, moving inwards from the cosmic, v. 1, to the personal, v. 16.

Circle number one is *universal worship*, vv. 1-4. The psalmist confidently anticipates its fulfilment as he looks ahead to the blessedness of the Saviour's earthly reign, v. 4. Such world-wide praise is not currently ascending to God, nor will it do so until "the earth shall be full of the knowledge of the Lord, as the waters cover the sea", Isa. 11. 9. Then, and not before, will "The kingdoms of this world ... become the kingdoms of our Lord, and of his Christ", Rev. 11. 15. During the Messiah's direct and righteous rule all will be subject to Him, Psa. 66. 3. When the believer feels grieved at the godlessness of the present age, or isolated amidst a hostile and rebellious environment, he would do well to remember that the Saviour will be honoured in the same world where He was rejected, Phil. 2. 10-11.

The second circle is that of *national worship*, vv. 5-12. As a nation, Israel had been recipients of God's redemptive deliverance at the miraculous crossing of the Red Sea, v. 6, and of His righteous discipline during the wilderness wanderings, vv. 10-12. The same is true of God's people today. We have been redeemed from worse than Egyptian bondage at infinitely greater cost, that "of the precious blood of Christ, as of a lamb without blemish and without spot", 1 Pet. 1. 18-19, and daily we experience God's fatherly correction, Heb. 12. 6-11.

The innermost circle is *individual worship*, vv. 13-20. Note the shift from "ye", v. 1, through "we", v. 6, to "I", v. 13. At the centre of all praise is the thankful heart of the individual believer, v. 16. There is much to learn from a worshipper who says, "I will go ... I will pay ... I will offer ... I will declare", vv. 13, 15, 16. Universal millennial praise is not yet a reality. Until it is, let us catch the psalmist's enthusiasm and make personal worship a priority.

"When they saw him, they worshipped him", Matt. 28. 17.

236

READING: **Psalm 67**

JOY IN JUSTICE

LIKE PSALM 66, this is a millennial psalm, picturing the blessings of the earthly reign of Christ. It anticipates a period when salvation extends to all, v. 2; the nations are governed in justice, v. 4; the earth itself gives of its abundance, v. 6, and when Israel especially enjoys the gracious favour of God, vv. 1, 7. And although believers today are waiting primarily for God's Son from heaven, 1 Thess. 1. 10, the Israelite's vision of a peaceful, prosperous earth is not foreign to our hope, for the Saviour who is coming to collect His Church is also coming to claim His rights in this world.

But notice the specific grounds for worship mentioned in the central verse of the psalm, v. 4. To praise God for His *greatness* in creation and His *grace* in salvation is easily understood. After all, every child of God is both the creature of His hand, Psa. 139. 14, and the object of His redeeming love, 107. 2. But here are worshippers who rejoice in God's righteous *government*. How often do we do that? During the present personal absence of the Lord Jesus, "the whole world lieth in the evil one", 1 John 5. 19 R.V. But the time is coming when "a king shall reign in righteousness", Isa. 32. 1, and "the government shall be upon his shoulder", 9. 6. How encouraging to know that this earth will be ruled as it should be by the One who made it!

The character of Christ's rule is total righteousness, and because of that all nations will "sing for joy", Psa. 67. 4. We sing hymns about grace, mercy, love and kindness, but do we ever rejoice in God's righteousness? Calvary, remember, displays it to the full, for there He proved Himself "just, and the justifier of him which believeth in Jesus", Rom. 3. 26.

> The love of God is righteous love,
>   Seen in Christ's death upon the tree;
> Love that exacts the sinner's debt,
>   Yet, in exacting, sets him free." (Bonar)

When Christ reigns, there will be universal justice, peace, freedom and joy. Is it any wonder that the nations will burst into praise?, Psa. 67. 3, 5.

"All nations shall come and worship before thee; for thy judgments are made manifest", Rev. 15. 4.

READING: **Psalm 75**

THY NAME IS NEAR

FOR THE BELIEVER, the truths of God's glorious character and His gracious closeness to His people have always been a source of delight. Asaph wrote Psalm 75 nearly three thousand years ago, but he, too, finds cause for thanksgiving in the Lord's Name, and in the Lord's nearness, v. 1.

Psalm 75 reveals Jehovah as the *God of Judgment*, who "putteth down one, and setteth up another", v. 7. The sobering truths touched on in Psalm 67 are here elaborated so as to emphasize that universal sovereignty is uniquely in His hands, v. 6. How foolish for feeble man to boast, v. 4, when it is God alone who "removeth kings, and setteth up kings", Dan. 2. 21. In days of international crisis, when men's hearts fail them for fear, the believer can rest in a God who reigns. But He is also the *God of Jacob*, v. 9. What a marvel of grace that the Eternal One should be willing to associate His Name with such a trickster as Jacob the supplanter, Isa. 41. 14. By nature, each one of us is a Jacob, rebelling against God's purposes and reliant upon our own cunning. Yet grace has stretched out and saved us, making us princes with God, Gen. 32. 28; Rev. 1. 6. The use of the old name Jacob reminds us of the continuing, debilitating presence of the flesh in God's people. Yet God never deserts His own. The Lord Jesus would not turn His back on the disciple who had denied any knowledge of Him, Luke 22. 61. And He is still the God of Jacob, and of Simon, and of all His saints, for His unchanging mercy and faithfulness mean that the "sons of Jacob are not consumed", Mal. 3. 6.

This God condescends to be near His children. The Son of God humbled Himself and stooped to us in our desperate need as the *Incarnate Lord*, John 1. 14. One so infinitely high became so low! As the *Invisible Lord*, He remains the close companion of the believer, James 4. 8, delighting to walk with those who will humbly walk with Him, Isa. 57. 15. But shortly, faith will give place to sight and He will return as the *Intervening Lord*, whose coming "draweth nigh", James 5. 8. Let us give thanks for a Saviour whose very name, Immanuel, tells that He is "God with us", Isa. 7. 14. *"Jesus himself drew near, and went with them"*, Luke 24. 15.

READING: **Psalm 81**

LISTEN BEFORE YOU PRAISE

PSALM 81 teaches us that before our mouths can be filled with God's praise, our ears must be open to God's voice, v. 8. It is sobering to learn that in ourselves we are incapable of expressing even our heart's gratitude to God without a divine initiative. Faith was generated in our hearts by the Word, Rom. 10. 17; our deep realization of God as Father is the work of the indwelling Holy Spirit, 8. 15; and our adoration too is the result of His gracious activity, for "we worship by the Spirit of God", Phil. 3. 3 R.V. True worship is the response of those who spend time with the Word.

Israel was exhorted to praise the right object, "God our strength", v. 1, with the appropriate accompaniment, "the timbrel, the pleasant harp", v. 2, and at the appointed time, "on our solemn feast day", v. 3. Today, the believer's worship has God as its object, Christ as its subject, and the Holy Spirit as its energy, for "through him we both have access by one Spirit unto the Father", Eph. 2. 18. Our accompaniment now is a whole-hearted devotedness to God, Rom. 12. 1, for pious words are of no value unless they proceed from a thankful heart and are reflected in godly living. In place of Israel's annual feasts we have the privilege of eternal, unbarred access into the immediate presence of the living God on the basis of the finished work of Calvary, Heb. 10. 19, 22. Although the Lord's Supper is our special weekly appointment for corporate worship, adoration is to be our constant attitude of heart towards God, 13. 15.

But Israel could never effectively fulfil these instructions without heeding God's Word. Thus God reminds His people of their redemption, vv. 5-7, their separation to Himself, vv. 8-10, and their subjection to His divine discipline, vv. 11-13. The foundation of our relationship with God is redemption, speaking of an infinitely costly deliverance, "ye are not your own ...For ye are bought with a price: therefore glorify God", 1 Cor. 6. 20. Separation is a joyful responsibility, and discipline the token of a Father's love. Should not such high honours fill our mouths with praise?

"As the Holy Ghost saith, Today if ye will hear his voice", Psa. 95. 7; Heb. 3. 7.

August 11th

READING: **Psalm 89**

UNFAILING FAITHFULNESS

THE ABSOLUTE trustworthiness of God is an insistent theme of Scripture. Along with the equally precious attribute of loving-kindness, God's faithfulness is the recurring idea in Psalm 89. Seven times we are reminded that the God to whom we belong is reliable. Men may fail, the universe itself (in the sovereign will of God) may change, but "thou art the same, and thy years shall have no end", Psa. 102. 27. Let us ponder on this celebration of divine faithfulness.

First, it is the subject of the believer's testimony, v. 1; every child of God is a living tribute to the Lord's reliability, being a recipient of His salvation, His preservation, and His tender care, 1 Cor. 1. 9. Do *our* mouths bear witness to this? Second, divine faithfulness is eternal, established "in the very heavens", v. 2. If mortal power or Satanic cunning could somehow cause God to be untrue to His Word, how miserable we should be! But God's trustworthiness is as enduring as Himself, James 1. 17. Further, this divine excellence provokes angelic delight, v. 5. It is encouraging to know that in praising God's worth we are in harmony with heaven. "The congregation of the saints", v. 5, reminds us of our responsibility to the local assembly, itself an evidence of God's faithfulness.

Lest we consider God's attributes mere enlargements of human qualities, the psalmist next emphasizes His uniqueness, v. 8. This is specially associated with God's blessings upon David and the Jewish nation, "my faithfulness ... shall be with him", v. 24. With us today is the Lord Jesus, Matt. 28. 20, whose name is "Faithful and True", Rev. 19. 11. Although David failed, Israel failed, and we regularly stumble and fall, our God will not suffer His faithfulness to fail, v. 33. From first to last, salvation depends entirely upon Him. Away for ever with the lie that makes eternal security rest one iota upon human works! Alas, Israel did backslide, vv. 38-48, but even amidst defection the psalmist's appeal is to God's unchanging promises, v. 49.

Thus we can make the Lord's faithfulness the subject of our praise, v. 1, and the basis of our petitions, vv. 49-51.

"Faithful is he that calleth you", 1 Thess. 5. 24.

240

August 12th

READING: **Psalm 89**

WHO IS LIKE THE LORD?

YESTERDAY we discovered that one characteristic of divine reliability is its uniqueness, v. 8. What God says, He does! And faith is the simple but life-changing assent to this precious truth, as we are persuaded, like Abraham, that what He has promised He is able also to perform, Rom. 4. 21. But the Christian soon begins to appreciate that God is incomparable in *all* His ways. "Who in the heavens can be compared unto the Lord?", Psa. 89. 6. In order to aid our limited understanding, God graciously provides illustrations in His Word (He has an eagle's strength, Exod. 19. 4; a mother's love, Isa. 49. 15; a shepherd's care, Psa. 23. 1), but He Himself is far beyond all such comparisons. What, then, does Psalm 89 teach about divine uniqueness?

First, God is unique in His *power*, vv. 9-14, for He is the Creator. Each time we look at the universe around us, we should be struck by its immensity, its complexity, and its unfailing testimony to the One who made it, Psa. 19. 1. If creation honours Him, should not we, who have been redeemed by blood?

Second, God is unique in His *purposes*, vv. 27-29. The nations of this world plan their strategies, and individual men struggle to fulfil their petty ambitions, Psa. 2. 1-2, but God's purposes alone will prevail. Notice the emphatic "I will" of verses 23, 25, 27, 28, 29. God's covenant with David and the nation of Israel is irrevocable, for human failing brings not rejection but discipline, vv. 30-37. And God is as unyielding in His purposes for believers today—see the thrilling summary in Romans 8. 28-30. Even His chastening hand is a proof of fatherly love. As J. G. Bellett wrote, "Let every tried believer know that discipline is not forgetfulness but remembrance".

Finally, our God is unique in His *possessions*, v. 11. Count the possessive pronouns relating to God in the psalm. It starts with "thy faithfulness" and continues in celebration of God's mercy, wonders, name, throne, righteousness, holiness, covenant, commandments, servants. Ponder each one, and praise! All these belong to God—and so do we, 1 Cor. 3. 22, 23.

"The only true God", John 17. 3.

241

August 13th

READING: **Psalm 95**

THE ROCK OF OUR SALVATION

ONE SURE WAY of appreciating God's excellence is to meditate upon the titles by which He reveals Himself in Scripture. Psalm 95 presents Him as the Rock, v. 1, the King, v. 3, and (implicitly) the Shepherd, v. 7. What does it mean to speak of God as a rock?

(i) It clearly suggests the idea of *strength* and *stability*. Israel, moving through a hostile wilderness towards the land of promise, needed to know that the God who had redeemed them was a God of unshakeable power. Other nations had their deities, but they were as nothing compared with Jehovah, Deut. 32. 31; Psa. 95. 3. Whether we look down, or up, or all around, we see what His hands have made, vv. 4-5.

(ii) He is the "rock of our *salvation*", v. 1; Deut. 32. 15; does it not dispel all doubts to know that salvation is firmly grounded? Before we were saved, we were sinking deep in the quicksands of sin, but, like David, we have been gloriously rescued, Psa. 40. 2. If we are on the Rock, we cannot be moved.

(iii) A rock speaks of *shelter*, for God is "the rock of my refuge", Psa. 94. 22. When Moses desired to see God's glory, he was sheltered in the cleft of a rock, covered from the dazzling sight of divine splendour by God's own hand, Exod. 33. 21-22. Today believers are both on and in the rock Christ Jesus, for our position "in Christ" is the guarantee of eternal acceptance in God's sight, Eph. 1. 6. What better refuge from the storms of trials and temptations than the Lord Jesus.

(iv) The rock portrays *supply*; out of a rock God provided life-giving water for His thirsty people, Exod. 17. 6. Thus the God of enduring strength is also the God of shepherd care who abundantly meets His children's needs. But note that the rock had to be smitten before the streams could flow. Worship can never bypass Calvary; there is not a single blessing we receive which does not stem from the atoning death of Christ, Rom. 8. 32.

What, then, should be our response? Psalm 95 encourages worship, v. 1; thanksgiving, v. 2; reverence, v. 6; and sensitivity to God's voice, v. 8. May we lean upon the Rock and enter fully into His rest, v. 11.

"And that Rock was Christ", 1 Cor. 10. 4.

242

READING: **Psalm 96**

SING A NEW SONG

A NEW SONG, of course, presupposes an old one. And the first song recorded in Scripture takes us back to the moment of creation, "when the morning stars sang together, and all the sons of God shouted for joy", Job 38. 7. Creation in all its splendour testifies to the magnificence of God, Rom. 1. 20. But God is also our Redeemer, for He who made us by His mighty power has, in matchless love and grace, bought us for Himself. Whenever the O.T. speaks of a "new song", it seems to be looking forward to the coming of the Lord Jesus and the blessings resulting from His redeeming work.

We start with the *call* to sing, Psa. 33. 3. Worship is no optional extra but a solemn, yet joyful, responsibility for every child of God. Too often, perhaps, we assail God's ears with old sighs instead of new songs! Then we discover the *cause*, which is nothing less than perfect, divine salvation, Psa. 40. 1-3. When we remember what we have been saved from, that new song should come naturally, Psa. 96. 2.But what of the *choir*? Psalm 96 has a universal vision: "Sing unto the Lord, all the earth", v. 1. True, "the whole world lieth in the evil one", 1 John 5. 19 R.V., but the Lord Jesus who holds its title deeds will shortly claim His rights, so that worship will ascend to God from the entire planet. Even though the choir is not yet complete, God looks for willing worship now from His people, Psa. 149. 1. The *context* of the song is one of absolute divine victory over all enemies, because "his right hand, and his holy arm, hath gotten him the victory", Psa. 98. 1. Our Saviour will return in resplendent glory as King of kings, to deliver His ancient people Israel from all her oppressors, 144. 9-10. The new song is not a lament but a song of triumph.

Finally, what is the song's *content*? Unlike some believers today, Scripture is consistently concerned with the matter rather than with the music of hymns. And the subject of heaven's worship is the Lord Jesus Christ, once crucified but now eternally glorified, Rev. 5. 9-10. All our material for proper worship is found in Him.

"And they sung a new song, saying, Thou art worthy ... for thou wast slain", Rev. 5. 9.

August 15th

READING: **Psalm 96**

GIVING TO THE GIVER

HAVE WE ever paused to wonder how creatures of the dust (for that is what we are) can possibly offer anything to God? After all, He is the self-sufficient "I AM", whose very name declares His independence and sovereignty. If God could have any needs of any kind whatever, how could we be certain of His ability to meet ours?, Phil. 4. 19. No, from Genesis 1. 29 onwards, HE is the ultimate Giver of all things, we merely being the humble recipients.

And yet, such a God desires our worship. The psalmist encourages us to "give unto the Lord glory and strength", Psa. 96. 7. Glory and strength are His in abundance already, eternally and infinitely, for "Honour and majesty are before him: strength and beauty are in his sanctuary", v. 6. All we can do is simply to acknowledge what He is, and what He has done for us in Christ. "Bring an offering", says the psalmist, v. 8. Like king David we have to confess that our offering at best is only giving back to God what He first gave us, 1 Chron. 29. 14. The Living God can accept nothing less than perfection, and therefore our worship will involve presenting to God the Lord Jesus in all His beauty, spotlessness and whole-hearted devotion to His Father's will, Matt. 3. 17; Eph. 5. 2. If God gave us such an "unspeakable gift", 2 Cor. 9. 15, surely we can express to Him our delight in His well beloved Son.

The Lord Jesus is the *subject* of our worship, and holiness is its *spirit*. True praise can only ascend from a heart wholly separated to Him. "O worship the Lord in the beauty of holiness", v. 9, reminds us that the divine idea of beauty is very different from ours. While we see only the outward appearance, God's eye penetrates to the centre of our being, assessing our thoughts, our motives, our reality, 1 Sam. 16. 7. How important, therefore, that our spoken or silent appreciation of the Lord Jesus in worship should be the fruit of a life genuinely set apart for Him. Anything less than that will be empty words. May our offerings of praise, "the fruit of our lips", Heb. 13. 15, bring pleasure to God today.

"Blessing, and honour, and glory, and power, be unto him that sitteth upon the throne, and unto the Lamb", Rev. 5. 13.

244

August 16th

READING: **Psalm 98**

THE PROPER FOCUS OF WORSHIP

PSALM 98, like so many others, deals primarily with corporate rather than individual worship. It envisages a praising company of people, extending its embrace from "the house of Israel" to include "all the ends of the earth", v. 3; even the natural world joins in celebration of Jehovah's majesty, vv. 7-9. And yet, despite this most impressive gathering of worshippers, the object of attention remains God Himself, for all is done "*unto* the Lord", vv. 1, 4, 5, and "*before* the Lord", vv. 6, 9.

Is our praise ever distracted by a consciousness of one another? On the one hand, corporate worship demands mutual consideration, 1 Cor. 11. 33, mutual courtesy amongst those who participate, 14. 30, and clarity of expression so that all the saints can appreciate the thanksgivings offered on their behalf, 14. 9, 16. We must remember that there are others present. Sometimes, an anxiety to avoid periods of silence provokes brethren into hasty or unprofitable speech. But the command "Let all things be done decently and in order", 14. 40, encourages neither a sluggish apathy nor an unseemly rush to take part. May our praise ascend to God worthily as from one heart, Acts 4. 24, "that ye may with one mind and one mouth glorify God, even the Father of our Lord Jesus Christ", Rom. 15. 6. On the other hand, it is "Jesus only" whom we would see, Matt. 17. 8. Our praise is for His pleasure, not for self-display. How sensitive we need to be to the Spirit's leading.

Our worship is also "before the Lord". There is no need to travel to some ornate temple, nor even to wait until the Lord takes us to our heavenly home before we can appreciate Him. By grace, *all* our adoration now is offered in His very presence. Properly understood, this truth will promote in us a spirit of reverence and godly fear. How carefully, how solemnly we would prepare our hearts if we fully grasped that we were coming, not before the saints, but before the Lord. Yet reverence does not preclude joy, for each time the psalmist speaks of God's presence it is in the context of rejoicing, vv. 8-9.

"*Now unto him ... be glory in the church by Christ Jesus*", Eph. 3. 21.

August 17th

READING: **Psalm 100**

SERVE WITH GLADNESS

PSALM 100 is the climax of a series of five psalms, beginning with Psalm 96, which anticipate the blessings enjoyed by Israel and the Gentiles under Christ's earthly reign of righteousness. Not surprisingly, it overflows with praise, for here prominence is given to the nature of the offerings brought before God. To approach Him empty-handed is unthinkable, Deut. 16. 16-17, so the worshippers in Psalm 100 draw near with gladness, singing, v. 2, thanksgiving and praise, v. 4.

Gladness speaks of a settled attitude of heart, a deep-rooted delight in God that makes serving Him not a burden but a pleasure. The word appears in the O.T. primarily in connection with the worship of Jehovah, for there only can true joy be found. "Let the heart of them rejoice that seek the Lord", Psa. 105. 3. And since we "joy in God through our Lord Jesus Christ", Rom. 5. 11, our delight will be as lastingly satisfying as its eternal object. *Singing*, Psa. 100. 2, comes from a root meaning "a shout of jubilation". It first occurs when the Lord publicly accepted the burnt offering, provoking a holy exultation amongst the people who "shouted, and fell on their faces", Lev. 9. 24, and is only used in the context of worship. A sacrifice that pleases God should move us to express our adoration. Only those who know the value of the cross can come with singing, for it is purely in the merits of Christ Jesus, our burnt offering, Eph. 5. 2, that we have a perfect standing before God, 1. 6. Are we learning more about Calvary?

Thanksgiving, Psa. 100. 4, translates a Hebrew word basically meaning to confesss, either one's sin, Ezra 10. 11, or God's excellence, Lev. 7. 12. Here it is the latter thought, for we are approaching Jehovah in the light of His goodness, mercy and truth, v. 5. The great indictment against sinful man is his ingratitude, Rom. 1. 21. May we, as redeemed ones, have an intelligent and thankful appreciation of all God is in Himself. Finally, *Praise* is our homage to God who is incomparably great. "Who is like unto thee, O Lord ... glorious in holiness, fearful in praises, doing wonders?", Exod. 15. 11.

"Give glory and honour and thanks to him", Rev. 4. 9.

246

August 18th

READING: **Psalm 103**

REMEMBERED BENEFITS

NOTHING CAN be more calculated to stimulate worship than the recounting of divine blessings. Human memory, however, is notoriously fickle, Gen. 40. 14, 23, and God, in His knowledge of our weaknesses, Psa. 103. 14, has graciously provided suitable aids. The Holy Spirit, John 14. 26; the Lord's Supper, 1 Cor. 11. 25, and the fellowship of believers, Psa. 78. 35, all serve to kindle our memories of God's goodness. And as we daily read the Word we are confronted with what our God has done, 2 Pet. 3. 2, so that an awareness of His benefits might cause us to "bless the Lord", Psa. 103. 22.

David starts with five distinct aspects of Jehovah's goodness to him. First, He *"forgiveth* all thine iniquities", v. 3. Note that precious word "all". There is not a sin committed by the child of God which has not been fully and eternally pardoned because of Calvary. Can we think of our forgiveness without also remembering what it cost the Saviour?, 2 Cor. 5. 21; 1 John 1. 7. Next, He *"healeth* all thy diseases", v. 3. In Israel's wilderness experience this, an aspect of God's covenant with the nation and dependent upon their obedience, was literally true, Deut. 28. 58-60. Today, our bodies await a glorious future transformation, Phil. 3. 20-21, but we still delight to acknowledge that all physical healing, direct or indirect, comes from the Lord.

He, too, *"redeemeth ...* from destruction", v. 4. David is probably thinking of specific deliverance from his enemies, but we are bound to see here a much grander rescue from everlasting bondage to sin and futility, 1 Pet. 1. 18-19. Nor should we forget who *"crowneth"* us with love and tender protection, v. 4. The word means to compass, as with a shield, Psa. 5. 12; just as Saul once surrounded David with his troops, so God surrounded David with His mercy, 1 Sam. 23. 26. How marvellous to be so perfectly garrisoned against all ills! Finally, our God *"satisfieth ...* with good things", v. 5. Is there not enough in the Lord Jesus to thrill our hearts? "Bless the Lord, O my soul and all that is within me, bless his holy name".

"Do ye not remember?", Mark 8. 18.

247

August 19th

READING: **Psalm 103**

SO GREAT IS HIS MERCY

THE HEART of David dwells delightedly upon the truth that God is "abundant in lovingkindness", v. 8 J.N.D. Our planet may be plagued with shortages, famines and droughts, but God's mercy can never run dry. Every believer is a living testimony to the lavishness of sovereign grace, Eph. 1. 7-8, and it is only fitting that we "bless the Lord" for His kindness to us.

His mercy is *unmerited*", vv. 8-10, because there is nothing is us to deserve it. Like Mephibosheth we can only respond in amazed gratitude to the honours heaped upon us, 2 Sam. 9. 7-8. And yet the psalm does not minimize our guilt. We are stained with sins, iniquities and transgressions, vv. 10, 12, each word unambiguously spelling out our total ruin before God. But the Lord is "merciful and gracious", v. 8, and truly it is only by His grace that we have been saved, Eph. 2. 11-12, because it exceeds all human measurement. If we could calculate the height of the heavens we could estimate the vastness of divine mercy (and thereby limit it), but all God's attributes are gloriously boundless, Job 38. 4-5. "So great salvation", Heb. 2. 3, is just too big for the believer's mind to grasp, but not too big for the heart to enjoy!

Because of His tenderness, wisdom, and intimate knowledge of each of His people, God's mercy is *fatherly* in its compassion, vv. 13-14. The N.T. reveals that this is more than mere poetic license, for the Lord Jesus came specifically to reveal God as Father, John 1. 18. How encouraging, then, to read of the God who has redeemed us as "the Father of our Lord Jesus Christ, the Father of mercies, and the God of all comfort", 2 Cor. 1. 3. By virtue of His deity, His mercy is *eternal*, vv. 15-18, enduring as long as God Himself, "from everlasting to everlasting", Psa. 90. 2. May we find strength in knowing that, though we are but dust, v. 14, and our days as grass, v. 15, our Father's loving attitude towards His children will never, never change.

> Change and decay in all around I see;
> O Thou that changest not, abide with me.

"Bless the Lord, O my soul".

"God ... is rich in mercy, for his great love wherewith he loved us", Eph. 2. 4.

August 20th

READING: **Psalm 107. 1-22**

GIVE THANKS UNTO THE LORD

PSALM 107 is the last of three psalms focussing on God's dealings with Israel. Psalm 105 commemorates redemption from Egypt, 106 catalogues the nation's rebellions, and 107 celebrates her ultimate regathering to the land. It establishes a recurring pattern of distress, deliverance and declaration as God repeatedly rescues His people, deserving their endless gratitude. And yet the four-fold refrain, "O that men would praise the Lord for his goodness", vv. 8, 15, 21, 31, suggests that, like the nine cleansed lepers of Luke 17. 12-19, men are tragically slow to give thanks to God.

Verses 17-22 provide an example of the basic pattern. Like Israel, because of personal folly and sin we find ourselves in *distress*, v. 19. The value of such misery is that it turns us to the Lord, that we might experience His *deliverance*, v. 20; Psa. 120. 1. "He sent his word": we are bound to think of the Lord Jesus, the living Word, sent down from heaven for our blessing, John 1. 14. And notice the fulness of that blessing: "he saveth ... healed ... delivered", vv. 19-20. No half measures, here, but a total salvation!

It is therefore only reasonable that we should respond with a hearty *declaration* of God's goodness, v. 21, through the offering of "sacrifices of thanksgiving", v. 22. This was a species of peace offering which marked a special display of divine mercy, Lev. 7. 12-15. The remarkable feature of *all* peace offerings was that God, and the priest, and the offerer partook of the sacrificial victim. Here was fellowship indeed, as men shared in the same object which brought pleasure to God. Of course, like all the offerings, it speaks of the Lord Jesus Christ. He is our peace, Eph. 2. 14, the One whose atoning death delights the hearts of God and His people. "Truly our fellowship is with the Father, and with His Son Jesus Christ", 1 John 1. 3. But here is the point: O.T. thanksgiving involved joyously feasting upon a slain animal, Deut. 27. 7. Our thanksgiving today can never be divorced from the work of the cross, for that is the basis of all our blessings, Rom. 8. 32. When you give thanks, think of Calvary.

"Thanks be unto God for his unspeakable gift", 2 Cor. 9.15.

August 21st

READING: **Psalm 107. 23-43**

SEE AND REJOICE

OUR WORSHIP is helped if we have a keen eye for God's hand at work. Psalm 107 concludes with the intriguing comment that the way to understand God's lovingkindness is to "observe" or "give heed to" His doings, v. 43 R.V. And true understanding will certainly lead to praise, Psa. 47. 7. How real and fresh would be our adoration if, like the mariners, we had an eye to "see the works of the Lord, and his wonders", v. 24. There is nothing like a personal acquaintance with God's ways to stimulate worship. Those who witnessed the Saviour's miracles "marvelled, and glorified God", Matt. 9. 8.

In this psalm, for example, we observe that our God is *active*, for the whole poem is crammed full of verbs powerfully expressing His deeds. He is the One who redeems, v. 2; gathers, v. 3; delivers, v. 6; leads, v. 7; satisfies, v. 9; saves, v. 19; heals, v. 20; and blesses, v. 38. It is glorious to belong to a God who is at work, John 5. 17.

Further, we learn that He is *gracious*, for His blessings are directed towards a people guilty of weakness, vv. 4-5; rebellion, vv. 10-12; folly, vv. 17-18; and helplessness, v. 26. And Israel is no worse than us. Despite their sin, each time they call to Him, He hears, vv. 6, 13, 19, 28, for His longsuffering is without end. Since He is the unchanging One, we can guarantee that He is still as patient with His children. So when anyone is at his wit's end, v. 27, let him not forget to cry to the Lord.

Finally, He is *tender*, because all His ways towards His people are guided by a loving heart that desires the very best for its object. Verse 41 spells this out, teaching that God provides both protection and fellowship for His own. Are we needy? Then He has set us "on high", for we are seated "in heavenly places in Christ Jesus", Eph. 2. 6, and there is no higher or safer place than that. Are we lonely? Then He has brought us into the family fellowship of His people, placing us in the body of Christ, and linking us in practical partnership with a local assembly of saints where we can experience the warmth of heaven itself, Acts 2. 46-47.

"The brethren ... came to meet us ... whom when Paul saw, he thanked God, and took courage", Acts 28. 15.

August 22nd

READING: **Psalm 113**

PAUPERS, PRINCES AND PRAISES

THAT "some have greatness thrust upon them" is one of our favourite stories from childhood—the sudden rise to fame and fortune of the nobody. But no human fiction can be more amazing than the reality of divine salvation. Psalm 113 reminds us that God has not only condescended to involve Himself with His creatures, v. 6, but has also raised up the lowly to a position of stupendous dignity, vv. 7-8. "But God hath chosen the foolish ... the weak things of the world", 1 Cor. 1. 26-27.

Unquestionably we were poor, for our spiritual bankruptcy before God is spelled out clearly in the Lord's parables, Luke 7. 41-42. The dust was our natural element, speaking eloquently both of human frailty, Eccl. 12. 7, and of the dirtiness of the sin which clogs our steps from birth, Psa. 51. 5. We do not need a handbook about ancient Israel to understand that the dunghill, Psa. 113. 7, is a striking metaphor for utter degradation and shame, Lam. 4. 5. If only we saw sin as God sees it, in all its ugly defilement, and smelt the stench of its corruption! In the light of heaven, unregenerate man is nothing but "wounds, and bruises, and putrifying sores", Isa. 1. 6. But from such depths we have been plucked, and raised to even greater heights of blessing, Psa. 113. 7-9, for paupers have been made princes. Paul's case is especially noteworthy, Eph. 3. 8.

What, then, have we become? Princes are noted for their *prosperity,* and none are wealthier than those in the royal family of heaven, sharing in the riches of God's mercy, Eph. 2. 4; grace, 2. 7; and glory, 1. 18. Besides those we enjoy now, there are infinite blessings in store, far beyond our comprehension, 1 Cor. 2. 9-10. No wonder the psalmist says of the believer, "wealth and riches shall be in his house", Psa. 112. 3. Further, we possess a *power* unknown to the natural man, for every saint is, from the very instant of conversion, indwelt by the Holy Spirit whose divine energy enables him to speak and live for the Saviour, Acts 1. 8. And finally, as sons of God, we have the *privilege* of access into His throne-room to solicit His help in time of need, Heb. 4. 16. Is that not a good reason for praise?

"Blessed ... with all spiritual blessings", Eph. 1. 3.

August 23rd

READING: **Psalm 117**

THE VALUE OF BREVITY

THIS, the shortest psalm, proves conclusively that any particular act of worship does not have to be long-winded. One of the dangers facing those who become accustomed to leading in public prayer is that they lose the art of brevity. Of couse, there *is* a place for prolonged praise. The next psalm but one is the longest in the Book, and its 176 verses celebrating the varied excellencies of God's Word are neither tedious nor redundant. The Lord Jesus Himself set us a challenging example by spending much time alone with His Father in prayer, Luke 6. 12, and few of us would deny that our personal communion with God could profitably be extended and enriched. Too often the Lord has to say to us, "could ye not watch with me one hour?", Matt. 26. 40. But in corporate worship we must ever bear in mind the weakness of the flesh and the very real possibility of wearying our brethren by over-lengthy prayers. It is perhaps significant that all the expressions of public worship recorded in Scripture are remarkably concise. Even Solomon's marvellous prayer at the dedication of the temple takes no longer than six minutes to read slowly, 1 Kings 8. 22-53.

Psalm 117, then, says much in little—whereas, alas, many of our prayers do quite the opposite, as did those of the heathen, Matt. 6. 7. Notice, it *encourages* worship by calling the nations of the earth to exalt Jehovah's name, v. 1. Do we encourage or extinguish praise amongst God's people? Remember, the spiritual state of each believer will either aid or hinder the worship of the local assembly. It *explains* worship by rejoicing in those delightful divine attributes of "merciful kindness" and "truth", v. 2, both of which are blessedly directed "toward us", for God's goodness is ever poured out on the unworthy, Matt. 5. 44-45. It *exemplifies* worship by practising what it teaches. Too often we talk about praise instead of doing it. Yet, though our words be few (and there is wisdom in that, Eccl. 5. 2) they can be full of matter. Surely even the youngest believer can say with Thomas, "My Lord and my God", John 20. 28.

"When ye pray, use not vain repetitions ... for they think that they shall be heard for their much speaking", Matt. 6. 7.

252

August 24th

READING: **Psalm 145**

DAVID'S PSALM OF PRAISE

THE CENTRAL VERSE of this psalm provides today's topic for meditation, because it emphasizes a significant but neglected responsibility. Worship and praise should not be limited to the formal gatherings of the assembly, but should be a vital part of the staple diet of our normal intercourse with the saints, v. 11.

The good sense of this is obvious. If praise is merely an attitude artificially cultivated for a few hours each week when we assemble to break bread or spend time in collective prayer, our hearts may well become hardened and coaxed into the complacency of a lifeless ritualism, Matt. 15. 8. Surely a praising spirit should *always* characterize God's redeemed ones! David promises to bless the Lord daily, v. 2, and since God's greatness is unsearchable, v. 3, there is no danger of running out of material for thoughtful adoration. It is only wise, then, to nurture our heart's affections for God by filling our regular conversation with an appreciation of His majesty. When we read that the God-fearers in the O.T. "spake often one to another ... (and) thought upon his name", Mal. 3. 16, we can guarantee that the theme of their discourse was not the trivialities of the passing world, for "the world passeth away", 1 John 2. 17, but the eternal excellencies of their God.

David's psalm is the ideal guide to uplifting Christian conversation. When you are feeling low, get a friend to read it aloud to you, so that your thoughts may be brought into line with heavenly truths. Its content is simple but profound, rehearsing God's *greatness*, vv. 3-7; *grace*, v. 8; and *goodness*, vv. 9, 14-20. How in all conscience can we remain gloomy when confronted with the glories of Jehovah, especially when told, "happy is that people, whose God is the Lord" ?, Psa. 144. 15. If only we were to grasp what our God is, we would find ourselves blessing His name, v. 10, encouraging other believers with what we have learned of His splendour, v. 11, and testifying to the unsaved, v. 12. Is *your* conversation filled with "the praise of the Lord", v. 21, or is it composed of "salt water and fresh"?, James 3. 11-12.

"And they talked together of all these things which had happened", Luke 24. 14.

253

August 25th

READING: **Psalm 146**

HALLELUJAH

THIS IS the first of the five Hallelujah Psalms which conclude the Psalter, and are so called because they each begin and end with the expression, "Praise ye the Lord". Since some believers seem to think that the perfunctory repetition of this phrase is a sure mark of spirituality, it is perhaps important to notice that the psalmist goes on to catalogue in detail the mercies of his God. In other words, he knows the God whom he praises! Every new experience of Jehovah should provide fuel for fresh and informed adoration of His grandeur. It was only when they saw God's hand at the Red Sea that Israel burst into song, Exod. 15. 1.

Twelve precious activities of God are listed to justify the psalmist's call to worship, vv. 5-10. The despondent saint would do well to consider these, for they have the healthy effect of drawing attention away from self (always depressing) towards the Saviour. Some concern His *power* as Creator, v. 6; King, v. 10; and Victor over the forces of evil, v. 9, but the majority of the reasons for praise in this psalm relate to God's *tenderness* towards His needy people. He intervenes on behalf of the oppressed, feeds the hungry, and releases the captives, v. 7. Such blessings are true literally and spiritually, for He who will righteously solve the world's problems at His return already meets our needs for protection, 1 Pet. 1. 5; food, Matt. 4. 4; and deliverance, Gal. 1. 4. Before conversion, we were blind, bowed down, and alienated from the life of God, vv. 8-9, but Christ has given us sight, 2 Cor. 4. 6; lifted us up, Eph. 2. 6; and received us into His eternal family, where we are "no more strangers and foreigners, but fellowcitizens with the saints, and of the household of God", 2. 19.

All this suggests that only those who know themselves to be entirely inadequate and helpless are qualified to worship, for worship involves the acknowledgement of dependence. He who loves (and therefore praises) the Lord most is he who has been forgiven most, Luke 7. 43-47. Next time you say "Hallelujah", make sure that you know why!

"All men glorified God for that which was done ... they lifted up their voice to God with one accord", Acts 4. 21, 24.

READING: **Psalm 147. 1-11**

IT IS GOOD TO SING PRAISES

IT IS A GENERAL principle in Scripture that God's requirements of His people are always for their benefit as well as for His glory. Praise is no exception. It is, indeed, the key to a happy and healthy Christian life, Psa. 146. 5, for it occupies our minds with the only object in which we shall ever find complete satisfaction, God Himself. As Augustine wrote, "Thou movest us to delight in praising Thee; for Thou hast formed us for Thyself, and our hearts are restless till they find rest in Thee".

This psalm declares three distinct benefits of praise: it is good, pleasant, and comely, v. 1. It is *good* for us because it prevents our thoughts from dwelling on evil. The way to quench Satan's fiery darts of wickedness and to counter the insidious temptations of the world and the flesh is not to strive for their expulsion from our minds. That we cannot do; rather, we must fill our hearts with an alternative and superior object. Thus Paul encourages positive thinking in the believer: "if there be any praise, think on these things", Phil. 4. 8. When the enemy attacks today, we must dwell upon God's greatness, Psa. 147. 5-6, and sing praises, v. 7.

Second, praise is *pleasant*. Never forget that it brings pleasure to God's heart when His saints worship Him, vv. 10-11. His delight is not in our human assets, be they physical strength, intelligence, business successs, or personal charm (although all come from Him), but in our adoration. May our worship show that we are those who fear Him, v. 11. And praise should also delight us. It is no drudgery to worship our Redeemer but an infallible antidote to misery, v. 7; 149. 5.

Finally, "praise is *comely*", v. 1. That is, it is both appropriate and beautiful. Meditate upon the works of God that feature in this psalm, and discover how fitting it is that He should be magnified. Scanty praise always indicates an inadequate appreciation of Jehovah. The remedy for that is to read the psalm again—and yet again! By then its beauty may grip us as we learn how lovely it is to glorify God; "Whoso offereth praise glorifieth me", Psa. 50. 23.

"We should be to the praise of his glory", Eph. 1. 12.

August 27th

READING: **Psalm 147. 12-20**

PRAISE THY GOD, O ZION

IT IS THRILLING to learn that we are the *special* objects of God's kindness. True, He so loved the world that He gave His Son, but His distinct Fatherly concern is for those who have become His children through faith in Christ, Gal. 3. 26; 1 John 3. 1. Like Israel of old, we can count our blessings and say, "He hath not dealt so with any nation", v. 20.

The Jews were particularly the object of His *protection*, v. 13, located in the midst of hostile powers, yet garrisoned by God Himself. Our personal weakness (and even after conversion the believer is frailty incarnate) is cause for much grief, but our God is "of great power", v. 5. If He is for us, "who can be against us?", Rom. 8. 31. True blessedness is the knowledge that "he careth for you", 1 Pet. 5. 7. Israel also enjoyed internal *peace*, v. 14, and so should we in our hearts, Phil. 4. 7, and in the assembly, 1 Thess. 5. 13. This God-centered serenity will not always still the storms, but it will give the confidence to endure them, Acts 27. 25.

Further, God made material *provision* for the Israelites, v. 14, supplying the best that this earth could produce as they obeyed Him, Deut. 28. 1-14. But in Christ our blessings are not tied down to the old creation. Rather, we are made rich with heavenly benefits, Eph. 1. 3. One of the significant differences between the O.T. Israel and the believer today is that our wealth, our worship, and even our warfare are primarily spiritual. Are we rejoicing in what God has provided? Let us "go in to possess the land, which the Lord your God giveth you to possess it", Josh. 1. 11.

As if to reassure the reader about God's ability to fulfil His pledges, the psalmist devotes several verses to His *power*, vv. 15-18. The stability of the created universe is a token of His goodness, for He gives "rain from heaven, and fruitful seasons, filling our hearts with food and gladness", Acts 14. 17. Israel's greatest privilege was God's Word, Psa. 147. 19-20, and we too are entrusted with His *precepts* to cherish, John 17. 14. Simply to mention these blessings is to strike a note of worship!

"How much more shall your Father which is in heaven give good things", Matt. 7. 11.

READING: **Psalm 148**

PRAISE FROM THE HEAVENS

As THE Psalter draws to its close, the volume and intensity of its worship increase. We have come a long way from the solitary "blessed man" who stood for truth despite the pressures of the ungodly crowd, Psa. 1. 1-4. Now we find nothing but a vast adoring host involved in continual praise, anticipating the day when all enemies are subdued and righteousness reigns supreme, Isa. 32. 1: 2 Pet. 3. 13.

The first half of Psalm 148 teaches that the very heavens are alive with worship. It is chastening to realize that the universe, which engages so much of man's scientific curiosity while ultimately eluding his final understanding, is made to honour God. At the forefront of this magnificent creation is "an innumerable company of angels", Heb. 12. 22; Psa. 148. 2, all involved in adoration. Despite our ignorance of these spirit beings, we can at least grasp something of their power and splendour. They guard God's people, 2 Kings 6. 15-17; deliver from imprisonment, Acts 12. 7; and destroy the enemy, 2 Chron. 32. 21. Yet they strictly refuse man's veneration, Rev. 22. 8-9, and devote themselves to God's praise, Isa. 6. 1-3. How wonderful to know that He whom we worship is "so much better than the angels", Heb. 1. 4, and that, as our psalm indicates, "all the angels of God worship *him*", 1. 6.

Just as these spiritual intelligences prostrate themselves before Jehovah, so too does the inanimate creation in the skies. Sun, moon, stars, the heavens, the waters above the heavens, all resound God's praise, vv. 3-4. This they do simply by being what He has made them to be, vv. 5-6, and "fulfilling his word", v. 8. What a lesson: God is glorified when His creatures, intelligent or otherwise, do His will; see Luke 19. 40. Thus sun and moon honour Him by fulfilling their illuminating function around the earth, Gen. 1. 14-18. In the same way, redeemed man glorifies God *when he obeys His Word*. Each act of obedience is an act of worship. As we have said before, praise should colour the whole Christian life. The universe is faithfully glorifying its Maker, as He intended. Are we?

"*For by him were all things created ... all things were created by him, and for him*", Col. 1. 16; Rev. 4. 11.

READING: **Psalm 148**

PRAISE FROM THE EARTH

IN THE FIRST six verses of Psalm 148 contemplate those elements of creation mentioned in Genesis 1. 6-19, the rest of the psalm turns the spotlight upon the immediate environment of man as described in the latter half of that chapter. Once again, all the praise is God's, ascending spontaneously from the whole of His infinitely varied and beautiful handiwork.

There is a rich texture to the worship generated in this psalm. The seas and their inhabitants, v. 7; the weather, v. 8; the landscape, v. 9; plant, animal and insect life, vv. 9-10, all combine in perfect accord to give God the glory. How much we can learn from the world around us!

Notice the *diversity* involved: there is nothing that God has made that is too small to receive His care, Matt. 10. 29, or too lowly to join in His praise, Luke 19. 40. Perhaps we would complain less about the weather if we remembered that it was obediently "fulfilling his word", v. 8. Consider, too, the *harmony* implied here. Despite the vast range of the animal kingdom, there is no discord in the orchestra of adoration, for a great fish, Jonah 1. 17; an ass, Matt. 21. 2-3; or even a bird, 1 Kings 17. 4, can each bring God pleasure by doing His bidding. May we be "of one heart and of one soul" in our corporate worship, Acts 4. 24, 32; Rom. 15. 6, as we seek to obey the Lord's command and remember Him, Luke 22. 19.

Continuity is suggested by the mountains and the hills, v. 9. Their very existence is a silent but majestic testimony to God's purpose for them. Since our breath is in His hands, Dan. 5. 23, and every heartbeat a token of His constant love, should not we sing praise as long as we live?, Psa. 104. 33.

Man, as the climax of God's creative acts, is the final participant in this paeon of praise, vv. 11-14. Whoever we are, great or small, young or old, male or female (and the psalmist carefully lists them all), we have a personal responsibility to honour His excellent name. Surely every believer, realizing that he is the Lord's by creation, Gen. 1. 27, by purchase, 1 Cor. 6. 20, and by gift, John 10. 29, will gladly join to exalt the Saviour.

"Give glory to him ... worship him that made heaven, and earth, and the sea, and the fountains of water", Rev. 14. 7.

READING: **Psalm 149**

LET ISRAEL REJOICE

THIS PSALM is an exhortation to Israel, God's own chosen people, to fulfil its responsibilities in worship. After all, that nation had a knowledge and an experience of Jehovah enjoyed by no other, Psa. 147. 20, and "unto whomsoever much is given, of him shall be much required", Luke 12. 48. Yet this was no burdensome duty but a high privilege, "this honour have all his saints", Psa. 149. 9.

Israel is reminded of its divine *formation*, v. 2. That miraculous deliverance from Egyptian bondage by blood and power was the nation's birthday, Exod. 12. 2. We too are redeemed, and love to look back to Calvary as the basis of our eternal relationship with God, for there "Christ our passover" was sacrificed for us, 1 Cor. 5. 7.

But Israel was not rescued to wander aimlessly; rather it was given a king, Jehovah Himself, Psa. 149. 2, who provided His people with divine *legislation* governing every aspect of life. The Mosaic law, with its civil, ceremonial and moral instruction, set Israel apart as a nation under God. Similarly, the local assembly is a theocracy where God's Word, not man's fashions or traditions, holds sway.

Again, Israel was distinguished by *jubilation*, as it rejoiced in a God who had done so much for His people, condescending even to dwell in their midst, vv. 3, 5, 6. Christian worship involves reverent joy tempered with holy astonishment as we recall that God "spared not his own Son, but delivered him up for us all", Rom. 8. 32. And He is always present where His saints gather to Him, Matt. 18. 20.

Being owned by Jehovah ensures continuing *salvation*, v. 4, and just as the Israelites were guaranteed national preservation, Jer. 31. 35-37, so we are sustained all the way, Jude 24. Those whom God saves He keeps! But whereas Israel's *occupation* was as the effective instrument of divine government in the world, vv. 6-9, we today are strangers and pilgrims, submitting ourselves to earthly rulers, 1 Pet. 2. 11-14, and patiently awaiting the Lord from heaven. When *He* comes, and not before, we shall reign, Rev. 20. 4; 22. 5.

"Unto him be glory in the church by Christ Jesus throughout all ages, world without end", Eph. 3. 21.

August 31st

READING: **Psalm 150**

LET EVERY THING PRAISE THE LORD

WE HAVE observed a significant progression in these final three psalms. Psalm 148 called for Jehovah's praise to be sounded from the heavens and the earth, while Psalm 149 focussed primarily upon Israel as "the congregation of saints", v. 1, from whom God expects a new song of worship. The closing psalm sums it all up by encouraging "every thing that hath breath" to praise the Lord, v. 6. Truly, praise is going to be a universal phenomenon!

Three simple thoughts arise from the major prepositions used in the psalm: "in", v. 1; "for", v. 2; and "with", vv. 3-5.

Where is God to be worshipped? "*In* his sanctuary ... in the firmament of his power", v. 1. Note that we have lost sight of the heavenly bodies, the earthly creation, mankind and Israel, for here all fades into obscurity in the light of His "excellent greatness", v. 2. Psalm 150 takes us forward into the eternal state where God is "all in all", 1 Cor. 15. 28, where the supreme object of attention is the Lamb of God, where the ultimate blessedness is to "serve him ... (and) see his face", Rev. 22. 4. Our worship down here is at best impoverished, but in glory all will be utter perfection for we shall "see him as he is", 1 John 3. 2.

Why is He to be praised? "*For* his mighty acts" and "his excellent greatness", v. 2. To list the great and gracious activities of Jehovah will take eternity, for even the "many other things which Jesus did" in His brief earthly ministry are too numerous for their record to be contained in the world, John 21. 25. Take time today to start cataloguing what God has done in your life over the past few years, and you will find abundant evidence of His mercy and strength.

How is He to be praised? *With* trumpet, lute, tambour, pipe, stringed instruments, organ, cymbals, vv. 3-5. The language, of course, relates to the musical accompaniment of Jewish temple worship, and provides a powerful impression of enthusiasm, concentration, variety, harmony and vigour. May our N.T. appreciation of God in Christ be equally zealous, equally glorifying to Him whom we adore.

"*(They) fell down before the Lamb...saying, Thou art worthy*", Rev. 5. 8-9.

260

The Word of God

THE PSALMS are a part of the Word of God as we know it today. It is true of the writers that they "spake as they were moved by the Holy Spirit", 2 Pet. 1. 21. They were partakers, in the hand of God, in that great work which over the centuries culminated in the Book which we today call the Bible. The Bible of the psalmists was very limited when compared with the finished work which we enjoy, possibly little more than the five books of Moses. But how they loved what they had! In Psalm 19 written by David, and again in Psalm 119 whose author is unknown, we have evidence that the godly in Israel prized beyond everything else the revelation that God had given to them. They used it as their authority in every experience of life.

As we speak of the "Word" of God, we can think of it not only as the revelation of God's thoughts, but also as the record of His promises; we remember that He always keeps His Word. Some of the psalms to which we shall refer contain no more than one or two verses dealing with God's Word; others, like Psalm 119, contain many references.

For our readings, subject headings have been prepared, and verses from the psalms have been used as they are deemed to be appropriate. Of necessity this will mean that there will be a degree of overlapping in the readings chosen for each day, particularly from Psalm 119. But the lover of the Word will not object to occasional repetition.

As we share together the thoughts that others had concerning the Word of God, we shall discover its relevance for today. We shall find that these men have been through experiences which are common to man; they have known disappointment, failure, depression, persecution, doubts, and in these experiences they have found the Word of God to be their support and strength. But we shall also find that their delight in the Word, and their submission to its authority, have led them in triumph and rejoicing. They learned something of what the Lord Jesus taught later, "If ye continue in my word, then are ye my disciples ... and the truth shall make you free", John 8. 31-32.

READING: **Psalm 1**

THY TESTIMONIES ARE MY DELIGHT

IT IS GENERALLY recognized that Psalm 1 is an introduction to the whole of the Psalter, and it is fitting that we should commence here in our consideration of the place that the Word of God finds in the psalms. Immediately God shows us the sharp division between the "blessed (happy) man" and the "ungodly", and in verse 2 He indicates the vital place that His Word has in maintaining this distinction. It is a God-made distinction. But clearly the regard that the blessed man has for God's Word is not a mere formality. Here is a man who "delights" in it. Reading it is not a drudge but a delight—he revels in it. In Psalm 19. 8, David gives voice to a similar sentiment, "The statutes of the Lord are right, rejoicing the heart" and the unnamed writer of Psalm 119. 111 could say, "Thy testimonies ... are the rejoicing of my heart".

Surely in this day of a completed revelation, when we have learned from it something of God's ways in grace through the redemption that is in Christ Jesus, and when we have learnt that through this work of grace the Author of Scripture has become our Father, then our reading of His Word and our meditation upon it should cause our hearts to rejoice. As we read it, "The Spirit breathes upon the Word and brings the truth to light". Being taught of the Spirit, we can experience "delight" as God opens His treasures, and whether the word is a word of comfort or a word of rebuke, we may know rejoicing of the heart. Whether we read of blessing or judgment, we can rest in the fact that a loving God (our Father) will make no mistakes. As we apply to our own pathway the truths that we read, we shall be able to say in the words of Psalm 119. 14, "I have rejoiced in the way of thy testimonies, as much as in all riches".

Our great Example in this, as in all other matters, is our Saviour. In Luke 10. 21, we find Him rejoicing that God has revealed Himself "unto babes". This is just what He does as we turn to His Word. Although we are "babes", He reveals Himself to us, and our hearts delight in this, as we find ourselves rejoicing in the Lord.

READING: Psalm 19

THE WORD—PERFECT

IN THIS PSALM the writer, David, first points to the majestic revelation of God in nature. Looking around him, he could see clear evidence of divine wisdom and power. He sees His glory, He sees His handiwork. But did this cause a sense of distance? He is the Creator and Sustainer, and man is so dependent. What he sees touches his mind and causes him to marvel, but it does not touch his heart, neither does it deal with his great spiritual need, and so the distance remains.

His thought then turns to another revelation of God—the law of the Lord. He did not speak of God's work in creation as "perfect", maybe because he knew that sin had left its mark on what had been declared by God to be "very good", Gen. 1. 31. But as he thinks of this other revelation of the divine purpose, he is led by the Spirit of God to call it "perfect". To quote from Ecclesiastes 3. 14, "nothing can be put to it, nor any thing taken from it". Indeed, solemn judgment is pronounced in Revelation 22. 18-19 upon any who dare to take away from, or add to God's Word. It is complete and perfect.

Note what David says about the action of the perfect word: it "converts the soul". Creation could not do that. In verses 12 and 13 of Psalm 19, he speaks of "secret faults", and also of "presumptuous sins" and "great transgressions". What can creation do about these? Nothing! But David has something in his hand, the law of the Lord, which can turn him round completely and make a new man of him. It does not ignore his sin, because as Psalm 119. 172 puts it, "all thy commandments are righteousness"; this is one aspect of its perfection—absolute righteousness. The righteousness of the Word reveals the sin and points the way to deliverance.

Peter takes up the thought in 1 Peter 1. 23, "being born again, not of corruptible seed, but of incorruptible, by the word of God, which liveth and abideth for ever". And following this "conversion", the perfect Word becomes the guide and mentor through life: "Thy word have I hid in mine heart, that I might not sin against thee", Psa. 119. 11. Have we done that?

September 3rd

READING: **Psalm 12**

A PURE WORD

VERSE 6 of this psalm declares that "the words of the Lord are pure words", and they are likened to silver which has been purified in the furnace. Notice that the writer speaks of "words" and not of "the word". Led by the Spirit of God, the writer is drawing attention to the fact that the individual words, used by God in the giving of His revelation, are pure. In making his declaration concerning the purity of the words, David uses a word which has within it the thought of purging, of being uncontaminated or unadulterated.

Some years ago, a Bible teacher made a suggestion that another comma should be placed after the word "furnace". This would then indicate that the words of the Lord are of earth, but purified seven times, that is, completely. It may well be that this is what is intended. God has used the words of men, human language, in writing His Book, but He has exercised His divine control to ensure that the very words used are the words of His choice. It is pure, unadulterated, because of this control. He did not merely convey a thought to the penman and then leave him to express it in his own way. He gave the very words.

In Psalm 19. 8, David again stresses the fact of the purity of the commandment of the Lord, and declares the effect of this to be "enlightening the eyes". If we are satisfied that God has controlled what is written, then we can see plainly what is meant, there is no dubiety. How confused we would be if we felt that what we were reading was only the words of men.

In John 17. 8, the Lord Jesus in speaking to His Father said, "I have given unto them the words which thou gavest me", and frequently in the course of His public ministry He stressed that the words that He uttered were given to Him by God.

In like manner, when the apostle Paul spoke of God's revelation, much of which came through him, he said, "Which things also we speak, not in the words which man's wisdom teacheth, but which the Holy Spirit teacheth", 1 Cor. 2. 13. God used the words of men in which to give His revelation to us, but He kept them free from error, so that we may have pure words and a pure Word.

READING: **Psalm 119. 121-136**

BETTER THAN GOLD

Is THE PSALMIST using exaggerated language as he speaks in verse 127 of God's commandments as being "above gold, yea, above fine gold"? Was it just a momentary, emotional exclamation? In verse 14 of this psalm, he had already said, "I have rejoiced in the way of thy testimonies, as much as in all riches", and in verse 72, "The law of thy mouth is better unto me than thousands of gold and silver". To the testimony of this man we may add the words of David in Psalm 19. 10, "More to be desired are they than gold, yea, than much fine gold". But were they right? Is the Word of God so precious? A more recent writer, Murray McCheyne, wrote, "One gem from that ocean is worth all the pebbles from earthly streams".

These testimonies lead us to a little self-examination. What value do we place upon them? What time do we devote to them? How does the time that we give to reading them compare with the time that we spend on secular literature, to the newspaper, the radio and television?

From time to time, there have been wild gold-rushes when men have risked their lives and incurred great hardship all to find gold—gold which perishes. We have, in the Word of God, far greater treasure, of heavenly origin, and which will last for ever. In the introduction to the Authorized Version of the Bible, the translators referred to the Bible in these terms: "that inestimable treasure, which excelleth all the riches of the earth". Men have gone to the stake, to the lions, have been prepared to suffer the loss of everything, rather than give up God's Word. Their example, their courage, their devotion, challenge our half-hearted attitude to that Word today.

Devotion to the Word brings spiritual enrichment. Was this the thought in Peter's mind as he closed his second Epistle, "grow in grace, and in the knowledge of our Lord and Saviour Jesus Christ" ?, 2 Pet. 3. 18. Growth in spiritual knowledge, namely a deeper knowledge of Christ, is the enrichment which comes from a love for the Word of God. The reverse is seen in 2 Peter 1. 8, "barren ... unfruitful". Spiritual poverty!

September 5th

READING: **Psalm 119. 9-24**

A YOUNG MAN'S RESOURCE

WE DO NOT KNOW the age of the writer of this psalm, but in verse 9 he has a special word for the young: "Wherewithal shall a young man cleanse his way?". Older people need to have their ways cleansed as well as those who are young, so why leave them out? The period of one's youth is the time for the formation of character, and a good start is essential. Lessons learnt in youth are seldom forgotten. The Bible tells us, "There is a way which seemeth right unto a man", Prov. 14. 12, and if it appears to be right, why should he not take it? But the remainder of the verse warns of its end. Whatever that way may be, it is man's way and ends in disaster. How can a young man start on the *right* way, and keep his way clear of defilement? "By taking heed thereto according to thy word". In verse 11, the writer then speaks of his own experience, "Thy word have I hid in mine heart, that I might not sin against thee".

What strong support this gives to Sunday School work and all activities that are for the purpose of teaching young people the Word of God. There was a day when the Scriptures were taught in the day schools, but alas, this is being discontinued on every hand. It is not difficult to see a link between this omission and the upsurge of youthful crime. In Genesis 39, we read of a young man, Joseph, sorely tempted to sin by his master's wife. His refusal was definite: "How can I do this great wickedness, and sin against God?". He was more concerned about God's thoughts than his master's. He knew that his God hated sin. How did he know? In whatever way he had learnt it, this stood him in good stead at that time.

The New Testament tells us of another young man, Timothy, concerning whom it is written in 2 Timothy 3. 15, "from a child thou hast known the holy scriptures". What a privilege! A firm foundation had been laid when impressions were strong. Now he was a teacher of others, but still young and still needing the secret of cleansing. Paul, writing to his young friend, recognizes this, and gives good advice, "Flee also youthful lusts: but follow righteousness", 2 Tim. 2. 22: go back to the Word.

READING: **Psalm 119. 97-112**

A SOUND EDUCATION

IN OUR READING today, we shall concentrate on verses 98-100, and bring in Psalm 19. 7 as a support. At the first reading, it might seem that the writer is claiming to know more than anyone else—that he has "all the answers". But he is not—he is stating facts. He is not only speaking for himself, but for all who have been taught of God through the Word. Psalm 19. 7 may seem a little more restrained in the words "the testimony of the Lord is sure, making wise the simple".

Let us look a little closer at verses 98-100. First the writer claims that God's commandments had made him wiser than his enemies. This may be illustrated from Acts 4. 13, where Peter and John are before the Sanhedrin, the highest Jewish council. As the council listened to Peter, "they marvelled" as they "perceived that they were unlearned and ignorant men", men who had not been through the recognized channels of education. They had wisdom that could not be resisted. The explanation? "They had been with (and listened to) Jesus". Similarly in Acts 6. 10 in relation to Stephen when he was confronted with opponents, "they were not able to resist the wisdom and the spirit by which he spake". Stephen's subsequent address in chapter 7 shows his knowledge of the Word of God.

In verse 99, the writer declares, "I have more understanding than all my teachers". May we consider the greatest of all examples? In John 7. 15, we read "And the Jews marvelled, saying, How knoweth this man letters, having never learned?". The reply of the Lord is instructive, "My doctrine is not mine, but his that sent me", v. 16. The word of His God was His constant delight.

In verse 100, it is not the young man saying, "all the old ones are out of date"; he is really saying, as the Lord Jesus said later, that heavenly wisdom is given to the "babes", Luke 10. 21. Age itself does not guarantee wisdom. A modern writer, Francis Schaeffer, wrote, "The ordinary Christian, with his Bible in his hand, can say that the majority is wrong".

If you want to be wiser than your enemies, to have more knowledge than your teachers, and to have more understanding than the ancients, dwell deeply in the Word. "The testimony of the Lord is sure, making wise the simple", Psa. 19. 7.

September 7th

READING: **Psalm 85**

LISTENING FOR GOD'S VOICE

"Speak Lord in the stillness, while I wait on Thee; Hushed my heart to listen, in expectancy." In the first three verses of our psalm, the writer is recounting, very gratefully, what God has done for His people, and in verses 4-7 he continues in petition for further blessing. He then seems to pause in verse 8, "I will hear (listen to) what God the Lord will speak". It may well be that verse 9 onwards is what God told him. If so, while the psalmist listened, he learned some very precious truths.

We read the Word of God, but is this a formality? As we read, do we really listen to hear what God wants to say, or are we in such a hurry that we move quickly away, so that there has been no time to "listen" ?

One hymn-writer wrote, "Speak to me by name, O Master; Let me know it is to me". In 1 Samuel 3. 10, we are told of a boy to whom God spoke by name: "Samuel", He said. The lad's reply is very lovely: "Speak; for thy servant heareth". Sometimes when we are reading the Word, it is obvious that the passage we are reading is not specially for us, but do we never hear the Lord saying, "This is for you"? Perhaps we are not really listening.

There are many voices in the world today, many of them claiming to speak with authority, and the constant repetition of their claims makes an impression. In consequence, we hear folk say, "I do not know what to believe". Alas, this operates in the realm of spiritual things too, but the wise Christian will hear so as to determine "*what the Lord* will speak". There is the final authority.

In Revelation 1. 3, there is a blessing pronounced on the one who reads, and hears (listens to), and then keeps the Word of God. In Matthew 7. 24, the man who hears (listens to) the Word and obeys it is likened to one who builds his house upon a rock—he has a firm foundation.

May the Lord give us all an increasing longing to hear the voice of God speaking to us in a personal way as we read His Word.

"I am listening Lord for Thee; What hast thou to say to me?"

September 8th

READING: **Psalm 50**

THE WORD AND THE SINNER

WE LOOK at verse 16 today. God is speaking to "the wicked" (the sinner of our title), for there is little doubt that this is like a person whom we would call "unsaved", or the ungodly man of Psalm 1. If we are Christians, then God calls us saints (set-apart ones). We must acknowledge that saints sin at times, but this is not the character of the one found in this verse.

It is interesting to contrast verses 15 and 16. In verse 15, we read, "call upon me in the day of trouble: I will deliver thee". Then notice the change in verse 16, "But". Earlier in the psalm, God had been speaking to "my saints", v. 5, "my people", v. 7. They were not a perfect people, but God would not include them in verse 16. The difference between them is shown (and caused) by their attitude to God's Word. In verse 17, in describing the attitude of the wicked, God says, "thou hatest instruction, and castest my words behind thee". In Psalm 119. 158, the writer speaks of "the transgressors ... they kept not thy word".

It is plain that if these men had obeyed the Word they would have ceased to be wicked. The language implies that they had heard it, and·had said "No"! We should note in Psalm 50. 18-20 the result of casting away God's Word. When God's Word is spurned, it leads to disaster.

God has ordained that it should be by His Word that men are brought from the place of rebellion into the place of liberty. The Lord Jesus said, "He that heareth my word, and believeth ... hath everlasting life, and shall not come into condemnation", John 5. 24. Paul wrote, "it pleased God by the foolishness of preaching to save them that believe", 1 Cor. 1. 21.

Psalm 119. 158 mentions the writer's grief on account of men's waywardness, and in verse 136 he says, "Rivers of waters run down mine eyes, because they keep not thy law". We think of the Lord Jesus as He looked over Jerusalem, "he ... wept over it", Luke 19. 41. He could see the tribulation that was to come because of the city's rejection of Him (the Word), and He sorrowed deeply. If we believe the Word of God as we read it, we know that judgment is coming on the wicked, on the ungodly. Perhaps someone dear to us is in this category. Is the love of Christ in us so real that we share His compassion?

269

September 9th

READING: **Psalm 78. 1-11**

A NATION'S GUIDE

As a nation, Israel was privileged above all others. As Paul expressed it, "unto them were committed the oracles of God", Rom 3. 2. In the psalm we have read, Asaph says, "he established a testimony in Jacob, and appointed a law in Israel, which he commanded our fathers", v. 5. Verse 7 adds, "that they might set their hope in God, and ... keep his commandments: and might not be as their fathers, a stubborn and rebellious generation". The Word of God was intended to be the nation's constitution. So important was this that God gave the instruction, even before a king was appointed, that any future king "shall write him a copy of this law ... and he shall read therein all the days of his life", Deut. 17. 18-19. God knew that writing a thing impresses it upon the mind, and that constant reading deepens the impression.

Alas, these exhortations were largely forgotten. and in consequence the nation so often was justly described in the words of verse 8, as "a stubborn and rebellious generation".

In the days of king Josiah, 2 Chron. 34. 14, the book of the law (which had been lost, and therefore not consulted) was found amid the rubble in the temple. It was brought to the king, and as it was read it was realized how far the nation was from God's standards. Reformation followed. The Word of God exerted its power in national life. There was a time in the history of England when it was called "the land of the Book", and during that period an Englishman's word was his bond. It is said that a visiting foreign potentate asked Queen Victoria the secret of Britian's greatness, and she replied "the Bible". Now, alas, all this has changed. In national life, there is no reference to God's authority, and of recent years vices which are denounced and forbidden in God's Word have been legalized by Parliament. In our schools, the teaching of the Bible is being abandoned, and the young are growing up in ignorance of God. Shall we soon deserve the words of Psalm 78. 8, "a stubborn and rebellious generation"?

Could it be that this has partly come about because we have failed to obey 1 Timothy 2. 1-2, "supplications, prayers ... be made ... for kings, and for all that are in authority"?

September 10th

READING: **Psalm 119. 161-176**

THY WORD IS TRUTH

IT IS a sad word that is written in Isaiah 59. 14, "truth is fallen in the street". This was true in the day of the prophet; it is true today. Truth is a casualty. Men do not trust each other any more. Why? In other pages, reference has been made to the abandonment of Bible reading, and it must be insisted that this is the cause.

In verse 163, the psalmist makes a positive statement: "I hate and abhor lying: but thy law do I love". Whoever the writer was, he was convinced that the two do not go together. Love for the Word of God will lead to a hatred of every form of deception and lying. Equally, a love for that which is not trustworthy will result in the setting aside of God's Word, the Truth.

In verse 128, the writer approaches the matter from the opposite direction: he commences with the Word, "I esteem all thy precepts concerning all things to be right; and I hate every false way". Here is a man who is prepared to say, "The Word of God is right", and all things must be judged according to their relation to this Word. What does not agree with it is not truth.

Down through the years, the opinions of men have clashed with the Word of God; scientific discoveries have been heralded abroad in an attempt to prove that the Old Book was wrong. One by one the claims have been discounted and the Word stands triumphant as the Truth.

The Bible is our authority for deciding what is right and what is wrong, in the realm of morals, and indeed in every realm.

One day, a Roman administrator asked sceptically, "What is truth?", John 18. 38. Standing before him was One who had spoken of Himself as "the truth", John 14. 6, and afterwards had said to His Father, "thy word is truth", 17. 17. That Person and that Word can so work in us that the psalmist's words will become ours, "I hate every false way". It is through Him (the Truth) and the Word (the Truth) that we can know the meaning of 1 John 4. 6, "Hereby know we the spirit of truth, and the spirit of error".

271

September 11th

READING: **Psalm 119. 65-80**

THE WORD AND AFFLICTIONS

SEVEN TIMES in this psalm the writer speaks of affliction that had come to him, and he sees (i) a link between his affliction and straying from the Word, and (ii) a close link betwen the Word and recovery. Before considering what he says about affliction, look at verse 65, "Thou hast dealt well with thy servant", and then at verse 67 where he speaks of affliction. This was part of God's goodness to him. The reason why affliction was with him seems to have been that he had gone astray, and the second half of verse 67 suggests that he had gone astray because of failure to keep God's Word. God sent the affliction in the spirit of verse 65, and the writer has now regained fellowship with his God.

In verse 71, he is looking back, pondering over God's dealings with him, and his testimony is, "It is good for me that I have been afflicted", and he sees why God has been dealing with him in that way, "that I might learn thy statutes". In verse 11, this man had written, "Thy word have I hid in my heart, that I might not sin against thee". Clearly, something had gone wrong, and it was necessary for God to bring him back again. How many times have travellers set out on a journey, being confident that they know the way so that they have not consulted a guide book, only to find themselves lost and compelled to say, "If only I had consulted the book". Our psalmist was like that; he had started well, but apparently he neglected the Book, and had gone astray.

In verse 75, he admits that the affliction was a testimony to God's faithfulness (note, not God's harshness), and in verse 107 he asks that he may know in the experience the quickening of God through the Word. Affliction covers a wide variety of experiences, illness, accident, domestic problems, financial difficulties. And while it is true that these things come upon us, yet it is not necessarily on account of some particular sin in our lives. Yet it is well to consider this possibility, and go to the Lord about it. Has there been a departure from the Word; do we need to get back to it?

A comforting word to close with: in Revelation 3. 19, the loving Lord is speaking, "As many as I *love*, I rebuke and chasten".

September 12th

READING: **Psalm 40**

THE MAN OF THE BOOK

HEBREWS 10. 5-9 establishes clearly that we have the Lord Jesus brought before us in this psalm, and in verse 8 of the psalm we see Him revelling in the Word of God, "I delight to do thy will ... thy law is within my heart". According to Hebrews 10. 5, He uttered these words as He left the glory and stepped into humanity. It would be right to say that the Word of God was His consuming passion. When He said, "in the volume of the book it is written of me", it may be that He had in mind the O.T. Scriptures, but there is the possibility that He also had in mind the volume of God's eternal counsel.

This Man of the Book was always obedient to the Word of God. Was it obedience to the Word of God that kept Him waiting patiently for the moment of resurrection?, v. 1. He knew that a period of three days and three nights was involved, and He would not forestall that by one moment. He also proclaimed the Word of God to others: "I have not concealed thy lovingkindness and thy truth from the great congregation", v. 10.

In the "blessed man" of Psalm 1, it is likely that we have the Lord Jesus, and in verse 2 we see that "his delight is in the law of the Lord; and in his law doth he meditate day and night". The result of this constant meditation is seen in His earthly ministry. When tempted by Satan in the wilderness, He replied to each temptation with the words, "It is written", and He quoted from the book of Deuteronomy. Satan also quoted from Psalm 91. 11-12, but took the words out of context. The Lord said, "It is written again", Matt. 4. 7. He did not use human argument; the Word was enough.

In Matthew 5. 17, when speaking of God's law, He said, "I am not come to destroy, but to fulfil". Later, He charged the Jewish leaders, "Ye do err, not knowing the scriptures", Matt. 22. 29. We can infer from this that *He* did not err because *He* did know the Scriptures. Even as sinless Man, He hid God's Word in His heart. Again, in John 17. 14, He said to His Father, "I have given them thy word". We leave Him with the two disciples on the Emmaus road, when "he expounded unto them in all the scriptures the things concerning himself", Luke 24. 27. He knew the Scriptures—He was the Man of the Book.

September 13th

READING: **Psalm 17**

THE SURE PROTECTION

IN VERSE 4, David is looking round, and he sees "the works of men". The expression may well include their religious works as well as their general behaviour. What he sees does not impress him, but rather he seeks a way of deliverance from them. He turns to the Book that he knows so well. When he spoke of being kept from "the paths of the destroyer", it is possible that he had in mind the time when Saul the king was within his power, and he could easily have destroyed him, 1 Sam. 26. 8-9, and when he was determined to slay Nabal, but was restrained, 25. 26, he could say, "Lord, thou hast kept me".

There is a destroyer abroad today—God calls him Satan, the adversary. According to 1 Peter 5. 8, "your adversary ...walketh about, seeking whom he may devour". Peter adds, "whom resist stedfast in the faith". When the Lord of glory had dealings with him in the wilderness, He overcame him by the Word of God. We cannot find a better weapon than the one that He used. Keep close to the Word if you would avoid the paths of the destroyer.

Psalm 19. 11 gives the words of David again, "Moreover by them is thy servant warned". He had spoken of the sweetness of the Word, but he lived in a world of danger and trouble, and it was needful to heed the warnings of the Word. The coast of our land is ringed by lighthouses, warning of rocks and dangerous seas: it is at his peril that the mariner ignores the warnings. Sometimes the Word of God comes to us as a challenge when we read it, and in relation to some proposed course of action the voice of the Spirit says, "No!". When we are driving along the highway, we may foolishly decide to cross over at the red light, ignoring the warning—that would be a perilous business. Do not ignore the warnings of the Word.

Concerning the righteous, Psalm 37. 31 says, "The law of his God is in his heart; none of his steps shall slide". The Bible is useless, however excellent its binding may be, if it is kept on the bookshelf—it must be in the heart. One's steps are controlled by it; the walk is then firm and steady.

A final thought from 1 John 2. 14, "young men ... ye are strong ... the word of God abideth in you, and ye have overcome the wicked one".

September 14th

READING: **Psalm 33**

THE WORD IN CREATION

WE LIVE in a beautiful, wonderful world—where did it come from? Man is still groping for an answer that will satisfy his own theories, but we can afford to put them all on one side. Verse 6 of our psalm makes a positive statement, "By the word of the Lord were the heavens made; and all the host of them by the breath of his mouth". Verse 7 shows us the gathering of the waters together, while verse 8 pictures the inhabitants of the earth standing in awe before the Creator, marvelling at His handiwork. Verse 9 is a kind of climax, "he spake, and it was done; he commanded, and it stood fast".

What a majestic statement is Genesis 1. 1, "In the beginning God created the heaven and the earth". Verse 3 states, "And God said", repeated in verses 6, 9, 11, 14, 20, 24, 26. "He spake, and it was done." The Bible knows nothing of the theory of natural selection, nor of the emergence of living things from the slime. It sees the demonstration of God's mighty power and wisdom in calling into existence the universe in which we live by the Word of His power.

Hebrews 11. 3 speaks of the worlds being "framed by the word of God". 2 Peter 3. 5 informs us, "by the word of God the heavens were of old, and the earth". John 1 introduces us to the Son of God, here called "the Word", stating that all things were made by Him, v. 3.

In 2 Corinthians 4. 6, we see the work of creation in response to the command of God used as an illustration of His work in salvation. The One who said "Let there be light", Gen. 1. 3, is now seen coming into the darkness of the human heart, bringing light and life. When Paul wrote of the change which is effected in a life when Christ comes in, it is significant that he wrote of it as a new creation, 2 Cor. 5. 17. It is the Word of God operative in a human heart.

Note that in Genesis 1, after the initial act of creation, God continued to work in development. From darkness comes light, from chaos order and stability, and we see the appearance of beauty and fruitfulness. In each stage of development, "God said". So it is with the new life brought about by the sovereign act of God; there should be a continual progress, governed by the Word of God.

September 15th

READING: **Psalm 107. 1-21**

SPIRITUAL HEALING

IT IS almost certain that physical healing is in mind in verse 20, and verses 17-19 suggest that the sickness was there because of the people's own folly. As we read the record of Israel's wanderings in the wilderness, we must come to the conclusion that God's protection during those forty years included the preservation of the people's health. There were occasions when God withdrew that protection because of their wilful sin (e.g., when serpents were allowed to invade the camp, Num 21. 6), but normally He commanded health for them, and after lapses, He speedily restored them.

Today, as then, health is subject to God's commandment— He alone is the great Healer. We may choose to go to the doctor when unwell, but ultimately healing is in the hand of God.

More important than physical sickness is spiritual sickness, and C. H. Spurgeon wrote in relation to our verses, "these verses describe a sin-sick soul: foolish, but yet aroused to a sense of guilt ... To its own apprehension nothing remains but utter destruction ... Then is the soul driven to cry in the bitterness of its grief unto the Lord, and Christ, the Eternal Word, comes with healing power in the direst extremity, saving to the utmost".

There are many who are sick in soul today, sick because of worry, because of sorrow, of doubt, of sin, of self-will, because of eating wrong food (the Word of God neglected, and the world's food enjoyed). What is the remedy? In Psalm 107. 19 "they cry unto the Lord", and His response was immediate: "He sent his word". He still does this. Neglect of the Word permits these various spiritual sicknesses to develop, and the remedy is: Back to the Word. God does not send human philosophy nor does He send religion; rather He sends His Word. Psalm 147. 15 indicates that God does not waste any time in this matter: "He sendeth forth his commandment ... his word runneth very swiftly".

To a company of Christians, away from God and His Word, but priding themselves of their position, the Lord of the church said, "thou art wretched, and miserable, and poor, and blind, and naked", Rev. 3. 17. In such circumstances, God has one unfailing prescription for spiritual sickness—the Word.

September 16th

READING: **Psalm 147**

PRIVILEGE—RESPONSIBILITY

VERSES 19-20 of this psalm refer to Israel's privilege in having the Word of God, something that made them distinct from all other nations. Verse 20 should not be understood as an utterance of pride, but an exclamation of wonder and gratitude, leading to praise. The first part of the psalm is largely taken up with the recounting of God's mercies to His creatures in His ordinary everyday providence, and it is almost as though the psalmist paused a moment and then said, "In addition to all this daily provision, our God has given us this priceless treasure of His Word". This meant that they had a knowledge of God in His character and in His requirements that could not otherwise be known. Commenting on verse 19, C. H. Spurgeon says, "By that knowledge Jacob is ennobled into Israel".

The realization of this great privilege appears in other scriptures, e.g., Deut. 4. 32-34; 33. 2-4; Psa. 78. 5. In the N.T., Paul asked, "What advantage then hath the Jew?", Rom. 3.1. In verse 2, he answers, "Much every way: chiefly, because that unto them were committed the oracles of God".

Alas, Israel failed to recognize their responsibility to pass on to others (not so privileged as themselves) the great revelation that God had given to them, and in consequence they became a people shut in unto themselves, selfish and unfeeling. Their attitude was, "We are the people". They berated other nations for their idolatry, but withheld from them the revelation that could have freed them from it.

How do we stand in the matter? We have not only the O.T. Scriptures which were committed to Israel. We have the completed Bible with its wondrous unveiling of God's full and free salvation, including the revelation of the Son of God, the living Word of God! What a privilege! Yes, we have it, and missionary agencies tell us of countless men and women who have never heard of these precious truths, and remain in darkness. Around us there are many in a similar condition. Do we hug the Word to ourselves, as though it was intended only for us? The Lord Jesus said to His disciples, "Go ye into all the world, and preach the gospel to every creature", Mark 16. 15. Paul wrote of the responsibility of "holding forth the word of life", Phil. 2. 16.

277

September 17th

READING: **Psalm 119. 145-160**

ABSOLUTELY RELIABLE

SOME YEARS AGO, a book was published with the title, *Can a Young Man Trust his Bible?*. Is this question being asked today—not only by the young, but by the elderly as well? Is the Bible still worthy of trust? In verse 160, the psalmist had no doubt about this. Concerning God's Word (an overall description), he says that it is true "from the beginning", v.160, and then, speaking of the separate commandments comprising that Word, he says that they endure for ever. This surely is because of what he had already said in verse 89, "For ever, O Lord, thy word is settled in heaven". He is thinking of where it comes from—the throne.

As we take the Bible in our hands today, we can do so with complete confidence that not one of God's utterances will ever be repealed. We can be assured that the last book is as true as the first, and that this also applies to every book in between. We may read it as searching for history—in that realm we shall find it reliable. We may be looking for guidance in the matter of morals—we can have complete confidence in what we find. Our searching may be for the purpose of finding out where we came from—we shall find an authoritative answer there.

To the young man at the beginning of life, the assurance in verse 9 is still true, namely that by taking heed to the Word of God there will be ensured a clean life; this can be tested in everyday experience. To those advancing in life, the words of Psalm 23. 6 can still be trusted, "Surely goodness and mercy shall follow me all the days of my life". And for those at the end of life's journey, Psalm 23. 4 will come with comfort and conviction, "though I walk through the valley of the shadow of death, I will fear no evil: for thou art with me".

When the Lord Jesus rose from the dead, messengers from heaven said to the women visiting the tomb, "he is risen, as he said", or "because he said so", Matt. 28. 6. Because He said it, it must be true. This is so of every utterance of God, whether it be in warning or in comfort. Finally, let us note Matthew 5. 18, "Till heaven and earth pass, one jot or one tittle shall in no wise pass from the law, till all be fulfilled". It can be relied upon utterly.

September 18th

READING: **Psalm 37. 23-40**

THE WORD AND EVERY DAY

THE HYMN WRITER wrote, "I know not what awaits me, God kindly veils my eyes". This is a thought that we may have as we start each day. God has kept from us knowledge of the hours to come, and in consequence we cannot know in advance how we shall react to the various experiences that we shall meet. Concerning the righteous, verse 31 of our psalm says, "The law of his God is in his heart; none of his steps shall slide". The word "steps" reminds us that our progress day by day is a step at a time, not a series of large leaps and jumps, by which we clear the obstacles. And David is convinced that the righteous man can walk steadfastly and confidently because "the law of his God is in his heart". Note: in the heart, not the head.

There is a contrast in the psalm between the wicked and the righteous; the difference exists because of differing attitudes to the Word of God. Verses 9-21 make it very clear that there is a rebellion against God. His will is being flouted: "they were disobedient, and rebelled against thee, and cast thy law behind their backs", Neh. 9. 26. How can the righteous live day by day in such a polluted atmosphere?

Psalm 119. 18 gives us a suitable prayer with which to start the unknown day: "Open thou mine eyes, that I may behold wondrous things out of thy law", and it is well to note in verse 19 why this is so, "I am a stranger in the earth". With the Word in our hearts, and in dependence upon the Holy Spirit to bring it to our minds, we may go safely on our way.

Later in Psalm 119. 54 the writer speaks of his pilgrimage and affirms that as he has been on his journey homeward, "thy statutes have been my songs". Clearly his mind had been occupied with the things of God. He met enemies in his pathway, but, undefeated, he pressed on, because the Word of his God was with him—in his heart.

In Ephesians 6. 10-17, where the apostle sees a malignant enemy and conflict in the life of the righteous man, he urges that the believer should take "the sword of the Spirit, which is the word of God", v. 17, that is, the appropriate word given by God for that moment. And where does it come from? It is brought by the Holy Spirit out of the Word that has been hidden within the heart.

279

READING: **Psalm 78. 1-22**

PASS IT ON

IT IS not only a privilege to be a parent, it is also a great responsibility. What our children will become morally and spiritually will largely be determined by their early training at home, and by the influence of their parents. Verses 5-7 of this psalm show the importance that God attaches to the teaching of His Word in these early impressionable days, while the children are still within the reach of home influence: "he ... appointed a law in Israel ... that they should make them known to their children". In this context, the law was not given to enable leaders to govern the nation, but that children should be taught. Verse 6 shows that the purpose was that these children should in turn teach their children, and so on from generation to generation. And why? Verse 7 reveals God's intention: "that they might set their hope in God, and not forget the works of God, but keep his commandments".

That this was to be a constant practice is shown in Deuteronomy 6. 7, where it would seem to be implied that at all times and in all circumstances the parent would draw attention to God's requirements. The ways of God in His dealing with their nation was to be constantly asserted, Exod. 13. 8, 14.

Having wrecked their lives in reckless living, how many young men and women have said, "If only my parents had taught me the truth". This is old fashioned, according to modern views; yet, "Train up a child in the way he should go: and when he is old, he will not depart from it", Prov. 22. 6.

Are we challenged by these thoughts? Sitting quietly now, with our Bible before us, are we satisfied that our children have learned from our teaching and example the truth about God? Have we taught them from the Word their need of a Saviour, and how they may lead a God-pleasing life?

In the N.T. we have an impressive example of this: "from a child thou hast known the holy scriptures, which are able to make thee wise unto salvation", 2 Tim. 3. 15. In verse 14, Paul speaks of those "of whom thou hast learned them". And who are they? In 2 Timothy 1. 5, we discover the answer: "thy grandmother ... and thy mother". Moreover, Paul charged Timothy to do what his mother had done to him, "preach the word, be instant in season, out of season", 4. 1-2. See also 2. 2.

September 20th

READING: **Psalm 111**

THE WORD—ETERNAL

THE WORD of God takes its character from the One who gave it—the eternal unchangeable God: "all his commandments are sure. They stand fast for ever and ever", vv. 7-8. Again, "For ever, O Lord, thy word is settled in heaven", Psa. 119.89. This Word of God was not given in a time of emergency, just to meet an unforeseen contingency. Rather our God is One who knows the end from the beginning, therefore His Word will need no alteration or amendment. As the psalmist says, "his commandments are sure". There is no uncertainty or doubt. In Genesis 1. 26, we read, "God said, Let us make man in our image", but this was only bringing into operation what He had said in eternity. And so throughout the Word.

All human literature becomes out of date, as men's thoughts change in the light of increasing knowledge. But God's Word will never be out of date, it will continue unchanged for "ever and ever". W. E. Gladstone, one-time premier of Great Britain, spoke of it as "the impregnable rock of Holy Scripture". Opponents of the Bible have hammered at it for centuries, but they have gone, and the Word remains. Their little hammers made no impression on the rock.

The eternal character of His Word gives stability to every promise that He has made. He never alters His Word. When the Lord Jesus said of His sheep, "I give unto them eternal life: and they shall never perish", John 10. 28, He spoke a word which will remain valid "for ever and ever". And when He said, "him that cometh to me I will in no wise cast out", He had eternity in view, 6. 37.

The N.T. emphasizes this truth: "Heaven and earth shall pass away, but my words shall not pass away", Matt. 24. 35; "the word of God, which liveth and abideth for ever", 1 Pet. 1. 23; "the word of the Lord endureth for ever", v. 25. In Revelation 19. 11-13, we see One coming from heaven to deal with the final revolt of men prior to the commencement of the millennium. The past has been a sad story of unbelief, denial and rebellion. Now in verse 13 the One who comes is called "the Word of God". As men had tried to get rid of the written Word, so they had tried to banish the Living Word, and it is in that character that He comes. God will have the last word.

281

September 21st

READING: Psalm 94

CHASTENING AND THE WORD

EARLIER IN this series, we considered the fact of affliction in the lives of God's people, and recognized that sometimes this comes from God's hand in chastening. We now look a little closer at this. There is a very close link between chastening and the teaching of God's Word, v. 12; the writer proclaims the one who is chastened and taught to be "blessed". Matthew Henry writes, "When we are chastened we must pray to be taught, and look into the law as the best expositor of providence. It is not the chastening itself that does good, but the teaching that goes along with it and is the exposition of it".

In the psalm, the background is the cruelty and hardness of the wicked, but "The Lord knoweth the thoughts of man", v. 11, so verse 23 speaks of His judgment. In verse 12, however, God is looking at His child when something has gone wrong, yet His thoughts are not thoughts of judgment but of chastening, that is, training or instructing. God loves His children so much that He will not let them go in spite of their waywardness.

In Luke 22. 31-34, we read of the pride and self-confidence of Peter as he rejected the thought that he could fail his Lord, and we notice the Lord's warning. In verses 54-62, we have the sad fulfilment of the Lord's prediction, the result being, "Peter remembered the word of the Lord ... And Peter ... wept bitterly", vv. 61-62. The spoken word was used in restoration, leading to a courageous Peter after Pentecost.

Commenting on verse 12, C. H. Spurgeon says, "The psalmist calls the chastened one a 'man' in the best sense, using the Hebrew word which implies strength. He is a man indeed who is under the teaching and training of the law". Let us pray that, as in the ministry of God's Word, so also in the ministry of His works and chastenings, we may be taught of God. Psalm 119.67 tells us of the experience of another child of God, "before I was afflicted I went astray: but now have I kept thy word" ; the chastening was effective. Hebrews 12. 5-11 makes much of the beneficial effects of chastening, and stresses that it is an evidence of the love of the Father to His child: "no chastening for the present seemeth to be joyous, but grievous: nevertheless afterward it yieldeth the peaceable fruit of righteousness unto them which are exercised thereby", v. 11.

282

READING: **Psalm 119. 17-32**

GOD'S WONDERS REVEALED

VERSE 18 is a cry from the heart of a man who had already discovered that the Word of God contained treasures beyond description. But beyond all that he had discovered, he felt that there was laid up great bounty, and he begs for the ability to perceive, appreciate and enjoy it. The language implies that he was conscious of a dimness of spiritual vision, but at the same time an assurance that God could remove it.

Do we sometimes feel like this as we turn to the Word? Do we find the reading of it hard-going, and when we have finished, do we feel that we have gained nothing, that it has been a profitless exercise? Never forget that we have a subtle enemy, who hates God's Word, and one of his activities is to blind the minds of men. But let us never forget that we have a priceless privilege today that the psalmist did not have, that is, the indwelling Holy Spirit whose work is to lead us "into all the truth", John 16. 13 R.V. As we turn to the Word, shall we also use the words of the psalmist, "Open thou mine eyes" ?

What are the wonders found in the Word? In Isaiah 64. 4, the prophet exclaims, "men have not heard, nor perceived by the ear, neither hath the eye seen, O God ... what he hath prepared for him that waiteth for him". Paul had this passage in mind when he wrote, "Eye hath not seen, nor ear heard, neither have entered into the heart of man, the things which God hath prepared for them that love him. But God hath revealed them unto us by his Spirit", 1 Cor. 2. 9-10. Some of these wonders are described in the N.T. as "mysteries", things which previously had been hidden, but now have been revealed. As examples, "the mystery of godliness" (the incarnation), 1 Tim. 3. 16; the mystery of the church, Eph. 5.32; the mystery of the resurrection and the rapture of the church, 1 Cor. 15. 51; and "the mystery of iniquity", 2 Thess. 2. 7.

Note what the psalmist says in verse 19, "I am a stranger in the earth", so since we belong to heaven, may we be taught heavenly things:

"The heavens declare Thy glory Lord,
 In every star Thy wisdom shines;
But when our eyes behold Thy Word,
 We read Thy Name in fairer lines."

September 23rd

READING: **Psalm 119. 129-144**

SPIRITUAL UNDERSTANDING

GOD HAS given to man a wonderful brain, and the use of that brain has brought to humanity many benefits. But God has decreed that human wisdom shall not be the channel by which men shall come to know Him, 1 Cor. 1. 21. The reason for this is plain: man must not pride himself that by his own wisdom he has come into relationship with God; moreover, if human wisdom was to be the way, many of us would be excluded. Human wisdom has no standing in the realm of spiritual things.

Our writer ascribes to God the initiation into spiritual life and understanding, "The entrance of thy words giveth light", v. 130. This implies an initial stage: into the darkness comes the Word of God. But this is only a beginning; there is a continuing process, "it giveth understanding unto the simple". It is, of course, inferred that there is a readiness to admit the light, and then it immediately begins to work. Genesis 1 illustrates this. We are there introduced to "darkness ... upon the face of the deep", v. 2; "And God said, Let there be light", v. 3. Read through the chapter, and see how everything was changed because of the entrance of light.

When the psalmist speaks of "the simple", he is talking of those who are sincere and willing to be taught. This is the attitude in which to read the Word. And when we approach the Word like this, the Holy Spirit is there to increase understanding. Experience has shown that so-called "simple believers" may possess such a spiritual understanding that the wisdom of the world is baffled. In verse 104 we find a further consequence of having this understanding, "therefore I hate every false way". It enables the believer to judge what is true and what is false.

This is God's sovereign way of imparting truth, not to the wise, but to the simple. Matthew 11. 25-26 gives us the Lord's words, "I thank thee, O Father ... because thou hast hid these things from the wise and prudent, and hast revealed them unto babes. Even so, Father: for so it seemed good in thy sight". Shall we thank God for the truth of 1 John 5. 20, "the Son of God is come, and hath given us an understanding" ? And since this understanding is a continuing process, may we pray, "give me understanding according to thy word", Psa. 119. 169.

September 24th

READING: **Psalm 102**

IN ORDER THAT WE MIGHT KNOW

WHY WERE the Scriptures written? One answer to this question is found in verse 18, "for the generation to come". As we think of this, we realize that God wants us to know about Himself and His ways. The immediate context of this verse is interesting. It is generally accepted that the psalm consists of a prophetic unfolding of the exercises of the Lord in Gethsemane. Note the heading of the psalm, "A Prayer of the afflicted, when he is overwhelmed, and poureth out his complaint to the Lord". Verses 25-27 are definitely quoted as the words of the Father to the Son in Hebrews 1. 10-12. This being so, the psalm enables us to appreciate more deeply the holy exercise of the Lord as He faced Calvary. Our verse 18 is startling, in the position it occupies. It is as if suddenly the divine voice said, "This must be placed on permanent record, so that those to come may know, and be led to praise".

This may well be considered to be one of the principles governing the giving of a written record: God wants us to know what He has done, what He is doing, and what He will yet do. He has not left us in ignorance.

Accepting that Scripture was written for the generations to come, we may well ask ourselves, How do I treat it? Do I believe it? Do I obey it? Do I communicate it? Pondering these questions convinces us that the existence of these holy Writings brings not only privilege but responsibility.

The N.T. continues this thought: "whatsoever things were written aforetime were written for our learning, that we through patience and comfort of the scriptures might have hope", Rom. 15. 4. God knew what our experiences would be, our trials, our persecutions, our failures, and in His Word He has given us strength and encouragement, telling us of triumph and glory. 1 Peter 1. 10-12 takes up the theme. After speaking of the words of the prophets, he says, "unto us they did minister the things, which are now reported unto you". Note in verse 11 that he speaks of "the sufferings of Christ, and the glory that should follow", taking us back again to Psalm 102.

"We thank Thee Lord indeed, that Thou Thy Word hast given; to light our path in this dark world, and safely guide to heaven."

READING: **Psalm 138**

GOD'S WORD EXALTED

VERSE 2 gives us a somewhat startling declaration concerning God's Word, "thou hast magnified thy word above all thy name". Is this possible? Derek Kidner, quite rightly, points out that, although the Scriptures make high claims concerning themselves, they do not encourage bibliolatry. When reference is made to the divine Name, it normally speaks of God's perfections—His justice, majesty, greatness, glory, love. Can anything be exalted above these?

In 1664, a Hebrew scholar gave an alternative rendering, which may well deal with our problem, "Thou hast magnified Thy Name above all things, in Thy Word". This is something that our minds can grasp. If this rendering is right, the psalmist is declaring that God has revealed Himself in His Word in a way that He never could have done in His universe. In this Word are found truths concerning God that science can throw no light upon, that cannot be discovered in the schools of human philosophy. This Word tells of an atonement being made by God, of men's sins being pardoned, of souls being saved, of men being brought into the family of God, of believing men and women being made heirs of heaven. These things magnify the Name of God beyond anything in the material world around us. And these things are found only in His Word.

As the psalmist meditates along these lines, he says, "I will worship toward thy holy temple, and praise thy name for thy lovingkindness and for the truth", v. 2. This surely must be our response as we contemplate the God revealed in the Word. In the N.T., we read, "these are written, that ye might believe that Jesus is the Christ, the Son of God; and that believing ye might have life through his name", John 20. 31. This purpose of God is found only in His Word. Colossians 1. 5 speaks of "the hope which is laid up for you in heaven, whereof ye have heard before in the word of the truth of the gospel". This revelation of God's purpose is declared only in the Bible. So all the grand foundation truths in which we rejoice, and which magnify the Name of the Lord, did not come to us by the skill of men, using microscope and telescope with human wisdom; they were revealed only through the Word.

READING: **Psalm 119. 25-40**

REVIVAL AND THE WORD

THE MAN who wrote this psalm was much concerned about revival—he called it quickening, being the same word in the Hebrew. He mentioned it in verses 25, 50, 93, 107, 149, 154. He was evidently a man whose spiritual experience was in a state of constant fluctuation—"sometimes trusting, sometimes doubting, sometimes joyful, sometimes sad". Verse 83 is almost a lament, "I am become like a bottle in the smoke". He felt parched, cracked, shrivelled, "My soul cleaveth unto the dust", v. 25; "I am afflicted very much", v. 107. Poor man! But who has not been there with him? Who has not yearned for a revival in personal spiritual life?

Where shall we turn for revival? Is it to be found in emotionalism, or any other energy of the flesh? Judging from our writer, he viewed true revival as being Bible-based, "according to thy word". As we think of his words in verse 25, "My soul cleaveth unto the dust", our minds go to the Emmaus road in Luke 24. Here were two despondent disciples, all hope gone, until a Stranger drew near and turned with them to the Scriptures. What was the result? "Did not our heart burn within us?", v. 32, and the joyful proclamation "The Lord is risen" to the other disciples, v. 34. This was personal revival.

Let us follow the psalmist. "O Lord, quicken me according to thy judgment", v. 149, namely, "Lord, Thou knowest my need; revive me as Thou seest best". No two of us are alike, but He is able to judge what is just right for us, and is able to take us to the right word. "Quicken me according to thy word", v. 154; we dare not ask Him to go outside His Word to bring new life to us—how could we? Looking back on a past experience, he said, "This is my comfort ... for thy word hath quickened me", v. 50. Did he pause to say "Hallelujah" ? Again, "I will never forget thy precepts: for with them thou hast quickened me", v. 93. Perhaps he had forgotten them before; hence the need for revival. Look also in the N.T. "the word of God ... which effectually worketh also in you", 1 Thess. 2. 13; "All scripture is ... profitable for doctrine, for reproof, for correction, for instruction in righteousness", 2 Tim. 3. 16; "these things write we ... that your joy may be full", 1 John 1. 4.

September 27th

READING: Psalm 119. 49-64

THE WORD AND THE DAY OF TESTING

As WE READ Psalm 119, we are reminded of the words of the Lord Jesus to His disciples, "In the world ye shall have tribulation: but be of good cheer; I have overcome the world", John 16. 33. Persecution has always been the lot of Christians. The psalmist had his share of this, and in verse 51 he tells us that the derision of sinners should not lead to a turning away from the Word of God. Verse 61 implies that the action of sinners should not lead the Christian to sin. We should leave the matter in the hands of God, and continue to feed on the Word of God, v. 78. Verse 157 suggests that, in spite of opposition, we should not swerve from God's Word.

Looking at these verses more closely, we discover that, though many attempts were made to turn the psalmist away, the effect was to drive him closer to the Word. There he found strength and consolation. It is hard to stand up to ridicule, v. 51. When we are taunted for being a "goody-goody", and worse, when our Saviour is taunted through us, what can we do? This man refused to turn from God's teachings in order to comply with the wishes of men. Having considered his position, he said "no". What would he have done without the Word?

"The bands of the wicked have robbed me", v. 61. What to do now? Many times Christians have suffered the spoiling of their goods, Heb. 10. 34. The believer does not retaliate in like fashion—he does not do wrong to avoid wrong. He does not forget the law of his God which bids forgiveness for those who harm. In verse 78, we see that, although men dealt perversely with him, it was without a cause. His meditation in the Word was standing him in good stead. His life could stand the test of inspection. Thus Daniel's enemies looked at him and they could find "none occasion nor fault", Dan. 6. 4. They persecuted, but failed to move him; he knew his God. Many were the persecutors and enemies of the psalmist, v. 157, yet because of the influence of the Word, he continued with God.

Listen to men in the N.T. "Lord, behold their threatenings: and grant unto thy servants, that with all boldness they may speak thy word", Acts 4. 29; "they that were scattered abroad went every where preaching the word", 8. 4; "I suffer trouble ... the word of God is not bound", 2 Tim. 2. 9.

READING: **Psalm 119. 97-112**

SWEETER THAN HONEY

"How sweet are thy words unto my taste". Verse 103 is an exclamation of delight. Here is a man who knew his Bible, limited though it was, and it was out of the depths of his experience that he uttered these words. He not only read the Word, he fed upon it, and his verdict was "how sweet". C. H. Spurgeon wrote, "God's words are many and varied, and the whole of them make up what we call 'the Word'. The psalmist loved them each one, individually, and the whole of them as a whole: he tasted an indescribable sweetness in them ... He who put the sweetness into them had prepared the taste of His servant to discern and enjoy it".

This is remarkable when we consider the experience of the writer as indicated in this psalm. He had been challenged and rebuked. He had known times of spiritual depression, as well as times of joy. In his varied experiences, he had been enabled to test and taste the Word. He made no distinction between promises and warnings, between doctrines and threatenings—they were sweet to his taste. Psalm 19. 10 also proclaims the Word of God to be "sweeter also than honey and the honeycomb", and it is significant that in verse 11 David adds, "by them is thy servant warned". We may also think of the words of the prophet Jeremiah, "Thy words were found, and I did eat them; and thy word was unto me the joy and rejoicing of mine heart". 15. 16.

In speaking of his own enjoyment of the Word of God, the writer speaks of his "taste". He then goes on to say, "yea, sweeter than honey to my mouth". Not "taste" now, but "mouth", where speech comes from. He is now speaking of his utterance; not of receiving, but giving. How precious to note that what had been so sweet to him is now reflected in his speech to others. What comes forth is sweetened by what he had digested.

"O teach me Lord, that I may teach the precious things thou dost impart", wrote F. R. Havergal. In the N.T. we read, "out of the abundance of the heart the mouth speaketh", Matt. 12. 34; "Let you speech be alway with grace", Col. 4. 6. And for our perfect Example, "all bare him witness, and wondered at the gracious words which proceeded out of his mouth", Luke 4. 22, because He delighted in feeding on His Father's Word.

September 29th

READING: **Psalm 119. 1-16**

ACCORDING TO THY WORD

SADLY, it must be acknowledged that much that is done in Christendom today is not "according to thy word". Much of it is based on human wisdom. Some of the things we find in our own lives may also justify this criticism. Seventeen times in this psalm the writer uses these words, and clearly we must be selective. We shall look at verses 9, 28, 41, 65, 169.

Verse 9. Here the question is, How to adjust life? The psalmist's answer is, "by the Word". Human advice may be helpful, but can never take the place of the Word. The best human advice is that which directs us to the Scriptures. As the traveller needs an accurate map, so in the journey of life we need accurate guidance.

Verse 28. Here is a man in tears because of life's experiences. In his depression, he listens to the voice of God, and finds strength. He finds his remedy through prayer. Paul was in trouble in Acts 18; he went to bed a frightened man, v. 9. There is no doubt that he prayed. Then the Lord spake to him in the night, "Be not afraid ... no man shall ... hurt thee", vv. 9-10. In the strength of God's Word Paul continued, and souls were saved in Corinth.

Verse 41. Here the writer sees the Word of God as the channel for the full understanding of the mercies and salvation of God. Human books are good, but The Book is better. The way of salvation is found in the Word, and in all respects the salvation which is in Christ is in accordance with the Word. Saul (once a Pharisee) said, "I ... thought ... I ought to do many things contrary to the name of Jesus", Acts 26. 9, but the word from heaven revealed God's salvation which became his.

Verse 65. "Thou hast dealt well with thy servant". In the N.T., the Lord said, "When I sent you without purse, and scrip ... lacked ye anything?", Luke 22. 35. They answered, "Nothing". He had promised to provide, and He did.

Verse 169. In the prayer, "give me understanding according to thy word", this was not the understanding of the schools or of ancient wisdom. In Galatians 1. 14, Paul speaks of his religious knowledge prior to his conversion, "above many my equals"; then he speaks of God revealing the truth to him—only then he understood "according to thy word".

READING: **Psalm 40. 6-11; 119. 89-96**

THE LIVING WORD

TODAY WE close our thoughts concerning the Word in the psalms. As we do so, let us also think of the Living Word, the Lord Jesus Christ. At the opening of the Gospel of John, we have the majestic words, "the Word was God", and in verse 14 "the Word was made flesh", and immediately we are introduced to the One who is the fulfilment of all that is found in the written Word. These two are in such harmony that love for the written Word will drive me to the Living Word, and love for the Living Word will drive me to the written Word. In both the heart of God is revealed.

In Psalm 119. 89, we thought of the eternal character of God's Word—for ever "settled in heaven", and this brings to mind the lovely words of the hymn, "Thou art the everlasting Word, the Father's only Son". Revelation 1. 4 speaks of the Author of the letters to the seven churches as being the One "which is, and which was, and which is to come". From eternity to eternity—the ever-living Word.

We thought, too, of the written Word as pure gold, priceless treasure. What believer can deny that these words appropriately describe the Living Word? John Newton was right when he wrote, "my never failing treasury filled with boundless stores of grace". The Spirit emphasized this when He caused Peter to write, "unto you ... he is precious", 1 Pet. 2. 7.

In Psalm 1, we considered the Word as the believer's delight—"his delight is in the law of the Lord". All that he needed he found there. He could not find it elsewhere. Is not this true of our beloved Lord? In John 6. 67, the Lord Jesus speaks to His disciples, "Will ye also go away". Peter's answer will come from every believing heart, "Lord, to whom shall we go? thou hast the words of eternal life". "Thou, O Christ, art all I want, More than all in Thee I find."

This verse speaks of the Living Word and the written Word:

> "In want my plentiful supply,
> In weakness mine almighty power:
> In bonds my perfect liberty,
> My light in Satan's darkest hour,
> In grief my joy unspeakable,
> In death my life, my heaven, my all."

Christ in the Psalms

To FIND Christ in any part of the Holy Scriptures is to meet up with that blessed One to whom Christians owe whatever blessing they can ever know and evermore enjoy. Just as the two forlorn disciples long ago actually walked alongside Him, listening while He literally interpreted to them in all the Scriptures the things concerning Himself, may it prove to be another month of communion with Him in the Psalms, that will send us on our way to strengthen and cheer others whose faith in Him, for many reasons, may have become dimmed.

This month, then, we shall keep company with Him who said, "I am Alpha and Omega ... which is, and which was, and which is to come, the Almighty", Rev. 1. 8. Hopefully, we shall discover "Jesus Christ the same yesterday, and to-day, and for ever", Heb. 13. 8, drawing near and going along with us. What a change this could make in our lives and circumstances! How wonderful that He, who has pledged Himself to be with us all the days, never more to leave us nor forsake us, should show us by His Spirit more of His unique glories. "Then were the disciples glad, when they saw the Lord", John 20. 20.

The Psalms declare that Christ is the Everlasting One, the Creator, the One for whom a body was prepared. They tell of His boyhood and public earthly ministry; of His reproaches and enemies, even of His betrayal and rejection. In speaking of His first coming to this earth, they give the most graphic details of His sufferings to be found in all Scripture. His incorruptibility, resurrection and ascension are also very clearly marked. But what of the glory (really glories) that should follow? We shall see Him exalted, crowned and as Sovereign, and it will thrill us to consider Him as the High Priest, the Man at the right hand and as the Firstborn. Then, when He returns to this earth, it must be to fulfil all that is said of David's Son, to reign in righteousness and to fill the earth with His glory. All these themes, and many more beside, will be our daily fare. May God grant to us an appetite for them, and hearts overflowing with thankfulness and praise. (D.C.)

October 1st

READING: **Psalms 90 & 93**

THE EVERLASTING ONE

PSALM 90 is probably one of the oldest psalms, written by Moses during the time of the penal wanderings of God's people through the wilderness. It is best understood by keeping Israel's experiences in mind at that time. Prophetically it is a remnant crying for restoration, and implies the second advent of the Messiah. Psalm 93 proclaims Jehovah as the universal King. The references chosen all speak of Christ in the light of such N.T. passages as John 1 and Col. 1. In 1 John 1. 1, the apostle writes about *from* the beginning, not *at* the beginning, and that the Word *was* (past tense). Colossians 1. 17 talks of Christ as *before* all things (in time). Let us look at Christ in relation to:

1. *Things Terrestrial*, Psa. 90. 2. He is "Before the mountains", whereas the mountains were considered, by man, to be the most ancient part of the earth. He is before the earth and the world; i.e., a world capable of being inhabited. He is from everlasting to everlasting in His essence and in His providence. It is not just that "He is", but that "He is God".

2. *Things Temporal*, Psa. 90. 4. To the Christ of God, time has no existence, but all is an eternal present. To a rich man, a thousand pounds are as a penny, so to God a thousand years are but a day. If we could outlive Methuselah, it would be as yesterday with God. In 2 Peter 3. 8, the phrase is also quoted in reverse—a day as a thousand years. A watch in the night suggests the unconscious sleeper for whom the night passes so quickly—hence a thousand years.

3. *Things Transcendent*, Psa. 93. 2. Note here the progression backwards in time—"established", "old", "everlasting". It also states that the Christ of God is *from* everlasting. We are taken here beyond eternity, if we can use that expression. In this, we are trying to explain and understand eternity, the essential characteristic of Deity, and we shall never be able to do this because our minds are finite. Christ is from everlasting to everlasting, and in this we take encouragement.

Endless has beginning and no end, but everlasting has no beginning and no end. (D.R.)

293

October 2nd

READING: **Psalms 102 & 104**

THE CREATOR

PSALM 102 is characterized by sorrow and solace, and has long been recognized as Messianic. Verses 24-27 are the key verses, to be read in conjunction with the opening verses of Hebrews 1. For example, "heir of all things, by whom also he made the worlds", Heb. 1. 2. Again, we read, "For by him were all things created, that are in heaven, and that are in earth", Col. 1. 16. They were "created by him, and for him". Psalm 104 adopts for its general arrangement the pattern of Genesis 1, emphasizing the maintenance rather than the process of creation. Christ, in sharp contrast to the achievements of man, is:

The Master of Master-Builders, Psa. 102. 25; 104, 2-3. He alone laid the foundations of the earth, and the heavens in all their grandeur are His handiwork. He is the Architect and the Builder—He is everything. Sir Christopher Wren, the former well-known architect, was once asked for examples of his work; his answer was, "Look around you". Similarly, we look around and see Christ's handiwork. In Psalm 104, the heavens are described as a canopy that protects the earth, a tent-curtain under which we all dwell. Psalm 104. 3 refers to the upper chambers of a house, built for solitude and retirement. The cloud-chariots and the wings of the wind suggest the swiftness of His coming for His people.

The Head of the Head-Gardeners, Psa. 104. 14, 16. These verses talk of the grass that He makes to grow, and the trees that He has planted. Grass seems a very simple thing to grow, and yet this cannot be done without God's help.

King of Astronomers-Royal, Psa. 104. 19-20. Astronomers only study what the Christ of God has created. He appointed the moon that governs the seasons and the calendar, and He controls the sun. Note the order—moon then sun—night then day—darkness then light—always the order in Scripture.

The Top of the Top Scientists, Psa. 104. 20. Man can make artificial light, but how can darkness be created? Only God can do that!

The Provider for the Providers, Psa. 104. 21, 27. All creatures that provide for their young wait upon the Lord.

Is He resident or president in our lives? (D.R.)

October 3rd

READING: **Psalm 40**

A BODY PREPARED

PSALM 40. 6-8 is quoted in the N.T. in Hebrews 10. 5-7, and by careful examination it will be seen that one phrase changes. The Holy Spirit who inspired the Word is free, of course, to requote in another form without changing the accuracy of the original statement. This is internal evidence for the inspiration of the Scriptures, and here one passage explains the other.

Psalm 40. 6b states, "mine ears hast thou opened", while Hebrews 10. 5b states, "a body hast thou prepared me". Both of these statements have an important common link discovered in the context: "Lo, I come: in the volume of the book it is written of me, I delight to do thy will". The common link is *obedience*. The custom of boring a servant's ears was a mark of perpetual servitude and willingness to obey; for the servant loved his master and would not go free. In the case of the Lord Jesus Christ, His obedience to His Father's will is seen in His incarnation and the body that was prepared for Him. Hence Simeon could say in Luke 2. 30, "mine eyes have seen thy salvation".

The Purpose. Christ is the antitype of all the O.T. offerings and sacrifices. They were not willing to die, but Christ, in obedience to His Father's will, was willing to die. Romans 8. 3 states, "God sending his own Son in the likeness of sinful flesh, and for sin, condemned sin in the flesh". Note that it is the *likeness* of sinful flesh, and note also how sin was condemned—*not* in the soul, or mind, but in the flesh—the weakest part of the human frame.

The Preparation. And so Christ was born into this world, or as Galatians 4. 4 puts it, "made of a woman". This may seem an obvious statement because every man came of a woman. But Christ is unique, and this statement had to be made, because Christ is eternal, from everlasting to everlasting, and yet "made of a woman"; cf. Luke 1. 30-35. The Song of Solomon could well describe Christ's unique beauty, "My beloved is white and ruddy, the chiefest among ten thousand ... he is altogether lovely", Song 5. 10, 16.

The Person. "I delight to do thy will"—He did the will of His Father, and fulfilled the O.T. Scriptures. (D.R.)

READING: **Psalm 119. 97-104, 121-128, 137-144**

BOYHOOD KNOWLEDGE

THE COMPOSITION of this psalm is a perfect and regular alphabetical acrostic employing the 22 letters of the Hebrew alphabet. There are 22 stanzas of 8 verses each, giving a total of 176 verses. Stating it in English, it is the "A B C" of God's Word, and what better place to start to appreciate God's Word than this psalm!

Luke 2. 46, 47, 49 and 52 highlight the boyhood knowledge of the Lord Jesus Christ: "hearing ... and asking questions", v. 46; "astonished at his understanding and answers", v. 47; "about my Father's business", v. 49; and "increased in wisdom", v. 52. Christ was a student of Scripture! He used the Scriptures for both defence and attack, and His use of the Word can help us understand how He studied the Scriptures.

In Psalm 119, the Scriptures are referred to in many ways, and the whole psalm is taken up with this theme. For instance, we find:

The Motive, "O how I love thy law", v. 97. The construction of this sentence is emphatic, and stresses the measure of His love for the Word. How much better can we study the Word when we love it!

The Means. There are too many references in this psalm to table here, but the Word is described thus:

Statutes means "to engrave on a stone", and are the decrees of a king; *commandment* is the will of a father; *judgments* refer to the decisions of a judge; *law* means "to point out", showing the will of God; *testimonies* are God's witness to what He is; *precepts* are directions from God, as from a master to a pupil; *word* is that which is spoken, and *way* represents a principle of action. In the life of Christ we can trace these various avenues through which the Word of life came from His lips.

The Mission was to be about His Father's business, and these words in Luke 2 were His first recorded words, whilst His last recorded words before He died were "It is finished", John 19. 30. "My zeal hath consumed me, because mine enemies have forgotten thy words", Psa. 119. 139; "It is time for thee, Lord, to work: for they have made void thy law", v. 126. Let us ponder well these verses when associated with Christ. (D.R.)

October 5th

READING: **Psalm 69. 1-9**

HIS LIFETIME ZEAL

VERSES 22-23 from the pen of David are confirmed by the Holy Spirit in Romans 11. 9-10. The prophetic overrules the historic in this psalm, being Messianic, and quoted many times in the N.T. It concerns itself with suffering for the sake of righteousness, and in particular in verse 9 it speaks of the zeal of Christ for the honour of His Father's house.

His Dedication. His zeal, never misplaced like that of man, can be described as godly jealousy for the honour of His Father's house. Jealousy *must not* be confused with envy. Due to careless speech, these two words have become interchangeable, and we should be careful to define our words clearly. The person who betrays envy has no right to possess that which is the cause of such jealousy. But jealousy can be a legitimate reaction in relationships. Our God is a jealous God, because He has every right to all that we have and are.

His Duty was the honour of His Father's house, and this can best be stressed by turning to the N.T. references in Matthew 21. 12-13 and John 2. 17. The house of God had become a den of thieves and a house of merchandise. Let us beware that we do not fall into the same error. There must be reverence at all times in the house of God. It is His house, and He makes the rules. These two N.T. references stress the high regard that the Lord had for the house of God.

His Devotion was such that it was a fire consuming within Him. The phrase is "hath eaten me up"; His zeal had engulfed Him, it was His consuming passion and was the reason for His drastic action in the temple on more than one occasion. Our feelings and devotions cannot match His, but we get the measure of His attitude here to the house of God and all that it stands for, and to its functions today, 1 Tim. 3. 15. In a world that has lowered its moral sights and has turned prodigal, we need jealously to guard the things that are believed among us, and to have no fellowship with the world. We must shrug off its rival suitors, and give our allegiance to the Lord, so as to guard the honour of His house.

Zeal is only fit for wise men. (D.R.)

October 6th

READING: **Psalm 91**

CHRIST'S LIFE OF VICTORY

"WHAT MANNER of man is this!", Matt. 8. 27. There is little doubt that Moses wrote this psalm, probably at the beginning of the wilderness journey, portraying how God gave His people shelter because He promised to do so. The relevant verses here are 11-13, and these should be carefully compared with the N.T. quotation in Matthew 4. 6. The devil quotes from Scripture, but the Lord's reply is "It is written again". In considering the victorious life, it is good to remember that the devil's weakness is seen in his misuse and misquoting of Scripture. It was the scriptural phrases he omitted that were significant, *not* the phrases he quoted.

Three points arise about the victorious life of Christ.

Its Source, "For he shall give his angels charge over thee", v. 11a. Not one angel, but many, sent direct from God and on His authority. Thus overshadowing the triumphs of Christ is the authority and command of God, who is still on the throne!

Its Secret, "to keep thee in all thy ways", v. 11b. Now this is the phrase that the devil omitted. He would have found it difficult to use, because it implied obedience to the will of God. Thus the secret of Christ's victory over Satan's temptation lay in His obedience to the will of His Father.

Its Success, "They shall bear thee up in their hands", vv. 12-13, implying special love and care. "Dash thy foot against a stone" suggests stumbling and falling, difficulties and objections, perils within and perils without. "Thou shalt tread upon the lion and adder" is a phrase that was conveniently omitted by the devil, because it could refer to himself! He only masquerades as a lion, and the thought behind treading upon him is not as an accident but the intentional action of a conqueror. "The young lion and the dragon shalt thou trample under feet" refers to two aspects of hostility: the lion roars in open hostility and the dragon (or serpent) lurks in subtle hostility. No perils overcame Christ because His was a triumphant life.

If we would seek for a victorious life, we must be prepared to follow Him in every sense of the word.

Glory is the reward of victory. (D.R.)

October 7th

READING: **Psalm 78. 1-22**

THE TEACHINGS OF CHRIST

"THE PEOPLE were astonished at his doctrine", Matt. 7. 28.

The writer of Psalm 78 may well be Asaph of David's day; he traced the history of Israel, underlining the mighty power of the word of God. He commanded, and it happened! The teachings of Christ and everything that the Word of God means are not frozen on the pages of a book, but lived out in the experiences of life. Verse 2 is quoted in Matthew 13. 35.

OUR RESOURCE. In verses 1-2, the teachings of Christ are represented in four ways:

1. *Authority*, "Give ear ... to my law". One feature that characterized all that Christ taught was the authority that He commanded; cf. Matt. 7. 28-29.

2. *Vitality*, "the words of my mouth". This refers, not to mere words, but to the Word of life. The Bible is a book that speaks; do we read the Bible, or does the Bible read us?

3. *Sagacity*, "open my mouth in a parable". The teachings of Christ penetrate the mind and soul, and when they are understood, they make a deep and unforgettable impression.

4. *Gravity*, "utter dark sayings of old". This relates to the wise man and his sayings, where old truths are best and there is no room for new truths. It implies a weighty speech and Christ's teaching is weighed rather than measured.

OUR RESPONSE, v. 3. (i) "We have heard"; obedience revolves around hearing and then putting it into practice. (ii) "And known"; we have a great responsibility if we have heard because it implies a knowledge of the facts and action to follow. (iii) "Our fathers have told us"; we have been told and we must tell others. This leads to the third main point.

OUR RESPONSIBILITY, v. 4. Here is indicated the importance of not hiding the truths from the children; they should be shown to the generation to come. In 2 Timothy 2. 2, we see the Paul-Timothy relationship and the charge that Paul gave to his child in the faith. "Thou hast heard" is past; "commit thou" is present; "shall be able to teach" is future. This must also be our solemn duty before God.

Teach me to feel another's woe,
That mercy I to others show.   (D.R.)

READING: **Psalm 45**

THE VOICE OF CHRIST

"NEVER MAN spake like this man", John 7. 46. Psalm 45 is described as "A Song of Loves". It speaks of a royal marriage, and describes the king in all his beauty. It points to the beauties that are in Christ, and the beauties of His voice for today are indicated in verses 1-2.

Its Source, "My heart is inditing a good matter", v. 1, or overflowing, bubbling over. Some suggest that there is here a picture of the meal offering in preparation and presentation; as prepared in the frying pan and with the mingled oil in Leviticus 2, it is bubbling over. The source here is the heart—those things that we give outward expression to must begin within the heart. So it is with Christ—everything that He said came from the heart.

Its Subject, "I speak of the things which I have made touching the king", v. 1. The subject is the king. Christ had many things to say, but He spoke so much of His Father in heaven. His object was always to glorify His Father, and the Father always honoured His Son. There could be no better subject about which to talk than that of the two on the road to Emmaus, Luke 24. 13-27.

Its Service, "my tongue is the pen of a ready writer", v. 1. These words could suggest the thought of a reporter or observer making detailed notes, ensuring that nothing is omitted. So it was with Christ—no words were wasted, but nothing that had to be said was omitted. Note that the writer is described *not* as a penman but as a pen. God is the Craftsman; we are the tool. He is the potter; we are the clay.

Its Sweetness. The stress here is on moral and spiritual beauty rather than on anything physical, namely on inward perfection and a readiness to impart to others what He has to say. The voice of Christ is a still, small voice, and it behoves us to draw near to Him and to stay there so that we can hear His voice speaking to us. John heard the voice of Christ in connection with the charge concerning Mary, the mother of the Lord Jesus Christ—and this was because he was standing near the cross, John 19. 25-27. Are we standing by Him at the cross?; can we hear His voice?

Speech is the gift of many, but thought of few. (D.R.)

October 9th

READING: **Psalm 35. 1-16**

CHRIST AND THE ENEMY

"MARVEL NOT, my brethren, if the world hate you", 1 John 3. 13. Psalms, such as 35, 59 and 64, deal with the nations in opposition to Israel, and with their endeavours to exterminate the people of God. Relating this subject to Christ and also to ourselves, we see the techniques that the enemy uses.

The Enemy's Tenacity, "strive with me", 35. 1. This shows how our archenemy persisted in his endeavours to overthrow Christ. But the persistence met with a greater resistance.

The Enemy's Trap, "hid for me their net in a pit", 35. 7, a method used to catch a wild animal. Christ's answers to His enemies' verbal traps are a joy to read and study; Matt. 22. 15ff.

The Enemy's Threats, "rise up against me", 59. 1. This stresses the strength and the violence of the enemy. Whenever Christ was so threatened, He committed His cause to His God, the One who judges righteously, 1 Pet. 2. 23.

The Enemy's Task, "workers of iniquity", 59. 2. This highlights not only the corruption that exists, but activities which are aimed at undoing the work of God.

The Enemy's Treachery, "lie in wait", 59. 3. This shows the subtilty of the enemy in terms of place and timing in his endeavour to attack us. With respect to Christ, subtilty was met with open rebuke; cf. Matt. 16. 22-23.

The Enemy's Technique, "run and prepare themselves", 59. 4. This brings with it the idea of sudden assault and readiness to meet it. Christ knew what was in man!

The Enemy's Taunts, "a noise like a dog", 59. 6. This suggests wild, savage and hungry dogs completely out of control. When the enemy shouts, it is a sign of weakness, not of strength—he cannot control himself.

The Enemy's Tongue, "swords are in their lips", 59. 7; this emphasizes the wounding effect of words. The sharp tongue of the enemy was no match for the gentle voice of Christ.

The Enemy's Thoughts, "the secret counsel of the wicked", 64. 2. This brings out their design and calculated tactics.

The Enemy's Triumph, "encourage themselves in an evil matter", 64. 5, laying bare the pleasure of the enemy in their evil design. We can rejoice that Christ completely destroyed Satan and his works; cf. Heb. 2. 14-15; Rev. 17. 14. (D.R.)

October 10th

READING: **Psalm 69. 1-29**

THE REPROACH OF CHRIST

"THEREFORE the world knoweth us not", 1 John 3. 1. The writers of the Psalms were often prophets as well as poets, and often wrote of matters outside their own experience. The two Psalms 69 and 89 deal with the suffering of God's people: but the only Person in whom all these sufferings met was the Person of Christ.

Reproach and Honour, "Thou hast known my reproach, and my shame, and my dishonour", 69. 19. We cannot say that our sufferings are unnoticed, when Christ was so acquainted with grief and reproach, with its attendant shame and dishonour. This shame and dishonour speak of the offence of the cross. The world has a form of honour in which none of God's people have a part, but in the Lord's case it was the Father that honoured Him, John 8. 54. "By honour and dishonour", 2 Cor. 6. 8.

Reproach and the Heart, "Reproach hath broken my heart", 69. 20. But "none of the ransomed ever knew, how deep were the waters crossed"; no matter how near we may be to Him, we shall always be a stone's throw away, as were the disciples in the garden of Gethsemane, Luke 22. 41. Even in our ordinary day-to-day experiences, we look for sympathy; yet remember Him who "looked for some to take pity, but there was none; and for comforters, but I found none".

Reproach and Hope, "Remember, Lord, the reproach of thy servants", 89. 50-51. This is a prayer that the Lord hears and answers. He did not forget His Son, and He will not forget us. We are called upon quietly to accept these reproaches, and to endure them in silence. Our hope is in God, and we must keep our eyes upon Him. Verse 51 both expresses our hope, and highlights the attitude of the world in unbelief. "They have reproached the footsteps of thine anointed" portrays a picture of a crowd, a rabble, insulting Him wherever He goes, and the idea of footsteps could suggest His return, and the ridicule of the people that have not seen Him, such as the appearance of scoffers in the last days proclaiming, "Where is the promise of his coming?", 2 Pet. 3. 3-4.

The people of the world may *expect* good or bad, but we *hope* for the good. The Lord is coming back!

Answer reproach with silence. (D.R.)

October 11th

READING: **Psalm 41. 1-13**

THE BETRAYER

IT WAS as a rejected king that David crossed the brook Kidron, 2 Sam. 15. 23. He had been betrayed by Ahithophel, his companion and trusted counsellor, v. 12. It is likely that the words of Psalm 41. 9 originally referred to Ahithophel.

History repeated itself some 970 years later. The Lord Jesus crossed the Kidron, John 18. 1, having been betrayed by one of His companions, Judas Iscariot. It was of Judas that the Lord spoke when He said, "I know whom I have chosen: but that the scripture may be fulfilled, He that eateth bread with me hath lifted up his heel against me", John 13. 18. Interestingly, both traitors subsequently hung themselves, 2 Sam. 17. 23; Matt. 27. 5.

First, note *the words quoted* by the Lord. He spoke of Judas as one who had *eaten bread* with Him. Earlier, Jesus had said to His disciples, "One of you which eateth with me shall betray me", Mark 14. 18. To accept hospitality carried great significance for a Jew; it placed the recipient under considerable obligations. The fact that Ahithophel had formerly enjoyed David's hospitality rendered his treachery all the more base and contemptible. The same was true of Judas. The idea behind *lifting the heel* may be that of a horse kicking violently at its master. Certainly the expression describes the deliberate infliction of an injury.

Second, note *the words omitted*. The Lord did not quote the description, "mine own familiar friend, in whom I trusted". These words could not have been applied truthfully to Judas. And the Lord Jesus was never insincere. When He later addressed Judas as "friend", Matt. 26. 50, the word employed is not the normal word used to describe a friend—such as He used, for instance, when speaking of Lazarus, John 11. 11. The word used of Judas denotes an associate or companion.

Third, note *the words added*. John reports not only a mention of Judas' *heel*, and the *scripture* which was fulfilled, 13. 18. He refers also to Judas' *heart* and to *Satan* who deposited there the idea of betraying Christ, v. 2. Finally, he alludes to Judas' *hand* and to the *sop* which he was given to identify him, v. 26 read with Matt. 26. 23, "He that dippeth his hand with me in the dish, the same shall betray me". (M.H.)

303

October 12th

READING: **Psalm 2. 1-12**

REJECTED OF MEN

THE OPENING VERSES of Psalm 2 have yet to receive their *complete and final fulfilment*. This will come at the end of the age, in the period preceding the Lord's return to reign.

The early church, however, saw a *partial fulfilment* of the passage in the rejection of the Lord Jesus at His first coming. Faced with fierce opposition from the Jewish chief council, the apostles quoted verses 1 and 2 in prayer, adding, "For of a truth against thy holy child Jesus, whom thou hast anointed, both Herod, and Pontius Pilate, with the Gentiles, and the people of Israel, were gathered together", Acts 4. 27. The four categories of men mentioned in the psalm correspond to those specified by the apostles. "The kings of the earth" were represented by Herod Antipas, Luke 23. 7-11, and "the rulers" by Pontius Pilate. "The heathen" denote the Gentiles who played a crucial part in the rejection of Christ, and "the people" indicate the nation of Israel, Acts 4. 10, 27.

The apostles took encouragement from the fact that those who opposed the Lord and His anointed were able only to "do whatsoever thy hand and thy counsel determined before to be done", v. 28. Even God's enemies acted by His permission! The Lord informed Pilate that he possessed no power against Him except that which came from above, John 19. 11. He went to the cross only because "it was determined", with His rejection taking place according to God's "determinate counsel and foreknowledge", Luke 22. 22; Acts 2. 23. God was in control of every event, and His foes were the unwitting instruments of His will and purpose. Praise God, He still reigns today! Without violating or destroying man's free will and responsibility, He still works all things according to the counsel of His own will.

The Christian appreciates that the Lord's rejection was no accident or tragic happening. It formed an essential part of God's eternal purpose. The Lord was "delivered" not only by Judas, the Jewish leaders and Pilate, Matt. 26. 15; 27. 2, 26, but by God Himself, "for us all", Rom. 8. 32. By God's grace, we have renounced all association with those who were "gathered together" *against* the Lord and are numbered among those who "gather together" *to* Him and in His Name, Matt. 18. 20. (M.H.)

October 13th

READING: **Psalm 22. 1-21**

FORSAKEN!

PSALM 22 foretells both "the sufferings of Christ, and the glory that should follow", 1 Pet. 1. 11. The hinge of the psalm comes at the end of verse 21, "thou hast heard me". This stands in marked contrast to all that has gone before and, in particular, to the words "thou hearest not", v. 2. The section down to verse 21 is concerned with the sufferings of the Lord Jesus, and the remaining section with the glory into which He was later to enter, Luke 24. 26.

The Holy Spirit first draws attention to the Lord's spiritual suffering, expressed in His cry, "My God, my God, why hast thou forsaken me?". The description of that which He suffered from men comes later. His physical sufferings represent, as it were, only the door through which He passed to enter into the fearful region beyond.

When on the cross, for three hours He was "made ... sin for us", 2 Cor. 5. 21. During that time, abandoned and forsaken by God, He was alone! True, He had been forsaken earlier by His disciples as, in Gethsemane, they left Him and fled, Matt. 26. 56. But of that occasion, He had said, "ye ... shall leave me alone: and yet I am *not alone*, because the Father is with me", John 16. 32; cf. 8. 29. Now, however, He is forsaken by God also. The darkened heavens bore silent witness to it. No angel descended to minister to Him or to strengthen Him. Truly, there was "none to help", Psa. 22. 11.

David speaks also of our Lord's sufferings from men. Verses 7-8 received their fulfilment in the derision that He faced from the *Jews*. The people who passed the site of the crucifixion shook their heads at Him in a gesture of contempt and reproach, Matt. 27. 39; cf. 2 Kings 19. 21; Job 16. 4. The chief priests, elders and scribes laughed Him to scorn, Luke 23. 35, using the very words foretold, Matt. 27. 43. Verses 16 and 18 tell of His sufferings from the *Gentiles*. In accord with the Roman method of capital punishment, His hands and feet were pierced. Roman soldiers parted His garments, and cast lots for His coat, John 19. 23-24.

What mysteries! The beloved Son is forsaken. The Fount of living water thirsts, v. 15. The One "clothed with honour and majesty", 104. 1, is stripped of all earthly attire. (M.H.)

October 14th

READING: **Psalm 69. 1-36**

REVILED

THE N.T. suggests at least four applications of Psalm 69 to the Lord Jesus. Three take the form of fulfilments and the fourth represents a contrast.

1. *Hated*, v. 4. Both the words and the works of the Lord left the Jews of His day without any excuse for their unbelief and hatred of Him, John 15. 22-24. Their hostility towards Him was truly "without a cause", v. 25. This expression translates the same word as that rendered "freely", Rom. 3. 24. Just as we have done nothing to merit our justification, so He did nothing to merit men's hatred.

2. *Reproached*, v. 9. He suffered the harsh censures and reproaches of men. Faithful as God's representative, the taunts aimed at God were directed at Him. Paul quotes from this verse to demonstrate that "even Christ pleased not himself", Rom. 15. 3. In the light of His supreme example of unselfishness, we ought not to insist on pleasing ourselves at the expense of harming other believers, vv. 1-2.

3. *Determined*, v. 21. Immediately prior to His crucifixion, the Lord was offered a drink of sour wine drugged with gall or myrrh, Matt. 27. 34. The drink was intended to deaden the sense of pain, but He refused it. Clearly, His voluntary death for others required the full exercise of His will and consciousness. He was unwilling, therefore, to spare Himself anything of the suffering which lay ahead.

4. *Forgiving*. In verses 22-28, David gives vent to some of the fiercest prayers for vengeance in the Bible. It is true that the words of verses 22 and 23 were fulfilled in the blindness and unbelief of Israel following the Lord's rejection and death, Rom. 11. 9-10, and that verse 25 received a fulfilment in the doom and replacement of Judas, Acts 1. 20. Yet at no time did the Lord Jesus pray for these things. In striking contrast to David's prayer, "Pour out thine indignation upon them", Psa. 22. 24, He requested, "Father, forgive them", Luke 23. 34. No bitter threats or cries for revenge escaped His lips. When He was reviled, He "reviled not again; when he suffered, he threatened not", 1 Pet. 2. 23. The Son of man had "not come to destroy men's lives, but to save them", Luke 9. 56. (M.H.)

October 15th

READING: **Psalm 31**

INTO THY HANDS

THE WORDS of Psalm 31. 5, "Into thine hand I commit my spirit", were quoted by the Lord Jesus as His very last utterance before He died, Luke 23. 46.

Yesterday, we referred to Peter's statement concerning the Lord that, "when he suffered, he threatened not", 1 Pet. 2. 23. "But", the apostle added, He "*committed* himself to him that judgeth righteously".

The context of Psalm 31 makes it clear that, when David committed his spirit to God, he was entrusting himself to God for the preservation of his life. With confidence he looked to God to continue to protect the life which He had previously delivered. In our Lord's day, the words "into thy hand I commit my spirit" formed part of the evening prayer used by all pious Jews. It expressed their expectation of God's care and protection, particularly during the night ahead. The words were, however, ideally suited for use at the approach of death. The Lord quoted the words about "the ninth hour", Luke 23. 44, 46—possibly at the very time of evening prayer, Acts 3. 1; 9. 30; cf. Psa. 55. 17.

We notice that the Lord Jesus addressed His prayer to God in a manner in which David neither would nor could. His opening word was "*Father*". O precious word! The darkness was past; He was forsaken no longer.

It is Luke who provides us with the first and last of the recorded utterances of our Lord during the days of His flesh. In both the Lord used the word "Father". The first concerned the Father's business with which He occupied Himself, Luke 2. 49. The last concerned the Father's "hands" into which He committed Himself, 23. 46.

In His spirit the Lord had "waxed strong", 2. 40, had "rejoiced", 10. 21, had "sighed deeply", Mark 8. 12, had "groaned", John 11. 33, and had been "troubled", 13. 21. Now the time had come for Him to "release" His spirit, Matt. 27. 50 *lit.* But before He did so, He would commit it, in firm and unwavering trust, to His Father for safe keeping. His flesh rested in hope of His resurrection, Acts 2. 25-32. No man took His life from Him; He laid it down of Himself; *He would take it again!* (M.H.)

307

October 16th

READING: **Psalm 16**

THE INCORRUPTIBLE CHRIST

PSALM 16 is one of the Messianic Psalms, being quoted by Peter and by Paul in the N.T. Both apostles explain it as referring to the resurrection and exaltation of Christ, Acts 2. 31-32; 13. 35-37. It is one of the psalms with the title "Michtam" meaning "golden", and has been called "David's golden jewel". In it, there is a goldmine of exquisite teaching concerning the Lord Jesus. One such gem relates to the incorruptibility of the Saviour, v. 10. This refers to the period covered by His death, burial and resurrection. In contrast to David himself, Acts 13. 36, our Lord's body saw no corruption because of His absolute holiness, 13. 34, 35, 37. He is the impeccable Son of God—without sin, Heb. 4. 15; without fault, Luke 23. 14, 41; without corruption, Psa. 16. 10.

He truly is the Holy One who has abolished death, and has brought life and incorruption to light through the gospel, 2 Tim. 1. 10 R.V. His incorruptibility relates directly to His sinlessness. The N.T. leaves us in no doubt that He was sinless and perfect. Consider what was said of Him as follows:

Judas—"innocent blood", Matt. 27. 4.

Pilate—"this just person", Matt. 27. 24.

Pilate's wife—"that just man", Matt. 27. 19.

The repentant thief—"this man hath done nothing amiss", Luke 23. 4.

Add to this the testimony of the apostles:

Peter the *active* man—"who did no sin", 1 Pet. 2. 22.

Paul the *analytical* man—"who knew no sin", 2 Cor. 5. 21.

John the *adoring* man—"in him is no sin", 1 John 3. 5.

Furthermore, He proved that He was apart from sin, Heb. 4. 15. He Himself could say, "Which of you convinceth me of sin?", John 8. 46; and Satan also had nothing in Him, 14. 30.

We thank God for the impeccability of our Lord. He was tempted, not to discover if He could sin, but rather to prove that He would not sin. How we rejoice to know that He, the just One, gave Himself for the unjust in order to bring us to God. Having described His holiness, Psalm 16 ends with His exaltation to God's right hand to experience fulness of joy and pleasures that never end. Because of our union with Him, our joys, too, are full and will never decay, John 15. 11. (J.M.)

October 17th

READING: **Psalm 16**

THE RISEN CHRIST

Both Peter and Paul quote from Psalm 16 in their preaching, Acts 2. 25-28; 13. 35. Furthermore, they both interpret the latter section of the psalm as referring to the resurrection and exaltation of Christ. Verses 8-11 find their adequate realization only in the risen Christ Himself. Some view His resurrection as a *fraud*; others as mere *fancy* or even *fable*, but the hundred or more references in the N.T. affirm it to be a *fact*, and that a fact of history. In addition, the resurrection is the *fulfilment* of prophecy, Psa. 22. 21-22; Jonah, Matt. 12. 40, and is the very *foundation* of Christianity, 1 Cor. 15. 16-20. The resurrection of Christ is attributed to the Persons of the Godhead: the Father, Rom. 6. 4; Col. 2. 12; the Son, John 10. 18; Luke 24. 6-7; the Holy Spirit, 1 Pet. 3. 18; Rom. 8. 11.

In 1 Corinthians 15, Paul speaks much of Christ's resurrection. In the opening verses he emphasizes its *power*, vv. 1-2; its *promise*, vv. 3-4, and its *proof*, vv. 5-11.

The resurrection of Christ is affirmed in each of the four Gospels, and is at the very heart of the preaching of the apostles in The Acts. This truth was presented fearlessly by the early Christians, despite antagonism and opposition from many quarters. Certainly it is a *fact* for *faith*. Yet Paul tells Timothy, "Remember Jesus Christ, risen from the dead", 2 Tim. 2. 8 R.V. It is not only important to believe the fact of the resurrection but also constantly to call to mind the Person who has been raised from the dead, even Jesus Christ. We are to exercise our minds in thinking about Him, and to realize in our hearts that He has conquered even death. Paul's earnest desire was to be in the good of knowing Him and "the power of his resurrection", Phil. 3. 10. The early Christians certainly believed that Jesus was alive. They saw in His resurrection the fulfilment of O.T. prophecy and verification of His own claims, John 2. 19; 10. 18. It transformed a disillusioned and disappointed group of men into fearless witnesses to His saving power.

Like David in Psalm 16, we rejoice in (i) the *truth* of the resurrection, (ii) the *triumph* of the resurrection, and (iii) the *testimony* of the resurrection. (J.M.)

October 18th

READING: **Psalm 68. 1-20**

THE ASCENDED LORD

Psalm 68 is "The Victory Psalm". This magnificent psalm traces God's march to victory, linking past victories connected with Israel to the future and final victory of God. The Messianic passage is, "Thou hast ascended on high, thou hast led captivity captive: thou hast received gifts for men", v. 18. Paul applies the verse to the ascension of Christ, Eph. 4. 8. The apostle sees the victory of Deborah and Barak over the Canaanites, Jud. 5. 12-13, as illustrating the ascension of the victorious Head of the church, giving gifts for the benefit of His people. Paul interprets three statements as follows: "When he ascended up on high"—the *ascension* of the victorious Christ; "he led captivity captive"—the *annulling* of the opposition; "and gave gifts unto men", the *allocation* of gifts to the church.

"The Victory Psalm" points on to the idea of the victorious Captain, having effected deliverance, 2 Cor. 2. 14; Heb. 2. 15, proceeding with the distribution of the spoils of victory. So with our glorified Head in heaven, God's method of producing unity is to give gifts with a view to the perfection of His people, Eph. 4. 12. The *gifts*, both the men and the spiritual endowments, Rom. 12; 1 Cor 12 and Eph. 4, are given to produce *growth* in the saints (as well as to present the gospel to sinners), the ultimate objective being the *glory* of Christ, Eph. 4. 13. Because of the exalted Man in heaven, the Holy Spirit has been sent, John 7. 39, so that the message of salvation might be presented to men, Rom. 10. 9, and the saints encouraged in the ways of the Lord, 1 Thess. 4. 8; 2 Tim. 1. 14.

The ascension of Christ took place near Bethany on the mount of Olives, Luke 24. 50. From there a cloud received Him into heaven, Acts 1. 9-11. He was "received up", Mark 16. 19; "carried up", Luke 24. 51; "taken up", Acts 1. 9; "went up", 1. 10; and He "ascended up", Eph. 4. 10. As the Hebrew Epistle makes clear, He is in heaven, Heb. 9. 24; and we await His return, Phil. 3. 20. As the foregoing scriptures are considered, we see His ascension was *actual*, *literal* and *visible*. His return to this earth will be likewise, when He accomplishes the ultimate victory foretold in Psalm 68.

"*Blessed be God*", Psa. 68. 35. (J.M.)

READING: **Psalm 2**

THE EXALTED CHRIST—UPON MY HOLY HILL

VERSES 6-8 emphasize the exalted Christ in contrast with the opening verses, where the nations are seen in all their pride, stubbornness and self-assertion.

The Unshakeable Power, v. 6. Here the "I" is emphatic, and the word "set" means not only placed, but settled, established and appointed, stressing the permanence of the things of God in contrast to the things of the world. Zion was an ancient stronghold that became the city of David, 2 Sam. 5. 7.

The Undeniable Position, v. 7. "Declare" brings with it the idea of giving notice and notifying. God's mighty weapon is His own Word! "Decree" implies an order, a command; God is still on the throne. The nations may rule, but God overrules. The second half of verse 7 is quoted three times in the N.T. (i) Acts 13. 33 where His manifestation at His baptism is in mind—heaven saluted Him as the Son. (ii) Hebrews 1. 5 links with His exaltation above angels. (iii) Hebrews 5. 5 links with His eternal priesthood. We conclude that this declaration emphasizes the greatness of Christ, and ensures that He is entirely unique. He is begotten in relation to God, and the Firstborn in relation to man. Notice the order in the declaration: "Son ... this day ... begotten". The word is begotten, not born. First He was the Son; then "this day" suggests time, and then begotten. Therefore He is the Son before time, and hence there is a stress on His eternal Sonship. This is the point that is expounded in Hebrews 1. 5, where this verse from Psalm 2 is employed.

The Universal Possession. The nations and the earth are His for the asking, thus undermining the power and the authority of all nations of the world. The word "ask" means to ask for oneself, to ask for one's own use and to ask for a purpose. Thus all God's purpose and promises will be fulfilled in Christ. The uttermost parts of the earth imply the opposite side, the west as opposed to the east. So much for world domination by the great powers, and so much for the aspirations of would-be world dictators. The possession of the nations and the earth will go to Christ, and He will hold it fast, as the word implies. As He has received, so He promises to share this rule with His people, Rev. 2. 26-27.

Kings of the earth set *themselves; God* sets His King. (D.R.)

October 20th

READING: **Psalm 68. 14-35**

THE EXALTED CHRIST—EXALTED ON HIGH

HERE WE look at verse 18, which according to the spirit of the text of the psalm, stresses the greatness of Christ and refers to Zion in the expression "ascended on high". The thought of Zion in verse 18 is set in contrast with Sinai in verse 17. At Sinai, in effect, God descended, put a yoke of the law upon the people and demanded obedience, whereas in verse 18 we see Christ ascending on high, leading captivity captive, and receiving gifts for men.

Heaven High. "Ascended on high" originally suggested the ark conducted to the summit of mount Zion, but now we see the ark whose antitype is Christ, ascending into heaven. Notice the repetition of the idea of exaltation in the two words "ascended" and "high". This is not a mere repetition, but the emphasizing of a very important truth—i.e. the exaltation of Christ.

Captivity Captive. These words emphasize both the resurrection and the triumphs of Christ. The cross was the greatest victory of all time—a victory over all our foes and in particular, Satan himself. The campaign is finished, the enemy has been routed, and in Colossians 2. 15 Christ has "spoiled principalities and powers, he made a show of them openly, triumphing over them in it". The picture given is of a victorious army parading in triumph through a captured city, exhibiting its triumphs and humiliating its prisoners.

Gifts Given. Verse 18 is quoted in Ephesians 4. 8, but with the significant difference: instead of the word "received", Paul used the word "gave". There is no contradiction here, but receiving and giving are both part of one grand and glorious action of our Mediator, the Man Christ Jesus. In the context of the psalm, the writer is exalting God in connection with a recent victory, and also thinks back to the deliverance from Egypt, the crossing of the Red Sea, the journey through the wilderness, and the ultimate entry into the promised land. Under the influence of the Holy Spirit, in Ephesians 4. 8 Paul ascribes all to Christ. We are blessed with all spiritual blessings in Christ Jesus.

Christ passed angels twice, once in His humiliation and once in His exaltation. (D.R.)

312

October 21st

READING: **Psalm 110**

THE EXALTED CHRIST—AT GOD'S RIGHT HAND

FROM THIS psalm, four verses under three headings are extracted to stress the great truth of the Exalted Christ.

Exalted and Waiting, v. 1, "Sit thou at my right hand, until I make thine enemies thy footstool". He is seated, indicating that the work of the cross is completed. The tone of the verse is one of rest and triumph, the ease of victory, a new order and an act of justice. Many people make much of the world and its fame, fortune, ambition, politics, riches and achievements, but in the final analysis it is only God's footstool.

Exalted and Interceding, v. 4. This verse is quoted in Hebrews 5. 6, and stresses the eternal priesthood of Christ in contrast to that of men. But the whole subject looks back to Genesis 14. 18, where we read of Melchizedek for the first time, and what is more important, we read there the word "priest" for the first time. Under the "law of first mention", important clues can be learnt from the use and meaning of a word. Genesis 14. 18 stresses the authority "of the most high God", and the office of priest, for "he blessed him", v. 19. Thus in Psalm 110. 4, we have the authority: "The Lord hath sworn"; the assurance: "and will not repent"; the office: "Thou art a priest"; the duration: "for ever"; the character: "after the order of"; and its royalty: "Melchizedek", the word meaning, "King of righteousness ... King of peace", Heb. 7. 1-2.

Exalted and Acting, vv. 5-6. Our God is a God of action, as these two verses show. We need to remember this when we pray, in order that we may encourage ourselves in the Lord. The word "strike" in verse 5 means not only complete victory, but full confusion and an incurable wound. Such is the power of the exalted Christ. Wrath is the most significant passion that man can display, and we shudder to think of what it means in relation to God! The greatness of the victory is further stressed in verse 6 by the devastation that is left behind. There is none left to bury the dead, and the enemy have been shamed and dishonoured. Proud and powerful political leaders will be wounded. How have the mighty fallen! How great is our God!

"Until" has lasted nearly 2,000 years, but He has been ready all the time. (D.R.)

October 22nd

READING: **Psalm 45**

THE BRIDEGROOM-KING

PSALM 45 describes the marriage of the King with a king's daughter and their subsequent posterity and renoun. It is a Messianic psalm, verses 6-7 being quoted in Hebrews 1. 8-9. The King is the main subject of the psalm, which points to our Lord Jesus as the King of kings and Lord of lords. He will come to earth in order to put down all rebellion and inaugurate His glorious reign, Rev. 19. 11-16.

The glories of the King occupy the psalmist in verses 1-9 of the psalm, and as verse 1 shows he finds it difficult to give expression to the wonders and glory of his great subject. The earlier part presents the glories of the Bridegroom-King.

His Moral Glory. He is "fairer than the children of men". There is none to compare with Him; all others stand in contrast. Having said who He is, the psalmist is now concerned with what He says, "grace is poured into thy lips". We recall the "gracious words" of our Lord, Luke 4. 22. The excellence of His moral character is revealed in the Gospels. The perfect blend of grace and truth is found uniquely in Him. He is like us, yet unlike us. He shared our human nature, but not our sinful nature. The perfect balance of His character, without weakness on the one hand, or overbearing on the other, is completely different from that of all others. He is fairer, more beautiful, and that by far.

His Official Glory. We read of "thy sword ... thy glory ... thy majesty ... thy right hand ... thy throne", besides a sceptre and anointing with the oil of gladness, vv. 3-7. As King, the Lord Jesus will take the kingdom by defeating His foes, Rev. 19. He is superior to any and every monarch, and He has the moral and official right to rule.

His Personal Glory. The full Deity of the King is seen, as we observe the Spirit's interpretation of verse 6 in Hebrews 1. 8. Also note that verse 8 explains that He is as gracious as He is glorious.

The queen is at His right hand, v. 9. On this wedding day, her beauty, attire and attendants are described in some detail, pointing on to a glorious time yet future for Israel and the church. The psalm closes with the bridal procession, vv. 14-15, anticipating the future time of rejoicing for God's people. (J.M.)

314

October 23rd

READING: **Psalm 110**

THE MELCHIZEDEK HIGH PRIESTHOOD

PSALM 110 is another Messianic Psalm. In fact, it is quoted in the N.T. more frequently than any other O.T. passage, and on every occasion it relates to the Lord Jesus Christ. The Lord Himself used this psalm to prove that He was not only David's Son, but also David's Lord, Matt. 22. 41-46. This emphasizes His essential Deity. In fact, verse 1 stresses His Deity, and verse 7 His true humanity. But in verse 4 His priesthood after the order of Melchizedek is established by divine oath.

In Hebrews, the priesthood of Christ is explained in two ways: firstly, after *the pattern* of Aaron, and secondly, after *the order* of Melchizedek.

Hebrews 9 is a divine commentary on Leviticus 16; it explains the *pattern*. The typical detail associated with the Day of Atonement has found its fulfilment in Christ and His sacrificial death. Unlike Aaron, however, the Lord needed no sacrifice for Himself, and His death accomplished what all the repetitive animal sacrifices could never effect.

The *order* of His priesthood is said to be after Melchizedek, who is referred to in only three places: historically in Genesis 14. 17-24; prophetically in Psalm 110, and doctrinally in Hebrews 5-7. He combines together the offices of king and priest. He is an eloquent type of the Lord Jesus who is the Priest-King, Zech. 6. 12-13. He has already been saluted by God as a High Priest after this order, Heb. 5. 10, but Psalm 110 looks forward to His manifestation as Priest-King. In presenting Melchizedek, Hebrews 7 shows the superiority of the priesthood of Christ over that of Aaron's. Not only is He the Priest-King, but He is eternal and therefore so is His priesthood, v. 3, and the value of His sacrifice, v. 27.

Although Christ's High Priesthood after the order of Melchizedek looks on to millennial times, we can say, "We have such an high priest who is set on the right hand of the throne of the Majesty in the heavens", Heb. 8. 1. And He is able "to succour", 2. 18, sympathize, 4. 15, and to "save", 7. 25.

Psalm 110 shows that He will defeat His foes when He comes to reign. If He is our Great High Priest, is He also our Lord? Do we willingly offer ourselves to Him now?, Psa. 110. 3 R.V.

"Such an high priest", Heb. 8. 1. (J.M.)

315

October 24th

READING: **Psalm 23**

THE GREAT SHEPHERD—SATISFACTION GUARANTEED

HERE IS the Great Shepherd because He rose again from the dead, Heb. 13. 20. We must not forget that He is the Good Shepherd, because He laid down His life, John 10. 11, and the Chief Shepherd because He is coming back, 1 Pet. 5. 4. There are so many ways in which this psalm can be enjoyed, but here we shall see how the truths of this psalm affect every side of our lives.

Beneath Me, v. 2, not just pastures, but green pastures and only the best for the feeding of the soul. "He maketh me to lie down": sometimes we have to lie down in order to look up.

Beside Me, v. 2, "still waters" to calm the troubled breast. The restlessness of the world is portrayed in its art, music, speech, conduct and attitude as if it is looking for something it cannot find. Having Christ, we shall not want.

Leads Me, v. 3. Unlike the shepherds of the western world, the shepherd in the middle east will lead his sheep rather than drive them. A leader must lead. The leaders in the assemblies today must lead and not follow behind.

With Me, v. 4. We may talk *about* Christ in many places, but when we are in the valley, we talk *to* Him, for where there is a shadow there must be a light.

Before Me, v. 5. Can we still accept and believe that the Lord is able to feed us in the wilderness? Are we content with the things that we have? Notice where the table is!

Around me, v. 5. The table is in the presence of our enemies. As in the world but not of it, we are surrounded by hostility.

Above Me, v. 5, "thou anointest my head with oil". Oil to soothe in the heat of the day, and to treat wounds, speaking of the work of the Holy Spirit. It is not a stagnant pool but a cup that runneth over that others may see what I have.

After Me, v. 6. The Great Shepherd leads, and goodness and mercy bring up the rear. This is not an occasional blessing, but a blessing that pursues me "all the days of my life".

Ahead of Me, v. 6, "and I will dwell in the house of the Lord for ever". The path may be rough and narrow, and dangerous at times, but we are surely getting there!

Look to the Son, and the shadows will fall behind. (D.R.)

October 25th

READING: **Psalm 80**

THE MAN OF THY RIGHT HAND

THE PRIMARY reference in this psalm is to Israel in her national recovery through the imagery of the vine, and consequently pointing to Christ, the True Vine. The Jewish custom was that the master of the feast should place at his right hand the person whom he loved best, and then he would lay his right hand on his friend as a testimony of his regard for him. Thus a picture is formed of the relationship between God and Christ, the Man at His right hand. It is a place of power, privilege and pre-eminence. There are a number of references in the N.T. to this position of Christ at the right hand of God, and many of them occur in the Epistle to the Hebrews. Some references are solely about Christ Himself, while others deal with the blessings that believers receive.

FOR CHRIST with respect to:

His Death, "when he had ... purged our sins", Heb. 1. 3; "after he had offered one sacrifice for sins for ever", 10. 12. The emphasis here is on His finished work.

His Resurrection, "yea rather, that is risen again", Rom. 8. 34; "when he raised him from the dead", Eph. 1. 20. At God's right hand we find security in Him, and also we see His mighty power in resurrection. He is far above all.

His Exaltation, "Therefore being by the right hand of God exalted", Acts 2. 33. In his witness to the resurrection of Christ, Peter pointed to the fact of His exaltation—made both Lord and Christ, v. 36.

His Priesthood, "We have such an high priest, who is set on the right hand", Heb. 8. 1, in contrast to the earthly priesthood, showing that Christ is the superlative in all things.

His Pre-eminence, Heb. 1. 13. We see the inferiority of the angels as compared with Christ, and His pre-eminence over the world. How can we love the world which is only His footstool?

FOR BELIEVERS.

Our Consolation. Acts 7. 55-56 shows the vision of the martyr Stephen as he pays the price for his faithfulness to Christ.

Our Consecration, Col. 3. 1. We seek those things which are above, where Christ sits on the right hand of God.

Our Cheer, Heb. 12. 2. We look unto Jesus as we run the race that is set before us. (D.R.)

October 26th

READING: **Psalm 89. 19-37**

MY FIRSTBORN

"THE CHIEFEST among ten thousand", Song 5. 10.

As we consider David, we find it remarkable that Jesse's youngest son became the firstborn with respect to the privileges enjoyed under Jewish customs. In the narrative it seems that everyone had forgotten about the youngest in the family, and God had to remind them that He sees not as man sees, but He looks on the heart, 1 Sam. 16. 7. But here we are looking at great David's greater Son, the Lord Jesus Christ. He is "higher than the kings of the earth", and who can rival heaven's firstborn? The word "firstborn" and its parallel word "first-begotten" is found in the N.T. under four headings.

The Relationship. Colossians 1. 15 tells us that He is "the image of the invisible God, the firstborn of every creature". This verse not only shows His pre-eminence over all creation, but His unique relationship with God, His Father. He is the very essence of God, and Christ has told Him out, John 1. 18. As we look at Christ, we begin to understand what the invisible God is like.

The Resurrection. In Colossians 1. 18 we read that Christ is the firstborn from among the dead. The reason given is that He might have the pre-eminence in all things. In Revelation 1. 5, He is the firstbegotten of the dead, and His pre-eminence is expressed in that He is "prince of the kings of the earth". His pre-eminence in resurrection in 1 Corinthians 15. 20 is expressed as "the firstfruits of them that slept". In all things, He is FIRST.

The Redeemed. He is the firstborn among many brethren, Rom. 8. 29, and here it is in relationship to the redeemed and their conformity to His image as God's Son. We need to ask: Are we growing more like Christ, for God looks for family likeness?

The Return. The better rendering of Hebrews 1. 6 is, "when he *again* bringeth in the firstbegotten into the world". This places the word "again" in its right place, and therefore refers to His return to earth in contrast to Christ's first advent in the preceeding verses. Thus, in Psalm 89. 27, the phrase "higher than the kings of the earth" refers to His return to earth in glory. Hence as the firstborn, He is the first, and He should also come first in our lives. (D.R.)

October 27th

READING: **Psalm 91**

CHRIST'S RETURN TO EARTH

"Who shall stand when he appeareth?", Mal. 3. 2.

Here we extract verses from Psalms 91, 96, 48, 45 to highlight the magnificence of Christ's coming in glory.

The Man, 91. 11-13. Compare these verses with Matthew 4. 6, where Satan quotes (or rather, misquotes) these verses in connection with Christ's temptation in the wilderness. Satan omits the phrase "to keep thee in all thy ways". This implies obedience. Christ did the will of His Father in heaven. Satan completely omits verse 13 because it refers to himself and his ultimate defeat. As Christ was victorious in the wilderness, so He will be victorious when He returns to this earth.

The Monarch, Psa. 96. The new song in verse 1 suggests the times of the Messiah, and the psalm is a coronation anthem, extending to all nations and embracing the renovated earth. The heavens rejoice, the earth is glad, the sea will roar approval, the field will be joyful and the trees will rejoice.

The Metropolis, Psa. 48. The holy city Jerusalem will one day be a great administration centre of the world. Note how it is referred to in this psalm: "the city of our God", v. 1; "the mountain of his holiness", v. 1; "mount Zion", v. 2; "the city of the great King", v. 2; "palaces", v. 3; "the city of the Lord of hosts", v. 8; "thy temple", v. 9; "towers", v. 12; "bulwarks", v. 13. Here we have a measure of what God thinks of His city, and it behoves us to pray for the peace of Jerusalem.

The Might, Psa. 45. The measure of the might of God in that day is seen in such expressions as "sword, mighty, glory, majesty", v. 3; "ride prosperously, truth, righteousness, terrible things", v. 4; "Thine arrows are sharp ... the people fall under thee", v. 5. This catalogue of events serves to indicate the might of the return of Christ in terms of the international situation and world politics. In the light of territorial claims and the aspirations of world domination, v. 6, puts everything in its right perspective by asserting that the throne of God is "for ever and ever", stressing not only its duration but its quality and equity. Note:

Heaven to earth: "Lo, I come", Psa. 40. 7.

Earth to heaven: "I come to thee", John 17. 11.

Heaven to earth: "I come quickly", Rev. 22. 20. (D.R.)

October 28th

READING: **Psalms 8, 24 & 103**

DIVINE SOVEREIGNTY

"CLAY in the potter's hand", Jer. 18. 6.

Extracts from these three psalms show how God is sovereign on three counts. A study of Romans 9 will show this subject dealt with to a fuller extent.

Sovereign in Creation, Psa. 8. 3, 6-7; 24. 1-2. The heavens in all their vastness are only the work of God's fingers; we should remember that the nearest star to earth is 25 million million miles (four and one third light-years) away, while the most distant nebulae are many thousands of millions of light-years away. Man seems so small in comparison with this, yet Christ died for us! The sheep, oxen, all beasts, birds and fish are all under His control. We read in Scripture how the animals obey God, and therefore they can teach us a lesson. In Psalm 24, the territorial dispute of man is settled once and for all: "The earth is the Lord's". Man is a tenant, a leaseholder upon a precarious tenure, The word "fulness" suggests the riches of the earth including all its mineral wealth. He who built the house and bears up its foundations has first claim.

Sovereign in Compassion. The tender mercies of God are heaped upon us, "I will have mercy on whom I will have mercy", Rom. 9. 15. Psalm 103. 8 shows that God is merciful and gracious, slow to anger and plenteous in mercy; verse 10 shows that our rewards are unmerited, while verse 12 shows that the removal of our transgressions is an unmeasured distance, for the distance of the east from the west is undefinable. Consider the quality of mercy (tender, v. 4), the measure of mercy (plenteous, v. 8), the extent of mercy (as high as heaven, v. 11), and the duration of mercy (everlasting, v. 17).

Sovereign in Conquest, Psa. 24. 7-10. Twice over the gates and everlasting doors are addressed as approached by the victorious King of glory. Some would apply this to the ascension of Christ into glory. But here we have the Messiah—the King—approaching the gates of Jerusalem, in millennial splendour, with the spoils of battle as the LORD of hosts. In that day only, will the gates of Zion be readily opened to welcome the rightful Monarch and He will reign in peace. (D.R.)

320

October 29th

READING: **Psalm 89**

GREAT DAVID'S GREATER SON

"The fruit of thy body", Psa. 132. 11.

The eventual restoration of Israel rests on God's faithfulness to the Davidic covenant, all fulfilled in Christ. It is a covenant of grace ratified by the precious blood of Christ. Big issues hinge on seemingly small details; thus Ruth's choice at the crossroads in the presence of Naomi and Orpah resulted in a great grandson by the name of David. Here we are looking at great David's greater Son.

A Royal Precedence, v. 26. "He shall cry unto me, Thou art my father". One Son without sin, but never a Son without a prayer. The Son acknowledges the Father and the Father honours the Son.

A Royal Prerogative, v. 27, "my firstborn". Christ has by inheritance a more glorious name than all of the angels, Heb. 1. 4. The Jews would recall this, as they thought of the eldest son in a family, with all his privileges and his birthright.

A Royal Promise, v. 28, "my covenant shall stand fast with him". A promise that is ratified by an oath of God, and by the blood of the sacrifice of Christ, is a covenant of grace that is sure to all because it stands fast with Him. "For all the promises of God in him are yea, and in him Amen", 2 Cor. 1. 20. In other words, all the promises of God are fulfilled in Christ.

A Royal Progression, vv. 29, 36-37. David's seed lives on in his greater Son, Christ, and His seed in every believer, thus answering the dilemma of the enquirer in Isaiah 53. 8, "who shall declare his generation?". The duration of God's throne is as the days of heaven and *not* as the days of earth. And how long is a day in heaven?, Psa. 89. 29. And again, His throne is "as the sun before me", v. 36, not just as the sun, but as the sun *before Me*. God commands and controls the sun and the entire universe; in other words, God is on the throne. "It shall be established for ever as the moon", v. 37. The moon fixed the Jewish calendar and the feasts in Leviticus 23, which are described as "statutes for ever". So the throne of God is for ever.

The kings of the world are like stars—they rise and set. (D.R.)

October 30th

READING: **Psalm 10**

THE MILLENNIAL REIGN

GOD HOLDS the key. Today we consider thoughts from four psalms, namely Psalms 10, 29, 47, 72.

Time for Recompense, Psa. 10. The background of this psalm is the man of sin who precedes the millennial reign, and these references could well be compared with those in Daniel chs. 7-8 and Revelation 13. The triumphant return of Christ to earth will bring help to the fatherless, Psa. 10. 14, when the arm or strength of the wicked will be broken and all wickedness will disappear, v. 15. The desire of the humble has been heard, v. 17, and equity and justice will be the order of the day as indicated in verse 18.

Time for Renewal, Psa. 29. Such is the might of the voice of the Lord that it will bring about the renewal that will characterize the millennial reign. Seven times the voice of the Lord sounds: "upon the waters", v. 3; "powerful", v. 4; "full of majesty", v. 4; "breaketh the cedars", v. 5; "divideth the flames of fire", v. 7; "shaketh the wilderness", v. 8; and "maketh the hinds to calve", v. 9.

Time for Rejoicing, Psa. 47. Such a reign of equity and justice can only bring rejoicing especially in the light of the world in which we live today. Why clap hands and shout?, v. 1; because God is a great King, v. 2; because He shall subdue the people, v. 3; and because there is an inheritance, v. 4. Why sing praises to God?, v. 6. Because God is King of all the earth, v. 7; because He reigns over the nations, v. 8; and because He is on the throne, v. 8.

Time for Righteousness, Psa. 72. The righteousness of God is seen in His character, His actions and in all that He is. It is displayed when He judges, v. 2; it results in peace, v. 3; it brings salvation, v. 4; it produces godly fear, v. 5; it brings blessing to those who adopt it, v. 7; it is shown in His dominion, v. 8; it is shown in its effects on His enemies, v. 9; it brings obedience, v. 11; it brings deliverance, v. 12; it brings redemption, v. 14. Such is the catalogue of the effects of God's righteousness. This is also the great and glorious theme of the Epistle to the Romans: "And so all Israel shall be saved: as it is written, There shall come out of Sion the Deliverer, and shall turn away ungodliness from Jacob", Rom. 11. 26. (D.R.)

October 31st

READING: **Psalm 132**

THE MILLENNIAL REIGN

IN THIS psalm the Davidic promises are fulfilled in Christ, and following on from yesterday we see that His reign will be a *Time for Restoration*, which is expressed in three ways:

In Covenant, v. 11. The certainty of the promise is stressed in the fact that the Lord has sworn, and that in truth. But added to this is the name by which God calls Himself here, namely, Jehovah, the God who makes the promises and keeps them. The Hebrew word translated Jehovah implies a God that continues and never ceases, both in being, and in action. God will not turn from it as verse 11 states, and the word of the Lord is sure and powerful. "The fruit of thy body will I set upon thy throne".

In Choice. God's choice is Zion, which is to be His habitation, v. 13. This is His rest, v. 14, for He has desired it. Why did God ever choose us? We cannot understand, but we can believe this and worship Him, giving Him our lives in service and devotion. He rests in those who rest in Him. "Jesus, I am resting, resting, in the joy of what Thou art. I am finding out the greatness of Thy loving heart."

In Care. In verses 15-16 we see provision, the satisfaction of the poor with bread, and the clothing of the priests with salvation. Notice that the provision is bread, a necessity of life, so we have to learn in this life that God only promises the necessities of life; luxuries are things that the world seeks after. No doubt we have all learnt from bitter experience in the past that the luxuries of the world do not satisfy.

The priests are clothed in salvation in contrast to His enemies who are clothed in shame, v. 18. The sinner is naked before God, and needs to be clothed in righteousness, Zech. 3. 4. Our salvation is like the clothes that we wear—it should show clearly. Many people are assessed by their appearance, and therefore some are judged by the clothes that they wear. Let our salvation, and therefore Christ Himself, show through us, that others may see Him.

There will be no second death for those who partake in the first resurrection. (D.R.)

Experiences of the Covenant People

WE RECALL that the appeal of the psalms lies largely in their intensely personal nature. They express and reveal the hopes and fears, the joys and sorrows, the regrets and shame of the individual human heart. Nothing could be more essentially personal than the confessions of king David recorded in Psalm 51. They were words uttered for the sacred ear of God Himself, though in His wisdom they have been recorded for our benefit.

Yet the psalmists often speak and sing with a vivid sense that they are not alone. They speak as members of the nation of Israel; the nation chosen by the sovereign will of God to become the head of the nations; the nation with tremendous privileges, descended from Abraham "the friend of God", and later entrusted with "the oracles of God", Rom. 9. 3-5.

The group of psalms which we are now to consider have to do with the earthly nation of Israel in covenant-relationship with God, with their king chosen and anointed by God, and with Jerusalem, the God-appointed centre to which their menfolk had to bring their sacrifices every year. The psalms give us reviews of Israel's history, Psa. 78; prayers for national recovery, Psa. 80; and praise for national deliverance, Psa. 126.

It was an earthly nation as such that had been redeemed from slavery in Egypt. There was not faith "to the saving of the soul" in every member, 1 Cor. 10. 5; Heb. 4. 2. The priests served and were given privileges not because of personal faith, but because they were descended from Aaron. They ministered in a material tabernacle, "a worldly sanctuary", Heb. 9. 1, with animal sacrifices, and they resorted to musical instruments to aid them in worship. Today we have no earthly centre, and our worship is essentially spiritual, not soulish, John 4. 21-24.

Moreover, the land given by God to Israel was often invaded by the unspeakably cruel and immoral nations around, and Israel's kings sometimes acted as the executors of God's judgments upon them. But we must love our enemies, and in this "day of salvation" we must bring to men the gospel of peace.

November 1st

READING: **Psalm 18**

MY DELIVERER, MY GOD

THIS IS the song of king David's triumph after his final deliverance from his inveterate and murderous enemy king Saul.

First of all he gives a ninefold description of all that God has become to him through his chequered career. When hunted by Saul in the wilderness of Judaea, he needed a fortress, a rock in or behind which he could hide, or a high tower, and in this God had become his unfailing resource. What has God become to us? Is He our strong habitation whereunto we continually resort?, Psa. 71. 3.

Note the fivefold repetition of the title "my God", vv. 2, 6, 21, 28, 29. David had had personal dealings with God; ultimately everyone will have to do with God personally. "Every one of us shall give account of himself to God", Rom. 14. 12. Evidently early in life David had confessed the sins of his youth, and had found the blessedness of the man "whose transgression is forgiven, whose sin is covered", Psa. 32. 1. To speak of the Almighty as "my God" is to imply that He is the highest Object of my trust, my obedience, my devotion and my adoration. Is He really so?

On the morning of our Lord's resurrection, Mary exclaimed, "They have taken away my Lord, and I know not where they have laid him", John 20. 13. She thought of Him as her own, almost as if there were no other to claim Him. A week later, Thomas confessed Him as "My Lord and my God", v. 28.

Doubtless God became dear to David through answered prayers when alone with his sheep. But when repeatedly saved from Saul's javelin and later from Saul's armies, with what heartfelt gratitude and affection he exclaims, "my God"!

Hudson Pope's hymn, "What is He to you?", ends with the verse:

> "Everything to me! Everything to me!
> Prince and Saviour all along,
> Light so clear, and Friend so strong,
> Shield, and Food, and Joyful Song,
> Everything to me!"

"The excellency of the knowledge of ... my Lord", Phil. 3. 8.

November 2nd

READING: **Psalm 20**

THE GOD OF JACOB IS OUR REFUGE

HERE IS the key to David's triumphs. He exclaims, "Some trust in chariots, and some in horses: but we will remember the name of the Lord our God", v. 7. He had learned to trust in the Lord with all his heart and not to lean on his own understanding. So he faced the lion and the bear in his youth, and so he overcame the giant Goliath of Gath. He doubtless practised patiently with his sling, but in each case he trusted in the Almighty. Everything ultimately depends on what God is. His name declares His character. To call Him "the God of Jacob" is to recall God's amazing grace and patience with the man who lied to his father Isaac and cheated his brother Esau. He is the God of all grace; He deals as patiently with us today as He did with Jacob.

When the stripling shepherd boy faced Goliath the giant, he said, "Thou comest to me with a sword, and with a spear, and with a shield: but I come to thee in the name of the Lord of hosts, the God of the armies of Israel, whom thou hast defied", 1 Sam. 17. 45. David's trust was in the Eternal, the God of Abraham, Isaac and Jacob, the Lord (this word in capitals in the A.V. means "the Eternal", as some French versions translate the title, the self-existing, Jehovah, unchanging), This made all the difference.

David had learned, like Daniel, that ultimately the most High does according to His will in the army of heaven and among the inhabitants of the earth, Dan. 4. 35. Today we wrestle not against flesh and blood, and we seek to live peaceably with all men. Yet we may, like Paul the apostle, be "troubled on every side", with fightings without, and fears within, 2 Cor. 7. 5. The world system characterized by "the lust of the flesh, and the lust of the eyes, and the pride of life", 1 John 2. 16, may impress us temporarily. But our Lord Jesus says, "Let not your heart be troubled ... In the world ye shall have tribulation: but be of good cheer; I have overcome the world", John 14. 27; 16. 33.

"Ye believe in God, believe also in me", John 14. 1.

READING: **Psalm 21**

GOD MY EXCEEDING JOY

DAVID BEGINS his song, "The king shall joy in thy strength, O Lord; and in thy salvation how greatly shall he rejoice", v. 1.

A king has more to rejoice in than most people: wealth, power and comfort such as few enjoy. But David found his joy in God Himself. "We also rejoice in God through our Lord Jesus Christ, through whom we have now received the reconciliation", Rom. 5. 11 R.V. Here the word "rejoice" ("joy" A.V.) means to exult, to boast.

Maybe a boy joys in his collection of foreign stamps or other hobby; then he joys in athletic achievements or examination successes; later, in manhood, in his business and family. But the believer in the Lord Jesus rejoices supremely in Him, the Giver of every ability and greater than all His gifts.

How much God had done for David, making him the king of all Israel. How much more has God done for us!, "exceeding abundantly above all that we ask or think", Eph. 3. 20. His response to the repentant sinner in the forgiveness of sins is but the beginning of blessings innumerable and eternal. So our heart must therefore rejoice in the Lord.

This joy is not something merely emotional, such as is stirred by musical instruments. King Saul was calmed by David's harp, but he remained a murderer still. Most folk experience superficial and transient joys. But the apostle Paul, who knew the most painful of sufferings, described his life as "sorrowful, yet alway rejoicing", 2 Cor. 6. 10; and he confidently urged his brethren to "Rejoice evermore", 1 Thess. 5. 16. Circumstances change; even friends change. But the Lord says, "I am the Lord, I change not", Mal. 3. 6. So we can say, "Rejoice in the Lord alway", Phil. 4. 4.

Finally, let joy find expression in outspoken thanksgiving and praise. "Is any merry?", asks James, "let him sing psalms", James 5. 13. Thus our psalm ends with praise, "Be thou exalted, Lord, in thine own strength: so will we sing and praise thy power", v. 13.

"Rejoice in the Lord alway: and again I say, Rejoice", Phil. 4. 4.

November 4th

READING: **Psalm 44**

PAST TRIUMPHS AND PRESENT PROBLEMS

PSALM 44 is a collective confession and appeal to God. We recognize that private prayer is vitally important, but "Two are better than one ... and a threefold cord is not quickly broken", Eccl. 4. 9-12. Let us seek the active fellowship of the godly; there are problems common to all for which to pray together.

How happy to hear of past prosperity and triumphs. Happier still to hear that it was not the military prowess of Joshua and Israel's ancestors that gained them the land of Canaan, but the "right hand" (the mighty power) of God Himself, Psa. 44. 3. Thus the first section of the psalm confidently concludes, "In God we boast all the day long, and praise thy name for ever", v. 8.

But now God seems to have forgotten His people: "But thou hast cast us off, and put us to shame", v. 9. What a weighty word "but" can often be. Note the words, "reproach, scorn, derision, byword, confusion, shame". And Israel acknowledge that this is not "chance" but the Lord's doing. They say with Job, "shall we receive good at the hand of God, and shall we not receive evil?", Job 2. 10. They say effectively, Thou hast given us like helpless sheep to be slaughtered; Thou sellest Thy people like slaves in the market place, vv. 11-12.

Now note verse 22 that Paul quotes in Romans 8. 36, "for thy sake are we killed all the day long; we are counted as sheep for the slaughter". This was evidently as true in apostolic days as of old; and still there are many martyrs today. The people of God, when faithful to Him, have met violent opposition from the world ever since Cain slew his brother Abel. The Lord Jesus said to His disciples, "Behold, I send you forth as sheep in the midst of wolves", Matt. 10. 16. So let us not be surprised if we suffer for doing right, but heed our Lord's words, "Rejoice, and be exceeding glad", Matt. 5. 12.

"If any man suffer as a Christian, let him not be ashamed; but let him glorify God on this behalf", 1 Pet. 4. 16.

November 5th

READING: **Psalm 50**

OUR GOD SHALL COME

HAVE YOU EVER stood at the railway station, at the quayside, or at the airport, watching the eager, expectant faces of those who await their loved ones? What smiles, what embraces, what tears of relief, when the longed for reunion takes place! It is a very faint foreshadowing of the joyous meeting of our Lord Jesus Christ with His people. We are converted "to serve the living and true God; and to wait for His Son from heaven", 1 Thess. 1. 9-10.

Then will come the day of review and reward for His servants; He says, "behold, I come quickly: and my reward is with me, to give to every man according as his work shall be", Rev. 22. 12. He comes to take account of His servants, and to show what each one of us has gained.

The psalmists knew nothing of Christ's coming to the air to snatch away His own as described in 1 Thessalonians 4. 13-18. But, like the prophets, they frequently warn of the unparalleled tribulation that the nation of Israel must yet suffer and the coming of the Lord to deliver the godly and punish the wicked among them. Then the godly remnant of Israel will exclaim, "Lo, this is our God; we have waited for him, and he will save us", Isa. 25. 9.

In Psalm 50, God calls heaven and earth to witness His fiery coming in judgment. For centuries He has been silent, but He will gather His saints, the godly, to instruct them, vv. 1-15; and He warns the ungodly of impending judgment, vv. 16-23.

Those who have made a covenant with God by sacrifice are Israel, the nation who solemnly pledged at Sinai, "All that the Lord hath said will we do, and be obedient", Exod. 24. 7. But this Mosaic covenant they repeatedly broke. Therefore God will make a new covenant with Israel dependent wholly on His own faithfulness, Jer. 31. 31-34. At the Lord's Supper we learn that believers today benefit by that new covenant.

We gather together now, like Israel, to hear our Lord's instruction, v. 5; Matt. 18. 20, and to anticipate our future gathering together unto Him in the air, 2 Thess. 2. 1. "Watch ye therefore ... lest coming suddenly he find you sleeping", Mark 13. 35-36.

"Maranatha! (Our Lord is coming)", 1 Cor. 16. 22.

329

November 6th

READING: **Psalm 60**

GIVE US HELP FROM TROUBLE

WHEN IN serious trouble, have we ever felt that God has failed us or even forgotten us? This psalm reveals the nation of Israel in a situation like this. They were shocked and confused, like people in an earthquake, vv. 1-3. This was despite the fact that they had been given a banner, a rallying point, by God Himself. They are ashamed at having been defeated by such cruel and immoral nations as Syria in the north, Moab and Edom in the east, and the Philistines in the south-west. Indeed, David and his commanders found that, when dealing with one enemy, they were attacked by another from an opposite direction. So we have to face the world, the flesh and the devil.

"Man is born unto trouble, as the sparks fly upward", Job 5. 7. This is as true today as in Job's day. We might expect it, in view of the universality of sin; sin is acting in independence of the God of love and grace.

But God says, "call upon me in the day of trouble: I will deliver thee, and thou shalt glorify me", Psa. 50. 15. So the psalmist cries, "save with thy right hand, and hear me", 60. 5. Then God speaks exultingly, vv. 6-8; He asserts His authority over Israel, over tribes east and west of the Jordan river, and also over the pagan nations around them. Moab and Edom are regarded as the meanest slaves, one to act as a washtub, and the other to be thrown cast-off sandals. Even the apparently impregnable fortress of the Edomites, still impressive for modern sightseers, presents no difficulty to the Almighty.

At times we, like Israel, must acknowledge that we have displeased God, and that He appears to have cast us off. But, reassured of His power and faithful love, we turn again to our Refuge and our Strength, praying, "Give us help from trouble: for vain is the help of man. Through God we shall do valiantly: for he it is that shall tread down our enemies", vv. 11-12.

"In all these things we are more than conquerors through him that loved us", Rom. 8. 37.

November 7th

READING: Psalm 72

HE MUST REIGN

How often do we hear people criticize the government, the king or queen, or president, the judge, the magistrate, the police, indeed anyone, good or bad, in authority. It is a fatal flaw in human nature. None of us, not even children, readily submits to authority, and if given it ourselves we often fail to use it wisely. God invested Noah with worldwide authority to re-establish the sacredness of human life, because the earth had become "filled with violence" before the flood, Gen. chs. 6, 9. Later He gave the law to Israel to reassert His own supreme authority, and to re-establish the authority of leaders and parents who are answerable to Him, Exod. 20. 1-17.

Think of the grievously lawless state of mankind today. It is very clearly described in Paul's Epistle 2 Tim. 3. 1-4. How much the world needs a wise, just, merciful and powerful Ruler! How happily reassuring is the promise, "a king shall reign in righteousness, and princes shall rule in judgment (justice)", Isa. 32. 1. God has in reserve His Son, a perfect Ruler who will have perfectly suitable subordinates.

In this psalm, David prays for, and prophesies concerning this coming King, for David was a prophet, Acts 2. 25-31. But before his death, he had Solomon installed and acclaimed as king. Like a compassionate shepherd-king, he prays in this psalm that righteousness and justice, the foundation of the throne of God, will be the foundation of Solomon's also.

But a greater than Solomon is in view. For "all kings shall fall down before him", v. 11, and "all nations shall call him blessed", v. 17. Moreover, His name shall last as long as the sun and moon endure, "throughout all generations", vv. 5, 17. Our Lord's death is prophesied in Psalm 22, His resurrection in Psalm 16, and His reign on earth in Psalm 72. Then "the work of righteousness shall be peace; and the effect of righteousness quietness and assurance for ever", Isa. 32. 17. This is the prospect when the present period of God's patience is ended and the ungodly are judged: our Lord Jesus Christ will be over all, blessed for ever.

"He is Lord of lords, and King of kings", Rev. 17. 14.

November 8th

READING: **Psalm 73**

HOLD UP MY GOINGS

To lose one's foothold can be a very frightening and even fatal experience. Whether it is an elderly person on an icy road, a venturesome lad on a cliff face, or a hardened mountaineer crossing a crevass, the very thought can be unnerving.

Psalm 73 records a time in Asaph's life when he had just avoided an experience like this. He first thanks God for saving him, "Truly God is good to Israel", v. 1. He wanted to be like Nathanael, "an Israelite indeed, in whom is no guile", John 1. 47. He wanted to live with a good conscience before God. But he had a problem; the age-old question as to why the wicked often prosper and good men suffer. It tended to make him envious. He forgot the warning, "Fret not thyself because of evildoers, neither be thou envious against the workers of iniquity. For they shall soon be cut down like the grass, and wither as the green herb", Psa. 37. 1-2. He found that "envy is the rottenness of the bones", Prov. 14. 30.

Asaph observed how healthy and prosperous were these blatantly wicked men. The rich boasted that God was ignorant of, or quite indifferent to, their evil ways. They had no qualms about death or of having to answer to God for their behaviour. Asaph was tempted to live like them, and blot out the thought of the life to come. But he was afraid to discuss the matter with others. He feared that he might dangerously influence his brethren by such foolishly immature thoughts. If the Levite who leads the praise slips, others will slip too.

Then comes a turning point: "until I went into the sanctuary of God", v. 17. This means not merely a building, but into the very presence of God, the All-wise, Himself. There, foolish thoughts are banished. "In thy light shall we see light", Psa. 36. 9. It is important, not only to study, but to draw near to God in secret prayer. "Hold up my goings in thy paths, that my footsteps slip not", Psa. 17. 5. Then we too shall confidently say, "Thou shalt guide me with thy counsel, and afterward receive me to glory", Psa. 73. 24.

"Bringing into captivity every thought to the obedience of Christ", 2 Cor. 10. 5.

November 9th

READING: **Psalm 74**

WHY? HOW LONG?

Two questions are asked in this psalm, two questions often asked in prayer. "Why?", vv. 1, 11, and "How long?", v. 10. Why? We are sure that the only wise God has the very best of reasons for all that He does, "wonderful in counsel, and excellent in working", Isa. 28. 29, in all that He permits. How long? We can be sure that He never allows more suffering than is necessary, for He delights in mercy.

The psalm is a passionate plea from the godly remnant of Israel after the desecration and destruction of Solomon's temple by the Chaldean armies, 2 Kings 25. 9-17.

No nation had been so blessed, not only with a most fruitful land, but with laws to preserve peace and justice. Yet, self-willed, like all men, they imitated the pagan nations around, and grew progressively worse. "They mocked the messengers of God, and despised His words, and misused His prophets, until the wrath of the Lord arose against his people, till there was no remedy", 2 Chron. 36. 16.

Why was the temple left destroyed and desolate? It was to provide further evidence that:

1. God's warnings are not empty threats.
2. Disobedience to the commands of God is fatal.
3. Religious observances (though outwardly correct as in this case) are worthless without heart-submission to the will of God.
4. God sometimes deals with nations, when the wicked and the godly prosper or suffer together.

It is the godly remnant of the nation who suffer with the rest and feel the shame more keenly than others. They are concerned for the honour of God's name. "How long shall the adversary reproach? shall the enemy blaspheme thy name for ever?", Psa. 74. 10. They remind God of His mighty power through which their ancestors were saved from slavery in Egypt, vv. 13-15, and then of His control of creation, vv. 16-17, His power was certainly more than sufficient; but they next appeal to His compassion for the oppressed, the poor and the needy, vv. 21-22. These are earnest appeals, but their prayers, like ours, must end, "not as I will, but as thou wilt", Matt. 26. 39.

"Let patience have her perfect work", James 1. 4.

November 10th

READING: Psalm 76

DO YOU KNOW GOD?

HERE THE psalmist celebrates the mighty victory that God gained over enemies attacking Israel, His chosen people, and Jerusalem His chosen dwelling place.

"In Judah is God known" : this is the highest knowledge that man can have. Adam knew God, and he was given such a long life that his great great grandchildren could have had a knowledge of the true God who, hating sin and punishing the wicked, was merciful to the penitent. Yet wilful men did not like to retain the true knowledge of God, Rom. 1. 18-28. So God had to reveal Himself afresh to Noah and later to Abraham. Then Moses came to know Him as the God of Abraham, Isaac and Jacob. His dealing with them showed much of His holy character; the giving of the law to Moses made things clearer still.

Finally, though no man has seen God at any time, the only-begotten Son who is in the bosom of the Father has declared Him, as He only could, John 1. 18. To say that you know someone may mean that you could recognize him in a crowd, but nothing more; his servants would know him much better, and his family better still. "And this is life eternal, that they might know thee the only true God, and Jesus Christ, whom thou hast sent", 17. 3. It is the life of eternal ages, imparted to the believer on the Lord Jesus Christ, that makes possible an intimate knowledge of God Himself, not merely about Him. Today, He is known in the hearts of those who love Him because He first loved them; and also in the local churches of His people amidst whom He dwells.

The psalm praises God known in His victory over the oppressors of His people, and who establishes justice for the meek and defenceless among them, vv. 8-9. He dwells in Jerusalem the city of peace, and the impregnable fortress of Zion, vv. 1-2. Despite their powerful weapons, Israel's enemies were cast into the sleep of death, v. 5. "Selah" means "Pause, and think calmly of that". God is more glorious than the mountains of Judaea, suggesting unchanging stability, v. 4. We really come to know God when we are converted to Christ, Gal. 4. 8-9; but we all need to know Him more.

"Walk worthy ... increasing in the knowledge of God", Col. 1. 10.

November 11th

READING: Psalm 78. 1-11

THE VALUE OF ISRAEL'S HISTORY

DIVINELY RECORDED history, fascinating though it is, is not given to entertain us. History is rather like a lighthouse, warning us of danger. Yet, often moved by passing pressures and pleasures, we rarely learn from it as we should.

Here Asaph the Levite reminds Israel of the history of their nation. They had learned this from their forefathers, so that they in turn could pass on the truth to their children and grandchildren. He recalls the wonderful works that God had wrought for His people from the time of their deliverance from Egyptian slavery till the reign of king David. This was to preserve them from the follies of their fathers. It was "that they might set their hope in God, and ... keep his commandments", v. 7. It was that they might not forget God's intervention in mercifully delivering them from their enemies. Their ancestors benefited from God's goodness, but their heart and their spirit were wrong. Forgetting how much they were indebted to God, they refused to obey His law, v. 8.

Asaph then refers to a typical episode in Israel's history, "The children of Ephraim, being armed, and carrying bows, turned back in the day of battle, v. 9. They failed to face and drive off the decadent and grossly immoral nations that attacked them. They had arms, but failed to use them.

So with ourselves; we have powerful foes. "The flesh lusteth against the Spirit", Gal. 5. 17. But God has given us all things that pertain to life and godliness. There is no sound reason for a true believer turning back. The Holy Spirit lusts "against the flesh", and the apostle John says, "greater is he that is in you, than he that is in the world", 1 John 4. 4.

We are armed, so let us go on. We have our Lord Jesus Christ above interceding for His own, and the help of the Holy Spirit on earth. We have also the guidance of the Holy Scriptures. So using the sword of the Spirit which is the Word of God, and praying always for more grace, we shall go on.

"We are not of them who draw back unto perdition; but of them that believe to the saving of the soul", Heb. 10. 39.

335

November 12th

READING: **Psalm 78. 12-72**

HIM WITH WHOM WE HAVE TO DO

Two FUNDAMENTAL elements of truth are brought vividly before us in this psalm: one, the amazing ingratitude and perversity of the human heart; the other, the character of the God with whom we have to do. We see that:

1. *God is the Almighty*, the God who does wonders. Centuries pass without the more obvious intervention of God in human affairs, but on two outstanding occasions, God accredited his messengers by mighty miracles—when saving Israel from Egyptian slavery, and when sending His Son for our salvation. He enabled Moses to work "marvellous" miracles in Egypt which completely baffled the heathen magicians, and then miraculously made a way through the Red Sea, vv. 12-13.

2. *God is a Generous Giver*. In the desert He "caused waters to run down like rivers ... the waters gushed out" and when food was needed He "rained down manna" and then "he rained flesh also upon them as dust", quails so that His people were "well filled", vv. 16-29. He gives liberally, upbraiding not.

3. *God is a Faithful Shepherd*. It is striking that in the Scriptures mankind is often likened to a flock of sheep; "All we like sheep have gone astray; we have turned every one to his own way", Isa. 53. 6. Sheep are defenceless, without the strength of the ox, the speed of the deer, the camouflage of the zebra, or the cunning of beasts of prey. So sheep need a shepherd. Robbers might threaten as well as wild beasts. In the mountainous land of Judaea were dangers for straying sheep.

Human weakness calls for divine power: God "made his people to go forth like sheep, and guided them in the wilderness like a flock. And he led them on safely, so that they feared not ... So he fed (shepherded) them according to the integrity of his heart: and guided them by the skilfulness of his hands", Psa. 78. 52-53, 72.

4. *God is a Longsuffering Creator* whether with Israel or mankind in general. "Many a time turned He his anger away", v. 38. There is a limit to His patience as in the days of Noah, and we cannot sin with impunity, but His longsuffering is designed for our salvation, 2 Pet. 3. 9, 15.

The Lord Jesus said, *"I am the good shepherd: the good shepherd giveth his life for the sheep"*, John 10. 11.

November 13th

READING: **Psalm 80**

THE SHEPHERD, THE VINE, THE MAN

HAVE YOU or your Christian friends ever been ridiculed or persecuted for faith in Christ or for your simple obedience to His commands? Such has always been the lot of the godly in this wayward world. Such was the experience of the psalmist. It was the more painful because God seemed deaf to His people's prayers. But the Lord Jesus bade us on such occasions to "Rejoice, and be exceeding glad: for great is your reward in heaven", Matt. 5. 12.

1. *The Flock*, vv. 1-7. When suffering for Christ, how happy it is to say, "The Lord is my shepherd", my personal Saviour who cares for me. Here He is called the Shepherd of Israel, concerned for the whole nation whom He led out of Egypt. Further, while on earth the Saviour said to His disciples, "Fear not, little flock; for it is your Father's good pleasure to give you the kingdom", Luke 12. 32. Each little company of His people may count on His divine support; each one of the seven churches in Asia was His personal concern. Although that at Philadelphia had but a little strength, He commended it for keeping His Word and not denying His name, Rev. 3. 8.

2. *The Vine*, vv. 8-16. Next, Israel is depicted as a vine brought out of Egypt, and planted in Canaan to bring forth fruit for the pleasure of God. In the days of David and Solomon, her influence spread to the Great Sea on the west and the river Euphrates on the north-east, vv. 8-11. God protests through the prophet Isaiah that He had done everything possible to make the nation prosperous and pleasurable to Him. But Israel had become a monument to the ingratitude and perversity of the human heart, Isa. 5. 1-7. It explains the words of the Lord Jesus to Nicodemus, "Ye must be born again", John 3. 7; men needed a new nature in order to please God.

3. *The Man*, vv. 17-19. God said to Pharaoh, "Israel is my son, even my firstborn", Exod. 4. 22. But now Another comes into view, the Firstborn who never failed, the Man whose name is the Branch, the Son of man who will have the glory of universal and eternal dominion, Zech. 6. 12. Note the Branch and the Son of man made strong for God and for His pleasure, Psa. 80. 15-17.

November 14th

READING: **Psalm 81. 1-7**

SING ALOUD

GOD GAVE man a voice so that he could commune with his Maker, to make requests and to express his appreciation of all God's goodness.

We read of the morning stars singing together at creation; but singing is first mentioned in Scripture in connection with Israel's deliverance from the angel of death in Egypt and from Pharaoh's hosts at the Red Sea. Then sang Moses and the children of Israel, "I will sing unto the Lord, for he hath triumphed gloriously" ; and Miriam led the women in the same song, Exod. 15. 1, 20.

In this psalm, the call is to express ourselves collectively in song. It is not David the shepherd boy alone on the hillside singing as he watched the sheep. It is a call for collective song; "For this was a statute for Israel", v. 4. It was appointed by God. God's law bade Israel blow the trumpets in His praise at the beginning of each month and at their God-appointed feast days. Then, as today, the godly would say, "O magnify the Lord with me, and let us exalt his name together" ; this is fellowship in song, Psa. 34. 3.

Believers today are liberated from what Scripture calls "the weak and beggarly elements" of the ceremonial law. Paul wrote to the Galatians, "Ye observe days, and months, and times, and years. I am afraid of you", Gal. 4. 8-11. Yet with his back lacerated by the human scourge, with feet fast in the stocks in the inner prison, he could pray and sing with Silas at midnight; "and the prisoners heard them", Acts 16. 25.

We hear our Lord in resurrection triumph, "I will declare thy name unto my brethren; in the midst of the congregation will I praise thee", Psa. 22. 22; Heb. 2. 12. There was a partial fulfilment on the resurrection day: "I ascend to my Father, and your Father", John 20. 17. But what a dignity this gives to a local congregation (a church, or assembly) gathered unto His name with Him in the midst. He leads the praise!

"Making melody in your heart to the Lord", Eph. 5. 19.

338

November 15th

READING: **Psalm 81. 8-16**

NO STRANGE GOD

IN THIS PSALM, we have already seen God calling for praise from His people. Now He is calling also for their ear, but, sadly, He is doubtful whether they will respond. He reiterates the first of the ten commandments given through Moses: "Thou shalt have no other God before me", vv. 9-10; Exod. 20. 3-4. He must have the first place in our lives. He has the first claim upon us all as our Creator, giving to us life and breath and all things. He had a further claim on Israel in saving them from slavery in Egypt.

Yet they ignored His command to keep clear of "strange" (i.e., foreign) gods. They had only to open their mouths wide like nestlings awaiting eagerly the return of the parent bird, and God would have supplied their need. But they followed the superstitions and immoral practices of the heathen idol-worshippers, vv. 10-11.

The second commandment in Exodus 20. 4 forbids men making any kind of image to represent the Eternal and the Almighty, for He is incomparable. "He is to be feared above all gods. For all the gods of the nations are idols: but the Lord (Jehovah, the Eternal) made the heavens", Psa. 96. 5. The Hebrew word for idols here means things of nought, nonentities, vanities. In general, the word "idol" refers either to the carved or molten image or to the spirit-being linked with it. The Corinthians were bidden to keep themselves from idols because of the demon-worship involved, 1 Cor. 8. 4.

What is an idol such as referred to by John, "Little children, keep yourselves from idols"?, 1 John 5. 21. An idol is anything that takes the place in our hearts and lives that God alone should have. Man's heart is too big for any god but the true God. He alone can satisfy the longing soul, and fill the hungry soul with good things. We say that a man makes a god of his garden, or a woman makes a god of her house. We may ask, "What dominates our thoughts in our leisure time?". Covetousness is called idolatry, Col. 3. 5, for the love of money or other possessions can easily become an obsession. It causes us to break the two great commandments, to love God with all our heart and to love our neighbour as ourselves.

"Wherefore ... flee from idolatry", 1 Cor. 10. 14.

339

November 16th

READING: **Psalm 83**

A THREATENING ALLIANCE

"KEEP NOT THOU silence, O God ... be not still, O God", v. 1. The silence of God and His apparent delay in answering our prayers is certainly not indifference. But how often have such prayers arisen when men are in trouble. People often ignore God's claims upon them, and fail to thank Him for His mercies, but they turn to Him or blame Him when their lives are seriously in danger.

As the psalmist sees Israel's enemies threatening the very life of his nation, he cries, "let them be put to shame, and perish", v. 17. This sounds harsh, but it is no petty plea, for the writer speaks of those who are enemies and haters of God. They aimed at nothing less than the complete destruction of the nation; "that the name of Israel may be no more in remembrance", v. 4. They formed an impressive alliance of pagan foes which completely surrounded Israel's land. Appalling cruelties threatened men, women and children.

The members of the confederation had often fought one another; but now they united in opposing God and His people. Similarly, when Christ came, the materialistic, agnostic Sadducees and their constant opponents, the religious, ritualistic Pharisees, joined together to condemn the Lord Jesus Christ to the cross. Similarly king Herod and Pilate, the Roman governor, sank their political and personal differences in handing over the Saviour to His murderous enemies. No wonder the apostle John says that the whole world lies in wickedness, 1 John 5. 19.

Those who have tasted that the Lord is gracious must long to see Him vindicated in dealing with the oppressors. The psalmist is not concerned just for himself and his country, but for the glory of God; "that men may know that thou, whose name alone is JEHOVAH, art the most high over all the earth", v. 18. That is good; it is a cry for simple justice.

But the day of judgment has not yet dawned. Christ still shows mercy, and He taught, "Love your enemies, bless them that curse you, do good to them that hate you, and pray for them", Matt. 5. 44. Thus Christ prayed when men crucified Him, and so did His martyr Stephen as he was being stoned.

"Father, forgive them; for they know not what they do", Luke 23. 34.

READING: **Psalm 89**

GREAT IS THY FAITHFULNESS

THIS PSALM celebrates two of the great attributes of God seen vividly in His dealings with king David. The keynote is struck at the outset, "the mercies" and "the faithfulness" of God. Each of these two words occurs seven times in the psalm; the first is sometimes happily translated "lovingkindness", meaning much more than withholding punishment, though it includes that. It means positive practical "goodness" and in recent versions is often translated "stedfast love".

God is not only merciful and gracious, but faithful, reliable, trustworthy. His goodness and faithfulness are seen in His covenant to make Jesse's son the king of Israel. These two attributes cause Him to be reverenced by both the godly on earth and the holy inhabitants of heaven.

The righteousness of God condemning sin may seem to prohibit God's grace being lavished on us. But mercy and truth met together, righteousness and peace embraced and kissed each other at the crucifixion of the Lord Jesus Christ. In dread darkness, He suffered for sins, the Just for the unjust, to bring us to God, who now righteously dispenses mercy freely to the penitent, Psa. 85. 10.

The psalm is a reminder that God's purposes will never be thwarted and His promises will never be broken. The psalmist warns of God's governmental dealings, but He says, "My covenant will I not break, nor alter the thing that is gone out of my lips", v. 34. The psalm was written when it seemed that God had "made void the covenant of thy servant", v. 39, but the gifts and calling of God are without repentance, irrevocable.

The N.T. confirms the O.T. Our Lord Jesus is called "the faithful and true witness", Rev. 3. 14; He is faithful as God's messenger to men in reaching them with the gospel. He is also "a merciful and faithful high priest in things pertaining to God", Heb. 2. 17; faithful in His ceaseless intercession for His own. God Himself is called faithful as having called us into the fellowship of His Son Jesus Christ our Lord, 1 Cor. 1. 9. Again, when Paul prays that believers may be preserved blameless till the coming of our Lord, he concludes, "Faithful is he that calleth you, who also will do it", 1 Thess. 5. 24.

"He abideth faithful", 2 Tim. 2. 13.

November 18th

READING: **Psalm 93**

THE LORD REIGNETH

THERE ARE few sights as awesome as the pounding of a rocky coast by the fierce waves of the sea during a storm. With destructive violence and deafening noise, the fearsome waves relentlessly expend their fury. The onlooker is most thankful to be beyond their reach. Yet the rock remains unmoved.

God is a rock, as both Moses and David testify, while the wicked are like the troubled sea that cannot rest, Isa. 57. 20.

This psalm presents a picture of the forces of evil which challenge the throne of God, and challenge it in vain. It begins with "The Lord reigneth", and continues, "the floods have lifted up their voice ... The Lord on high is mightier than the noise of many waters, yea, than the mighty waves of the sea". It is a comfort to know that the throne of God is unmoved; but it is better still to be assured that the Creator is positively mightier than all who may presume to challenge His supreme authority. Surely, "happy is that people, whose God is the Lord (the Eternal)", Psa. 144. 15.

He rules and overrules to make all things work together for good for those who love Him. We see this in the life of Jacob's son, Joseph, hated by his brothers, sold as a slave, outrageously maligned and unjustly imprisoned, but becoming the saviour of his family and of the land of Egypt. God's overruling is just as real when it is less obvious.

The three Psalms 93, 97 and 99, which begin with "The Lord reigneth", all end in speaking of His holiness. He is not only exalted above all gods, 97. 9. He is absolutely distinct from His creation, set apart and untainted by defilement. When Isaiah saw Jehovah "sitting upon a throne, high and lifted up", Isa. 6. 1, he saw the seraphim ceaselessly voicing God's praise, crying, "Holy, holy, holy, is the Lord (Jehovah) of hosts", v. 3. They are themselves holy beings, literally "burning ones" like our God who is a consuming fire; but each covers his face with two wings as unable to look on the glory, and covers his feet as unworthy to be seen. So each had two wings to fly at the bidding of the King of kings.

Isaiah *"saw his glory, and spake of him"*, John 12. 41.

READING: **Psalm 97**

FAR ABOVE ALL

PSALMS 96-99 speak of God coming to judge the world, just as Enoch foretold before the flood, and just as our Lord Jesus Christ Himself prophesied.

Psalm 96 reads, "Say among the heathen that the Lord reigneth ... for he cometh to judge the earth", and Psalm 97 begins, "The Lord reigneth". Clouds, darkness, fire, lightnings and earthquakes declare the intervention and presence of God, "the Lord of the whole earth", vv. 2-5. This is the language of faith; soon it will be the language of sight also.

Today the kingdom of God is the moral and spiritual realm in which souls bow the knee to God's appointed King, the Lord Jesus Christ, Rom. 14. 17. It is a sphere of righteousness, peace and joy in the Holy Spirit, into which we enter by being "born again" (from above), John 3. 3-5.

The prophetic psalms speak of the kingdom set up in manifest glory and power when Christ returns. Here the call is, "Confounded be all they that serve graven images, that boast themselves of idols: worship him all ye gods", v. 7. The word "gods" is often used in the Psalms of those "in authority like judges to whom we pay respect and homage". It is amazing today that the hearts of millions are still set on their idols, whether carved or molten images, or the imaginations of self-centred hearts. According to the psalm, an idol is something that we regard so highly that we boast in it. An idol is someone or something that takes the place that the living God should have in our interests, affections and reverence.

After the mention of Jehovah, the Eternal One, and the warning against idolatry, comes the exhortation, "worship him all ye gods", v. 7. However great the dignity of the creature, it is not to be compared with the dignity of Him who is "exalted far above all gods". Worship is the bowing of the heart as well as the bowing of the knee, Eph. 3. 14. It includes both service and boasting.

"Thou shalt worship the Lord thy God, and him only shalt thou serve", Matt. 4. 10.

READING: **Psalm 105. 1-7**

GIVE THANKS UNTO THE LORD

HAVE YOU ever had a long-cherished ambition, and after disappointing rebuffs been really exultant in seeing your hopes ultimately fulfilled? This was king David's experience reflected in this psalm.

He had long desired that God should have the highest place of honour amid His people Israel. The ark of the Lord was a token of His presence; now at last it had been brought to the place prepared for it in Jerusalem. The psalm is David's call to remember, rejoice, and revel in the goodness of God.

We today should pray that God would raise up men gifted not only to teach, but to exhort us as David does here, urging us to respond to the love of our God. Here are David's nine exhortations, reinforced by other scriptures:

1. "*O give thanks* unto the Lord", v. 1. "Giving thanks always for all things unto God and the Father in the name of our Lord Jesus Christ", Eph. 5. 20.

2. "*Call* upon his name", v. 1. "Call upon me in the day of trouble: I will deliver thee, and thou shalt glorify me", Psa. 50. 15.

3. "*Make known* his deeds among the people", v. 1. The Lord Jesus said, "Whosoever therefore shall confess me before men, him will I confess also before my Father which is in heaven", Matt. 10. 32.

4. "*Sing* unto him", v. 2. "Singing and making melody in your heart to the Lord", Eph. 5. 19.

5. "*Talk ye* of all his wondrous works", v. 2. "Talk of them when thou sittest in thine house, and when thou walkest by the way, and when thou liest down, and when thou risest up", Deut. 6. 7. Make God and His works the subject of your conversations.

6. "*Glory* ye in his holy name", v. 3. "He that glorieth, let him glory in the Lord", 1 Cor. 1. 31.

7. "Let the heart of them *rejoice* that seek the Lord", v. 3. "Rejoice in the Lord alway", Phil. 4. 4.

8. "*Seek* the Lord, and his strength: *seek* his face evermore", v. 4. "Seek, and ye shall find", Matt. 7. 7.

9. "*Remember* his marvellous works that he hath done", v. 5.

"*Suffer the word of exhortation*", Heb. 13. 22.

November 21st

READING: **Psalm 105. 8-45**

REMEMBER

MEMORY IS a remarkable gift of God. There are events in life that we gladly remember; others that we call to mind with sorrow, and yet others that we would rather not remember at all. But memory is invaluable to those who wish to avoid repeating past mistakes.

When the Israelites ended their long journey from Egypt to Canaan, Moses commanded them, "thou shalt remember all the way which the Lord thy God led thee, to know what was in thine heart", Deut. 8. 2. We also do well to recall Israel's experiences, for we are men "of like passions", liable to make the same mistakes, having to do with the same unchangeable God.

Events do not just happen. There is a cause for every event, but God Himself is behind every cause. Note how the psalmist puts is, "He called for a famine ... He sent a man before them ... He sent Moses his servant ... He sent darkness" and other plagues in Egypt. Then despite the repeated complaints of ungrateful Israel, "he brought quails ... He opened the rock, and the waters gushed out ... he brought forth his people with joy". It is a happy recollection of God's goodness and mercy.

When the ageing patriarch Jacob thought that Joseph had long since been destroyed by a wild beast, and that he was to lose his treasured son Benjamin, he exclaimed, "all these things are against me", Gen. 42. 36. But all these things were working together for the good of the whole family. Jacob did not know then that Joseph's brothers had sold him as a slave, and that he had now become the Lord of all Egypt, controlling the only food that could save them all from famine. When Joseph confronted his conscious-stricken brothers with their sin, he said, "God did send me before you to preserve life ... it was not you that sent me hither, but God", Gen. 45. 5, 8; 50. 20.

Israel's history is the story of a gracious, longsuffering God seeking to overcome the evil of a proud self-centred people. It is the story of mankind. It is the story of each one of us. It is the story of God's triumph over evil. No wonder the psalm ends, "Praise ye the Lord".

"Wherefore remember", Eph. 2. 11.

November 22nd

READING: **Psalm 106. 1-26**

WE HAVE SINNED

THIS PSALM reviews Israel's history of failure and God's patience with man. But first hear

1. *The Psalmist's Call: Praise*, vv. 1-2. First comes a call to thanksgiving, praise and worship. Those who have tasted that the Lord is gracious can never praise Him enough. Thanksgiving shows an appreciation of what God has done for us. Worship expresses appreciation of what God is in Himself. There is an element of wonder in the words, "Who can utter the mighty acts of the Lord? who can show forth all his praise?", v. 2. This is the spirit of worship. Men will worship the future last world emperor much as they worshipped Nebuchadnezzar, Rev. 13. 4. But God alone, Jehovah, is incomparable. Thus Moses, when saved from the Egyptian army, worshipped, saying, "Who is like unto thee, O Lord among the gods? who is like thee, glorious in holiness, fearful in praises, doing wonders?", Exod. 15. 11.

2. *The Counsel: Do Right*, v. 3. Both saint and sinner need reminding that the righteous Lord loves righteousness and hates iniquity. Doing right does not come naturally to fallen man. But God insists on just dealings "at all times", in the family, in business, and in the church.

3. *The Cry: Save Me*, vv. 4-5. This cry is not only for personal salvation, but for others too. Israel is recognized as a nation in which God had a special interest because of His promise to Abraham. It was His peculiar possession in a rebellious world. Moses said long before, "the Lord's portion is his people; Jacob is the lot of his inheritance", Deut. 32. 9. Should not we also appeal to God, not only for ourselves, but for our local church testimony? The seven churches mentioned in Revelation 1-3 are all viewed as golden lampstands, but what a feeble light some emitted!

4. *The Confession*, vv. 6-7. Now comes an unreserved confession of sin, not merely the psalmist's but that of the nation. Like Daniel, he humbly associated himself with his wayward brethren, "We have sinned". The man who walks with God never feels himself superior to his brethren. He is too keenly aware of his own failures for that.

"If we confess our sins, he is faithful and just to forgive us our sins", 1 John 1. 9.

READING: **Psalm 106. 34-48**

MINGLED AMONG THE HEATHEN

GOD CALLED Israel out of Egypt to be separated from the increasingly immoral nations, whose evil threatened to corrupt the whole of mankind. He saved them to be holy as He is holy. For four centuries, He had waited patiently, but the Canaanites grew worse and worse. "Because sentence against an evil work is not executed speedily, therefore the heart of the sons of men is fully set in them to do evil", Eccl. 8. 11. So at last God commanded Joshua to deal with the canker and cleanse the land.

Today we are not to execute judgment like Israel did. Elijah called down fire from heaven, but the Lord Jesus forbade His disciples to do so, Luke 9. 55. But we are "sanctified", that is, set apart for the pleasure of God, holy as He is holy. We are bidden, "come out from among them, and be ye separate, saith the Lord, and touch not the unclean thing", 2 Cor. 6. 14-17; Rev. 18. 4. This does not imply living a monastic life, but acting as salt in the earth, arresting corruption by our conduct, and not following the crowd on the road to destruction.

But Israel disobeyed and mixed with the Canaanite, first tolerating and then imitating their ways. They "learned their works", Psa. 106. 35, and became slaves to the idolatrous practices of the dissolute pagans. "Yea, they sacrificed their sons and their daughters unto devils (demons)", v. 37. Beware of the world's idols, not only pop stars and film stars, but the love of money and the love of pleasure.

The believers in Corinth were warned, "Be not deceived", for evil company corrupts good manners and morals, 1 Cor. 15. 33. My younger brothers and sisters in Christ: cultivate friendship not with merely professing Christians, but with those who are set to serve our Lord Jesus Christ. Follow the psalmist's example, saying, "I am a companion of all them that fear thee, and of them that keep thy precepts", Psa. 119. 63. To know and to keep God's commandments are two very different things.

To walk in the counsel of the ungodly leads to standing in the way of sinners, and then to sitting in the seat of the scornful, Psa. 1. 1.

"Keep thyself pure", 1 Tim. 5. 22; 1 Cor. 15. 33.

November 24th

READING: **Psalm 114**

SANCTUARY AND DOMINION

AGAIN WE RECALL the mighty power of God in delivering His people from thraldom in Egypt and bringing them into Canaan.

The nation's twofold description shows that it can be viewed in two ways. (i) Jacob means "Supplanter", describing Isaac's son naturally from his birth, a man who aimed by fair means or foul to wrest from his elder brother the rights of the firstborn son, Gen. 25. 20-23.

(ii) Israel means a "Prince", one who has power with God, 32. 27-28. It speaks of the dignity conferred upon the nation which later He called His son. It was the name given to Jacob, not at birth but at Jabbok after he had confessed his sinnership; then, with his pride overcome, he clung to God for blessing. Of Nathanael the Lord Jesus said, "Behold an Israelite indeed, in whom is no guile", John 1. 47, that is, an Israelite true to his God-given name, in whom was none of the scheming deception which marked Jacob's early life.

Today a true believer in Christ may to his shame show his old Jacob-character by actions which are grievously sinful, but he will also give evidence of a new life characterized by righteousness and self-denial. Let us beware of Jacob-like tendencies, "the old man" as Scripture puts it, and live to manifest the character of God our Father.

When God delivered the nation from Egypt, they were called to be His sanctuary, His holy dwelling-place. He manifested His presence in the cloud which gave light to Israel, but was darkness to the Egyptians. Then He deigned to give evidence of His presence in the tabernacle that Moses built, saying, "there will I meet with thee", Exod. 25. 22. Where the King of kings dwells, He must needs rule; so Israel became His dominion also.

Since the Lord's ascension, there have been local churches owning His authority. Paul wrote, "Ye are the temple of God (the inner shrine, the sanctuary)". In one sense, God is omnipresent; but He cannot tolerate evil. So Paul continued, "the temple of God is holy, which temple ye are. If any man defile (corrupt) the temple of God, him shall God destroy", 1 Cor. 3. 16-17. God is still known amongst His gathered people.

"God is in you of a truth", 1 Cor. 14. 23-37.

READING: **Psalm 115**

TRUST IN THE LORD

THERE IS one thing that we cannot exaggerate, the infinite greatness and glory of God. Despite Israel's waywardness, there were always some among them, maybe a very small remnant, who exulted in the God of Abraham, Isaac and Jacob. Of Him David said, "Great is the Lord, and greatly to be praised; and his greatness is unsearchable". This psalm contrasts Him with the helpless idols of mankind. True Israelites had no molten or graven image, so the pagans taunted them saying, "Where is now their God?" When our longsuffering God refrains from executing summary judgment, the wicked will say, "Where is your God now?". One reply is, "Where is *your* God now—if indeed you have one?", 1 Kings 18. 27. The psalmist replies, "our God is in the heavens". He is far beyond the reach and the influence of earthdwellers below, although still accessible to the humble. "He hath done whatsoever he hath pleased": he is sovereign in all His ways, not to be called to account by any of His creatures. He is contrasted here with idols (gods) that cannot speak, see, hear, smell, work or walk. Our conception of God is certainly far too small. Since God is so great and His understanding is infinite, He is to be trusted and relied upon absolutely. There are three calls to put trust in Him.

(i) "*O Israel*, trust thou in the Lord", v. 9. This is an appeal to the whole nation. They took the name Israel (a prince with God) given to Jacob by God, when he ceased relying on his own strength and cunning, when he clung to God alone. God became his help and shield, and then the help and shield of the nation. (ii) "*O house of Aaron*, trust in the Lord", v. 10; this is a call to the priests, descended from Aaron. They had the high and holy privilege of serving God by offering sacrifices, and also of teaching their countrymen the commandments of God. (iii) "*Ye that fear* the Lord, trust in the Lord", v. 11. All the nation professed to fear the Lord, but this has in view not those who merely professed allegiance to the only true God, but those who had a reverent regard for Him and so kept His commandments. We should ask, "Do I?".

"Ye believe in God, believe also in me", John 14. 1.

READING: **Psalm 122**

GOD IS IN THE MIDST OF HER

A NATION is naturally proud of its capital city. It is the centre of government, and generally contains the most magnificent buildings and impressive monuments.

The nation of Israel had special reason for their admiration of, and reverence for Jerusalem. When God gave Moses His law, He spoke of a place where He would dwell among His people, to which all the men were to bring their sacrifices at the three great annual festivals. That place was a rallying centre to maintain the unity of the nation, Deut. 12. 5-14.

The first thing mentioned in this psalm is not Jerusalem but the house of God in it. "Will God indeed dwell on the earth? behold, the heaven and heaven of heavens cannot contain thee; how much less this house that I have builded?". So said Solomon, as he dedicated the temple in Jerusalem, 1 Kings 8. 27.

Not until God had redeemed a people from slavery and given them His law did He say, "Let them make me a sanctuary; that I may dwell among them", Exod. 25. 8. Then Moses made the tent of meeting. Later God chose Jerusalem for His dwelling place; but today, He dwells not in temples made with hands, but in the "spiritual house", His people, John 4. 21-24; Acts 7. 48; 1 Pet. 2. 5. That imparts a high dignity to an assembly of His people.

This psalm is a "song of ascents", probably sung as the godly went up to the hill of the Lord. Well might we pray like David, "Peace be within thy walls, and prosperity within thy palaces", v. 7. Salem means "peace", Heb. 7. 2, and peace is necessary for prosperity. We should go to normal church gatherings with the same zest that the godly had when they went to the temple, first seeking the face of the Lord in private, and then expecting His presence in the assembly.

Finally, in Isaiah 2. 2-5; Micah 4. 1-2 and Zechariah 14. 16-21 we read of Jerusalem becoming the metropolis of the whole earth: "in the last days, ... the mountain of the Lord's house shall be established in the top of the mountains, and shall be exalted above the hills; and all nations shall flow unto it". Then the name of the city will be, "The Lord is there", Ezek. 48. 35; Psa. 46. 5.

"There am I in the midst of them", Matt. 18. 20.

November 27th

READING: **Psalm 126**

GREAT THINGS

THIS IS a record of the relief and rejoicing of the people of Judah on their return from Babylon to their homeland. God had allowed them to be carried as captives into Babylon seventy years earlier because of their persistent idolatry. They had "mocked the messengers of God, and despised his words ... till there was no remedy", 2 Chron. 36. 16. Their enemies had overrun the land, and destroyed the temple.

Now, in answer to the prayers of Daniel, God had moved the heart of Cyrus, the Persian king who had recently displaced the Babylonians, to provide for their return. So about 50,000 chastened Jews had returned to build a house for the God of heaven in Jerusalem.

They had no heart to sing while in captivity, but now they revelled in their deliverance. Everyone who has truly called on the Lord Jesus can say with them, "The Lord hath done great things for us; whereof we are glad", v. 3. The unconverted also must confess this. They can surely see a change in a liberated soul, v. 2. The change was like a dream, hardly believable.

To the south of Jerusalem was semi-desert, whose dried-up water courses became torrents of life-giving water in the wet winter season. The former captives pray that fresh streams of their brethren also may join them. They recall their tears of repentance, and look forward to further rejoicing in the Lord, v. 6.

Then came the problem of cultivating and sowing the land that had been largely left fallow for seventy years. They had to reserve some of their precious corn to ensure a harvest the next year. So when a man went forth with a basket of seed for sowing, he had a hard decision to make. Maybe his wife and children were crying for more bread, but he must use his seed wisely, and would in due time reap a rich reward. We expect to reap, not just what we sow, but more than we sow, whether thirty, sixty, or one hundred fold. We go out with a basket; we return with sheaves. This is sobering. The way we use our time and abilities now will make all the difference to us in eternity.

"Above all that we ask or think", Eph. 3. 20.

November 28th

READING: **Psalm 132**

A PLACE FOR THE LORD

HERE WE FIND king David's earnest and dominant desire to find a suitable place for the ark as the sacred symbol of the presence of the living God among His people, vv. 1-10. Then comes the equally earnest pledge of God to find a resting place among them for ever, vv. 11-18. This promise must yet be fulfilled.

What is the most important object to have before us in life? In David's case he swore, he pledged himself, to take no rest till he had found a suitable dwelling place for God amid His people. This, indeed, is the ultimate object of God Himself. In the new creation, "the tabernacle of God is with men, and he will dwell with them, and they shall be his people", Rev. 21. 3.

This singleheartedness marked our Lord Jesus Himself. "I must be about my Father's business ... I must work the works of him that sent me, while it is day", Luke 2. 49; John 9. 4. It marked His apostle Paul, "this one thing I do ... I press toward the mark for the prize of the high calling of God in Christ Jesus", Phil. 3. 13-14. It marked David, "One thing have I desired of the Lord, that will I seek after; that I may dwell in the house of the Lord all the days of my life, to behold the beauty of the Lord, and to enquire in his temple", Psa. 27. 4.

To bring the ark to its place of honour caused David real trouble. At the first attempt, God's instructions about carrying the ark were ignored and Uzzah was smitten for his irreverence; at the second David danced with delight to see his ambition fulfilled, but Michal his wife met him with scorn and contempt; 2 Sam. 6 gives all the details. So he prayed, "Lord, remember David, and all his afflictions".

We, too, will have opposition if we seek to give the Lord Himself the pre-eminent place that He should have in our private life and also in our church life. Sometimes, as with David, opposition comes from those from whom we least expect it. This should move us to prayer, and with John the Baptist, we say, "He must increase, but I must decrease", John 3. 30.

"That in all things he might have the preeminence", Col. 1. 18.

READING: **Psalm 135**

PRAISE YE THE LORD

PRAISE IS the outcome of a consideration and estimation that moves us to pleasure, approval and admiration. The word means to exclaim with a loud voice, and so to express our worship of God. The psalm bids us praise His name which describes His character, the Eternal, who was and is and will be, the Same yesterday, today and for ever. It was especially a call to the priests privileged to serve in the house of God. Those believing in Christ today are privileged to come boldly to the throne of grace to obtain mercy, Heb. 4. 16. As priests to God, we must offer the sacrifice of praise continually, the fruit of lips which confess His name, Heb. 13. 15.

"Sing praises unto his name", v. 3. What weighty reasons there are to do so! First, He is good and His lovingkindness is over all His works. Secondly, He is great, great in His mercy to men, and great in His universal control "in heaven, and in earth, in the seas, and all deep places", v. 6; great in His deliverance of Israel of old, great beyond our ken. No wonder the refrain in Psalm 107 is "Oh that men would praise the Lord for his goodness, for his wonderful works to the children of men!". One gladly says, "O magnify the Lord with me, and let us exalt his name together", Psa. 34. 3. An assembly of His people today, like the temple of old, is not only a "house of prayer", but a house of praise also. The more earnest and persevering our prayers, the more genuinely spiritual will be our praise.

If someone says, "I don't feel like praising", remember that we have a High Priest touched with the feeling of our infirmities, and ever living to make intercession for us. Say, "Why art thou cast down, O my soul? and why art thou disquieted in me? hope thou in God: for I shall yet praise him", Psa. 42. 5. We must pray for God to give us the oil of joy for mourning and the garment of praise for the spirit of heaviness. He delights to do this so "that he might be glorified", Isa. 61. 3.

"Singing and making melody in your heart to the Lord", Eph. 5. 19.

READING: **Psalm 137**

A PSALM OF REFLECTION

It is sometimes good to recall the gracious disciplinary acts of God in our spiritual education. In this psalm, the Israelites who had been deported to Babylon and had endured years of cruel captivity look back with mixed feelings.

(1) They recall with bitterness the taunts of their captors calling on them to sing songs in praise of Zion. Zion had been their great delight, the fortress and the city of David, "beautiful for situation, the joy of the whole earth", this being its description in the palmy days of David and Solomon foreshadowing its future when Messiah shall return in glory, Psa. 48. 2. But Zion lay waste, and the captives could but hang their harps on the willows beside the Euphrates. May we too value God's chastening which yields the peaceable fruit of righteousness to those who are exercised thereby, Heb. 12. 11.

(2) Their sufferings failed to quench their admiration of Zion and their devotion to the city of God's choice. With Zion in ruins, they cannot play their harps on foreign soil; they would rather be dumb and never sing again. They loved Jerusalem above their "chief joy", for there they had brought their gifts to the altar of God Himself. They pledge their loyalty to His appointed centre. May we, too, value our local gatherings (the people rather than the place) whither we come to worship.

(3) They cry for justice. The barbarous cruelty, which keeps prisons full and leaves broken homes and weeping souls unnumbered in some countries today, is but a reflection of the unspeakable cruelties of the Babylonian and Edomite hosts, 2 Kings 8. 12; Obad. 10-12. It would be only justice for Babylon's infants to be treated as she had treated Israel's.

Ultimately, justice must be done when God arises "to shake terribly the earth", Isa. 2. 19. But it is very difficult for men to avoid personal animosity when their own interests and comfort are involved. "Avenge not yourselves ... Vengeance is mine; I will repay, saith the Lord", Rom. 12. 19. May we therefore, like our Master, "pray for them which despitefully use you, and persecute you", Matt. 5. 44, and thank God that the day of vengeance has not yet dawned!

"Now is the day of salvation", 2 Cor. 6. 2.

Prospects, Hopes and Aspirations

ENTERING THE last month of the year, our thoughts instinctively look forward with anticipation to the advent season with its renewed opportunities for musing on the wonders of the Incarnate Saviour. Yet not only do we look with expectation, but with mixed feelings as we await another New Year with its increasing uncertainties and shadows of the unknown.

What better preparation for it than these exquisite Songs of Israel, containing such ministry that lifts our souls daily to levels that are above all the vicissitudes of time, anchoring them to the throne of sure Almightiness and unerring providence.

Our selection of Psalms will proceed in sequence through these five great volumes, each largely taking its character from the corresponding volume of the Pentateuch to which it is linked. Hence there will be thoughts of Walking with God (Genesis); the Work of Redemption (Exodus); the Worship of the Lord (Leviticus); the Wilderness Pilgrimage (Numbers); and the Word of the Law (Deuteronomy).

As the people of God are seen moving through the Pentateuch, whether as patriarch or as the redeemed nation of Israel, theirs was the forward look. Abraham looked for the city which has the foundations; he and his family saw and greeted the promises afar off, seeking a country of their own. Isaac blessed Jacob concerning things to come; Joseph spoke of the nation's departure; Moses looked unto the recompence of reward, and looked to Him who is invisible. To Israel, it was said, "I have set the land before you", Deut. 1. 8.

Perhaps more than ever, these are days when we need our spiritual prospects illuminated, our soul's true hopes deepened, and our life's aspirations clarified. Let us therefore adjust our sights daily to the spiritual foci determined by these psalmodic strains, in order that our day's life-cycle may be regularly tuned to our heavenly prospects, to sure and certain hopes, and to true soul-aspirations. Then, though the road may be uphill all the way, our progress will be truly rooted and fixed in God.

The Lord make us a people marked by the onward and upward look, "*forgetting those things which are behind*", Phil. 3. 13-14.

December 1st

READING: **Psalm 4**

THE SOUL'S GREAT CERTAINTIES

WHAT A PSALM with which to begin our month's forward looking exercises, providing us with solid rock beneath our feet as our sure vantage ground. What an octave of melodic notes to confront us on our first day! In this "Genesis psalm" truly Abraham in spirit is here, v. 3, and Isaac too, v. 1, with Jacob, vv. 4, 5, 8, and lastly Joseph, vv. 6-7. Can you find them here? Let us listen carefully to each succeeding chord so that its strains may rejoice our hearts despite the cloudy day perhaps facing us, or the dark day that we have just completed.

1. *"Thou hast enlarged me"*, or "set me at large", v. 1 R.V., whether or not our day has been restricted and cramped. Is this not true? What broad acres are measured by our redemption, great depths to plumb, heights to scale and areas to explore and possess. Is the Jabez-prayer ours?, 1 Chron. 4. 10.

2. *"Know that the Lord hath set apart him that is godly for himself"*, v. 3. Enlarged, yet set apart—what consolation. I am His alone, for He has chosen me—what confidence.

3. *"Stand in awe ... and be still"*, v. 4. Here is the necessary pause-note in our melody. Halt and reflect; wonder and worship. In view of these certainties, read Psalm 46. 10.

4. *"Put your trust in the Lord"*, v. 5. In the light of the foregoing, should we not do this? The day will be different in the light of faith. If this injunction is obeyed, sacrifices will be made, v. 5a.

5. *"Lord, lift thou up the light of thy countenance upon us"*, v. 6. Was this not Israel's portion?, Num. 6. 24-26; and is it not ours? This will disperse shadows and lighten the way.

6. *"Thou hast put gladness in my heart"*, v. 7. Then are we sad? This sixth chord is but the grand flute of the anthem to be sung "double forte". Yet there is a sequel of peaceful rest.

7. *"In peace will I both lay me down and sleep"*, v. 8 R.V.; this is a calm epilogue with verses 1-7 as a pillow; a soft "Amen" at the end of a day's walk with God. Maclaren translates, *"lay me down and sleep at once"*. So another lap of life's pilgimage may end with the golden sunset of a pianissimo of rest. Then we can say, "I laid me down and slept; I awaked; for the Lord sustained me", Psa. 3. 5.

Is this the new song in my heart and on my lips?

December 2nd

READING: **Psalm 23**

FROM HEATH TO HOME

WHILST THIS psalm is initially a song of Israel's remnant, the eye of the singer being fixed on the earthly goal of "the house of the Lord, to length of days", v. 6 marg., what a Christian heritage it has become, supplying us with heavenly prospects. The psalm has three stanzas:

1. *The Unchanging Care of the Ministering Shepherd*, vv. 1-3. How busy we see Him to be in these verses, not just for the flock in general, but for each individual sheep. He never rests: He makes, leads, restores, guides. It is all action for them. He feeds and refreshes, and then He is seen restoring and guiding. With our Shepherd, it is always "grace" and "truth"; cf. John 1. 14. He makes us *lie* in the luscious pastures, demanding that we "chew the cud" after having eaten; then He leads beside the quiet waters. Does this suggest the work of the Holy Spirit to aid us after receiving spiritual food so as to obtain the greater benefit? Lying down is not mere rest, but occupation with the pasture received. His treatment of the sheep is good, since He is the Good Shepherd.

2. *The Unfailing Presence of the Attending Shepherd*, vv. 4-5. There are dangers, shadows and enemies along the way, but His rod and staff give comfort in the darkest hours. "Thou art with me" implies a continuously present boon, not just past history or future promise. Also, when enemies lurk, we still eat of His provision without fear, and it is a banquet indeed, prepared by Him personally, with heads anointed. The enemies look and long, but stand aloof. He can deal with the sheep's enemies; see Mark 1. 13. Moreover, His provision and protection are always plenteous, Matt. 16. 9-10.

3. *The Unending Shelter of the Hosting Shepherd*, v. 6. The desert pathway will one day terminate, the temporary fold be left behind, for that road converges on our permanent home. This is no earthly bivouac, for there we shall *dwell*. On the desert track the Shepherd was with us, but there we shall be with Him. The desert way was good with Him near, but what will home be like? Sometimes we cry, how much longer is the path? Never fear, long or short, for He who leads provides faithful followers, and they are guaranteed.

The desert's bleat is followed by home's Hallelujahs.

357

December 3rd

READING: **Psalm 24**

THE SANCTUARY'S PRESENT EXPERIENCE

OUR PSALM is primarily millennial, cf. Isa. 2. 1-3, yet in grace its principles are appropriate now for our application.

Yesterday's psalm warmed our hearts with the prospect of our eternal entrance into that holy place, but what about our practice of it now? Verses 3-6 show our going up into the hill of the Lord as a present spiritual experience. Because the Lord has gone up already in ascension, we may enter now: "Having therefore, brethren, boldness to enter into the holiest ... let us draw near with a true heart in full assurance of faith", Heb. 10. 19-22. Is this the real aspiration of our hearts? These verses give the way of our approach. The steps leading to the sanctuary demand:

1. *An Ascent*, v. 3. The soul needs to leave the earth level and seek the pure atmosphere of the heavenlies; see Matt. 6. 6. The intrusions of earth must be deliberately left behind; worship must be on "one of the mountains", Gen. 22. 2.

2. *It is "Hill Territory"* , v. 3. This is characteristic of the divine presence; cf. Psa. 2. 6; 15. 1; 68. 15; 87. 1; Isa. 2. 2. It demands purpose of soul, energy of spirit, and effort of mind. The "hill country of Judaea" is the place where wonderful things are heard and learned, Luke 1. 39.

3. *It is a Place of Great Sanctity*, v. 3. This holy place debars defilement. How the priests of old had to wash carefully before entering. The laver was much in use. Hence,

4. *Strict Requirements are Demanded* of those who stand there, v. 4: clean hands, pure hearts, humble spirits, circumspect lips. "This is (and must be) the generation of them that seek him", for holiness becomes His house. It is here, of course, that real blessing is received.

5. *The Encouragement to Draw near.* He who desires our entry is "the God of Jacob", v. 6 R.V. How gracious is our holy Lord; how He welcomes us. He Himself "by the blood of Jesus" has opened the way in and bids us, the most unworthy yet cleansed, to enter with boldness. The Forerunner has entered for us, Heb. 6. 20; then let us not refrain from entering. If our eye is truly on heaven, then our heart will surely seek the holy place.

It is our right and privilege to enter as priests.

December 4th

READING: **Psalm 25**

DIRECTION FOR THE UNTRODDEN WAY

THIS CONTEMPLATIVE passage is encircled by troubled conditions: enemies, treachery, personal iniquities and sins, an
entangling net, desolation, troubles and distresses, affliction
and travail, vv. 1-3, 11-22. Round and within, there is only
besetment, but he looks up and cries to the Lord, vv. 1, 15, 21.
In doing so, he considers his prospective way. Does his lot
represent ours? Then let our cry match his. In the opening
verses, we have an introversion:

    1. The Lord's paths desired, v. 4.
      2. The Lord's guidance requested, v. 5.
        3. The Lord's past mercies pleaded, v. 6.
          4. David's faults recognized, v. 7.
        5. The Lord's present goodness affirmed, v. 8.
      6. The Lord's response conditioned, v. 9.
    7. The Lord's paths described, v. 10.
      8. David's faults confessed, v. 11.

At the heart of the cry is the ready acknowledgement of the
sins of immaturity and the failures of rebellion, v. 7, with a plea
for divine non-remembrance thereof based on the goodness of
God. The cry is completed by confession and a call for pardon,
v. 11. When the past is cleared, the prospect is clearer. Then
we hear the desire to know the Lord's ways (principles of
action) and the paths of His directing, v. 4, knowing the worth
of *all* His directives to the faithful, v. 10. Now David desires to
walk in those paths and requests guidance: "show me", "guide
me", "teach me". For such he will constantly wait, for
salvation is only in his God, v. 5. He is confident of the
response if conditions are met. The Lord will teach the
teachable, v. 9. David bases his confidence on the unchanging
character of God, v. 6, and strengthens it with the conviction
of the constant goodness and rectitude of God's present
character. What He has been, so He will be, v. 8.

The Lord will instruct in the way that *He* shall choose, v. 12,
giving with it soul-ease, v. 13. The secret of the Lord may be
known, v. 14. He will deliver from life's distresses, vv. 15-17;
He will forgive, v. 18, when confession of the past is made and
heart desire for His paths is expressed.

"This is the way, walk ye in it", Isa. 30. 21.

December 5th

READING: **Psalm 27**

THE PSALMIST'S SOLILOQUY OF FAITH

ONCE AGAIN we have an introversion as follows:

1. Confession expressed, v. 1.
  2. Confidence begotten, v. 2.
    3. Conquest assured, v. 3.
  4. Covert desired, v. 4.
5. Conviction founded, v. 5.

The psalmist's pathway is still troubled. He is encountering evildoers, adversaries, foes, opposition, v. 3, enemies, forsakings, false witnesses, vv. 10, 12. In this world, the saint of God must suffer tribulation. From such circumstances, however, he looks back, up and on. His aspirations are high and his prospect sure.

His soliloquy therefore begins with the *Confession of present facts*, v. 1. He knows Jehovah; his God *is* his light (for the darkness), salvation (for the dangers) and strength (for the difficulties), and he can thus confidently assert provision against fear. This is truth accepted. How often, however, we acquiesce to truth, but never submit to its power. Doctrine held must become doctrine proved.

Yet David turns his confession into *Conviction*, v. 5. Note the connecting word "for". The confession of his lips becomes the conviction of his heart. Contemplating the day of trouble, he says the Lord *shall* keep him "secretly" R.V., "hide him" in His pavilion (His light), A.V.; He *shall* hide him in the Covert of His tabernacle (His salvation), R.V., and He *shall* lift him up upon a rock (His strength), A.V.

Is our prospect a sure conviction? Such is founded on a *Confidence* begotten by past experience, v. 2. When evildoers came upon him (note the tense), they stumbled and fell, and will again. For Jesus Christ remains the same for ever as yesterday.

Now he moves into action, and seeks the desired *Covert*, v. 4. He has his priorities right, and pursues them, v. 5; this is to dwell permanently in the house of the Lord. Our privilege, even amidst confusion and stress, is also to dwell in this holy place, the centre of peace, beholding the beauty of the Lord; there problems are dismissed, and problems answered.

From the covert, the vista is always bright, bringing sacrifice, singing, seeking, security and serenity.

READING: **Psalm 28**

THE SOUL'S UPLOOK AND ONLOOK

NOTE THE TWO divisions of this psalm, with the break at verse 5. Also note that each has two sub-divisions, the breaks being at verses 2 and 7. In each division, the psalmist has an uplook and an onlook.

In the first section, he has an uplook of *Supplication*, vv. 1-2. His hands and eyes are lifted up in prayer, which is directed to his Rock and the holy oracle, the place whence God speaks, 1 Kings 6. 19. His cry is urgent, "be not silent", "if thou be silent", "hear my voice". His call is tense, "I cry", "I cry", "I lift up my hand". His soul is moved. Why?

Note his first onlook. He sees those who "go down into the pit". View with him the *March of the Sinful*, vv. 3-5; noting their character, "wicked", "workers of iniquity" and deceivers, v. 3, and seeing their course, the receiving of the reward of their deeds, v. 4. This is not malice, anger or imprecation, but the exclamation of one who knows the ways of his holy God and has intelligence in His laws of government. He knows his own deserts when he says, "Draw me not away with the wicked", v. 3, for he knows their crime, v. 5.

Attend now to David's second uplook, that of *Song*, vv. 6-7. With sorrow for the wicked, he praises with song for his own blessing. "Blessed be the Lord, because he hath heard", v. 6, and has strengthened, shielded and helped, v. 7. Note the individual confession, "my, my, my", "I am helped" and "will I praise". As we see the ungodly drift by, are we not only grieved as we remember their latter end, but thankful that the Lord is not rewarding us according to our deeds?

As he sings, he sees another movement, his second onlook, the *March of the Saved*, v. 9. Note how they go: they march with steady and sure step, for the Lord is their strength. They march with certainty, for the Lord is the stronghold of salvation, R.V., or the saving strength of His anointed. They have a tread of confidence, for their Lord will save them and bless them; He will feed them and they will know His daily support, for He will lift them up (or, bear them up, R.V.) for ever. Of the others, he says that God will not build them up, but break them down, R.V.

We are marching to Zion, the beautiful city of God.

December 7th

READING: **Psalm 39. 1-7**

WHAT IS MY LIFE?

WE ARE not here for ever, though at times, with many of us, it would appear as if it were so. Earthly-mindedness is often to blame. The psalmist strikes an important note: life is transitory, its term is limited. We are quickly moving on. David requests God to make known to him three things: (a) his end, (b) the measure of his days, (c) his frailty, moving backward from effect to cause, v. 4.

Life has a terminus for us all. It will come to an end, either by the return of the Lord or our return to dust, and both are imminent. Life has also a divinely measured span. The Lord has determined it, though our physical frailty demands it. One secret of Christian effectiveness is to be constantly aware of it. Verse 5 emphasizes the truth of this fact. God makes our days as handbreadths, each present day only being what our hands can hold and say is our own. And should age be extended ever so far, it is nothing in His sight, and man at his best is but a breath. We have thus expressed the frailty, brevity, vanity and poverty of life—a shadow, vapour, grass.

The fault with man is his failure to grasp realities and his waste of time on impermanencies, v. 6. The point therefore is, "now, Lord, what wait I for? my hope is in thee". In the span of this our quiet time, let us ask, "what wait I for?"; are we waiting for something to turn up, aimless and purposeless? Is my expectation the mere realization of personal plans and aspirations? Is self our sole goal? Or is our hope in God? Have our lives one absorbing focus? Do we consecrate our day-by-day lives to His will? Is the glory and pleasure of God our daily objective? Is each day a passing boredom, or another "handful on purpose" for Him? Is God, the One whom we profess to own, serve and worship, the one drive of our days, their present portion and ultimate prospect? These are searching questions in these fleeting days, and they require, as the Lord demands, an answer.

"Awake thou that sleepest, and arise from the dead, and Christ shall give thee light. See then that ye walk circumspectly, not as fools, but as wise, redeeming the time, because the days are evil. Wherefore be yet not unwise, but understanding what the will of the Lord is. And be not drunk with wine, wherein is excess; but be filled with the Spirit", Eph. 5. 14-18.

December 8th

READING: **Psalm 42**

HOPING IN GOD

AFTER yesterday's meditation, surely this psalm is appropriate for today. Is our hope in God?, 39. 7. If so, what are the inner stirrings of our hearts just now? Can we say now with fervour, "Hope in God"? The psalmist seems to be conscious of three important facts:

1. *A Remorseful Remembrance.* Three times he cries, "Why art thou cast down?". "I remember", v. 4, is (*a*) the cry of *Conscience*, v. 4. He remembers past days when he went with the throng, and *led* them to the house of God, R.V. Those were days of singing and holydays, but now his soul is disquieted within him, v. 5. (*b*) It is also the cry of *Conviction*, v. 10. His adversaries reproached him and said, "Where is thy God?". This was as a sword in his bones. Are we moved also—in our quiet place are we forced to think of our yesterdays? The thoughts of the psalmist are still carrying him back to such backsliding, and he remembers his God from the deathly wilderness experience (the land of Jordan); days when he was too self-exalted for God (the Hermons); yet days when he was reduced to conscious humiliation (the littleness of Mizar). Out of such soul-distress, however, we hear

2. *A Regretful Repentance.* The hand of the Lord had been heavy upon him, v. 7, and now we hear, "why go I mourning?", v. 9; see v. 3. His thoughts return to the goodness of God, "Yet the Lord *will* command his loving-kindness in the daytime, and in the night his song shall be with me", v. 8. He is "the God of my life". Hence he says, "hope thou in God: for I shall yet praise him for the help of his countenance", v. 5. This conviction is beginning to grip him more and more, and he repeats it, v. 11. His soul steadily moves towards

3. *A Restful Restoration*, vv. 1-2. The inner longings for God are reviving, "when shall I come and appear before God?", v. 2. His soul-vision is returning, and he beholds before him the rare prospect that is still inviting. His thirst for spiritual things rises, "My soul thirsteth for God"; the productivity of the land of Jordan is not to be compared with such fertile fields, since God is there. May our prayer today be, *"Lord, turn me from my careless past, to view what Thy love has prepared for me"*.

363

December 9th

READING: **Psalm 49**

THE FOOLISH AND THE FAITHFUL

THE PSALM is marked clearly by features of those who live *foolishly*, v. 13, behaving as if this life were all, never to end, v. 9. Their focus is solely on the accumulation of wealth in which they boast, v. 6, and time seems to be their only consideration, v. 11. They are similar to the "earthdwellers" seen in the Book of Revelation, upon whom divine judgments are to descend. Theirs, whether wise or unwise, v. 10, is the appointment to death, and they will perish, vv. 12, 14, leaving their substance to others, v. 10, with their glory departing, v. 17. At the end of life's efforts, they are seen meekly shepherded by death to the grave, v. 14. Such "shall never see light", v. 19, for "there is no morning for them", Isa. 8. 20 R.V. Life has had earthbound limits, and there has been no prospect beyond what is material; with all their efforts, they remain powerless to effect greater matters, vv. 7-9.

Here and there, however, there are flashes of light that characterize those who live *faithfully*, called the upright, v. 14. (i) They *live fearlessly* in evil days "when the perverseness of those that would trip them up encircleth" them, v. 5, F. W. Grant. In addition to peaceful ways, they have (ii) *prospects* of great certainty. (*a*) There *is for them* "a morning", v. 14. For the psalmist, this probably refers to the millennial glory; see Mal. 4. 2, but for N.T. saints it is the awaking on the other side when death is past. (*b*) They can say (with greater light than that of the psalmist), "God will redeem my soul from the hand (or, power) of the grave (Sheol): for he shall receive me", v. 15. Let us hold present riches and fame lightly, for we have wider horizons. Live not for time, but for eternity. Present things are temporary, and we are destined for eternal possessions and limitless prospect. The glory that we seek is heavenly, and our assets are spiritual and lasting. Hence we are not fearful but confident when we see others made rich and advancing in station, v. 16. A man's life consists not in the abundance of the things that he possesses.

Lift your sights to where Christ sits at the right hand of God, and strive for the riches which pass not away.

364

December 10th

READING: **Psalm 62**

THE ATTITUDE THAT ASSURES

THE believer's prospect has often to be viewed through the mist and confusion of surrounding factors of opposition. Such was the case of David here where, as so often, he is beset by enemies. Observe that the psalm is in four stanzas with a conclusion, forming a simple introversion:

1. David in prospective mood, vv. 1-2,
   2. His enemies described, vv. 3-4 R.V.
3. David in prospective mood, vv. 5-8.
   4. His enemies despised, vv. 9-10.
5. David in prospective mood, vv. 11-12.

Note, he fixes his eyes on God before viewing his enemies and thus they lose their fearsomeness. They are seen to be a mere breath (vanity), yea, lighter than a breath, vv. 9-10. Let us concentrate on his prospect.

1. *He can Afford to Wait*, or, "be silent", vv. 1, 5. This is the attitude of one who sees beyond the difficulties and fixes his eye on One who is his Rock (for his feet), Salvation (for his life), and High Tower (for his soul's focus or defence); see R.V.

2. *His Steady Vision* brings him increased certainty:
   "I shall not be *greatly* moved", v. 2.
   "I shall not be moved (*at all*)", v. 6.

3. *His Vision is Exclusive*. Note the difficult concept "only" which occurs twice in verses 1-2 R.V., and twice in verses 5-6. How often is our vision fixed upon God *plus* other expedients as if God might fail and we must provide against emergency. How long it takes us to learn the need of this "only". Our safeguard is not God plus, but God alone.

4. *His Waiting is Seen to Progress* in assurance, for in verse 1 his is but the confession of a fact, "from him cometh my salvation", but in verse 5 his is the conviction of a truth, "my expectation is from him". His conviction is personal and persuasive, v. 8.

5. *He Ends his Waiting* with a note of established assurance, vv. 11-12. God has spoken once, nay *twice*, that with Him is power to perform and mercy to attend. Again observe the exclusive note, "belongeth unto God", and to *no other*.

God renders to opposer and opposed according to their work.

December 11th

READING: **Psalm 63**

GOD SEEN FROM THREE POSITIONS

DAVID IS in three positions or stations, (i) in the wilderness, (ii) in the sanctuary, and (iii) in bed. He has learned the truth of yesterday's psalm. Psalm 63 is in three stages, and stage two, vv. 2-4, seems the pivot of the others.

Position One. In spirit he has been in the sanctuary, vv. 2-4; this came first, *"so as I have seen thee in the sanctuary"*. The remembrance of this supports him in the wilderness, v. 1, and satisfies him in his bedchamber, vv. 5-11, in desert and darkness. There he had seen the power, glory and lovingkindness of his God. The sight of power had strengthened him, of glory had stirred him, of lovingkindness had succoured him. If we would be strong for earth's frays, we must often kneel there and let the vision impress the soul; this moves to praise and worship, vv. 3-4. Why are our lips so dumb?

Posture Two, v. 1. This is affected by position one, "O *God*, thou art my God". David is now in the wilderness of Judah, thirsting, longing, wearying, but he remembers the sanctuary vision. Effectively, he says, "Jehovah (printed GOD), Thou art my Mighty One". This remembrance changes the nature of his desires. He thirsts for this faithful, mighty One; his very flesh longs for Him, and He alone will rest and refresh his weariness. Note the intensity of his desire, "early", "seek", "thirsteth", "longeth" (the word is pineth). Does his expressed soul-desire shame us? If so, is this why our wilderness of soul continues?

Position Three, vv. 5-11. Occupation in position one gives satisfaction in position two, and leads to contemplation in position three. Satisfaction and song become the exercises of the soul in the night watches. Instead of hours of sleeplessness and fear, his hours are times of even greater devotion. They are filled with soul-refreshment, "satisfied as with marrow and fatness", and like Paul and Silas he praises with joyful lips, Acts 16. 25. His waking hours are not fraught with tomorrow's cares, but are full of thoughts of Him, v. 6. He rests in the Lord's shadow, and rejoices in His care, vv. 7-8. He loses his fear of his enemies, vv. 9-11.

Seek often the sanctuary, finding there strength for the day's wilderness, and serenity for the darksome night.

December 12th

READING: **Psalm 73**

WHERE ASSESSMENTS ARE CORRECTLY MADE

WE MEET the value of the sanctuary again. Yesterday, the psalmist had a view there of the power, glory and lovingkindness of God which calmed his soul, and now he has the true view of man which corrects his thoughts. Note how the psalm turns around a twice-stated phrase: (i) "But as for me", v. 2, before he resorts to the sanctuary, and (ii) "But as for me", v. 28, F. W. Grant, after resorting thereto.

In verse 1, the psalmist expresses a truth which he cannot deny, yet which he failed to believe. He had not found it so; see v. 13. In verses 2-12 he surveys, by the mere sight of his eyes, the prosperity of the wicked, and what seemed apparent to him shook his foothold of faith, v. 2. He saw financial success, v. 3; establishment, v. 4; freedom from trouble, v. 5; abundance, v. 7, despite man's godlessness, vv. 8-9, and impiety, vv. 8-11, and he hurries to a rash conclusion, v. 12.

He does confess, however, that the seeming blessing was but a snare to them, v. 6, and he grieves as he sees the Lord's people following them, v. 10. Yet he is moved to envy, v. 3, and in his envy he muses on his own experience, vv. 14-16. It is the age-old problem, Why do the godly suffer?

There are many reasons. Chagrin fires his soul "until", v. 17. The calm seeking after the presence of God corrected his warped vision and soothed his soul. The sanctuary is the place of understanding, for there we see as God sees. There we see the true end of the ungodly, that their foothold is not as sure as it appeared to be, and that their seeming success is but for a moment. They have no lasting hope, for destruction, desolation and terrors are ahead. Their life has been at best but a dream, v. 20. What paupers are men without God, vv. 18-20.

The corrected outlook affects his heart, and produces confession, vv. 21-22. The sanctuary enables us to see ourselves and rightly value our assets. He now appreciated seven things: (1) the unceasing fellowship of God, (2) the divine grip upon him, (3) the Lord's unerring counsel, (4) the glory at the end of the road, (5) the greatest possible possession man can have in heaven or on earth, (6) the divine inward strength, and (7) an everlasting portion, vv. 23-26. How rich we are!

The soul's sights are rightly set in the sanctuary.

December 13th

READING: **Psalm 77**

THE SANCTUARY IS THE SOLUTION

THOUGH OUR hopes and prospects are bright, the world within us can often be dark. At such times, today's psalm can be encouraging and inspiring. Others before us have been in a similar condition, and have found an answer. The psalm is "after the manner of Jeduthun", R.V., that is, "the worshipper". It is encouraging to find soul-complaint and soul-distress in such a psalm.

1. *The Psalmist Looks Within*, vv. 1-3. His day was troubled and his night distraught, "my hand was stretched out and slacked not", R.V. His burden is not specified, so it could include ours. Note the intensity: "refused to be comforted", "I moaned (was troubled)", "I complained", the "spirit overwhelmed". He sought Adonhai, the Almighty Ruler, and was conscious of being heard, v. 1. After this comes inward confession.

2. *He Looks Back*, vv. 4-6. Thus he calls to mind the ancient times reflecting on the ways of God with men. Then he thinks upon his own past, v. 6, when days seemed brighter, when he could even sing in the night. This troubles him, v. 4, and he is agitated to speechlessness. Following this,

3. *He Looks Up*, vv. 7-19. Can his sustained trouble be attributed to God?; has He cast him off?; has He ceased to show favour?; is His mercy at an end?; has His promise (His holy word) failed?; has He forgotten grace?; has anger closed mercy's gates? Momentarily he chides himself. Nay, "This is my infirmity", my malady. Infirmity is in us, never in Him! Then he recalls the years of God's right hand, His works and wonders, His greatness, mighty redemption and universal creator-control and His faithfulness revealed therein. As he mediates, he learns (i) "Thy way is in the sea", v. 19. So His footsteps are untraceable, His ways past finding out. He also learns (ii) "Thy way ... is in the sanctuary", v. 13. God's ways may be beyond our tracing, but not beyond our trusting, for they are always in accord with His holiness and can be understood only in the holy place.

4. *He Looks On*, v. 20. Amidst his burdens and queries, he sees a faithful Shepherd leading His people on. This verse is truly the answer to his doubts in verses 7-9.

Let us stop fretting and start following; the Lord is ahead.

December 14th

READING: **Psalm 80**

THE PSALMIST REMINISCES

THE THOUGHTS of the psalmist revert to the days of his fore-fathers when Israel's march to Canaan was in progress; recall yesterday's reading, 77. 20. Asaph was a Kohathite, 1 Chron. 16. 4-7; hence his forebears carried the tabernacle furniture, including the ark, in the midst of Israel as they marched. We remember that the glory of the Lord resided over the ark when the tabernacle rested. The tribes which followed immediately were Ephraim, Manasseh and Benjamin; hence Joseph is included in verse 1. See Numbers 10. 21-24.

As Asaph (the chief singer) sings, he does so on behalf of Israel, and calls upon the Shepherd of Israel to shine forth, for such would guarantee Israel's salvation, v. 3. They were privileged tribes which immediately followed the sanctuary, marching daily with their faces ever toward that which spoke of the divine glory. As we wend our pilgrim way, are our eyes ever unto the Lord of the sanctuary, our Shepherd? Is this our prospect? Do we walk in the light of His shining face?

Our psalmist links this with "being saved". This psalm is punctuated with this certainty, vv. 3, 7, 19. Israel is seen as disconsolate, crying under the Lord's displeasure. They had turned away, and needed to turn again, so they cry thrice. Do we need to be turned again? Is the Lord of the throne ceasing to be the Lord of the heart? Let us turn again, and get Him fully in focus (and He will return, v. 14), and the shining of His face will bring the salvation that we need as pilgrims. If we walk with face averted, there is still a Saviour to be seen.

Note that somewhere in that same grouping of the march the body of Joseph is being carried in a coffin, surely by one of Joseph's tribes, Exod 13. 19. Whether they looked ahead or behind, they were reminded of God's salvation, either in the Lord's face, or in the bones of Joseph (called Zaphenath-paneah, the Revealer of Secrets) in a coffin.

Note the progress of thought: 1. "Turn us again, O God" (the Strong One), v. 3. 2. "Turn us again, O God of hosts" (the Victorious One), v. 7. 3. "Turn us again, O Jehovah God of hosts" (the Faithful One), v. 19; "cause thy face to shine" appears in these verses.

What cloud is hiding His face?

369

December 15th

READING: **Psalm 84**

MARCHING TO ZION

ISRAEL APPEARS still in a strange land, afar from beloved Jerusalem and the temple of God, but faithful hearts are longing for return. Their eyes are toward His house, and our psalm anticipates their heart-throb. To believers today, the psalm would speak of longings for their heavenly home, the Father's house. What a prospect and a hope we have. The psalm has three stanzas, as follows:

1. *The Prospect Ahead of us*, vv. 1-4. How lovely are the dwellings of the Lord. We know this, for the One who lives there has exquisite beauty; see Psa. 27. 4. Is this the expressed ecstasy of our hearts as we consider His glory? Are we longing and fainting for those holy courts, crying out for the living God? Or are we too much at home in the world to long for heaven? How jealous were the faithful in Israel of their feathered friends finding nesting places in the sacred precincts whilst they were still far away from temple courts and altars! It was not that the birds nested in the altars, for that was impossible; the longings of the faithful are expressed in metaphorical language. As we look upward to those gone before, do we say, "Blessed are they that dwell in thy house: they will be still praising thee"? But we *are* on our way, and will soon join them.

2. *The Path Before us*, vv. 5-8. They at home are singing, but we are still sorrow-beset. The pathway there still winds through the valley of weeping (as Baca indicates), yet our strength for the way is in God and we press on for "in our hearts are the high ways to Zion", R.V. The strength of God is in our hearts, therefore the spring is in our steps. The path at times may be wet with tears, but such turn to springs of blessing. We press on to appear before God in Zion, v. 7.

3. *The Persuasion Within us*, vv. 9-12. As we move onward to our home, note the *Assessment*, v. 10, and the *Assurance*. God is our shield for the way and our Sun for its weariness; He will give grace for every mile and glory at journey's end. Along the uphill course, no good thing is withheld, so let us walk erect, not bowed with care; God looks on the face of His Anointed, and through Him we shall conquer.

Mark the golden towers of the city of God, and press on.

370

December 16th

READING: **Psalm 88**

A DIMMED PERSPECTIVE

ROSSETTI wrote, "Is the road uphill all the way? Yes to the very end!", but where the road leads highest, the clouds are often heaviest and the prospect dim. Fellow-traveller to heaven, is the day before you foreboding? There have been many before you who have felt thus. Heman was a wise man (see 1 Kings 4. 31), but there were things that he did not know. Note his recurring "why", Psa. 88. 14, yet his psalm is entitled "Mahalath Leannoth", meaning "sickness for humiliation". The attaining of heights often demands a leveling of spirit.

All but unrelieved gloom hangs over this psalm. We are not informed as to the specific burden of the psalmist, but his case is bitter. He speaks of being "nigh unto Sheol", v. 3, indeed as if already dead, in the lowest pit, vv. 5-6. He feels the loneliness of estrangement, v. 8, and that heaven is brass-like in unresponsiveness, v. 9.

From a description of his condition he turns to expostulation with God, vv. 10-12. The psalm ends as it begins. He cries incessantly to God, and receives no reply. He asks only that he shall be heard, v. 2. He concludes that it is God's hand upon him in wrath, vv. 6, 7, 8, 14, 16, 18. Job-like he receives no explanation, yet he continues to cry as indicative of a faith still stirring in his soul, vv. 1, 9, 13. These three callings on the Lord are instructive. They were *persistent*, "day and night", v. 1, "daily", v. 9, "in the morning", v. 13. It is hard when importunate prayer seems but to rebound. His prayers were *consistent*, for he leans always on the Jehovah-name. He appeals to the faithfulness of his God, linked with His might. Though he seems to argue with God, he cannot overlook His care. His plea also was *confident* that the One to whom he cried was solely the source of help, "O Jehovah the God of my salvation", v. 1. Here is faith in the gloom holding on despite circumstances. The psalm leaves him in the darkness, distraction, silence and loneliness, vv. 15-18.

The psalm teaches us that "faith *is* the victory that overcometh", even though the way is hard and the prospect dim.

May our daily motto be, even though distresses abound, "Trusting though not Tracing".

371

December 17th

READING: **Psalm 93**

BEHOLD "THE KING"

THIS IS a millennial psalm presenting the hope of every true Israelite. How Isaiah constantly looked forward to the realization of this, and projected the minds of his people forward by repeating, "in that day". However, we too should pray "Thy kingdom come", for we also are to know the wonders of that coming age. Today, horrors abound in our world, vice, outrage, cruelty, faithlessness, injustice and the like, so that we often need to reassure our fearful hearts with the fact that God is still on the throne, Psa. 103. 19. The day is coming when the fact that "The Lord reigneth" will be manifest; the King will be on the throne.

In this psalm, the subject before us is twofold: (i) the Fact, vv. 1-2, and (ii) the Features of the kingdom, vv. 3-5. The throne is the same as of old, v. 2, though not now recognized or revealed, but then, with what visible majesty will it be seen when the Lord will appear girded for action, v. 1. Then the world will be truly established. The rule of peace will have dawned. The floods, whether physical or human, having lifted themselves up, will be stilled by the mightiness of the King. His testimonies will be sure, and munificence and holiness will be manifest.

But what of today? With our eye on the coming glory, are the principles of the coming reign in our hearts and lives? We are ready for the "regeneration", Matt. 19. 28, for such has already taken place within us, and therefore we should be living under that reign now. Is the Lord reigning within, enthroned in our hearts, and is the strength of the Lord now truly establishing our little world within? Has every adverse factor, every rising turbulence in our living been brought under control by His mighty hand? Are we proving the sureness of His testimonies and is holiness becoming His house now? Are we moving towards heaven as living witnesses of, and with likeness to, the coming One? The King awaits His coming, though now in heaven; "Yet have I set my king upon my holy hill of Zion", Psa. 2. 6. Sooner than we think, He will be acclaimed in Jerusalem; are we acclaiming His rule now in the places where we live and serve Him?

Set apart Christ as Lord in your heart, 1 Pet. 3. 15.

December 18th

READING: **Psalm 94**

ASSURANCE AMID THE RISING TIDE

THOUGH THIS month our sights are being set very high, we cannot disregard the morass of evil through which we travel. For us the heavens are bright, but the earth is dark and the sky is red. Thank God for a glorious prospect and a blessed hope. This psalm is fittingly a follow-up of Psalm 93, for it presents the floods, 93. 3, and the mighty One, v. 4. A reading of verses 3-11 truly pictures the conditions through which we are now passing, and which will worsen as the days go by. Note the moral landslide and the total disregard of God in verses 3-7. Today's distresses only foreshadow the coming great tribulation, but our hope is not from the earth-level but from the sky-level. We note the cry of the righteous, vv. 1-2, and the cognisance of God, vv. 8-11. He that sitteth in the heavens shall have them in derision.

There are words of uplift for us, however, as skies darken above us and world conditions worsen. On earth there are masses of ungodly men, described in the psalm as proud, wicked, arrogant, workers of iniquity, brutish, foolish, yet God has His eye on those referred to in the psalm as "thy people", "thine heritage", "the upright".

Here and there in these verses there are jewels of truth for us. Note the promise of *Serenity* amidst the dangers in verses 4-7; to those responding to the control of the Lord, and who answer to His teaching, there is the promise of "rest from the days of adversity", vv. 12-13. In verses 14-15, His people are given the assurance of *Security*. "The Lord will not cast off his people" or "forsake his inheritance"; and the "upright in heart" will follow a straight path. When oppression arises, divine *Support* is granted, vv. 16-19, for His mercy holds us and His comforts delight the soul. The underlying thought of the word "delight" is "His comforts cuddle my soul"; what a warming truth, reminding us of the promise in Isaiah 40. 11. Then finally in verse 22 is the present reality of the Lord's *Salvation*. When viewed by the enemy, v. 21, it may seem that God the Mighty One is inaccessible, but He is in reality available. Though earthly prospects are dim, we truly have all things and abound.

If clouds are lowering, fix your eyes on the silver lining.

December 19th

READING: **Psalm 95**

THE KING AND HIS PEOPLE

READ THIS psalm as if it relates, not to His coming nation, but to His present church, since there is a message in it for us. Amidst the storm clouds of Psalm 94, a song can be raised and heard. The joyous peals of happy hearts are greater than the thunder claps. There is a rock beneath our feet, v. 1, whilst sinking sands may surround us. We dare so to sing for we have a covert in the storm, v. 2, and before us, moving us to quiet worship, v. 6, is our LORD (Jehovah), a great God and a great King above all gods, v. 3. What a calming perspective! If the earth about us seems to quake and yawn, the deepest places are in His hand, and if the highest mountains should totter and fall, then they are His also, v. 4. If the sea should toss and roar, and the dry land shake, He the great Creator is in control, v. 5.

With such a God before us, the greatest storm and uprising floods become a quiet pasturage, and we are not wrecks of the tempest but sheep of His pasture, not submerged in the maelstrom but in His hand. Ours can be a stable experience within a storm-tossed world. If the shrieking of the rising outrage of man should increase, the call to the assured soul is to "come", "sing", "be joyful", "kneel", "bow down", "worship"; then the still small voice is heard, John 14. 27.

Is all this just rhetoric to us? Listen to the words, "Today, Oh that ye would hear his voice", v. 7 R.V., and "Harden not your heart as at Meribah, as in the day of Massah in the wilderness", v. 8 R.V. With all the encouraging ministry of the psalm before us, vv. 1-7, what is perhaps robbing us of a God-promised rest?, v. 11. Is not God able to provide in the severest circumstances: Meribah, Massah?, Exod. 17; Num. 20.

Here are two rock scenes: thirst, and desperation rising and a people ready for riot. They had not learnt the lesson of the first to strengthen them for the second. These occasions were never forgotten by God; see Num. 27. 14; Psa. 81. 7. The Lord's complaint is that Israel "have not known my ways". In Psalm 77. 13, we learned that the ways of the Lord are only known "in the sanctuary", and here in verses 1-6 we are invited there, so that this, when heeded, prepares us for verse 10.

Let not life's storms disturb our rest; God is greater.

December 20th

READING: **Psalm 96**

THE KING AND HIS GOSPEL

HAVING INCLUDED Psalm 93, we must also include Psalm 96, since the group 93-96 all hold together. Here is another millennial song, but again we are looking for a message for our hearts today, since "all scripture is profitable". Read Psalm 95 again, and as we enjoy the calm within the raging elements let us "look on the fields" of man's desperate need. If our present perspective has been particularly upward and onward, it must also be outward, for the one must needs inspire the other. At the time of the millennial fulfil-ment of this psalm, the Lord will have a message for the world (the gospel of the kingdom); so do we have a message now. This is given by the same Lord, the gospel of His grace, and we are responsible for sounding it out. The psalm informs us of the world's need, for the world is without God and "all the gods of the nations are idols", v. 5. As we testify of the only true (genuine) God and Jesus Christ whom the Father has sent, John 17. 3, we have:

A Message. Its character is joyous, "good news", and we go singing. What we proclaim is that:

1. The Lord is great, v. 4, and therefore is greatly to be praised, and not to be ignored.

2. The Lord is to be feared, v. 4; He is above all gods.

3. The Lord reigneth, v. 10; therefore He must be obeyed.

4. The Lord cometh, v. 13; men must be prepared. In proclaiming these truths, we are instructed to

1. Declare His glory among the nations, and His great works.

2. Show forth His salvation from day to day, vv. 2-3. In preaching this message, we are also reminded that we have

A Motive. This is twofold. To *Win*, vv. 7-12, and to *Warn*, v. 13. We preach:

1. To turn men to God, vv. 7-8; see 1 Thess. 1. 9.

2. As ambassadors, bringing an offering, v. 8b, this being the only one acceptable. Thus we seek worshippers, for the Father seeks such, John 4. 23; see Psa. 96. 9.

3. To stress the untold joy in returning to God, vv. 11-12; multiplied pardon is much to sing about, Isa. 55. 7.

4. To warn men of the coming judgment, v. 13.

With our own hopes secure, as we go we must throw out the lifeline to others along the way.

December 21st

READING: **Psalm 102**

THE VISION THAT VITALIZES

EVEN SAINTS can have dismal days, and move along paths of dark distress. The sombre clouds are all listed, vv. 1-11, and these seek to hide the glory of the soul's prospects. Read these verses again, noting once more the depths of the man's grief. No cause is given for it; as the title says, he is just "overwhelmed". No doubt we all have times when we see ourselves reflected here, scarcely knowing what is burdening the heart. The psalmist confesses to having enemies, v. 8, and feels as if his days are numbered, v. 24. We sometimes sing, "Days of darkness oft come o'er me". However, beyond the shadows of life, there is the glory on which our eyes need to be fixed—the glory of the unchanging God. If verses 1-11 are full of human gloom, then verses 12-22 are full of divine light: "But thou", v. 12, and again, "But thou", v. 27. Note the subjects of the soul's gaze:

1. *The "But thou" of Divine Eternity.* "Thou, O Lord, shalt endure for ever", v. 12. My days consume away, v. 3, my heart withereth like grass, v. 4, my days are like a shadow that declineth, v. 11, but the eternal God is my refuge. He is still there whilst my heaviness lasts, and is there when it ends. The psalmist may think that God has cast him away, v. 10, but in grace He is still there to receive him. But more:

2. *The "But thou" of Divine Constancy.* "But thou art the same", v. 27. At best, we are creatures of change and inconstancy, but "No change Jehovah knows". Even the great works of the Lord, v. 25, are limited and subject to change according to the purpose of the Creator. Yet the Creator is changeless and ever shall be, v. 7. This word "same" is not simply used adjectivally, as a mere description of God, but as a noun—surely a title of God, the Name that He assumes as denoting His changelessness. See Deut. 32. 39, where "I, even I, am He" is really "the Same". Follow this by observing Isaiah's frequent use of the same, though not evident in our English version, Isa. 37. 16; 41. 4; 43. 10, 13; 46. 4; 48. 12; 51. 9, 10; 52. 6. Hear Malachi's word, "I am the Lord, I change not", Mal. 3. 6.

In your distress, fix your eyes on Jesus (Jehovah the Saviour), and the things of earth will grow strangely dim.

December 22nd

READING: **Psalm 105. 8-22**

PROSPECTS DIMMED BUT REALIZED

FROM OUR psalm today we take a character study that provides us with details not contained in the historical record. Joseph had had dreams that seemed significant. His brethren hated him because of them, Gen. 37. 8, his father rebuked him for them, v. 10, and his brethren envied him. Why? They had all detected a prophetic significance about them. What did all this mean to the lad? How often had he consequently dreamed of distant glory? "Reign over us?" his brethren had said; "Bow down to thee?" his father had questioned. The lad was seventeen years old—the age for castle-building, but soon his castles crumbled. He must have thrown his dreams away when in the pit and prison. He had gone to see his brethren at his father's request, and did not know that the Lord had sent him, and that his going out of the vale of Hebron was the first step to becoming the mighty centre in an important movement of God. So watch your circumstances, and do not form conclusions hastily. Sold, and no longer free; a servant and no longer a son; hurt and no longer comforted; in irons, and a malefactor, it seemed. Where are his prophetic dreams now? The important word has yet to come: "until", v. 19.

Have you felt stirrings of divine leading with hopes raised high, yet strange happenings have left them a heap of ruins? Frustrating events are often the crucible of heavenly preparation. God's fulfilments have a time factor, v. 19, and patience is needed. In the meantime, God's word "tries" for sincerity. When God's time ripens, the needed machinery moves, v. 20. Circumstances which seem to hinder give place to circumstances which fulfil. "Shalt thou ... have dominion?", they said, Gen. 37. 8; Pharaoh "made him lord", Psa. 105. 21. No, God did! He sent a man—so it was God who made him lord. We see Joseph now, his calling fulfilled, his hopes confirmed. His is dominion over house and substance, v. 21, with authority and wisdom, v. 22, a Zaphnath-paaneah (revealer of secrets) for the God-determined catastrophe, v. 16. The Lord's goal for those of His appointing is often reached by devious and undesired paths; it is for the servant to wait for the divine "until", v. 19, giving serious heed to the Word.

Watch the diversions; they lead to true destination.

December 23rd

READING: **Psalm 115**

LIGHT FOR THE DARKNESS

WE HAVE reached the darkest stage of the year, the winter solstice, and the darkest day, typical of our spiritual day, yet to get darker still. For the reader, is the day, in some ways, a dark one? The psalm before us seems made for a dark path. The song begins well, v. 1, and ends well, v. 18, but the question is soon asked of us, "Where is now their God?". Is your answer, "our God is in the heavens". Is this all? Are our ways so dark that we cannot see Him near? Do we look around for help? Do we sense futility when we consider the gods of men who, they think, determine their well being and destiny? This is where verses 4-8 lead us. Truly men's gods today are "silver and gold"; such are irresponsive, without feeling, undemonstrative, who only make their devotees like unto themselves. There is no help for us in them. We reach the source of real help in our darkness at the centre of this psalm, "O Israel, trust thou in the Lord", v. 9. The only antidote to darkness is faith.

Note the faith-centre of the psalm. We hear a threefold call. "O Israel, trust"; "O house of Aaron, trust", "Ye that fear the Lord, trust". Whatever our nomination, as through the covenant, the sanctuary, or of the God-fearing—*trust*. If we have believed in the Lord for salvation, then trust Him for life; we must remember that the call is to trust in Jehovah, the everlasting, unchanging, faithful One. Note the threefold affirmation, "he is their help and their shield". Here is help to press on, with a shield to protect as we move on in the dark toward our prospect. As we look backwards, the psalm reminds us, "The Lord hath been mindful of us", v. 12. As we look forward, note the fourfold guarantee: "he will bless us; he will bless the house of Israel; he will bless the house of Aaron. He will bless them that fear the Lord, both small and great", vv. 12-13. Note the change in tense—what He has been He will yet be. All nominations are included in the divine blessing. So the promise is that we will be moving on to greater things, v. 14, greater light, greater blessing, clearer prospects, brighter hopes. The only light, therefore, for the dark is the candle of the Lord, the flame of faith.

Presently dark, prospectively lighter unto perfect day.

378

December 24th

READING: **Psalm 121**

GREAT EXPECTATIONS

To those of us who love the Lord and who think of the original anticipation of His birth, this day has perhaps a special significance. In anticipation, there is joy—that of promises fulfilled in Christ's coming to earth. We think of the shepherds who sat watching, and saw from heaven what they had never expected. With our psalmist, we too will lift up our eyes to the mountains. Not that our help comes from these. Today, we look higher, since, as at that first Christmastide, our help comes from the Lord, namely from Jehovah who always keeps promise. We look, awaiting a second return.

As we interpret this psalm in the light of the incarnation, what great thoughts it provokes. Note that the great theme of the psalm is "The Lord ... thy keeper", the One who keeps His word and who keeps His people. The thought of being kept resounds through the psalm six times (see R.V.), since "preserve" is the same word. In these verses, expectations and hopes become realities. Let us rejoice today as we feel the keeping power of our God about us. In Psalm 115 yesterday we were in the dark; today we are in His grip.

Let us learn, His keeping brings *Establishment*, v. 3. The foot shall never slide, for our Keeper does not slumber. He is never taken by surprise. The keeping of our Lord also provides *Encouragement*, v. 4. We know that He neither fitfully slumbers nor lengthily sleeps. How different to Baal, 1 Kings 18. 27. With what confidence we can rest in the Lord. Moreover, His keeping supplies *Refreshment*, vv. 5-6. By day or night, sunlight or moonlight, He is ever the corrective shade. Now, more deeply still, in Him we have safe *Encirclement*, v. 7; He keeps from evil, moral and physical. He keeps the soul, John 10. 29; what guardianship we enjoy. Again, in all our movements for Him, He inspires a true *Abandonment*, knowing that He "shall give his angels charge over thee, to keep thee in all thy ways", Psa. 91. 11. What precious gifts to receive and enjoy this very day from the Lord! So we can say, anticipatively, these things shall be ours in fulness "from this time forth (from *this very day*), and even for evermore".

"Kept by the power of God", 1 Pet. 1. 5.

December 25th

READING: **Psalm 130**

AT THE RIGHT TIME

WHAT BETTER psalm than this for Christmas Day! We note the time-point around which the O.T. swings into the N.T. Luther called this psalm a "Pauline psalm", and he, Paul, knew both the rigours of O.T. law and the redemption of N.T. grace. The psalm seems to be divided at verse 6. In part one, vv. 1-5, there is a sense of fear, but in part 2 there is a looking for the arrival of the divine Promiser, v. 7. True to the O.T., in verses 1-5 we have:

(i) The cry of one who knows the deep darkness of guilt from which he cries with intensity, vv. 1-2.

(ii) The consciousness of a holiness before which sinners are doomed, v. 3.

(iii) The confession of a forgiveness still associated with fear, v. 4.

(iv) The conviction of soul which waits hopefully for a fulfilled promise, v. 5. Then what a change of prospect appears in part 2.

Here in verses 6-8, no longer is there a patient waiting for a promise to be fulfilled, but an eager looking for a person, the arrival of the Lord of promise, v. 6. The night is ending, the dawn is breaking, and watchers (not particularly the official watchmen on the city wall, but those wearied by the long night) are ready to hail the sunrise. We remember how the N.T. opens, "Where is he that is born King of the Jews?", Matt. 2. 2. Why this eager watching? With the coming One, there comes mercy in verses 7-8 to meet the need in verse 3, and *plenteous* redemption to meet the demands of verse 4. This redemption from *all* iniquities, however, still leads to the fear of a reverential kind though not to one of abject terror.

Throughout the psalm, the writer's cry alternates between a call to God as Jehovah and to God as Sovereign Master (Adonhai). He therefore appeals to One (Jehovah the faithful One) whom he knows will and who can, for He has authority and power. See vv. 1-2, 3, 5-6, but in verse 7 Jehovah fills the verse—the great covenant Keeper. How both of these great characters are vested in the Christ of the incarnation—He is Jesus, Jehovah the Saviour, and He is Lord.

No wonder we can use the greeting, "A Happy Christmas".

December 26th

READING: **Psalm 131**

THE FOCUS, FROM THIS TIME FORTH

MANY IN THE WORLD will be waking this day with heads sore because of the foolish excesses of yesterday, but the Christian can wake with a calm and peaceful heart. So may we greet the day in the spirit of Psalm 131. This short psalm of three verses is potently sufficient to express the true blessing of Christmastide. Three ideas are latent in the psalm:

1. The Change of Mind, v. 1.
2. The Confidence of Soul, v. 2.
3. The Concept of the Heart, v. 3.

The great truths of yesterday's psalm have checked the self-life. Pride and self-esteem have gone, v. 1a, and egotism has been subdued, v. 1b. Meeting with the Christ of redeeming grace has changed the perspective: "Not I, but Christ!". The writer thinks not as he did, sees not as he did, seeks not as he did; his thoughts, desires and ambitions are changed. What a change Christ makes, since He now reigns within!

Secondly, there is now rest of soul. When Christ reigns, peace follows. A deep confidence is manifest in verse 2. There has been a new birth; the once arrogant-one has become a little child. Rest and contentment are now found in Another. The milk of new life has been received (note, "weaned"), and the softness of the bosom of God has become the place of assurance. Here is the joy and fulness consequent on simple dependence—the life of faith has now been entered.

If verse 1 reminds us of what used to be yesterday, and verse 2 of what is true today, then verse 3 now leads into a new realm for tomorrow and all the succeeding days. The mind has now a new concept. The focus, perspective, prospect and sole hope of the heart is the LORD. "Let Israel hope in the Lord", and that controlling and all-consuming hope is "from *henceforth* and for ever". Like our Lord before us, we can be described like the One who has made the change within us, "in that he died, he died unto sin once: but in that he liveth, he liveth unto God", Rom. 6. 10. The one ruling passion, prospect, hope and ambition is "hope in (and unto) the Lord", and the mind has now one focus, the soul one contentment, and the life one decided goal. As Paul wrote,

"*For to me (now) to live is Christ*", Phil. 1. 21.

December 27th

READING: **Psalm 132**

A MAN WITH AN ASPIRATION

WE WILL read the whole psalm, but will extract one thought for our meditation and heart-searching. It is David who conceives in his heart the desire to raise a permanent dwelling for the Lord, vv. 13-17. This was not true of Saul—he was a man after the flesh, and could have no thought for the divine habitation. But David was a man after God's own heart, so God's interests were his. Note the deep stirrings of David's heart, vv. 1-4, his self-forgetfulness and even self-sacrifice for the Lord's glory. We know the Lord's plan was otherwise, and why, 2 Sam. 7. 12-13. When we read such heart-yearnings, we think of David's greater Son and Lord who manifested a similar spirit of concern and interest in the house of the Lord—His Father's house, John 2. 17; Matt. 21. 13. How precious it was to Him, though defiled by man. See the Lord's manifest grief in Mark 11. 11, when He had entered into the temple and had looked round about on all things.

Today, our God has no dwelling-place of human construction, but an even more wonderful habitation, Acts 7. 48; Eph. 2. 19-20; God places His Name there. What is my attitude of heart toward it? Is this my present aspiration? Do I love to promote it and maintain its glory? Am I found there with regularity? Does the assembly have my heart-interest? Do David's sentiments move my heart?, vv. 3-4. In these days, this wonderful dwelling-place of the Lord is being neglected, nay, dare we say desecrated? Its pattern in the N.T. is being departed from, and its holiness disregarded. Where do I stand in relation to it? Moses was faithful in God's house of his day, Heb. 3. 5; are we faithful in God's house of our day?, for there our Saviour is Son and Lord, Heb. 3. 6. Do others see the zeal for God's house eating us up and gripping us?

How jealous God was with regard to the tabernacle which He commanded to be set up in the wilderness. We read that Moses was warned of God to comply with the heavenly pattern shown to him on the mount, Heb. 8. 5. Is God less interested in His dwelling-place today?

If our hopes are set on dwelling "in the house of the Lord for ever" when our little day is over, then our devotion now will be for the place where He dwells.

December 28th

READING: **Psalm 133**

THE PLACE OF BLESSING

WE MUST not exclude this psalm from our selection, for the lesson it brings has affinity with the challenge of yesterday's psalm. When the Lord promises blessing to any chosen place, it behoves us to give attendance there; verse 3 is therefore significant. Yesterday we saw a King associated with the house of God, but today it is the High Priest, and immediately our minds turn to Hebrews 10. 21. With our loyalties fixed upon the present habitation of God, the psalm presents three truths:

1. The Condition for Blessing, v. 1.
2. The Consecration for Blessing, vv. 2-3.
3. The Command for Blessing, v. 3b.

1. *The Condition.* Unity of spirit: the psalm states that such a condition is potently good and pleasantly lovely. This dwelling in unity expresses the oneness of the God in our midst. We are expected to behave in unity for we are a unity, not created by man but by the Spirit, Eph. 4. 3-6. We are exhorted to keep, to maintain it. Disunity mars the house, but unity opens the door to blessing. This should be the constant aim of the assembly of God.

2. *The Consecration.* This condition is likened to the occasion of the consecration of the high priest of Israel; see Lev. 8. 12. This unity is therefore linked with the holy anointing oil (emblem of the Holy Spirit). Just as the oil flowed down over the whole man, so the Spirit controlling the members of the house will produce consecration leading to unity of mind and action. Another symbol of the Holy Spirit is used here, that of the dew of Hermon descending on all the mountains of Zion, and so refreshing the whole.

3. *The Command.* Blessing is not humanly produced, rather it is God-given. If we fulfil our responsibility to maintain the necessary conditions, the Lord will fulfil His promise. Note again verse 3b: the promise of the Lord is emphatic, "for *there*"; and also positive, "commanded the blessing"; further it is guaranteed, "*even life for evermore*".

Does the company of saints to which we belong aspire to such a condition, and do they have such expectancy of blessing? If we have to grieve over no blessing—why?

READING: **Psalm 139**

THE IMMANENCE OF GOD

WE HAVE been moving through the month with our eyes and hearts fixed on great and coming matters. We have often been in the sanctuary, thirsting for God, and viewing our hopes and prospects. Our eyes have been up to Him, but it is good to remember that His eyes are upon us. The words of the ancient poet are still true, "in him we live, and move, and have our being", Acts 17. 28. How deeply God knows us; He is aware of our every act and thought, vv. 1-6. His awareness of myself I cannot avoid, vv. 7-12; He not only knows my every movement, but is in closest touch with every part of me, vv. 13-16. He knew me before I knew myself, and determined the fashion and function of my every member. As a confirmation of this, see the Lord's words to the prophet Jeremiah, Jer. 1. 4-5.

Now if God knows my every movement, this should surely stimulate holiness. If I cannot ever escape from Him, this deepens my assurance of His vigilant care. If he has even fashioned all my members (and that in view of my intended life, v. 16), then that fact should determine my consecration to His will. The question should long linger in our minds, "Why has He made me thus?". My life was therefore no accident, but is intended for divine purpose. It demands that I tread carefully.

Even so, the psalm includes great encouragement for us. Since God knows me as intimately as all this, how precious are His thoughts unto me—more than can be numbered, vv. 17-18. This quickens my trust in Him. He knows the worst about me and loves me still, for whenever I awake I find that I have not been forsaken, v. 18. Should not this psalm stir our resolutions for the year immediately ahead? As we therefore move onward through life toward our heavenly consummation, surely the prayer in verses 23-24 should also be ours? Search me, know me, try me, know my thoughts, lead me in the way everlasting. Our ways must conform to His ways for us. Hence verses 1-18 should purify our aspirations, clarify our prospects and make certain our hopes. If we have been fearfully and wonderfully made and are constantly under His surveillance, then what are our lives going to be from now on?

If this God is for us, who then can be against us?

READING: **Psalm 145**

THE CHARACTER OF OUR IMMANENT GOD

WE MUST have one more look at our God who is so immanent.
The view of Him will inspire our hearts for the unknown year
ahead. This psalm makes five arresting statements about Him,
and we will use them to direct our vision:

1. The Lord is Great: He is Unsearchable, v. 3.
2. The Lord is Gracious: He is Approachable, v. 8.
3. The Lord is Good: He is Impartial, v. 9.
4. The Lord is Righteous: He is Equitable, v. 17.
5. The Lord is Nigh: He is Available, v. 18.

In each case, the psalmist uses the Name Jehovah, the Name
of our God, the Everlasting, Unchanging, Faithful, Covenant
Keeping God; *He* has all these attributes. Since this is our God,
what should be our response to Him as we read? If He is
Great, then we will *Worship*, vv. 1-2, 5. Since He is Gracious,
we will *Work* for Him, v. 4. In the light of His Goodness, we
will *Witness* for Him, vv. 6-7. Since our God is Righteous, right
in all His ways, then we will *Wait* for Him and not run before
Him, v. 15, and because He is Nigh to all that call upon Him,
we will *Walk* with Him.

With such a God as ours, we should never be without a
song, vv. 1-3; never be without a testimony, vv. 4, 6; never be
without a subject for meditation, v. 5; never be heard uttering
a grumble, v. 7; never be without a spirit of appreciation, vv.
8-10; never be without a theme for conversation, vv. 11-12;
never be without hope, vv. 14-16; never be holden by fear, vv.
18-20.

As a Great God, He never lacks power to fulfil that which He
desires; as a Gracious God, He will ever minister to us even
though we ill deserve His kindness at times; as a God that is
Good He will ever provide for the needy, for "no good thing
will he withhold from them that walk uprightly", Psa. 84. 11;
as Righteous, we know that His benevolence will never be un-
principled but always wise; and as Nigh to them that call upon
Him, He will never fail to hear and answer prayer. Through a
long year, this God has demonstrated His love to us, and as
we view the distant road to our heavenly goal, the prospect
remains clear.

They "that do know their God shall be strong", Dan. 11. 32;
"that I may know him", Phil. 3. 10.

December 31st

READING: **Psalm 150**

THE FINAL PRAISE

THE OLD YEAR has almost gone, for some perhaps a gladsome thought, as the way may have been weary. For others perhaps the year has been a time of great blessing, as great things have been achieved for God. So this year is by now almost history, yet for all of us it is a lap nearer the glory of the Father's house. Soon the bells will be ringing the old year out and the new year in. Reviewing the path, we can say, "Surely goodness and mercy" have followed us. For this, let us join in the chorus of praise which closes the Psalter. This final Hallelujah Chorus tells us where to praise Him, v. 1; why, v. 2a; what measure to use, v. 2b; how, vv. 3-5; and who is to be praised, v. 6. Whether in the privacy of the holy place or out in the expanse of the firmament, our song should be of Him. In worship or in testimony, we sound His praise. God's mighty acts inspire us, and His excellent greatness should mark the volume of the song. The varied instruments, undoubtedly used in O.T. service, would induce the utilization of every means of speaking forth His worth.

In this age, when shadows have given place to the substance, surely the deep lesson here for us is that every capacity that we possess should be dedicated to His praise. This would include our voice in song, our lips speaking His Name, our hands in service, our feet readily obeying His call, and the inward unspoken praise of heart and mind. True praise is not measured by the volume, or even the sweetness of sound, but by the sincere exercise of the hidden man of the heart. Hence the apostle Paul writes of "speaking one to another in psalms and hymns and spiritual songs, singing and making melody with your heart *to the Lord*", Eph. 5. 19 R.V.

Praise is often infectious, and when we are seen to be a happy, praising people, others may be moved into singing. Thus the psalmist said, "Let every thing that hath breath praise the Lord". Let us then make this last day a day of praise, and let us enter the New Year with hearts aglow expectantly awaiting the coming of our Lord Jesus Christ. We are people of *prospect*, begotten unto a living *hope*, so may all our *aspirations* be unto and of the Lord.

"The night is far spent, the day is at hand", Rom. 13. 12.

Index

Aaron, 324, 349
Abraham, 58, 63, 346
Absalom, 54, 94
Abstain, 61, 139
According to, 290
Acrostic, 125, 296
Activity, 233
Adam, 45, 167
Adoration, 250
Adultery, 144
Adversary, 97, 274
Affliction, 51, 86, 137, 272
Against, 145
Ahithophel, 54, 210, 303
Almighty, 101, 138
Alone, 305, 329
Altar, 59, 131, 132, 204
Ambitions, 381
Angels, 257, 298
Anger, 320
Anointing oil, 314, 383
Antitype, 295
Apostasy, 189
Appointed, 294
Appreciation, 167, 244, 255
Ark, 32, 128, 204, 369
Arm, 34
Asaph, 176, 214, 332, 369
Ascension, 201, 310
Aspirations, 68, 360
Assembly, 350, 353
Assurance, 138, 157, 365
Assyrian, 222
Astray, 272
Atmosphere, 28
Attitude, 29
Attributes, 134, 136
Authorities, 87
Authority, 261
Authorized Version, 265
Awe-inspiring, 36

Babylon, 351, 354
Backsliding, 38
Bathsheba, 144, 206
Battle, 69
Beasts, 188
Beauty, 25, 185, 201, 211

Before, 293
Begotten, 311
Behaviour, 53, 170
Beholding, 133, 212
Believers, 215
Betray, 54
Blaspheme, 33
Blessing, 70, 216, 254, 383
Blood, 34, 55, 204
Body of glory, 191
Boldness, 358
Bondage, 31
Bridegroom, 172, 314
Bright, 166
Build, 351
Burden, 80

Calamities, 174
Calvary, 66, 177, 237, 249
Canaan, 345
Captives, 324, 356
Captivity, 151
Care, 50
Cave of Adullam, 107
Certainties, 356
Change, 168, 169
Character, 58
Chasten, 50, 179
Chastisement, 117, 241, 282
Cherubim, 14, 214, 228
Children, 280
Chosen, 211, 234
Christian, 142
Christ, The, 292
  Baptism of, 292
  Boyhood, 296
  Heir, The, 294
  Mediator, 312
  Spirit of, 307
  Teachings of, 299
  Word, The, 293
Chronological order, 160
Circle, 236
Circumstances, 79, 108
Citizen, 60
City, 60, 222
Cleanse, 266
Clothed, 219, 323

Clouds, 376
Comfort, 140
Coming of Christ, 302, 329
Commandments, 267, 347
Commitment, 148
Communion, 131, 292
Companion, 347
Compassion, 134, 136
Condescends, 48
Confession, 78, 360
Confidence, 71, 93, 98
Conscience, 99, 130, 170
Consolation, 65
Consuming fire, 342
Control, 264
Conviction, 62, 360
Counsel, 140, 301, 304
Courts, 370
Covenant, 37, 254
Creation, 57, 188, 212, 243, 258, 263
Creator, 37, 254
Cross, The, 31, 32, 52
Crowned, 292
Cry, 147
Cup, 67
Curse, 89

Daniel, 85, 346
Darkness, 49, 52, 119
David, 144, 325, 327, 338
Davidic covenant, 321
Day of Atonement, 315
Day(s), 47, 213, 344
Death, 49, 55, 161, 306
Decline, 168
Deeds, 250
Defence, 54, 81
Defilement, 251
Deity, 315
Delight, 63, 246, 262
Deliverance, 116, 231, 259
Dependence, 41
Depression, 290
Derision, 288
Desease, 50
Destroy, 41, 63, 378
Destroyer, 274
Determination, 147
Devil, The, 298

Devotion, 297
Diligence, 39
Distress, 72, 138, 187
Diversity, 258
Divine, 64
Divine purpose, 384
Doeg, 200
Dominion, 42
Doorkeeper, 220
Dwell, 45, 209

Early, 148
Earth, 169, 258, 260
Edom, 330
Encouragement, 288
End, 63
Endureth, 161
Enemies, 69, 79, 178, 223, 288, 357
Enemy, 301
Enjoyment, 289
Enriched, 252
Entertainment, 224
Enthroned, 372
Envy, 367
Ephraim, 335
Escape, 51, 141
Eternal, 281, 313, 315
Everlasting, 47, 248, 293
Everything, 260
Evil, 53, 61, 191
Exalt, 190
Exalted, 312
Examine, 170
Example, 280
Exceeding, 327
Excellent, 195
Exhort, 344
Exile, 54, 88, 149
Existence, 47
Expectation, 186
Experience, 54, 77, 139, 254
Expression, 139, 307
Eyes, 66

Face, 142, 369
Failure, 346
Faith, 181, 207, 241, 360
Faithful, 17, 306
Faithfulness, 240, 341, 371

False, 223
Family, 254
Favour, 34, 58
Fear, 58, 141
Fearfully, 43
Fear not, 142
Feasts, 208
Fellow, 118
Fellowship, 12, 68, 128, 247
Filled, 175
Finished, 38
Fire, 23, 223
Firstborn, 18, 318, 337
Fixed, 235
Flee, 108
Flesh, 189, 287, 307
Flourish, 104
Footsteps, 18
Forerunner, 358
Forget, 72
Forgiveness, 62, 139, 150, 159, 380
Forgotten, 149
Forsaken, 51, 305
Foundation, 38, 61, 109, 286
Frailty, 48, 256, 362
Freedom, 138
Friendship, 54
Fulfilled, 303, 306
Fulness, 48, 249, 320

Garments, 185
Gates, 127
Gathering, 234
Gifts, 310
Gladness, 94, 231, 246
Gloom, 49, 371
Glorified, 173
Glorify, 182
Glory, 166, 176, 180
Goal, 362, 385
God, 9
   All-Sufficient, 16
   Attributes, 153, 157
   Government, 115
   Mighty One, 373
   Most High, 20, 75
   Name, 10, 79, 101, 286
   Nature, 110
   of Israel, 177
   of Jacob, 326
   of my righteousness, 124
   Presence, 11, 99, 234
   the Father, 27, 296, 306, 307
Godhead, 156
Gods, 10, 114, 160, 161
Gold, 217
Gospel, 38, 44, 185, 375
Government, 125, 237
Grave, 49, 55
Groaning creation, 195
Guarantee, 185
Guilt, 135

Hallel, 127, 191
Hallelujah, 195, 229, 254
Hands, 46, 132, 307
Happy, 59, 232, 255
Harmony, 36, 258
Harps, 354
Harvest, 216
Healing, 276
Healthy, 255
Heart, 27, 68, 182, 217, 235, 274
   382
Heavenly, 364
Heavens, 52, 60, 68, 167, 199, 257
Hell, 54
Help, 98, 179
Hezekiah, 211
Hide, 35, 138
High Priest, 203, 315, 353
Holiness, 38, 182, 355, 381
Holy, 13, 46, 202
Holy hill, 46, 206
Holy occupations, 228
Holy Spirit, 58, 239, 264, 297
Home, 59, 370
Honour, 297
Household of God, 254
House of God, 197, 209
Human, 41, 284
Humility, 84
Hypocrisy, 99

Idols, 339
Idolatry, 90, 192
Impeccability, 308
Imprecation, 76
Incarnation, 164, 380
Incense, 102

Incomparable, 14, 339
Incorruptible, 308
Inheritance, 87, 179, 322
Iniquity, 62, 154
Injustice, 112, 140
Innocent, 122
Instruct, 58, 359
Integrity, 129
Intelligence, 58, 361
Intercession, 353
Intimacy, 58, 73
Isaac, 348, 349
Israel, 259, 348

Jacob, 238, 346, 348
Jealousy, 81, 297
Jehovah, 90, 101, 111
Jerusalem, 169, 198, 319, 334
Joseph, 377
Joy, 61, 196, 234, 308
Judah, 334
Judas, 303
Judge, 33, 111
Judgments, 37, 110, 119, 173, 329
Justice, 109, 237, 322
Justification, 306

Keeper, 30, 379
King, 169, 172, 300, 374
Kingdom, 215, 372
Know, 66, 101, 285, 361, 254
Knowledge, 43, 174, 265
Korah, Sons of, 180, 220

Law, 273, 296
Learn, 126, 163
Levites, 332, 335
Life, 60, 61, 148
Light, 74, 212
Living, 12
Local church, 212, 334
Longsuffering, 345
Lord of Hosts, 69, 180
Lord's Supper, 239, 247
Love, 26, 186, 205, 282
Lovely, 383
Lovingkindness, 136, 353
Loyalty, 54, 105, 354

Magnificent, 286

Majesty, 143, 194, 322
Man, 41
Man of sin, 70
Marvellous, 135, 227
Meditate, 255, 273
Meek, 137
Melchizedek, 121, 313
Memory, 65, 247, 345
Mercy, 64, 137, 192
Messiah, 175, 195, 320
Messianic, 186, 297
Mighty, 36
Millennial, 228, 237, 322
Moon, 321
Moses, 145, 184, 342
Mount of Olives, 310
Mount Zion, 96, 201, 234
Mystery, 52

Nathan, 78
Nation, 51, 270
Near, 142, 238
New, 243, 275
Night, 213

Obedience, 133, 295
Object, 26, 300
Offering, 204, 300
Oil, 316
Old age, 85
Omnipotent, 115
Omnipresent, 21
Omniscience, 107
Overflowing, 300

Pardon, 124, 139
Paths, 63, 359
Patience, 30
Peace, 63, 94, 139, 381
Penitential, 50, 145, 187
Perfect, 263, 314
Persecution, 288
Personal, 145, 154, 268
Perspective, 63, 138, 377
Pilgrimage, 68, 356, 369
Pine, 264
Poor, 55, 84
Possessions, 66, 311
Power, 30, 83, 233, 309
Praise, 41, 147, 229, 253

Prayer, 28, 95, 285, 328
Precepts, 256, 271
Precious, 65, 158, 254, 268
Pre-eminence, 318
Prepare, 245
Presence, 138, 350
Preserve, 165
Principles, 146
Prisoners, 38
Privilege, 60, 251, 277
Profitable, 106
Promises, 28, 323, 379
Prophetic, 169, 377
Propitiation, 24
Prospects, 355
Protection, 82
Proud, 53, 193
Punish, 120
Purged, 179, 317
Purify, 384
Purpose, 34, 87, 175, 384

Quicken, 287
Quiet time, 39, 155

Rebellion, 70, 270, 314,
Reconciliation, 327
Redeem(ed), 318, 350
Redemption, 34, 231, 239, 380
Red Sea, 189
Refuge, 62, 174
Reign, 259, 314, 381
Rejected, 169, 304
Rejoice, 60, 232, 259
Remember, 136, 149
Remission, 62
Remnant, 329, 333
Repentance, 78, 126, 178
Reproach, 226, 302
Response, 67, 239
Responsibility, 277
Rest, 157, 255, 323
Resting place, 219
Restoration, 323
Resurrection, 309, 317
Return of Christ, 319, 322
Revelation, 13, 134, 261
Reverence, 15, 46, 58, 350
Reviled, 306
Revive, 151, 287

Righteous, 66, 104
Righteousness, 116, 118, 322, 341
Right hand, 317, 328
River, 143, 221, 224
Rock, 35, 82, 242
Royalty, 118

Sacredness, 43
Sacrifice, 56, 95, 204, 295
Saints, 255, 269
Salvation, 30, 74, 181, 240
Same, 376
Sanctuary, 32, 148, 223, 367
Satan, 69, 225
Satisfied, 148, 188, 209
Save, 79, 214
Saviour, 40
Sceptre, 314
Search, 384
Second death, 323
Secret, 43, 73, 298
Security, 64
Selah, 334
Servant, 205, 341
Service, 67, 203
Settled, 278, 291
Sheol, 49, 371
Shepherd, 214, 316, 337, 368
Shield, 90, 370
Shiloh, 198
Silence, 52, 305
Sin, 50, 62, 188, 336
Sincerity, 46, 129, 132
Sing, 196, 243
Sky, 167
Sleep, 92
Solomon, 121, 175, 219
Song, 65, 230
Song of ascents, 350
Son of God, 9, 284
Son of man, 42, 306, 337
Sorrow, 65, 80
Soul, 276, 295
Source, 26, 53
Sovereign, 20, 51, 284, 320
Speak, 199, 268
Spiritual, 55, 99, 198, 224
Stability, 96, 242
Stand, 159
Statutes, 279

Stedfast love, 143
Steps, 63
Stone, 227
Storms, 374
Strength, 22, 171, 219, 288
Suffer, 328
Suffering, 50, 187, 302
Support, 366
Supremacy, 183
Sweetness, 35, 289

Tabernacle, 25, 171, 221
Teach, 162
Teaching, 117
Tears, 68, 158
Temple, 25, 171, 199, 333
Temptation, 141, 225
Tenderness, 30
Testimonies, 262
Testimony, 45, 132, 185, 222
Thanksgiving, 173
Thirsting, 208
Thoughts, 21, 56, 282
Thrill, 247
Throne, 24, 125, 183, 342
Time, 29, 184
Titles of God, 9
Tongue, 45, 54, 300
Tower, 325
Transgressions, 62, 126
Treachery, 54, 80, 210
Treasure, 291
Trial, 23, 146, 110
Tribulation, The, 373
Triumph, 50, 69, 221, 298
Trouble, 50, 98, 330, 368
Trumpet, 338
Trust, 50, 64, 140, 378
Truth, 64, 152, 233, 271
Types, 201, 202

Uncertainty, 349
Unchangeable, 281
Unchanging, 16, 281
Unclean, 347
Understanding, 18, 284
Unfailing, 29
Ungodly, 331

Unique, 160, 241
Universal, 236, 260
Unsearchable, 194
Urim and Thummim, 207

Vain, 330
Vanity, 48
Vastness, 248
Vengeance, 33, 254
Victory, 32, 196, 310
Violence, 301
Vision, 365
Voice, 37, 300
Volume, 257, 295
Vows, 31, 67

Wait, 28, 74, 329
Walk, 67, 210, 274
Warfare, 190
Warning, 274
Watch, 329
Ways, 29, 368
Waywardness, 349
Weakness, 22, 48, 250
Wealth, 56
Welcome, 59
Wicked, 53, 123, 269
Wickedness, 63, 119, 269
Wilderness, 349
Will, 67, 304
Willingly, 217
Wisdom, 18, 47
Wise, 55, 61, 267
Wonderful, 19, 43, 292
Wonders, 29, 283, 314
Word of God, 168, 263
Words, 45
Works, 19, 193, 233
Worship, 164, 197, 231, 252
Wrath, 86, 177, 179, 313
Wrong, 161, 233

Yoke, 163
Youth, 266

Zeal, 226, 296
Zion, 60, 206, 311, 354